THE RECEPTION OF JESUS IN THE FIRST THREE CENTURIES

7

Series Editors
Chris Keith, Helen Bond, and Jens Schröter

From the Passion to the Church of the Holy Sepulchre

Memories of Jesus in Place, Pilgrimage, and Early Holy Sites over the First Three Centuries

Jordan J. Ryan

LONDON • NEW YORK • OXFORD • NEW DELHI • SYDNEY

T&T CLARK
Bloomsbury Publishing Plc
50 Bedford Square, London, WC1B 3DP, UK
1385 Broadway, New York, NY 10018, USA
29 Earlsfort Terrace, Dublin 2, Ireland

BLOOMSBURY, T&T CLARK and the T&T Clark logo are trademarks of
Bloomsbury Publishing Plc

First published in Great Britain 2021
This paperback edition published 2022

Copyright © Jordan J. Ryan, 2021

Jordan J. Ryan has asserted his right under the Copyright, Designs and Patents Act, 1988,
to be identified as Author of this work.

For legal purposes the Acknowledgements on p. xiv constitute an extension
of this copyright page.

Cover design: Charlotte James
Cover image: The Good Shepherd, fresco (3rd century) in the Catacomb of Priscilla,
Rome, Lazio, Italy © De Agostini / G. Cargagna / Getty Images.

All rights reserved. No part of this publication may be reproduced or
transmitted in any form or by any means, electronic or mechanical, including
photocopying, recording, or any information storage or retrieval system,
without prior permission in writing from the publishers.

Bloomsbury Publishing Plc does not have any control over, or responsibility for, any
third-party websites referred to or in this book. All internet addresses given in this
book were correct at the time of going to press. The author and publisher regret any
inconvenience caused if addresses have changed or sites have ceased to exist, but can
accept no responsibility for any such changes.

A catalogue record for this book is available from the British Library.

Library of Congress Cataloging-in-Publication Data
Names: Ryan, Jordan J., author.
Title: From the passion to the church of the Holy Sepulchre : memories of Jesus in place,
pilgrimage, and early Holy sites over the first three centuries / Jordan J. Ryan.
Description: London ; New York : T&T Clark, 2021. |
Series: The reception of Jesus in the first three centuries; 7 |
Includes bibliographical references and index. |
Summary: "This book examines the history and archaeology of early Christian holy
sites and traditions connected with specific places in order to understand them
as interpretations of Jesus and to explore them as instantiations of
memories of him"– Provided by publisher.
Identifiers: LCCN 2020039971 (print) | LCCN 2020039972 (ebook) |
ISBN 9780567677457 (hb) | ISBN 9780567697745 (paperback) |
ISBN 9780567677464 (epdf) | ISBN 9780567677488 (epub)
Subjects: LCSH: Jesus Christ–Travel. | Bible. New Testament–Geography. |
Christian shrines–Israel. | Christian shrines–Palestine. |
Church history–Primitive and early church, ca. 30–600.
Classification: LCC BT303.9 .R93 2021 (print) | LCC BT303.9 (ebook) |
DDC 225.9/1–dc23
LC record available at https://lccn.loc.gov/2020039971
LC ebook record available at https://lccn.loc.gov/2020039972

ISBN: HB: 978-0-5676-7745-7
PB: 978-0-5676-9774-5
ePDF: 978-0-5676-7746-4
ePUB: 978-0-5676-7748-8

Series: The Reception of Jesus in the First Three Centuries, Volume 7

Typeset by Newgen KnowledgeWorks Pvt. Ltd., Chennai, India

To find out more about our authors and books visit www.bloomsbury.com
and sign up for our newsletters.

For Anders Runesson

Contents

List of Figures		ix
List of Translations Commonly Used		xi
Acknowledgements		xiv
List of Abbreviations		xvi
1	Introduction	1
	Methodological Foundations	5
	Conclusion	16
2	Remembering Golgotha: Memory and Interpretation of the Place of Crucifixion from the First to the Fourth Centuries	19
	The Site of the Crucifixion and the Tomb of Jesus in the New Testament	19
	Golgotha from the Second to the Fourth Centuries	23
	Pilgrim Experiences of Golgotha (Bordeaux, Egeria, Breviarius)	57
	Conclusion	62
3	The Tomb of Jesus in Christian Memory and Interpretation	65
	The Tomb of Jesus in the Gospels	65
	Between Easter and the Church of the Holy Sepulchre	75
	Interpretation of the Church of the Holy Sepulchre as Commemoration of the Burial and Resurrection of Jesus in Early Christian Writings	80
	Memory of Jesus in Pilgrim Experiences of the Space of the Holy Sepulchre	92
	Analysis and Conclusions	95
4	Locating a Memory: The Architecture of the Constantinian Church of the Holy Sepulchre as Jesus-Memory	99
	Meaning in Architecture	99
	The Archaeology and History of the Traditional Site of the Tomb of Jesus	103
	Establishing the Architecture	111
	Interpreting the Monument	119
	Conclusion	132
5	Bethlehem and the Mount of Olives	135
	The Birthplace of Jesus in the Second and Third Centuries CE	139
	The Church of the Nativity	152

	The Mount of Olives	159
	The Eleona and the Imbomon	170
	Conclusion	180
6	Galilee: "There They Will See Me"	183
	Constantinian Church Building in Galilee?	184
	Capernaum	186
	The Heptapegon	195
	Nazareth	203
	Conclusions: The Galilean Life-of-Jesus Churches	216
7	Conclusion	219

Gallery of Additional Photos	224
Bibliography	237
Index of Authors	259
Index of References	264

Figures

1	Floor plan of the Constantinian Church of the Holy Sepulchre	100
2	Floor plan of the Church of the Nativity	136
3	Floor plan of the Eleona	171
4	Floor plan and reconstruction of the Church of the Ascension	172
5	Reconstruction of the fourth-century Church of the House of Peter by Virgilio Corbo	187
6	The fourth-century Church of the Multiplication superimposed on the fifth-century structure	196
7	Floor plan of the excavations at the Church of the Annunciation at Nazareth	204
8	Reconstruction of the early Church of the Annunciation	205
9	The modern Church of the Holy Sepulchre	223
10	Façade of the Church of the Holy Sepulchre	224
11	The Anastasis and Aedicule in the modern Church of the Holy Sepulchre	225
12	The Chapel of Adam	226
13	Heavily reconstructed stairway from the monumental entrance to the Constantinian Church of the Holy Sepulchre in the Russian Hospice in Jerusalem	227
14	The modern Church of the Nativity	228
15	Interior of the Church of the Nativity	228
16	Mosaic floor beneath the current floor of the Church of the Nativity	229
17	Reconstructed façade of the Eleona	229
18	Reconstructed interior of the Eleona (now the Pater Noster Church)	230
19	Reconstructed Apse of the Eleona	230
20	Grotto of the Eleona	231
21	The Chapel of the Ascension	231
22	Remains of the Byzantine Church of the Ascension (Imbomon)	232
23	Jesus' footprint in the Chapel of the Ascension	233
24	Modern Church of the Multiplication interior, Tabgha (based on the plan of the fifth-century Church of the Multiplication)	234

25	The altar and "holy rock" at the Church of the Multiplication, Tabgha	234
26	Archaeological remains of the ancient Church of the Annunciation in the modern-day Basilica of the Annunciation	235

Permissions have been sought for all images and figures, but in case an image has not been duly credited for whatever reason, we ask that the institution or person contact us so that this can be corrected in the next edition.

Translations Commonly Used

All English biblical quotations are from the NRSV unless otherwise indicated. If not otherwise indicated, translations of the following works of ancient writers are from these editions.

<u>Basil the Great, *Commentary on the Prophet Isaiah*</u>

Nikolai A. Lipatov, *St. Basil the Great: Commentary on the Prophet Isaiah*, Texts and Studies in the History of Theology 7 (Mandelbachtal: Edition Cicero, 2001).

<u>The Bordeaux Pilgrim, *Itinerarium*</u>

John Wilkinson, *Egeria's Travels*, 3rd ed. (Warminster: Aris & Philipps, 2002).

<u>Cyril of Jerusalem</u>

Edward Yarnold, *Cyril of Jerusalem* (London: Routledge, 2000).

<u>Egeria, *Itinterarium*</u>

Anne McGowan and Paul F. Bradshaw, *The Pilgrimage of Egeria: A New Translation of the* Itinerarium Egeriae *with Introduction and Commentary*, Alcuin Club Collections 93 (Collegeville: Liturgical Press Academic, 2018).

Alternatively, where stated and when drawing on sections of Egerian origin in Peter the Deacon, *de locis sanctis*:

John Wilkinson, *Egeria's Travels*, 3rd ed. (Warminster: Aris & Philipps, 2002).

<u>2 Enoch</u>

Translation from F. I. Anderson, "2 (Slavonic Apocalypse of) Enoch," in *The Old Testament Pseudepigrapha*, ed. James J. Charlesworth, 2 vols. (Peabody: Hendrickson, 1983), 1: 91–221.

<u>Ephrem the Syrian, *Hymns*</u>

Kathleen E. McVey, trans., *Ephrem the Syrian: Hymns*, Classics of Western Spirituality (New York: Paulist Press, 1989).

<u>Epiphanius of Salamis, *Panarion*</u>

Frank Williams, trans., *The* Panarion *of Epiphanius of Salamis*, 2nd ed. (Leiden: Brill, 2009).

Eusebius, *Ecclesiastical History (EH)*

Kirsopp Lake and J. E. L. Oulton, trans., *The Ecclesiastical History*, 2 vols., The Loeb Classical Library (London; New York; Cambridge, MA: William Heinemann; G. P. Putnam's Sons; Harvard University Press, 1926–32).

Eusebius, *Life of Constantine*

Averil Cameron and Stuart G. Hall, *Life of Constantine*, Clarendon Ancient History Series (Oxford: Clarendon Press, 1999).

Alternatively, Richardson's translation of *Church History, Life of Constantine the Great, and Oration in Praise of Constantine* (cited below), is used where stated.

Eusebius, *De laudibus Constantini* and *De Sepulchro Christi*

Ernest Cushing Richardson, trans., *Eusebius: Church History, Life of Constantine the Great, and Oration in Praise of Constantine*, vol. 1, ed. Philip Schaff and Henry Wace, A Select Library of the Nicene and Post-Nicene Fathers of the Christian Church, Second Series (New York: Christian Literature Company, 1890).

Eusebius of Caesarea, *Demonstratio Evangelica*

W. J. Ferrar, *The Proof of the Gospel*, 2 vols. (Eugene: Wipf and Stock, [1920] 2001).

Eusebius of Caesarea, *Onomasticon*

G. S. P. Freeman-Grenville, Rupert L. Chapman III, and Joan E. Taylor, eds., *The Onomasticon by Eusebius of Caesarea* (Jerusalem: Carta, 2003).

The Gospel of Peter

Paul Foster, *The Gospel of Peter: Introduction, Critical Edition and Commentary*, TENT 4 (Leiden: Brill, 2010).

Jerome, *Commentary on Matthew*

Thomas O. Schenk, *St. Jerome: Commentary on Matthew*, The Fathers of the Church 117 (Washington, DC: Catholic University of America Press, 2008).

Jerome, *Epistles*

W. H. Fremantle, *St. Jerome: Letters and Select Works*, NPNF 2.6 (New York: Christian Literature, 1892).

Julius Africanus, *Chronographiae*

Julius Africanus, *Chronographiae*, ed. Martin Wallraff, Die Griechischen Christlichen Schriftsteller der ersten Jahrhunherte Neue Folge 15 (Berlin: Walter de Gruyter, 2007), 42–3 (T17).

Justin Martyr, *Dialogue With Trypho*

Thomas B. Falls, trans., *Saint Justin Martyr: The First Apology, The Second Apology, Dialogue with Trypho, Exhortation to the Greeks, Discourse to the Greeks, The Monarchy or the Rule of God*, The Fathers of the Church 6, repr. ed. (Washington, DC: Catholic University of America Press, [1948] 2008).

Life of Adam and Eve (Greek and Latin Recensions)

Translation from M. D. Johnson, "Life of Adam and Eve: A New Translation and Introduction," in *The Old Testament Pseudepigrapha*, ed. James J. Charlesworth, 2 vols. (Peabody: Hendrickson, 1983), 2: 249–95.

Melito of Sardis, *Peri Pascha*

Alistair Stewart-Sykes, *On Pascha: With the Fragments of Melito and Other Material Related to the Quartodecimans* (Crestwood: St. Vladimir's Seminary Press, 2001).

Origen, *Commentary on the Gospel of St. Matthew*

Ronald E. Heine, *The Commentary of Origen on the Gospel of St. Matthew: Translated with Introduction and Brief Annotations by Ronald E. Heine*, Oxford Early Christian Texts (Oxford: Oxford University Press, 2018), 740 n. 98.

Origen, *Contra Celsum*

Henry Chadwick, trans., *Origen: Contra Celsum* (Cambridge: Cambridge University Press, 1953).

The Protevangelium of James

Lily C. Vuong, *The Protevangelium of James*, Early Christian Apocrypha 7 (Eugene: Cascade, 2019).

Acknowledgements

The seeds of this project were planted when I was a student. Toward the beginning of my first season as a participant in the excavations at Magdala, I traveled with my friends and colleagues on the excavation to Jerusalem for the first time. It was on that trip that some of my colleagues insisted that I visit the Church of the Holy Sepulchre with them. My encounter with that place on that day sparked a fascination with early commemorative churches that eventually led to this book. Thus, my first word of thanks is to everyone who participated in the excavation at Magdala with me during the 2012 season.

This project has traveled with me over several years and through two institutional changes. It could not have been completed without the support, friendship, advice, and help of so many along the way. The years during which this book was written were difficult for personal reasons and because of the challenges of being a recent graduate of a PhD program. Although I can only name a few here, I do nevertheless want to acknowledge and thank all those of you who have journeyed through the past few years with me. A deep word of gratitude is due to Anders Runesson, my *doktorvater* and academic mentor. The ethos, methods, and approach of this research reflect the guidance and instruction that I have received from him over the years. The opportunity to visit and discuss some of the sites studied in this book with him during the 2018 excavation season at Magdala was also helpful for my research. This project would not exist were it not for his guidance and counsel. Wally V. Cirafesi deserves a special word of thanks and acknowledgment. Over the past few summers, he has traveled with me to several ancient churches and synagogues in Israel and Palestine, some of which are included in this study, and has been a frequent conversation partner throughout the process of writing and researching this book. I am grateful for his friendship and for his input on this research. Marcela Zapata-Meza deserves particular recognition and thanks for teaching me so much about archaeological fieldwork over the years, which has served me well at both Magdala and at Tel Shimron. I am also particularly grateful for the friendship and willingness of Matt Schlimm to act as a sounding board for some of the ideas that went into this book. Jonathan Bernier has also been a constant conversation partner throughout the process of research and writing this book, and has provided feedback on portions of the manuscript and on a number of ideas that went into this study. It is a richer study as a result.

Alan Kirk was extremely gracious in reading an early version of the manuscript of this study, and his input has been both encouraging and valuable. Chris Keith deserves my thanks and recognition for initially encouraging me to think of this research in terms of reception, which has helped to shape the final product immensely. I would also like to thank Karin Zetterholm, who recently invited me to participate in a colloquium at Lund University and to share some of the research that went into this book. The insights that came through the discussion, feedback, and conversation at that colloquium were very helpful as I entered into the final stages of the preparation of this manuscript. At that colloquium, Rina Talgam provided several encouraging thoughts and comments on some of the archaeological and architectural aspects of this project, for which I am also thankful. Andy Witt provided me with photographs of the archaeology museum at the Basilica of the Annunciation in Nazareth, which was helpful and generous. My teaching assistant, Tess De Pretis, helped immensely with the bibliography and has assisted me throughout the 2019–20 academic year in various capacities, which gave me more time to focus on this project. Grant Flynn has also assisted me greatly through his work on the indices.

My colleagues at Wheaton College have frequently been willing to listen and to provide feedback or thoughts on aspects of this project. In particular, Adam Miglio and Daniel Master have given an ear to my thoughts on early Christian archaeology on more than one occasion. I am also grateful for my students at Wheaton College. It has given me great joy to see the genuine interest that so many of you have expressed in the archaeology and history of early Judaism and early Christianity. Members of the University of Dubuque Theological Seminary community also deserve my thanks for being wonderful colleagues, especially Annette Huizenga, Mary Emily Duba, Jennifer Pattee, Chris Doll, and Chris James. I would also like to thank and acknowledge a few other colleagues for their friendship and encouragement throughout the writing of this project. I can name only a few here: Greg Fewster, Bruce Worthington, Andrea Garza Díaz Barriga, Rosaura Sanz-Rincón Michael Barber, Michael Johnson, Bill Heroman, and John Bolton. I am a better and more confident scholar because of all of you.

Additional thanks are also due to my immediate family, including my parents, Bill and Lillian, my sister Caitlin, and my mother-in-law Angeline. Without their steadfast support, this project would not have come to be. Finally, my wife, Joy Lee-Ryan, deserves my utmost thanks and recognition for being the best companion that I could have asked for, accompanying me to each of the sites included in this study, some on multiple occasions, and tirelessly photographing even mundane details at each one so that I could study them later. The photographs belonging to me included in this volume were taken by her with my direction. She has also joined me in the excavations at Magdala and at Tel Shimron, proving her mettle and skill as a digger time and again. I am grateful for the companionship and for the unsung time and effort that she too has put into making this project a reality.

Abbreviations

ABRL	Anchor Bible Reference Library
AYB	Anchor Yale Bible
BECNT	Baker Exegetical Commentary on the New Testament
CBQ	*Catholic Biblical Quarterly*
HdO	Handbuch der Orientalistik
IEJ	*Israel Exploration Journal*
JAAR	Journal of the American Academy of Religion
JECS	Journal of Early Christian Studies
JETS	Journal of the Evangelical Theological Society
JSHJ	Journal for the Study of the Historical Jesus
JSJSupp	Supplements to the *Journal for the Study of Judaism*
JSOTSupp	*Journal for the Study of the Old Testament* Supplement Series
JTS	Journal of Theological Studies
LA	*Liber Annuus*
LNTS	Library of New Testament Studies
LXX	Septuagint
NCBC	New Cambridge Bible Commentary
NIGTC	New International Greek Testament Commentary
NPNF	Nicene and Post Nicene Fathers
NRSV	New Revised Standard Version
NTL	New Testament Library
OCP	*Orientalia Christiana Periodica*
PEFQS	*Palestine Exploration Fund Quarterly Statement*
PEQ	*Palestine Exploration Quarterly*
PNTC	Pillar New Testament Commentary
PVTG	Pseudepigrapha Veteris Testamenti Graece
TENT	Texts and Editions for New Testament Study
THKNT	Theologischer Kommentar zum Neuen Testament
TSAJ	Texts and Studies in Ancient Judaism
WUNT	Wissenschaftliche Untersuchungen zum Neuen Testament
ZECNT	Zondervan Exegetical Commentary on the New Testament

Abbreviations of Ancient Texts

The abbreviations of ancient texts in this book follow the conventions of *The SBL Handbook of Style*, second edition.

The Bordeaux Pilgrim
Itin. Burd.   *Itinerarium Burdigalense*

Egeria
Itin. Eger.   *Itinerarium Egeriae*

The Piacenza Pilgrim
Itin. Piac.   *Itinerarium Piacenza*

Epiphanius
Pan.   *Panarion*

Eusebius of Caesarea
Dem. Evang.   *Demonstratio Evangelica*
Hist. eccl.   *Historia ecclesiastica*
Laud. Const.   *De Laudibus Constantini*

Cyril of Jerusalem
Cat.   *Catechetical Lectures*
Myst. Cat.   *Mystagogic Catecheses*

Jerome
lib. loc.   *Liber Locorum*

Peter the Deacon
de loc. sanct.   *de locis sanctis*

Pseudepigrapha
GLAE   Greek Life of Adam and Eve

1

Introduction

Place is central to the early Jesus tradition. The gospel narratives about Jesus are localized in the world of first-century Judea, Galilee, and Samaria. According to the traditions in the canonical gospels, Jesus was born in Bethlehem. He taught in Galilee. He died in Jerusalem. Beginning in antiquity, Christian visitors to Eretz Israel-Palestine have imagined themselves to walk in the very footsteps of Jesus of Nazareth. Likewise, today's pilgrims too can touch the place where Jesus was born, sit where he fed the five thousand, see the place where he had his Last Supper, pray at the spot where his body was laid, and even stand at the place where he ascended. At least that is what they are told by tradition, by their guides, and above all, by the existence of the monumental buildings that mark these spots as the places where the events took place.

In 2014, I spent a summer studying at the École Biblique et Archéologique in Jerusalem. During that summer, I once shared a vehicle on a journey from Jerusalem to Galilee with some travel companions, including a Roman Catholic priest, a seminarian, and another scholar. On that particular journey, we took a route that took us near Mt. Tabor. It was the seminarian's first visit to the region, and so the priest pointed to the mountain as it appeared in the distance and told him that Mt. Tabor was the place where Jesus was transfigured. The seminarian, like so many of us who have visited this region, asked how we can know that Mt. Tabor was the site of the transfiguration, since the location is not specified in the gospels. The priest's response was succinct and memorable: "Mt. Tabor is the place where we remember it."

The question of the "authenticity" of the traditional Christian commemorative sites is a valid one, but it is not the only question that can be asked about them in relation to Jesus and the gospels. To limit our inquiry of the relevance of early Christian commemorative sites related to the life of Jesus to the question of "authenticity" would miss the richness of the data that these sites provide us. Regardless of the historical "authenticity" of the site, the fact that the memories of Jesus and the traditions about him are given physical, geographical, even architectural expression through place in the form of holy sites is significant in itself. Moreover, the places themselves invite interpretation, and traditions can coalesce around them. The way that the sites connected to key events in the life of Jesus are interpreted can significantly impact the manner in which the events that they commemorate are interpreted. Thus, by considering a reception of significant places in the Jesus tradition of the first few centuries CE, we will be able to examine underexplored avenues of the history of the tradition and of the reception of Jesus of Nazareth in early Christianity.

The aim of the present project is to examine the reception of places connected to key events in the life of Jesus from the first century to the fourth century and to study the ways in which Jesus was commemorated at or in connection with those places. What did early Christians have to say about Golgotha? How did they understand the place of Jesus' birth? Of his burial? How did they interpret the significance of those places? What traditions, theological concepts, or narratives took root at these sites, and what can they tell us about the reception of Jesus over the first few centuries of the Common Era? The age of Constantinian commemorative church building in the fourth century at sites connected to the life of Jesus provides us with a bookend to cap off the study. More importantly, it affords us an opportunity to study the crystallization of memory and tradition in the form of the architecture of the monuments as we know them through the archaeological record. With this in mind, we will limit our study to places connected to key events in the life of Jesus for which churches commemorating those events were certainly or arguably constructed in the age of Constantine or slightly thereafter. This includes the place of Jesus' crucifixion, the place of his burial, the site of his birth, and the site of the ascension. Naturally, the events that loomed largest in Christian memory and tradition were among the first to receive monumental commemorative architecture. These places connected to central events in the life of Jesus, all of which are located in or near Jerusalem, are joined by a handful of ancillary sites in Galilee at which churches commemorating Jesus' miracles at Capernaum, the multiplication of the fish and the loaves, and the annunciation to Mary at Nazareth were constructed in the fourth century.

While commemorative churches are important, visible instantiations of the reception of places connected to the events of the life of Jesus, they are not the only object of our study. Nor should we conceive of the places that we will study only in terms of the geographic sites where the gospel narratives under discussion have been traditionally located. It is also essential to consider the reception of these places and its impact on the reception of Jesus himself in text, beginning with the gospel accounts. The early church had much to say about places such as Golgotha and the birthplace of Jesus. In order to fully appreciate and understand the contribution of the memory of these places to the way that Jesus was himself remembered, it will be essential to consider literary representations and interpretations of these sites.

In order to achieve our aim, we will need to examine the data from several perspectives. First, we will track and examine the presentation and discussion of each place in early Christian literature from the first century to the fourth century, beginning with the gospels. In the course of doing so, we will consider the various traditions, particularly extracanonical traditions, that were connected to the sites that we are studying. We will also consider the relationship of the traditions and interpretations of the sites in Christian literature to any parallels within early Jewish literature, if there are any. All of this will allow us to chart and track the reception of these places and the events of Jesus' life that were connected to them through the first few centuries. Then, with the advent of the construction of commemorative monuments at the traditional location of these places in the age of Constantine, we will turn our attention to the architecture of the commemorative churches in order to examine them as instantiations of reception and memory. Particular attention will be paid to ways in which the architecture itself communicated concepts, traditions, or ideas about Jesus. When the available evidence allows us to do so, we will also consider the ways in which these spaces, which served to anchor and locate the memory of Jesus in specific locations, were experienced by worshippers and pilgrims through liturgy and through pilgrimage itineraries and guides. We will also pay special attention to the roles that these places and the memory of them played in Jewish-Christian relations and in the intersection of Jewish and Christian traditions and concerns.

The data available to us are rich and complex. This makes it difficult to articulate a summary of what our study will uncover about each place that we will examine. However, there are a few themes that will emerge from the study. As we will see, the reception and interpretation of the key events in the life of Jesus that we are examining here were often impacted by the way that the place where the event happened was remembered. We will also see that the commemorative activity that took place at the traditional locations of key life-of-Jesus events, such as the crucifixion, contributed to Christian identity formation. Moreover, sites of Jesus-memory frequently functioned as vehicles and receptacles for the preservation of traditions, both canonical and apocryphal. Furthermore, these places and the memories attached to them were unfortunately sometimes leveraged to serve supersessionist, anti-Jewish purposes.

Place gives memory a tangible referent, grounding it, allowing it to take root. Thus, Gérôme Truc writes, "Our memory is framed by spatial reference points: places, sites, buildings, and streets give us our bearings and enable us to anchor and order our memories."[1] Memories of Jesus were attached to places very early on. Thus, the evangelists tell us that Peter's confession took place specifically at Caesarea Philippi,[2] that Jesus healed a sick man at the Pool of Bethesda,[3] that the "Bread of Life" discourse was given in the synagogue in Capernaum,[4] and so on. The specific identifications of place in early Christian memory anchored memories of Jesus in the physical space of the Land of Israel in the late Second-Temple period and allowed for the organization of those memories into coherent narratives of the past. Whatever we may think about the reliability of individual traditions, the memories of Jesus set in places such as the lake region of Galilee and Jerusalem are so solidly crystallized in the early Christian collective memory that a reasonable historian cannot but acknowledge that the man was active in these regions.

This, of course, speaks to the geography of the gospel accounts, both historical and sacred, but what about the holy sites of early Christianity? How did they come to be, and moreover, how did the process of commemoration through the building of monuments, the writing of accompanying liturgy that interacted with the places and monuments, and the oral spread of traditions coalescing around these sacred places

---

[1] Gérôme Truc, "Memory of Places and Places of Memory: For a Halbwachsian Socio-Ethnography of Collective Memory," *International Social Science Journal* 62, no. 203–4 (2011): 147–59 (148).
[2] Mark 8:27 (cf. Matt 16:13).
[3] John 5:2.
[4] John 6:59.

contribute to the reception, interpretation, evolution, and preservation of the Jesus tradition? How did place continue to play a role in Jesus memory beyond the writing of the gospels? What role did it play for the memorialization of Jesus in the Christianized Palestine of the fourth century? Furthermore, what can the history, traditions, architecture, and archaeology of places like the Church of the Holy Sepulchre, the Church of the Nativity, or the so-called House of Peter tell us about Jesus in memory, history, and reception?

The relevance of the commemorative churches to the church historian or archaeologist of early Christianity in Palestine is clear. However, the matter of their relevance to the things that interest New Testament scholars, such as the study of Jesus, the gospels, Jesus-memory, and gospel traditions has yet to be fully appreciated. The study of early Christian sites commemorating and localizing the events of the life of Jesus has long been the domain of the study of late antique Christianity, and with good reason. The great commemorative churches in Palestine were first built in the fourth century in the midst of the Constantinian shift. However, the events that they commemorate and claim to mark ostensibly took place in the first century, and the man that they commemorate lived in the first century. How, then, do they relate, if at all, to the first-century narratives and events that their very existence is meant to commemorate?

As R. A. Markus concludes in his study of the emergence of holy places in early Christianity,

> Christianity, when it finally endowed itself with holy places, did so almost inadvertently, certainly indirectly, *as a consequence of identifying itself with a historical past* ... A sense of sacred space, and of a sacred Christian topography, was, however, a late arrival on the Christian scene, and one in large measure produced by the enhanced sense of the past, and the need to experience it as present. Places became sacred as the past became localised in the present. *It was always the past that really mattered, and it was the impact of past human action that gave places their significance*: "You are here to kneel where prayer has been valid."[5]

The purpose of the establishment of the holy sites was to identify the present with the past, to connect the emerging Constantinian "Holy Land" of the Christian present with the past events that gave birth to the movement three centuries prior. The holy sites are themselves vehicles of remembrance, a sort of topographical history, witnesses in monumental form to key events in the life, ministry, and death of Jesus of Nazareth.

Through their very existence, the holy sites make historical claims about the biblical past that are, by definition, extracanonical. They concretize the abstract sense of place in the text of the gospels. While the gospels often tie events to places, they do so generally or abstractly. However, in the experience of a fourth-century pilgrim such as Egeria, it is no longer simply at Nain that the widow's son is raised— it happened at *this* specific location in Nain, at *this* specific church, a physical, architectural, monumental

---

[5] R. A. Markus, "How on Earth Could Places Become Holy?: Origins of the Christian Idea of Holy Places," *Journal of Early Christian Studies* 2, no. 3 (1994): 257–71 (271). Emphasis my own.

marker that existed in her own day.⁶ Similarly, the feeding of the five thousand did not simply take place "in a deserted place" (Mark 1:31–32; Matt 14:13), perhaps somewhere near Bethsaida (cf. Luke 9:10–11).⁷ Rather, it took place specifically at the Heptapegon (Arabic "Tabgha"), a location marked by the distinctive feature of its seven springs. The precise locations of these events are themselves non-biblical traditions, drawn from collective memory rather than from the gospels directly.

When I say that these traditions are drawn from collective memory, I am not making a claim about the accuracy, age, or truth of the traditions pertaining to the precise geographical locations of the gospel events.⁸ What I am in fact saying is that, regardless of the accuracy or age of the traditions, events in the life of Jesus were commemorated at these places, and they became *lieux de mémoire* as collective memory crystallized solidly around them. Thus, for local Christians as well as pilgrims, the geography, landscape, topography, and physical features of these *topoi* became part of the gospel stories, and facilitated and encouraged their retelling.

Methodological Foundations

It is important to clarify from the outset that the authenticity of the "holy sites" of fourth-century Palestine as the genuine locations of events in the life of Jesus is not the primary concern of this study. That is not to say that the question is completely irrelevant to the matter at hand but rather that it is ancillary to our primary goals. This approach comes, in part, out of current discussions in the study of Jesus and the gospels. Previous eras of scholarship typically placed "authenticity" at the core of the historical task, leading to what might be described as a premium placed on verifiable, "authentic" data. Perhaps it is this elevation of the "authentic" that has resulted in the neglect of the holy sites and associated traditions by New Testament scholars despite their ostensible claim to a historical connection to Jesus of Nazareth. The claims to the biblical past upon which the holy sites are founded are extremely difficult to verify and are far too easily dismissed as "legend," perhaps belonging to the study of "Patristics"

---

⁶ Concerning the importance of markers in early Christian pilgrimage in Israel-Palestine, see Blake Leyerle, "Landscape as Cartography in Early Christian Pilgrimage Narratives," *JAAR* 64, no. 1 (1996): 119–43; cf. Leyerle, "Pilgrims to the Land: Early Christian Perceptions of Galilee," in *Galilee through the Centuries: Confluence of Cultures*, ed. Eric M. Meyers (Winona Lake: Eisenbrauns, 1999), 345–57.

⁷ On the problem of Luke's location of the location of this event at Bethsaida, as opposed to the Markan "deserted place" (Greek ἔρημον τόπον), compare the views expressed in, e.g., Darrell L. Bock, *Luke*, 2 vols., BECNT (Grand Rapids: Baker, 1994), 1: 828–29; James R. Edwards, *The Gospel According to Luke*, PNTC (Grand Rapids: Eerdmans, 2015), 265; Joseph A. Fitzmyer, *The Gospel According to Luke*, 3 vols., AYB 28 (New York: Doubleday, 1981), 765.

⁸ Nevertheless, it is important to recognize that, as John Bodnar has argued, commemoration in monumental form (as with the early Christian *lieux de mémoire*) interweaves "official" memory driven by the institution and "vernacular" memory, memory driven by the ordinary people. See John Bodnar, *Remaking America: Public Memory, Commemoration, and Patriotism in the Twentieth Century* (Princeton: Princeton University Press, 1992). This is to say that there is local, organic collective memory within the fabric of these sites, regardless of the accuracy of that memory or of the institutional purpose driving the crystallization of it.

or "early Christianity," and thus outside the typical areas for study by New Testament specialists.

However, one of the key issues that has been highlighted in some recent publications on method is that there is a need to shift the scholarly discourse away from an inflexible dichotomy between "authentic" and "inauthentic" material. This has been promulgated especially by proponents of the use of social memory theory in research on Jesus and the gospels.[9] For example, Chris Keith writes,

> A significant problem with the criteria approach in this respect is that it detaches supposed later, purportedly inauthentic, traditions from the earlier stages of the traditioning process *entirely*, as if those alleged inauthentic traditions appeared out of thin air in the course of history … Alleged inauthentic traditions *exist* as historical artifacts, however, and, on that account if no other, demand a historical explanation.[10]

Likewise, Anthony Le Donne writes that the historian "is keenly interested in all interpretations, whether they are 'factual' or not."[11] So, too, Loveday Alexander observes that "the fact that stories are shaped for present needs does not mean they are no use to the historian."[12]

There is a need for a robust approach to the understanding of evidence and its role in historical inquiry in our discipline. Thus, in a different way from the proponents of the memory approach to the historical study of Jesus and the gospels, I have also advocated for a move beyond the confines that are created by the quest for "authenticity," though on grounds based primarily on the philosophy of history rather than on social memory theory.[13] Writing in the 1920s and 1930s, R. G. Collingwood cautioned against "scissors-and-paste" history, which is history done by excerpting "true" statements of witnesses and consigning the leftover "false" statements to the waste bin.[14] The primary question that scissors-and-paste history is concerned with is "Shall we incorporate this statement into our own narrative or not?"[15] The problem that Collingwood identified with scissors-and-paste history is that the historian may

---

[9] For an introduction to this matter, see the essays contained in Chris Keith and Anthony Le Donne, eds., *Jesus, Criteria, and the Demise of Authenticity* (London: T&T Clark International, 2012), esp. Anthony Le Donne, "The Rise of the Quest For an Authentic Jesus: An Introduction to the Crumbling Foundations of Jesus Research" (pp. 3–24), and Chris Keith, "The Indebtedness of the Criteria Approach to Form Criticism and Recent Attempts to Rehabilitate the Search For an Authentic Jesus" (pp. 25–48).

[10] Chris Keith, *Jesus' Literacy: Scribal Culture and the Teacher from Galilee*, LNTS 413 (London: T&T Clark, 2011), p. 63.

[11] Anthony Le Donne, *Historical Jesus: What Can We Know and How Can We Know It?* (Grand Rapids: Eerdmans, 2011), 78.

[12] Loveday Alexander, "Memory and Tradition in the Hellenistic Schools," in *Jesus and Memory*, ed. Werner H. Kelber and Samuel Byrskog (Waco: Baylor, 2009), 113–54 (152).

[13] Jordan J. Ryan, "Jesus at the Crossroads of Inference and Imagination: The Relevance of R.G. Collingwood's Philosophy of History for Current Methodological Discussions in Historical Jesus Research," *JSHJ* 13 (2015): 66–89 (76–8).

[14] R. G. Collingwood, *The Idea of History*, ed. Jan van der Dussen; rev. and enl. ed. (Oxford: Clarendon Press, [1946] 1993), 275 (e.g.).

[15] Ibid., 259.

be interested in a given statement regardless of whether it is literally "true" or "false." In actuality, the very fact that a statement is made at all may be significant and may be crucial or important evidence for a given investigation.

As others have noted, including Collingwood himself, the detective's role in a murder investigation provides a fitting parallel for the historian's task.[16] This is because both disciplines are concerned with reconstructing the past on the basis of evidence and both involve the criticism of testimony. In a murder mystery, a detective does not disregard planted evidence. Rather, the very fact that evidence has been planted is in itself evidence for something else. Rather than simply discarding it, the detective investigates why it was planted in the first place, since this may open up new avenues for investigation. Similarly, if a witness is caught in a lie, the statement is not set aside altogether. Rather, the very fact that the lie was told is in itself of interest to the detective. Why would the witness lie? Perhaps it was to protect someone else, or perhaps it points to the guilt of the person telling the lie. In either instance, that knowledge could serve to advance the investigation. Whether it is planted evidence or a lying witness, it is necessary to interpret and understand the data rather than discarding it out of hand.[17]

In order to break out of the confines of a scissors-and-paste approach to history, the historian needs to be willing and able to treat testimony as *evidence* for a given investigation. Collingwood posited that the primary question that history is properly concerned with asking of any given datum is "What does this mean?"[18] What does this mean, if anything at all, *for the question that I am pursuing*? It is essential at this juncture to break out of the dichotomy of taking testimony at face value or rejecting it and thus casting it aside. Testimony should be understood by the historian as an artifact of the past requiring interpretation and explanation.

The result of these recent developments in the methodological discussion is that the pool of data from which to draw upon for historical investigation on Jesus should now be greatly expanded to include data that were previously disregarded as "inauthentic."

As James Dunn has famously argued, the only Jesus to which the historian has access is the remembered Jesus.[19] The new postform critical paradigm has opened up new avenues for exploration of the remembered Jesus. Rather than asking only "Was Jesus remembered accurately?" we are now presented with the opportunity to instead ask "How was Jesus remembered?" We should treat the chronological distance between Jesus and the construction of the commemorative churches dedicated to events in his life in the fourth century CE as an opportunity to study collective Jesus-memory in oral form over the *longue durée* rather than as an insurmountable obstacle.

---

[16] Ibid., 266–82. For other examples, see the introduction and essays collected in Robin W. Winks, *The Historian as Detective: Essays on Evidence* (New York: Harper Torchbooks, 1970).

[17] For examples of other major twentieth-century historical theorists dealing with the problem of testimony, see Marc Bloch, *The Historian's Craft*, trans. Peter Putnam (New York: Alfred A. Knopf, 1953), 79–137; Jacques Barzun and Henry F. Graff, "A Medley of Mysteries: A Number of Dogs That Didn't Bark," in *The Historian as Detective: Essays on Evidence*, ed. Robin W. Winks (New York: Harper Torchbooks, 1970), 213–31; and Michael Oakeshott, *Experience and Its Modes*, repr. ed. (Cambridge: Cambridge University Press, [1933] 1994), 114–17.

[18] Collingwood, *Idea of History*, 275.

[19] James D. G. Dunn, *Jesus Remembered*, Christianity in the Making 1 (Grand Rapids: Eerdmans, 2003), 616.

As we have said above, the age of Constantinian commemorative church building in Palestine in the fourth century CE provides a bookend for our study. During this time, the first places connected with the events of the gospel narratives became enshrined within monumental architecture, which incorporated and instantiated the earlier memories that had coalesced around these places while also presenting novel or evolved interpretations of the past through their construction, location, and architectural elements. Although commemorative life-of-Jesus churches continued to be constructed in Palestine well after Constantine's time, the present study is limited to monuments constructed roughly around the age of Constantine and thus as close to the termination of the first three centuries of the reception history of Jesus of Nazareth as possible. Later commemorative churches in Palestine, particularly of the fifth century, are interesting instantiations of reception and memory in their own right but also incorporate new developments in architecture and are themselves conditioned by the historical events of their own time.[20]

Sites of Memory

Elsewhere, I have expressed the need to recognize the limits of memory-based approaches for historical investigations and have advocated instead for a method firmly rooted in the philosophy of history and historiography, particularly for historical Jesus studies.[21] That having been said, I nevertheless recognize the insight that has been brought to the study of Jesus by proponents of social memory theory in Jesus studies. While I am not confident that social memory theory can form the basis of a historiographical method, whether for studying the historical Jesus or otherwise, I do recognize that memory-based approaches have the potential to help us to better understand the history of the tradition.[22] Since what we are dealing with in this project is essentially an extension of the history of the tradition, we will consider some of the ways in which being attentive to the processes of collective remembering and commemoration will be helpful for our present aims.

---

[20] For example, it has been convincingly argued by Vered Shalev-Hurvitz that the commemorative buildings of the Kathisma and Mary's Tomb, both dated to the fifth century CE, should be understood in light of the historical context of the Council of Ephesus, after which these two churches with Marian foci were constructed; in Vered Shalev-Hurvitz, *Holy Sites Encircled: The Early Byzantine Concentric Church of Jerusalem*, Oxford Studies in Byzantium (Oxford: Oxford University Press, 2015), 138–9, 153–8.

[21] Ryan, "Jesus at the Crossroads of Inference and Imagination"; Jordan J. Ryan, *The Role of the Synagogue in the Aims of Jesus* (Minneapolis: Fortress, 2017), 12, 288. It is worth noting that Chris Keith has rightly preferred the term "approach" to "method" for historical investigations based in social memory theory. See Chris Keith, *Jesus against the Scribal Elite* (Grand Rapids: Baker, 2014), 81.

[22] I am greatly indebted to conversations with Alan Kirk for this conception of the potential role that collective memory studies can play in the study of the gospels and early Christianity. See also his publications, Alan Kirk, "Cognition, Commemoration, and Tradition: Memory and the Historiography of Jesus Research," *Early Christianity* 6 (2015): 285–310; Alan Kirk, *Memory and the Jesus Tradition*, Reception of Jesus in the First Three Centuries 2 (London: T&T Clark, 2018), esp. 1–7, 70.

Remembering is collective. Thus, in the words of Maurice Halbwachs, "each impression and each fact, even if it apparently concerns a particular person exclusively, leaves a lasting memory only to the extent that one has thought it over—to the extent that it is connected with the thoughts that come to us from the social milieu."[23] It is thereby essential to understand the process of remembering Jesus through the commemoration and interpreting the sites of the key events of the life of Jesus as a function of collective memory.

The places that are the focus of our study function as what Pierre Nora calls "*lieux de mémoire*."[24] *Lieux de mémoire* are sites where memory crystallizes. According to Nora, "A *lieu de mémoire* is any significant entity, whether material or non-material in nature, which by dint of human will or the work of time has become a symbolic element of the memorial heritage of any community."[25] We are concerned here with actual places, but *lieux de mémoire* can also be objects or events within the memory of a community. Furthermore, we need not necessarily conceive of *lieux de mémoire* solely in terms of monuments or of actual, geographical places. They can also exist in literary or ideal form. The tomb of Jesus was a *lieu de mémoire* long before the Church of the Holy Sepulchre was constructed, existing within the collective memory and writings of the early church.

Memory is intertwined with interpretation. This is because the past is remembered in light of the present. Thus, when we say that a particular event in the life of Jesus is "remembered" or "commemorated" by a particular ancient monument (for example), we must also recognize that, as it is remembered, so too it is interpreted. As Chris Keith has pointedly put the matter, "there is no memory, no preserved past, and no access to it, without interpretation."[26]

Two distinct tendencies or perspectives have been identified within memory studies.[27] The first, termed "presentism" or "constructionism," emphasizes the present's impact on the recollection of the past, to the point that the present essentially eclipses the past. Barry Schwartz summarizes it aptly, writing that in the presentist model, "social memory is context-depenent and constructed differently as it is invoked in different communities ... constructionist scholarship endeavors to show how beliefs about the past become hostage to the circumstances of the present, and how different elements of the past become more or less relevant as these circumstances change."[28] However, some have identified a problematic element to a hard, extreme presentism

---

[23] Maurice Halbwachs, *On Collective Memory*, trans. Lewis A. Coser (Chicago: University of Chicago Press, 1992), 53.
[24] Pierre Nora, "Between Memory and History: Les Lieux De Mémoire," *Representations* 26 (1989): 7–24.
[25] Pierre Nora, *Realms of Memory: The Construction of the French Past*, trans. Arthur Goldhammer (New York: Columbia University Press, 1996), xvii.
[26] Keith, *Jesus' Literacy*, 61.
[27] For a discussion of presentism and continuitism specifically in the context of research on Jesus, see Anthony Le Donne, "The Problem of Selectivity in Memory Research: A Response to Zeba Crook," *JSHJ* 11, no. 1 (2013): 77–97 (esp. 83–7).
[28] Barry Schwartz, "Christian Origins: Historical Truth and Social Memory," in *Memory, Tradition, and Text: Uses of the Past in Early Christianity*, ed. Alan Kirk and Tom Thatcher, Semeia (Atlanta: Society of Biblical Literature, 2005), 43–56 (44).

so far as historical interpretation and historiography are concerned. According to Barbie Zelizer, "This 'presentist' approach, which views memory as constantly shifting, facilitates the misinterpretation of historical data by viewing it through its own categories. It undoes history and risks tottering the establishment of continuity and stability, seen as instrumental for the group's identity."[29]

The other model, termed "continuitism," recognizes the impact of the present on the memory of the past, while also holding that the present is nevertheless "constituted by the past."[30] Thus, in the words of Schwartz, "society changes constantly, but social memory endures because new beliefs are superimposed upon—rather than replace— old ones ... As individuals acquire traditional understandings through forebears (either through oral culture, commemoration, or historiography), common memories endow them with a common heritage ... Every society, even the most fragmented, requires a sense of sameness and continuity with what went before."[31] Keith helpfully captures the essence of the continuitist perspective in saying that "memory is a much more complex social process of mutual influence. The present does not simply run roughshod over the past; the present acts on the past while the past simultaneously acts on the present."[32]

This study recognizes that the acts of remembering and commemorating involve a relationship between the past and the present (the time when the remembering is done). Any extreme overemphasis on one to the degradation of the other by the historian will result in a problematic interpretation of the data. Thus, this study recognizes both the impact of the present on the memory of the past, as well as the continuity of the past with memory of it in the present. Thus, the past is interpreted in light of present circumstances, but not necessarily so distorted as to be unrecoverable.

Maurice Halbwachs, the progenitor of social memory theory (also called "collective memory"), wrote on the holy sites in light of his theoretical work on collective memory.[33] Although that work espouses ideas that are now quite dated, from the perspective of the study of social memory as well as that of early Christianity, it nevertheless presents insights that are worth considering. In particular, Halbwachs observed that, although the search for the localization of the events of the life of Jesus in early Christianity may have some basis in local memory, the holy sites nevertheless represent the beliefs and ideas of the fourth century CE.

Thus, the epoch of Constantine and the epoch of the Crusaders respectively mark the two moments when the Christian memory—the collective memory representing the totality of the Christian community in these two epochs—searched for the sites of the evangelical facts and tried to find locations for its recollections. It tried, in a way,

---

[29] Barbie Zelizer, "Reading the Past against the Grain: The Shape of Memory Studies," *Critical Studies in Mass Media* 12 (1995): 214–39. Quoted in Le Donne, "Problem of Selectivity," 83, in relation to historical Jesus studies.

[30] Barry Schwartz, *Abraham Lincoln and the Forge of National Memory* (Chicago: University of Chicago Press, 2000), 302.

[31] Schwartz, "Christian Origins," 44.

[32] Keith, *Jesus' Literacy*, 58.

[33] Originally, Maurice Halbwachs, *La Topographie Légendaire des Évangiles en Terre Sainte: Étude de Mémoire Collective* (Paris: Presses Universitaires de France, 1941). The thesis is reproduced in the conclusion of *On Collective Memory*.

to situate itself in space, in Jerusalem and in the Holy Land. In each case it tried to use local memories as a basis, but it also introduced new localizations. As a result, the general organization of the holy places is strongly marked by contemporary Christian beliefs.[34]

This general observation, that the fourth-century holy sites tried to use local memories as a basis but are also marked by contemporary Christian beliefs, is insightful. Any interpretation of the early commemorative churches must consider them as representations of ideas and events of the time in which they were popularized and in which their monuments were constructed, as well as the events and ideas of the first century CE that they intend to commemorate.

While there are undoubtedly some insights contained in Halbwachs's study, there are also numerous shortcomings. Although Halbwachs recognized that there was an "early system of localization" in earliest Christianity, he also considered it to be built within a framework of earlier Jewish, typically biblical, localized memories.[35] This means that the localized memories of the life of Jesus were attached to places that were already significant in Jewish tradition. This is greatly overstated, to a degree that is problematic. Halbwachs's best example of this is the localization of the Nativity at Bethlehem in Matthew and Luke, which he rightly notes is connected to Jewish memories of David.[36] While there is a case to be made for a connection between the memory of the localization of the Nativity at Bethlehem and the Jewish traditions connecting David to the same place, other important events of the gospels that happen to be localized are not as clearly connected to earlier memories. For example, it is hard to imagine how the same could be said about key localizations at places like Caesarea Philippi, Capernaum, Nazareth, and Cana.

Moreover, Halbwachs holds that the first set of memories, the early "system of localization," lost its strength, became obscure, and "gave way, at the time of Constantine, to a new system, which prevailed during the centuries that followed."[37] This too is an overstatement, or at least a hypothesis that needs to be examined and weighed. Halbwachs here expresses a level of presentism that does not allow much room for any relationship between the first- and fourth-century memories of localization. Whether or not the fourth-century commemorative sites of the life of Jesus are based on earlier traditions is a point that we will need to address as our discussion progresses. At the very least, at the foundation of this project is a recognition that there is some relationship between the first-century memories of Jesus in the tradition and their reception in the commemorative architecture and activity of the fourth century. Even if all of the commemorative life-of-Jesus churches reflect localizations that go back no further than the fourth century, a prospect that is difficult to defend, they are nevertheless receptacles and interpretations of the Jesus tradition.

Another problem that hampers Halbwachs's study is his attitude toward the Galilean portions of the gospel narratives. He holds that "the Galilean part of the gospels had

---

[34] Halbwachs, *On Collective Memory*, 233.
[35] Ibid., 213–14, 233.
[36] Ibid., 214.
[37] Ibid., 233.

been imagined toward the end of the first century or at the beginning of the second by a group that knew the places and situated the discourses and miracles there in a more or less arbitrary manner."[38] It goes without saying that this position is not followed in modern scholarship, especially in light of the so-called Third Quest for the historical Jesus, which emphasized the historical Jesus' Galilean origins. Indeed, if we regard the Galilean localizations in the gospels as secondary additions to the tradition, it is difficult to explain the localization of Jesus' activities in relatively insignificant Jewish villages such as Capernaum, Cana, Nazareth, Bethsaida, and Chorazin.

Halbwachs espouses a hard presentism, wherein the present eclipses the past, to a degree that is problematic. Schwartz addresses the problem with Halbwachs's study, writing, "That commemoration is a selective celebration rather than an inferior version of history escapes Halbwachs. He cannot fully grasp what sacred sites accomplish, how they transmute reality to mobilize and sustain religious sentiment and, above all, elevate Jesus and sustain faith in what he did and represented."[39] Schwartz identifies the refusal of both Rudolf Bultmann and Halbwachs "even to ask how pericopae, texts, and physical sites reflected what ordinary people of the first century believed" as a common failure.[40]

Although Halbwachs's work concerning the holy sites has largely not been followed in contemporary scholarship, it is nevertheless worth recognizing that his theory of collective memory provides us with a helpful framework. Nora's concept of the *lieux de mémoire* similarly provides us with a way to think about the places connected with key events in the life of Jesus. They are sites where memories of Jesus have accumulated and crystallized in the form of the discussions and presentations of them in early Christian writings, monumental architecture, and other markers. That crystallized memory, available to us through historical sources and through the archaeological remains of commemorative monuments, when understood properly in their role as interpretive representations of the past, offers us a unique window into the reception and interpretation of Jesus from the first to fourth centuries CE.

Commemorating the Past

Commemoration will be a significant dimension of this study, so it will serve our purposes well to define it here. According to Schwartz, "Commemoration mobilizes symbols to awaken ideas and feelings about the past ... By marking events believed to be most deserving of remembrance, commemoration becomes society's moral memory. Commemoration makes society conscious of itself as it affirms its members' mutual affinity and identity."[41] Commemoration "sanctifies" the past[42] and contributes to the formation of group identity as well as to the establishment of official memory in the sphere of public memory. It is important to be attentive to the power dynamics involved

---

[38] Ibid., 211.
[39] Schwartz, "Christian Origins," 49.
[40] Ibid., 49.
[41] Schwartz, *Abraham Lincoln*, 9–10.
[42] Ibid., 11.

in this sort of commemoration, which takes place in the arena of public memory. According to Paul Connerton, "Control of a society's memory largely conditions the hierarchy of power."[43] This aspect of memory and how it is controlled will be helpful to consider as we explore the beginnings of the imperial commemorative church-building enterprise in Palestine under Constantine in the fourth century CE.

According to Kenneth Foote and Maoz Azaryahu,

> Commemorations assign significance to events and figures to create a "register of sacred history,"[44] a set of shared historical experiences and attitudes that define and bond a community ... In this capacity, public memory is a part of the symbolic foundation of collective identity, where the question, "who we are," is answered, at least partially, by answering the question, "where do we come from," and what we share and do together as a community.[45]

Commemoration is part of the foundations of a community, of its expression and formation of its identity. Through what it commemorates, it defines the identity of the community in the present in light of its origins. For early Christianity, that identity is naturally bound up in the life, works, and ministry of Jesus of Nazareth, who is ultimately the object of the commemorative activity expressed through the sites of memory that we will be examining. In particular, it will be of utmost importance to pay attention to the ways in which the commemorative activity expressed in text, architecture, exegesis, place, and pilgrimage, associated with these places, which be construed both literarily and geographically,[46] attempts to construct and control public memory.

John Bodnar and other like-minded theorists of commemoration distinguish between memory that stems from "vernacular" and "official" culture.[47] Cynthia Pelak has effectively and helpfully summarized this distinction in the following manner:

> Official memories are those supported by cultural and political leaders with state power to promote individual and group interests that confirm the status quo.

---

[43] Paul Connerton, *How Societies Remember* (Cambridge: Cambridge University Press, 1989), 1.
[44] Citing Barry Schwartz, "The Social Context of Commemoration: A Study in Collective Memory," *Social Forces* 61, no. 2 (1982): 374–402 (377).
[45] Kenneth E. Foote and Maoz Azaryahu, "Toward a Geography of Memory: Geographical Dimensions of Public Memory and Commemoration," *Journal of Political and Military Sociology* 35, no. 1 (2007): 125–44 (127).
[46] Golgotha, for example, can both be construed through an author's writing about the place, and through geographically locating it.
[47] Bodnar, *Remaking America*, 13–18. The distinction between "official" and "vernacular" memory in commemoration has been taken up by others in recent years, e.g., Aaron Hess, "In Digital Remembrance: Vernacular Memory and the Rhetorical Construction of Web Memorials," *Media, Culture & Society* 29, no. 5 (2007): 812–30; Ekaterina Haskins, "Between Archive and Participation: Public Memory in a Digital Age," *Rhetoric Society Quarterly* 37, no. 4 (2007): 401–22; David Charles Sloane, "Roadside Shrines and Granite Sketches: Diversifying the Vernacular Landscape of Memory," *Perspectives in Vernacular Architecture* 12 (2005): 64–81; Cynthia Fabrizio Pelak, "Institutionalizing Counter-Memories of the U.S. Civil Rights Movement: The National Civil Rights Museum and an Application of the Interest-Convergence Principle," *Sociological Forum* 30, no. 2 (2015): 305–27.

Vernacular memories are constructed and supported by nonelite, nonstate actors and communities that give meaning to everyday life and histories that are distinct but not necessarily in opposition to the politics of elites or official collective memories.[48]

According to Bodnar, the culture of official memory "originates in the concerns of cultural leaders or authorities at all levels of society ... these leaders share a common interest in social unity, the continuity of existing institutions, and loyalty to the status quo."[49] Vernacular culture, on the other hand, is concerned with "restating views of reality derived from firsthand experience in small-scale communities."[50] Tension can exist between the official and vernacular, as the concerns of the two clash, or as one ignores, or reformulates, the other. At the intersection of the two is what Bodnar calls "public memory," which is "a body of beliefs and ideas about the past that help a public or society understand both its past, present, and by implication, its future. It is fashioned ideally in a public sphere in which various parts of the social structure exchange views."[51] Bodnar observes that while public commemorations usually celebrate official concerns, the local and personal past is usually incorporated into public memory rather than the other way around.[52]

The distinction between vernacular and official memory, as well as the intersection between the two in public memory, is important to keep in mind as we examine the process of early Christian commemoration in the holy sites. As we will see, many of the commemorative churches clearly reflect what Bodnar calls "official culture." Even in these sites, it is important to be attentive to how vernacular memory interacts with the official. Other sites, particularly those in Galilee mentioned by Egeria in her *Itinerarium* that lack both canonical referents and architectural monuments, generally do not have the characteristics associated official memory. It may be that they instead have their roots in vernacular, local collective memory and *possibly* (though I am not making such claims here) even in personal memory, albeit personal memory that has undergone the usual processes of interpretation, accretion, and distortion that we would expect to occur over the course of three centuries.

For the purposes of this study, we will be particularly attuned to the geography of memory, which "locates history and its representations in space and landscape," and locates memory "in terms of places and sites that case a certain vision of history into a mold of commemorative permanence."[53] In order to do so, we will necessarily "focus on the spatial, locational, and material patterns and dynamics of these commemorative practices, generally in public spaces."[54]

---

[48] Pelak, "Institutionalizing Counter-Memories," 308.
[49] Bodnar, *Remaking America*, 13.
[50] Ibid., 14.
[51] Ibid., 15.
[52] Ibid., 17.
[53] Foote and Azaryahu, "Geography of Memory," 127.
[54] Ibid.

Meaning in Architecture

By the fourth century CE, commemorative activity and social memory that had been primarily located in text and collective imagination began to focus upon and manifest itself at specific geographical locations in the form of architectural monuments. One of the major methodological challenges of this project is that it requires us to consider the meaning not only of texts concerning the memory of places associated with the life of Jesus but also of the architecture of the commemorative churches. For example, what meaning, what ideas about Jesus, are communicated through the *architecture* of the Constantinian Church of the Holy Sepulchre?

Just as human thought and intention are conveyed through writing, so too are they conveyed through architecture. According to Collingwood, the father of the modern philosophy of history, "all history is the history of thought."[55] There is both an "inside" and an "outside" to every historical action, wherein the "outside" is that which can be described in physical terms, that which pertains to bodies and their movements, whereas the "inside" of an event is that which can be described in terms of thought.[56] Action, in history, is the unity of the inside and the outside of an event.[57] The historian does not seeks to understand one to the exclusion of the other, but both, as two sides of the same coin. The physical is informed and driven by the thought, expressed in terms of intention, which underlies it. Just as Ben F. Meyer argued for the primacy of the intended sense of texts in interpretation,[58] so too should we consider the intentions that lie behind and inform architecture such as the commemorative churches. Thus, we seek the inside of the event of the building of the commemorative churches, communicated through both historical and archaeological evidence, "to grasp it as motivated in some way, moving in some direction, significant in some context."[59]

In order to do this, we turn to the iconography of architecture.[60] Although the iconography of architecture as a methodological approach was developed particularly within the study of medieval Christian architecture, its basic premises have clear application for early Christian architecture as well. The foundational principle of the iconography of architecture is that architecture conveys meaning. In speaking of the iconography of medieval architecture, Richard Krautheimer writes that "any mediaeval structure was meant to convey a meaning which transcends the visual pattern of the

---

[55] Collingwood, *Idea of History*, 215.
[56] Ibid., 213.
[57] Ibid.
[58] Ben F. Meyer, *Critical Realism and the New Testament* (Allison Park: Pickwick, 1989), 17–55.
[59] Ibid., 167.
[60] As first articulated and elucidated by Richard Krautheimer, "Introduction to an 'Iconography of Mediaeval Architecture,'" *Journal of the Wartburg and Courtald Institutes* 5 (1942): 1–33; cf. Krautheimer, "The Carolingian Revival of Early Christian Architecture," *The Art Bulletin* 24, no. 1 (1942): 1–38. It is worth noting that early Christian architecture and its impact on medieval architecture played a key role in the formulation of Krautheimer's conception of the iconography of architecture. For a good overview of the method of the iconography of architecture, refer to Elizabeth Valdez del Álamo, "The Iconography of Architecture," in *The Routledge Companion to Medieval Iconography*, ed. Colum Hourihane (London: Routledge, 2016), 377–89. See also Catherine Carver McCurrach, "'Renovatio' Reconsidered: Richard Krautheimer and the Iconography of Architecture," *Gesta* 50, no. 1 (2011): 41–69.

structure."[61] The methodological upshot of this is that, in the words of Elizabeth Valdez del Álamo, "the study of a building's symbolic content is as important as the study of its formal or technical elements."[62]

The primary concerns (adapted for our purposes) that emerge from the study of the iconography of architecture are how architecture was understood by ancient authors and how modern scholars identify significance in ancient buildings.[63] We are fortunate in that we have a considerable amount of early documentary evidence pertaining to the early commemorative life-of-Jesus churches. The information concerning the life-of-Jesus churches provided by such authors as Eusebius, Epiphanius, Egeria, the Pilgrim of Bordeaux, Jerome, Cyril of Jerusalem, and others is of immense value. Context is of particular importance in the determination of the significance of architecture. Text is only one aspect of that context. Krautheimer's particular approach to the iconography of architecture emphasized the importance of determining how the "nonrepresentational medium of architecture could impart ideological meaning through reference to other structures."[64] Thus, understanding the architecture of the commemorative life-of-Jesus churches in relation to other buildings, both earlier and contemporary, can provide some interpretive clarity.

Conclusion

Our discussion thus far has determined the task set before us, as well as the theoretical framework that will orient and guide the investigation going forward. By recognizing the places connected to significant events of the life of Jesus and ecclesiastical monuments that were erected to commemorate them as *lieux de mémoire*, we are able to conceive of these places, understood both in terms of the presentation and discussion of them in early Christian literature as well as the traditional localizations of them, as instantiations of interpretation, memory, and reception. This allows us to think of how they relate to Jesus in a manner that goes beyond questions of their authenticity toward understanding what they *mean* and what they convey about Jesus, even apart from literal historicity. I am, for example, less interested in whether or not the feeding of the five thousand (Mark 6:30–44; Matt 14:13–21; Luke 9:10–17; John 6:1–15) took place in the area of the Heptagon, as the fourth-century tradition locates it so much as what the location of the Church of the Multiplication at Tabgha communicates about how the Multiplication was remembered, understood, and interpreted by early Christians in Palestine.

We will begin our investigation with the central sites associated with the passion narrative: the places of Jesus' crucifixion and burial. In the next chapter, we will examine the reception and interpretation of Golgotha. Chapter 3 will do the same for Jesus' tomb. Because the events of the crucifixion and burial were commemorated in the

---

[61] Krautheimer, "Iconography," 20.
[62] Valdez del Álamo, "Iconography of Architecture," 377.
[63] Adapted from ibid., who is speaking of medieval, rather than ancient, architecture.
[64] McCurrach, "Renovatio," 42.

same structure in the fourth century, we will hold off on analyzing the commemorative architecture dedicated to these places until Chapter 4, in which we will consider the meaning conveyed by the architecture of the Church of the Holy Sepulchre. Chapter 5 will examine the traditions and interpretations associated with the place of Jesus' birth and the Mount of Olives, which is the site of Jesus' ascension. It will also discuss the architecture of the commemorative structures dedicated to both of those sites, the Church of the Nativity and the Imbomon. In Chapter 6, we will investigate places in Galilee connected with the life of Jesus and will focus on the commemorative architecture and activity that were located at Capernaum, Tabgha (the Heptapegon), and Nazareth. Chapter 7 will present some of the overarching conclusions and patterns that have been discerned over the course of the project.

2

Remembering Golgotha: Memory and Interpretation of the Place of Crucifixion from the First to the Fourth Centuries[1]

The modern Church of the Holy Sepulchre is a composite patchwork of building phases and materials. Bustling with tourists and pilgrims, its interior is a sprawling maze of monumental architecture and pious artwork. It is filled with the sounds and smells of centuries of liturgy and devotion. It lies on the site of the fourth-century commemorative church complex built by Constantine the Great. However, its true significance derives from the claim that it stands on the very place where Jesus of Nazareth was crucified and buried. According to the Christian faith, it is also where he was raised from the dead. Nevertheless, visitors seeking a Jewish rock-cut tomb from the first century CE situated in a garden will be disappointed, as they are instead confronted with an *aedicule* in a rotunda. This church is an architectural manifestation of the memory of the crucifixion and burial of Jesus, which has crystallized at this particular place.

The aim of this chapter is to investigate the reception and development of the place of Golgotha as a site of interpretation, memory, and commemoration of Jesus in early Christian literature from the first to the fourth centuries CE. In order to proceed in our investigation, we must begin with the gospel accounts of the crucifixion and burial. It is crucial to recognize the gospels as products and instantiations of commemoration, collective remembering, interpretation, and reception of Jesus. The process of commemoration and interpretation includes the gospels, it does not postdate them. Thus, our examination of the place of Golgotha in that process begins with them.

The Site of the Crucifixion and the Tomb of Jesus in the New Testament

Perhaps the strongest memory about Jesus in the tradition is that he was crucified.[2] For example, writing in the decades between the life of Jesus and the destruction of the Temple in Jerusalem in 70 CE, Paul of Tarsus and his coauthor Sosthenes state that "we

---

[1] A version of this chapter was presented as an Oslo Lecture in New Testament in early 2020. The Oslo Lecture version of this chapter is published as Jordan Ryan, "Golgotha and the Burial of Adam between Jewish and Christian Tradition," Scandinavian Jewish Studies 32, no. 1 (2021): 3–29.
[2] There are early portraits of the remembered Jesus in the early church that are either uninterested in the crucifixion or that reject it completely. For the most part, the "uncrucified" Jesus is typically

proclaim Christ crucified" (1 Cor 1:23). The burial of Jesus, though less prominent in the theological discourse of the New Testament authors than Jesus' crucifixion, is also included by Paul among the things that were handed on to him and that he has handed on (1 Cor 15:4). Similarly, in Acts, Luke depicts Paul mentioning that Jesus was placed in a tomb during his speech in the synagogue at Pisidian Antioch (Acts 13:29).

Place plays a curious role in the evangelists' narrative of the crucifixion. It is localized, but in a manner that is remarkably vague, leaving much to the imagination of later readers of the gospels. Both John and the synoptic tradition situate Jesus' crucifixion at a place apparently called "Golgotha" in Aramaic (transliterated as Γολγοθά), or in Greek, *Kranion*. The fact that Golgotha is named at all likely indicates that a specific place is in mind. Luke omits the Semitic name "Golgotha" (23:33), although this is in keeping with his proclivity for removing Semitic terms, which is likely a reflection of his intended audience, for whom Semitic nomenclature would have little meaning. Indeed, as Raymond Brown notes, Luke similarly omits "Gethsemane" (22:39; compare Mark 14:32, cf. Matt 26:36).[3] The place of crucifixion is thus clearly named in the early tradition, and moreover, it is given a memorable and fitting name. As we will see later in the discussion to follow, the fact that the place is named "Golgotha" will have a major impact in later reception and interpretation.

Although the place of crucifixion is given a name, it is not given a description, nor is it given a clear location.[4] Moreover, the reader is not told *why* the place is called "Golgotha," simply that it means *kranion* ("skull"), which leaves the matter open to interpretive speculation. The lack of clarity concerning the location of the crucifixion in the canonical passion narrative is significant in itself. The vagueness of the evangelists' description of the site leaves room for the processes of commemoration and collective remembering to fill in some of the gaps created by the lack of specificity in the early tradition. As memories crystallize in the process of remembering, they become fixed elements of the tradition. The Chapel of Adam in the modern Church of the Holy Sepulchre is an example of this, and one that we will return to in due course.

The nomenclature of the location of the crucifixion requires further comment, since it bears directly on the matter of "place."

---

found in streams of the tradition outside of what modern scholarship would consider to be proto-Orthodox. For example, the Gospel of Thomas, though containing material parallel to the synoptic tradition that quite likely originated with Jesus in one respect or another, neither depicts nor clearly mentions the crucifixion. Early docetic accounts of the Passion, by their nature, present a kind of memory and reception of the crucifixion, insofar as they attempt to imaginatively explain the centrality of the memory of Jesus' crucifixion while nevertheless maintaining that, contrary to appearance, he was never truly crucified.

[3] Raymond E. Brown, *The Death of the Messiah*, 2 vols., ABRL (New York: Doubleday, 1994), 2: 936.

[4] Granted, this is not atypical of how named locales are presented in the early Jesus tradition. The evangelists vary in their specificity concerning named locales. Mark, for example, introduces Capernaum without elaboration or description, without clarifying or specifying its location (Mark 1:21). By contrast, Matthew indicates that Capernaum is in Galilee (4:12), "by the sea (of Galilee), in the territory of Zebulun and Naphtali" (4:13).

Mark 15:22	Matt 27:33	Luke 23:33	John 19:17
…τὸν Γολγοθᾶν **τόπον**, ὅ ἐστιν μεθερμηνευόμενον Κρανίου **Τόπος**	…**τόπον** λεγόμενον Γολγοθᾶ, ὅ ἐστιν Κρανίου **Τόπος** λεγόμενος	…τὸν **τόπον** τὸν καλούμενον Κρανίον	…τὸν λεγόμενον Κρανίου **Τόπον**, ὃ λέγεται Ἑβραϊστὶ Γολγοθα
"…the Golgotha place, which is translated 'Place of a Skull.'"	"…a place which is called 'Golgotha,' which means 'Place of a Skull.'"	"the place which is called 'Skull'"	"that which is called 'Of a Skull Place,' which means 'Golgotha' in Hebrew [Aramaic]."

We may make several observations about the evangelists' nomenclature for the place of crucifixion. First, there is general agreement that its Semitic (Aramaic) name is "Golgotha." Luke omits the Semitic name, but for reasons discussed above, this is neither surprising nor particularly significant for our purposes. All four evangelists correctly consider *kranion* ("skull") to figure into the meaning of the place's name, and moreover, all agree in regarding it as a *topos*. There are, however, a few differences worth observing. As Brown notes, "grammatical relationship between *topos* ('place') and *kranion* or 'Golgotha' varies in each Gospel."[5] As indicated by the genitive constructions, Matthew and Mark seem to consider *topos* to have been part of the Greek name ("Place of a Skull"). Luke, however, does not, instead regarding the name of the *topos* to be *kranion* ("the place which is called 'Skull'").

As Brown has argued, it is quite likely that the Aramaic name "Golgotha" ("Skull") and the designation of the site of the crucifixion as a *topos* derive from pre-evangelical tradition.[6] It is probable, as Joan Taylor has convincingly argued, that the *topos* of "Golgotha" refers to an area rather than a specific spot,[7] such as the rock spire that is located immediately to the right upon entering the modern Church of the Holy Sepulchre. The Greek translation offered by Mark and followed by Matthew, "Place of a Skull," is not a direct translation of the Aramaic name. We should rather regard it as a sort of interpretation.[8] Although Luke does not include the Aramaic name in his narrative, his nomenclature (*Kranion*, "Skull") actually more closely reflects the Aramaic "Golgotha." John's rendering of the Aramaic "Golgotha" is similar to that of Mark, though with *topos* in the accusative (Τόπον) case rather than in the nominative.

What Mark or John might have meant to convey by their interpretive rendering of the Aramaic is not entirely clear. Edward W. Klink offers a possible interpretation,

---

[5] Brown, *Death of the Messiah*, 2: 937.
[6] Ibid., 936.
[7] Joan E. Taylor, "Golgotha: A Reconsideration of the Evidence for the Sites of Jesus' Crucifixion and Burial," NTS 44, no. 2 (1998): 180–203 (183–6).
[8] Cf. R. T. France, *The Gospel of Mark: A Commentary on the Greek Text*, NIGTC (Grand Rapids: Eerdmans, 2002), 642.

writing, "the *place* of the Skull has been overtaken by the *presence* of the Savior!"[9] I find it difficult to be as certain about the intention underlying the interpretive renderings of "Golgotha," but the fact that the evangelists translate it at all is significant. Not every toponym is given a translation. Gethsemane, for example, is untranslated in Mark 14:32 and Matt 26:36. What we see is place, here in the form of the traditional toponym of the site of Jesus' crucifixion, being translated and interpreted, thus factoring into the reception and interpretation of Jesus already in the earliest extant passion narratives.

It is tempting to read theological meaning into the name of the place of crucifixion. Grundmann and Schlatter both saw *Kranion* as a theological feature of the text, meant to imply that the Jesus died in an unclean place for sinners who were themselves unclean.[10] However, this reads too much into the text without clear basis. As the early reception history (discussed below) shows, it is difficult not to associate a toponym meaning "skull" with death, especially since it is the place of execution in the gospels.

The Gospel of Mark, which is usually thought to be the earliest extant gospel, provides us with the earliest description of the sites of crucifixion and burial of Jesus to which we have direct access. Karel Hanhart has made a case for reading an intentional connection to the Jerusalem Temple in Mark's description of Golgotha and the sepulcher.[11] According to Hanhart, "Mark was not reporting the discovery of an empty grave as a *bare fact*, an event that took place two days after the crucifixion. Rather, he wanted to relate the death of Israel's Messiah to a different historical fact, namely, the destruction of the Temple, which had just become world news."[12]

Hanhart's argument depends heavily on Mark's use of the Greek term *topos* in 15:22 and 16:6 to describe Golgotha and the place of Jesus' burial.[13] He observes that *topos* typically translates the Hebrew *māqôm* (מָקוֹם) in the LXX. The significance of this is that "although it occurs some 363 times, it has a special theological significance in Scripture when it refers to Mount Zion, on which were built Jerusalem and its Temple."[14] Hanhart is, of course, aware that both the Greek and Hebrew terms could have a range of meanings. Nevertheless, he argues that "if read in a clear context of the Temple, the word *Maqom* was enough to remind the Judean reader of the 'holy place' of God's choosing."[15] Hanhart holds that from Mark 10:33 onward, the author builds up a "climactic linkage" between the death and resurrection of Jesus and the destruction of the Jerusalem Temple. This is done, he argues, through the narration of the entry into Jerusalem, the cleansing of the Temple, the cursing of the fig tree in ch. 11, the dialogues in the Temple court in ch. 12, the prediction of the Temple's destruction (13:2), and the accusation that Jesus will destroy the Temple and build another in

---

[9] Edward W. Klink III, *John*, ZECNT (Grand Rapids: Zondervan, 2016), 802. Emphasis original.
[10] Adolf Schlatter, *Der Evangelist Matthaüs* (Stuttgart: Calwer Verlag, 1948), 779; Walter Grundmann, *Das Evangelium nach Markus*, THKNT 3 (Berlin: Evangelische Verlagsanstalt, 1977), 431.
[11] Karel Hanhart, *The Open Tomb: A New Approach, Mark's Passover Haggadah* (Collegeville: Liturgical Press, 1995), 149–206.
[12] Ibid., 149–50.
[13] Ibid., 157–61.
[14] Ibid., 158.
[15] Ibid.

three days (14:58), which is repeated at the crucifixion (15:29).[16] Thus, in Hanhart's estimation, Mark has created a strong enough connection between the Temple and the scenes of Jesus' crucifixion and burial for the reader to see a link between the *topos* of the passion events and the *māqôm* of the Temple Mount.

Hanhart's argument is sophisticated, and it is simply not possible to reproduce it in its entirety here, nor is it necessary to do so. For our purposes, it is significant that his reading of Mark's use of spatial terms in reference to the site of crucifixion and burial raises the possibility that there may be elements of interpretation in even the earliest extant remembrances of the crucifixion and burial sites. That having been said, while Hanhart's argument is intriguing, it is difficult to accept with any measure of certainty, since it requires us to believe that Mark expected his readers to be able to make the connection between *topos* and Temple, which is hard to prove based on the available evidence.

Golgotha from the Second to the Fourth Centuries

The place of Golgotha remained a fixture of early Christian memory of Jesus beyond the first century CE. By this, I do not simply mean that the actual, topographical, geographical location of Golgotha continued to be known. Rather, the place of Golgotha continued to function as a site of memory, insofar as the very image and name of Golgotha continued to impact the collective remembrance of Jesus. Our discussion will now turn to the reception of Golgotha from the second century on.

The Place of Crucifixion in the *Peri Pascha* of Melito of Sardis

Melito was bishop of Sardis,[17] though he may have had connections to Palestine and access to Palestinian traditions.[18] Eusebius preserves a fragment of a letter by Melito to a person named Onesimus, which mentions that he "came to the east and reached the place where these things were preached and done, and learnt accurately the books of the Old Testament."[19] In this fragment, Melito (if he is indeed the author) seems to indicate that he traveled to the places where the events of the Old Testament took place, which would naturally be the same region where the events of the life of Jesus took place. As such, it is possible that he had knowledge of Jerusalem and some contact with Palestinian tradition. However, caution is in order. As Martin Biddle writes, "We do not know whether the sermon was written before or after this journey, nor if he

---

[16] Ibid., 159.
[17] That is, of course, assuming that the *Peri Pascha* attributed to Melito was indeed written by Melito of Sardis. On the question of the authorship of *Peri Pascha*, see Lynn H. Cohick, *The Peri Pascha Attributed to Melito of Sardis: Setting, Purpose, and Sources*, Brown Judaic Studies 327 (Providence: Brown Judaic Studies, 2000).
[18] See A. E. Harvey, "Melito and Jerusalem," *JTS* 17, no. 2 (1966): 401–4; cf., e.g., Jerome Murphy-O'Connor, "Argument for the Holy Sepulchre," *Revue Biblique* 117, no. 1 (2010): 74. See also Alistair Stewart-Sykes, *On Pascha: With the Fragments of Melito and Other Material Related to the Quartodecimans* (Crestwood: St. Vladimir's Seminary Press, 2001), 9.
[19] Translated from Kirsopp Lake, *The Ecclesiastical History and 2: English Translation*, ed. T. E. Page et al., trans. Kirsopp Lake and J. E. L. Oulton, vol. 1, The Loeb Classical Library (London; New York; Cambridge, MA: William Heinemann; G. P. Putnam's Sons; Harvard University Press, 1926–32).

visited Jerusalem, and so we cannot be sure whether he obtained his information on the spot or at second hand."[20]

In *Peri Pascha*, Melito makes several references to the place of Jesus' crucifixion being in the middle of the city:

> This is the one who has been murdered.
> And where murdered?
> In the middle of Jerusalem.
> By whom? By Israel.
>
> (*Peri Pascha* 72)[21]

> Therefore the feast of unleavened bread is bitter for you:
> as it is written, "You shall eat unleavened bread with bitterness."
> ...
> You killed the Lord in the middle of Jerusalem.
>
> (*Peri Pascha* 93)

> Listen all you families of the nations and see:
> a strange murder has occurred in the middle of Jerusalem;
> in the city of the law,
> in the city of the Hebrews,
> in the city of the prophets,
> in the city reckoned righteous.
> ...
> Now in the middle of the street,
> and in the middle of the city,
> in the middle of the day before the public gaze,
> the unjust murder of a just man has taken place.
>
> (*Peri Pascha* 94)

The interpretation of these passages is necessarily tied to the rhetorical context in which they appear. Because of this, I have attempted to include some of that context in the citations above. It is immediately clear that Melito's statements about the crucifixion's location in the middle of the city are related to his rhetorical aims and cannot be read as a mere report of geography.

Melito's insistence upon the location of the crucifixion in the middle of the city stands in stark contrast with the depiction of the crucifixion outside the walls of Jerusalem in the canonical New Testament (e.g., Heb 13:12; Mark 15:20, as discussed above). However, Herod Agrippa extended Jerusalem's fortifications to the north with the construction of the "third wall," which would have brought the traditional location of Golgotha within the limits of the city walls.[22] Hadrian's Aelia Capitolina covered

---

[20] Martin Biddle, *The Tomb of Christ* (Stroud: Sutton, 2000), 61.
[21] Translation from Stewart-Sykes, *On Pascha*, 56. All translations of *Peri Pascha* are by Stewart-Sykes unless otherwise noted.
[22] See discussion in relation to *Peri Pascha* by Harvey, "Melito and Jerusalem," 402; and Taylor, "Golgotha," 188–91.

ground up to that third wall, so it is plausible that Melito, writing in the second century, could have been referring to the traditional site of Golgotha, which was outside of the walls at the time of Jesus, but within the city limits at the time of Melito.[23] In fact, the traditional area in which Golgotha and the Church of the Holy Sepulchre are located may fit this description fairly well, since they were located in the vicinity of the Hadrianic forum at the intersection of the Decumanus Maximus and the Cardo.[24]

However, we are not only concerned with the geographical accuracy of Melito's claim about the location of the crucifixion but also interested in the interpretation of the place of crucifixion in *Peri Pascha*. The point of Melito's repeated references to Jesus' crucifixion in the middle of the city is that it was done in public rather than at night or in a desert place (*Peri Pascha* 94), and so Melito is unable to keep silent about the brazen injustice of the public crucifixion of an innocent man.[25] The fact that the aim of the references is rhetorical does not mean that it is ahistorical or unreliable. However, the claims about the location of the crucifixion in *Peri Pascha* are decidedly odd when they are cast alongside the accounts of the gospels and Hebrews, which place the crucifixion outside of the city. In my opinion, the best explanation for this is that Melito was aware of the traditional location of the crucifixion as it was in the second century and based his rhetorical claims on the location of the traditional site within the walls of Aelia Capitolina.

In this case, then, the geographical location of the traditional site directly impacted Melito's interpretation of the events of the crucifixion. A location within the "middle of the city" loans rhetorical force to his point about the injustice of a public execution of an innocent man carried out in Jerusalem, which Melito variously calls the city of the Law, the Hebrews, and the prophets, a "city reckoned righteous" (*Peri Pashca* 94). As von Wahlde rightly notes, the purpose of referring to the Law is that the Law forbids murder; the reference to the Hebrews is made because in Melito's view, Jesus was the Jewish Messiah; and the prophets are mentioned because they decried injustice, yet were killed themselves (at least, according to early Christian tradition).[26] There is, thus, in Melito's perspective, a sort of dark irony to the fact that the city reckoned "righteous" or "just" was privy to such injustice. In the logic of *Peri Pascha*, the fact that this act of injustice was carried out in public for all to see in a city as significant as Jerusalem enhances this all the more. This is really only effective if Melito has the traditional site of the crucifixion in mind, which would have been within the walls of second-century Aelia Capitolina (Jerusalem), and anachronistically applied it to the situation in the first century, of which it is doubtful that he could have been aware. The geography of the traditional site thus impacts Melito's interpretation of the event of the crucifixion and serves his rhetorical aims.

Melito uses the location of the crucifixion to further his rhetorical indictment of "Israel." Although there is some disagreement in scholarship as to the precise target of the invective, this is probably best understood as an instance of Christian

---

[23] Classically argued by Harvey, "Melito and Jerusalem."
[24] Harvey, "Melito and Jerusalem," 402–3. See also Taylor, "Golgotha," 188–91. Taylor argues for a location of the historical site of the crucifixion near the traditional site, but located slightly to the south, underneath the Decumanus south of the forum rather than beneath the Temple of Venus.
[25] In agreement with Urban von Wahlde, "The References to the Time and Place of the Crucifixion in the *Peri Pascha* of Melito of Sardis," *JTS* 60 (2009): 556–69.
[26] von Wahlde, "References," 562–3.

anti-Judaism.[27] If so, it is worth observing that the unfortunate rhetorical or symbolic use of the locations of sites connected to the life of Jesus within the traditional Jewish homeland to advance supersessionist ideas may have begun well before Constantine built the first commemorative churches in Palestine.

Origen and Adam's Burial at Golgotha

The curious name of Golgotha, and its interpretive translations provided by the evangelists, became a focal point for interpretation, opening the door for new Christological interpretations to become affixed to it. As these novel Christological interpretations accrued around Golgotha, they would eventually crystallize and become a fixed part of the memory of Jesus in Palestine. Some aspects of the layers of memory associated with the locality of Golgotha that first appeared in the intervening period between Easter and the Church of the Holy Sepulchre are so firmly crystallized around the place that they remain fixed in the tradition to this day.

Although the evangelists use the Aramaic name "Golgotha" to refer to the place of crucifixion, and speak of it as though it was a known toponym, the name does not appear in any known Jewish sources that can be securely dated prior to the reign of Constantine.[28] However, an explanation for the nomenclature of the place of crucifixion can be found in early Christian literature, in which it is frequently connected to the burial place of Adam. The earliest extant tradition connecting Golgotha to Adam can be found in Origen's *Commentary on Matthew*. Since it is the earliest and most significant attestation to the tradition, it is fitting to cite it in full here. It has been preserved in a Greek fragment as well as in the Latin translation. Though the two traditions are similar, there are some noteworthy differences. As such, it is fitting to cite both. The Greek fragment reads as follows:

> It has come to me concerning the place of the skull that the Hebrews hand down that the body of Adam has been buried there, so that, since we all die in Adam, Adam, on the one hand might arise, but on the other we may all be made alive in Christ.[29]

---

[27] See discussion in, e.g., A. Thomas Kraabel, "Melito the Bishop and the Synagogue at Sardis Text and Context," in *Studies Presented to George M. A Hanfmann*, ed. David G Mitten, John G Pedley, and Jane A. Scott (Cambridge: Harvard University Press, 1971), 77–85; Laurence Broadhurst, "Melito of Sardis, the Second Sophistic, and 'Israel,'" in *Rhetoric and Reality in Early Christianities*, ed. Willi Braun (Waterloo: Wilfred Laurier University Press, 2005), 49–74; Judith M. Lieu, *Image and Reality: The Jews in the World of Christians in the Second Century* (Edinburgh: T&T Clark, 1996); Miriam S. Taylor, *Anti-Judaism & Early Christian Identity: A Critique of the Scholarly Consensus* (Leiden: Brill, 1995), 67–74; Stephen G. Wilson, "Passover, Easter, and Anti-Judaism," in *To See Ourselves as Others See Us*, ed. Jacob Neusner and Ernest S. Frerichs (Atlanta: Scholars Press, 1985), 337–55. An alternative proposal has been advanced by Lynn H. Cohick, "Melito of Sardis's *PERI PASCHA* and Its 'Israel,'" *Harvard Theological Review* 91, no. 4 (1998): 351–72.

[28] For a classic but dated review of the material, see Joachim Jeremias, *Golgotha*, ΑΓΓΕΛΟΣ 1 (Leipzig: E. Pfeiffer, 1926).

[29] Translation from Ronald E. Heine, trans., *The Commentary of Origen on the Gospel of St. Matthew: Translated with Introduction and Brief Annotations by Ronald E. Heine*, Oxford Early Christian Texts (Oxford: Oxford University Press, 2018), 740 n. 98.

The Latin text reads:

> But the "place of Calvary" is said not to have any expansive meaning whatever, so that he who was to die for humanity died there. For some such tradition has reached me that the body of Adam, the first man, was buried there [Calvary] where Christ was crucified so that "just as in Adam all die, so in Christ all are made alive;" so that a that place, "which is called the place of Calvary, that is the place of the head," the head of the human race found resurrection with all people through the resurrection of our Lord and Saviour, who suffered there and arose. (Origen, *Commentary on Matthew*, 126)[30]

The Latin lacks the reference to the "Hebrew" character of the tradition.[31] That having been said, both the Greek and Latin identify "the place of the Skull" (Golgotha) with the place where Adam was buried as well as where Christ was crucified (Latin, "*quoniam corpus Adae primi hominus ibi sepultum est ubi crucifixis est Christus*"). As others have noted, the Latin tradition, dating to the fifth or sixth century, does not necessarily take priority over the Greek catena.[32] Moreover, it is possible that a "Hebrew" tradition is understood in the Latin text as well. Directly preceding the text cited above is a discussion of the Hebrew meaning and orthography of the names "Simon" and "Simeon," which concludes with the statement that "the Hebrews write both the name Simeon and Simon with the very same letters. But the 'place of Calvary'..."[33] Since the context of this point in the text is a discussion of Hebrew language and orthography, it is likely that Origen has Hebrew language and tradition in mind in his discussion of Golgotha ("place of Calvary").

Origen's exposition of the Golgotha tradition is complex and requires some discussion. It is important to separate Origen's own Christological interpretation of Golgotha from the tradition about the place of the crucifixion that he has received. The received tradition is that the body of Adam is buried where Christ was crucified.

Origen does not explicitly relate "the place of the skull" to Adam's skull. Instead, Origen makes a Christological connection. For Origen, the "skull" is "the head of the human race," that is, Christ. This idea clearly draws upon the concept of Jesus' supremacy depicted in terms of his being the "head" (κεφαλη) in the Pauline corpus.[34] Indeed, Origen's interpretation of Golgotha is deeply rooted in Pauline Adam Christology, citing 1 Cor 15:22. Similar Pauline Adam Christology appears elsewhere in Origen's work,[35]

---

[30] Translation from ibid., 740.
[31] As noted by Joan E. Taylor, *Christians and the Holy Places* (Oxford: Clarendon Press, 1993), 124, 127.
[32] Cf. Emmanouela Grypeou and Helen Spurling, *The Book of Genesis in Late Antiquity: Encounters between Jewish and Christian Exegesis*, Jewish and Christian Perspectives 24 (Leiden: Brill, 2013), 72 n. 86; John Anthony McGuckin, ed., *The Westminster Handbook to Origen*, Westminster Handbooks to Christian Theology (Louisville: John Knox, 2004), 30.
[33] Translation from Heine, *Origen on the Gospel of St. Matthew*, 740.
[34] 1 Cor 11:3; Eph 1:22; Col 1:18.
[35] On this, see John VanMaaren, "The Adam-Christ Typology in Paul and Its Development in the Early Church Fathers," *Tyndale Bulletin* 64, no. 2 (2013): 275–97 (286–8); cf. also C. P. Hammel, "Adam in Origen," in *The Making of Orthodoxy: Essays in Honour of Henry Chadwick*, ed. Rowan Williams (New York: Cambridge University Press, 1989), 62–93. On the Adam-Christ typology in other early

particularly in his commentary on Romans,³⁶ in which Origen elaborates on the typological relationship between Adam and Christ, noting that the acts of both Adam and Christ impacted all human beings, as through Adam condemnation came to all, while justification came to all through Christ. For Origen, the place of Golgotha is remembered and thus interpreted in light of the theological implications of a Pauline Adam Christology. This is apparently made possible by the name of the place and Origen's connection of that name to a tradition locating Adam's burial on Golgotha. Golgotha, and its significance of the place of the crucifixion, is thus remembered in light of the Pauline tradition of Adam Christology.³⁷

If we consider Golgotha as a sort of *lieu de mémoire*, a site where memory accumulates and crystalizes, this tradition forms a new stratum of crystalline memory stratum over the place. It is difficult to ascertain whether Origen would have known about the traditional site of Golgotha. As we will see below, there is reason to think that the *topos* of Golgotha was identified in Christian circles prior to Constantine's building projects. For example, Eusebius seems to have known about the place, since he lists it in his *Onomasticon*,³⁸ which was written before Constantine's building projects took place. This is not sufficient warrant to conclude that the traditional site is "authentic," but it does raise the possibility that Origen could have been familiar with it. Whatever the case may be, the place existed within early Christian literature, and thus within the living collective memory and consciousness of early Christianity. Its legacy as a site where the memory and interpretation of Jesus would be concentrated was already underway well before the place identified as Golgotha from the fourth century onward would emerge from the earth. This goes to show that a site need not be visible or even tangible for it to play a role in commemoration and interpretation.

Origen calls the Adamic burial tradition a "Hebraic tradition" that has "come down."³⁹ What are we to make of this? At the very least, Origen claims not to be the originator of the tradition of Adamic burial at Golgotha, though he is our earliest extant source for it.⁴⁰ There may be some indication of a precedent for the tradition in a fragment of the *Chronographiae* of Julius Africanus.⁴¹ The fragment, preserved by

Patristic literature, see, e.g., Maja Weyermann, "The Typologies of Adam-Christ and Eve-Mary and Their Relationship to One Another," *Anglican Theological Review* 84, no. 3 (2002): 609–26.

³⁶ Origen, *Commentary on Romans*, 5.1.7, translation from Thomas P. Schrenk, trans., *Commentary on the Epistle to the Romans, Books 1–5*, FC 103 (Washington, DC: Catholic University of America Press, 2001), 307–8.

³⁷ On the theological connection between the place of Adam's burial and Christ's crucifixion in early Christianity more generally, see Grypeou and Spurling, *Genesis in Late Antiquity*, 71–9.

³⁸ *Onomasticon* 74.19-21. On the date of this work, see the discussion below in this same chapter.

³⁹ Again, note that the Latin lacks the mention of the Hebraic origin of the tradition. However, the question as to whether the tradition that is mentioned here is of Jewish origin is valid and worth pursuing whether or not Origen explicitly identified it handed down by Hebrews (Greek Ἑβραῖοι παραδιδόασι)

⁴⁰ Although Melito of Sardis mentions the place of crucifixion in *Peri Pascha*, which predates Origen, the Adam tradition is not mentioned, and neither is the name "Golgotha."

⁴¹ Julius Africanus, *Chronographiae*, ed. Martin Wallraff, Die Griechischen Christlichen Schriftsteller der ersten Jahrhunherte Neue Folge 15 (Berlin: Walter de Gruyter, 2007), 42–3 (T17). On this, see Nikolai Lipatov-Chicherin, "Early Christian Tradition about Adam's Burial on Golgotha and Origen," in *Origeniana Duodecima: Origen's Legacy in the Holy Land – A Tale of Three Cities: Jerusalem, Caesarea and Bethlehem. Proceedings of the 12th International Origen Congress, Jerusalem, 25–29*

Symeon Logothete, reads, "It is said that Adam was the first to be buried in the ground, from which he was taken. And his tomb was in the ground of Jerusalem, according to what is reported in the Hebrew tradition."[42] Assuming that this fragment does indeed come from Africanus, it is our earliest attestation of the burial of Adam at Jerusalem in the Christian tradition. However, we must note that Golgotha is not specifically named here, so we cannot certainly connect it to the memory of the place of Jesus' crucifixion. Interestingly, the language of Adam being "the first to be buried in the ground" parallels the mention of Adam's burial in Jub. 4:29, although the place of Adam's burial is not mentioned there. The exact relationship between the tradition of Adam's burial at Jerusalem attested by Africanus and the more specific burial at Golgotha attested by Origen is uncertain, but the fact that both cite it as a "Hebrew" tradition may suggest at least a generic relationship. That having been said, we are concerned here specifically with the memory of the place of the crucifixion of Jesus, which is lacking from Africanus' account of the burial of Adam, leaving Origen as the earliest certain attestation of the Adam-Golgotha tradition. Scholars are understandably divided over the origin of the Adam-Golgotha tradition. Some scholars have argued for a Jewish-Christian genesis.[43] Nikolai Lipatov-Chicherin notes that the term "Hebrew" is an ethnic rather than a religious designation (as opposed to "Jews"), indicating "people of Hebrew origin but not of Jewish faith, which in the context of Origen's passage means Hebrew Christians."[44] He also observes that Basil of Caesarea identifies this tradition as having been preserved in the Church (*Commentary on Isaiah*, 5.141), indicating a Christian genesis. When combined with Origen's identification of the "Hebrew" origin of the tradition, this evidence supports the hypothesis of a Jewish-Christian (or "Hebrew Christian") genesis for the tradition of Adam's burial at Golgotha.[45]

Bellarmino Bagatti regards the Adamic Golgotha tradition as Jewish-Christian, particularly on the basis of evidence drawn from late antique Adamic literature, especially the Cave of Treasures, which situates Adam's burial at Golgotha.[46] Ignazio Mancini has likewise argued that its origin is Jewish-Christian, since it differs from the traditions about the location of Adam's burial place preserved by "the synagogue," by which he seems to mean rabbinic literature.[47]

June, 2017, ed. Brouria Bitton-Ashkelony, Oded Irshai, Aryeh Kofsky, H. Newman, and Lorenzo Perrone, Proceedings of the 12th International Origen Congress, Jerusalem, June 25–29, 2017 (Leuven: Peeters, 2019), 151–78.

[42] Translation from Wallraff, *Chronographiae*, 43 n. 1.

[43] For example, see the discussion in Georg Kretschmar, "Festkalender und Memorialstatten Jerusalems in altkirchlicher Zeit," in *Jerusalemer Heiligtumstraditionen in altkirchlicher und fruhislamischer Zeit*, ed. Heribert Busse and Gerog Kretschmar, Abhandlungen des Deutschen Palastinavereins 8 (Wiesbaden: Otto Harrassowitz, 1987): 29–111 (esp. 107–11). Somewhat more recently, see Oskar Skarsaune, *In the Shadow of the Temple: Jewish Influences on Early Christianity* (Downers Grove: IVP Academic, 2002), 185; Lipatov-Chicherin, "Early Christian Tradition," 163.

[44] Lipatov-Chicherin, "Early Christian Tradition," 163.

[45] Ibid.

[46] Bellarmino Bagatti and Emmanuel Testa, *Il Golgota e la Croce: ricerche storico-archeologiche*, Collectio Minor 21 (Jerusalem: Franciscan Printing Press, 1978), 27–30 (cf. 30–4). Bagatti also discusses the *Combat of Adam*, but this text is dependent upon the Cave of Treasures.

[47] Ignazio Mancini, *Archeological Discoveries Relative to the Judeo-Christians* (Jerusalem: Franciscan Printing Press, 1984).

However, Taylor has presented strong arguments against the positions of Bagatti and Mancini. Arguing against Mancini, she notes that the fact that the Adamic burial tradition referenced by Origen differs from traditions seen in rabbinic literature is not evidence that it is thereby Jewish-Christian.[48] Taylor also rightly observes that Bagatti's reliance on the Syriac Cave of Treasures to establish the Jewish-Christian origins of the Adamic Golgotha tradition is problematic, due to the late date of the text and to its questionable status as a "Jewish-Christian" text, since, at best, it is a Christian text making use of an earlier Jewish source.[49]

The Cave of Treasures is indeed quite late, likely dating to the fifth or sixth century CE at the earliest,[50] several centuries after Origen's time. The Adamic Golgotha tradition had already become common in Christian circles by the end of the fourth century CE,[51] presumably invigorated by the construction of the Church of the Holy Sepulchre. Thus, it is likely that the Cave of Treasures is a later reception of the tradition, not evidence of an earlier Jewish-Christian instantiation of the Adamic Golgotha story. Although Bagatti and Testa regard the legend of Adam's burial at Golgotha as reflecting a tradition stratum much earlier than the final text of the Cave of Treasures, there is no clear evidence to support this conclusion.[52] It is unclear that there is even an earlier Jewish source or version redacted by the Christian author of the Cave of Treasures at all. As Clemens Leonhard has demonstrated, the Cave of Treasures "should be read as a coherent work" and "no layer of an *Urschatzhöhle* ["original Cave of Treasures"] can be analysed within it."[53]

Taylor has argued that the Adamic Golgotha tradition could have originated from a misunderstanding by Origen.[54] She notes that, in Jewish tradition, rather than Golgotha, Mount Moriah or Hebron are regarded as the burial place of Adam.[55] Moreover, Jewish tradition regards Mount Moriah as the *axis mundi*, whereas in Christian tradition, it is Golgotha. This, combined with the fact that Golgotha was located under a temple in Origen's day, allowed for confusion. According to Taylor,

> If we know that Jews did not believe that Adam was buried under the temple of Venus, but under Mount Moriah or Hebron, how then did Origen come to make a mistake? Origen may have confused a "temple" (the Jewish Temple) possibly referred to by his source with the temple of Venus which had stood on the site

---

[48] Taylor, *Christians and the Holy Places*, 127.
[49] Ibid., 128.
[50] On the date of the Cave of Treasures, see Clemens Leonhard, "Observations on the Date of the Syriac *Cave of Treasures*," in *The World of the Aramaeans: Studies in Honour of Paul-Eugène Dion*, ed. P. M. Michèle Daviau, John W. Wevers, and Michael Weigl, 3 vols., JSOTSupp 324 (Sheffield: Sheffield Academic, 2001), 3: 255–88. See also Sergey Minov, "Date and Provenance of the Syriac *Cave of Treasures*: A Reappraisal," *Hugoye* 20, no. 1 (2017): 129–229. Both authors argue effectively for a late date. Minov dates the text somewhat later than Leonhard, placing it between the middle of the sixth century and the first decades of the seventh century CE.
[51] See the discussion that follows.
[52] Cf. Leonhard, "Observations," 278–80.
[53] Ibid., 288.
[54] Taylor, *Christians and the Holy Places*, 124–31.
[55] See also, following Taylor, William L. Krewson, *Jerome and the Jews: Innovative Supersessionism* (Eugene: Wipf and Stock, 2017).

of Golgotha since the days of Hadrian. Or else it is possible that his resiting of an event located by some Jews on the Temple Mount was polemical: it made the Adam Christology of Paul more poignant.[56]

Taylor's former suggestion probably has more explanatory power, as it takes the situation in Origen's own time into consideration, since the Jewish Temple no longer stood during his lifetime, although the Temple of Venus certainly did. While it is possible that Origen intentionally resited the tradition for polemical purposes, this may raise more questions than it answers. For instance, why call it a "Hebraic" tradition at all, especially if the intent is polemical? Origen's point could just have easily been made simply by connecting "skull" (*kranion*) with "head" (*kephalē*) without needing to appeal to an intentionally garbled Jewish tradition.

In my opinion, the scholarly discourse on this issue can be enriched by deeper examination of the Jewish sources pertaining to the burial of Adam.[57] The Jewish traditions locating Adam's burial on Mount Moriah are quite late. The Moriah traditions appear in *Pirqe de Rabbi Eliezer* (PRE) as well as *Abot de Rabbi Natan* B (ARN B).[58] Although PRE is attributed to Rabbi Eliezer, who was a Tanna, the text itself is clearly late and is typically dated somewhere between the seventh and ninth centuries CE.[59] The date of ARN B is a complicated matter.[60] The extant recensions of ARN (both A and B) presumably postdate *m. Abot*, since they cite and comment on it. However, the core of ARN relies on a version of *Abot* that diverges from the version extant in the Mishnah, and it may have its origin in the third century CE.[61] However, it is hard to determine how long the development of ARN continued, and which traditions might date to the earlier phases. The final redaction of ARN B is dated variously from the end of the third century CE (which would postdate Origen) to the end of the Amoraic period.[62]

While it is certainly possible in the case of both PRE and ARN B that the Adamic burial traditions may be older than the texts themselves, it is extremely difficult to know if this is the case, and if so, just how old they are. It is thereby impossible to determine whether the tradition of Adam's burial on Mount Moriah would have been current in Origen's day, nor is it possible to know whether the Golgotha burial tradition is a polemic derivative of the Moriah tradition or if the opposite is the case. An alternative Jewish tradition places the burial of Adam and Eve in Machpelah at Mamre (Hebron,

---

[56] Taylor, *Christians and the Holy Places*, 130–1.
[57] For a good introduction to Adam texts and traditions, see Alexander Toepel, "Adamic Traditions in Early Christianity and Rabbinic Literature," in *New Perspectives on 2 Enoch: No Longer Slavonic Only*, ed. Andrei A. Orlov and Gabriele Boccaccini (Leiden: Brill, 2012), 305–24.
[58] On the Moriah tradition in Jewish literature of late antiquity, see Grypeou and Spurling, *Genesis in Late Antiquity*, 50–4.
[59] For a recent, balanced review of the scholarly discourse surrounding the date of PRE, see Rachel Adelman, *The Return of the Repressed: Pirqe De-Rabbi Elizer and the Pseudepigrapha*, JSJSupp 140 (Leiden: Brill, 2009), 35–42.
[60] See discussion in Hermann Leberecht Strack and Günter Stemberger, *Introduction to the Talmud and Midrash*, 2nd ed., trans. Markus Bockmuehl (Minneapolis: Fortress, [1982] 1996), 226–7.
[61] Ibid., 227.
[62] A full review of this matter is beyond the scope of this project. See discussion in ibid., 226–7, esp. 227.

Kiryat Arba), attested in *b. Erub*. 53a and *Genesis Rabbah* 58:4, 9. Interestingly, Jerome also appears to have known this tradition and makes mention of it in his *Commentary on Matthew* (IV, ad Matt 27:33), which is dated to 398 CE.[63] In a letter dated to the first decade of the fifth century, he mentions that "the Hebrews suppose" that Adam was buried at Hebron (Kiryat Arba) along with Abraham, Isaac, and Jacob (Epistle 108.11).

Due to the problems involved with dating the Mount Moriah burial tradition in rabbinic sources, it is best to seek out Jewish traditions about the burial of Adam that are likely to have developed prior to Origen's time. A promising avenue for investigation can be found in the Greek Life of Adam and Eve (GLAE).[64] According to the traditions preserved in GLAE, Adam's body was brought to Paradise after his death (38:4). Abel's body was also brought (40:3–4) to the same place, and both Adam and Abel were "buried according to the command of God in the regions of Paradise (Gk. μέρη τοῦ παραδεισου) in the place from which God had found the dust."[65] This data provides us with yet another Jewish tradition about the location of Adam's burial, as GLAE situates Adam's burial place in the "regions" of Eden, the very place where Adam was first created. This tradition almost certainly stems from or, at the very least, cleverly alludes to the statement in Gen 3:19 in which God tells Adam that he will "return to the ground; for out of it you were taken; you are dust, and to dust you shall return."

Some scholars identify the place where Adam is buried in the Life of Adam and Eve with the site of Jerusalem Temple.[66] M. D. Johnson notes several places in the GLAE and the Latin Life of Adam and Eve (abbr. *Vita*) that mention a place with an oratory (GLAE 5:3; *Vita* 30:2) or an altar (GLAE 33:4). He identifies this place with the place where Adam was created and buried (GLAE 40:6), and refers to rabbinic sources that locate Adam's oratory on Mount Moriah (Midr. Pss. 92:6; Pesiq. Rab. 43:2; Pirqe R. El. 23, 31). Also of note is Adam's instructions for where he should be buried as narrated in the Latin recension: "if I should die, bury me against the East in the great dwelling place of God" (*Vita* 45:2). Combining this data, Johnson concludes, "There can be little doubt that the same site is intended in all such references and that the location is to be understood as the place of the Jerusalem Temple, where rabbinic sources fix the location of Adam's oratory."[67] Lois Dow also considers the burial of Adam in the Life

---

[63] See Grypeou and Spurling, *Genesis in Late Antiquity*, 77.

[64] Although the textual traditions are complex, the shorter Greek Life of Adam and Eve (abbreviated as GLAE) is regarded as the oldest extant version. See Marinus de Jonge and Johannes Tromp, *The Life of Adam and Eve and Related Literature*, Guides to Apocrypha and Pseudepigrapha (Sheffield: Sheffield Academic, 1997), 30–44; Marinus de Jonge, "The Literary Development of the *Life of Adam and Eve*," in *Literature on Adam & Eve: Collected Essays*, ed. Gary Anderson, Michael Stone, and Johannes Tromp (Leiden: Brill, 2000), 239–49. For the critical text, see Johannes Tromp, *The Life of Adam and Eve in Greek: A Critical Edition*, PVTG (Leiden: Brill, 2005).

[65] Translation from M. D. Johnson, "Life of Adam and Eve: A New Translation and Introduction," in *The Old Testament Pseudepigrapha*, ed. James J. Charlesworth, 2 vols. (Peabody: Hendrickson, 1983), 2:249–95. All subsequent translations of *Life of Adam and Eve* texts, both Greek and Latin, are from this source unless otherwise stated.

[66] Ibid., 254, 270 n. 3; cf. Lois Katherine Dow, "Eternal Jerusalem: Jerusalem/Zion in Biblical Theology With Special Attention to 'New Jerusalem' as the Name for the Final State in Revelation 21–22" (PhD diss., McMaster Divinity College, 2008), 137–8.

[67] Johnson, "Life of Adam and Eve," 254.

of Adam and Eve texts to be located on Mount Moriah, noting the rabbinic tradition that Adam went to live "on Mount Moriah, to cultivate the ground from which he had been created" (Tg. Ps.-J. 3).[68]

The argument for identifying the place of Adam's burial with Mount Moriah in the GLAE requires further critical investigation. There are a few issues to address. The Latin version of the Life of Adam and Eve appears to locate Adam's burial place on Mount Moriah, so long as we understand "the great dwelling place of God" to be the place of the Jerusalem Temple. However, text-critical scholarship on the Life of Adam and Eve has shown that the Latin version is a later recension of the text, the result of extensive editorial activities.[69] In fact, while the Greek text likely represents the earliest stages of the text, the Latin version represents the latest stage of development.[70] Moreover, some manuscripts disagree with the location, having Adam instead ask to be buried "towards open country" (*in agrum*) or "on land" (*in agro*).[71] Furthermore, the conclusion that the burial place of Adam is necessarily the site of the Jerusalem Temple is an inference relying on the combination of several different textual traditions.

The date of the GLAE is difficult to determine.[72] The state of the question in current scholarship is summed up by Marinus de Jonge and Johannes Tromp, who have suggested a wide range between the second and sixth centuries CE,[73] although they prefer a date between the second and fourth centuries.[74] Furthermore, Tromp and de Jonge prefer to view the GLAE as a Christian composition, though one that incorporates Jewish traditions.[75] Anne Marie Sweet has likewise argued for a date no earlier than the second century CE.[76] Johnson prefers a date toward the end of the first century CE,[77] which is quite close to the earlier end of de Jonge and Tromp's range. Jan Dochhorn has argued for a Jewish provenance for the GLAE within the first or second century CE in Palestine, partly on the basis of an argument for the author's possible familiarity with Hebrew.[78] By contrast, Rivka Nir has argued for a date closer

---

[68] As quoted in Dow, "Eternal Jerusalem," 137–8. Translation appears to be from John Wesley Etheridge, *The Targums of Onkelos and Jonathan ben Uzziel on the Pentateuch: with the Fragments of the Jerusalem Targum from the Chaldee* (London: Longman, Green, Longman, and Roberts, 1862).

[69] See de Jonge and Tromp, *Life of Adam and Eve*, 37–40; Tromp, "Literary Development," esp. 246–7; Johannes Tromp, "The Textual History of the *Life of Adam and Eve* In the Light of a Newly Discovered Latin Text-Form," *JSJ* 33, no. 1 (2002): 28–41.

[70] E.g., de Jonge and Tromp, *Life of Adam and Eve*, 77; Marinus de Jonge, *Pseudepigrapha of the Old Testament as Part of Christian Literature: The Case of the* Testaments of the Twelve Patriarchs *and the Greek* Life of Adam and Eve (Leiden: Brill, 2003), 230; Otto Menk and Merin Meiser, *Das Leben Adams und Evas*, Jüdische Schriften aus hellenistisch-römischer Zeit 2,5 (Gütersloh : Gütersloher Verlagshaus, 1998), 755–69.

[71] See Johnson, "Life of Adam and Eve," 286 (n. 45).

[72] For a review of various proposed dates for the GLAE, see the helpful review in Rivka Nir, "The Aromatic Fragrances of Paradise in the *Greek Life of Adam and Eve* and the Christian Origin of the Composition," *Novum Testamentum* 46, no. 1 (2004): 20–45 (45, n. 90).

[73] See de Jonge and Tromp, *Life of Adam and Eve*, 75–7; cf. discussion in Wanda Zemler-Cizewski, "The Apocryphal Life of Adam and Eve: Recent Scholarly Work," *Anglican Theological Review* 86, no. 4 (2004): 671–7 (674–5).

[74] de Jonge and Tromp, *Life of Adam and Eve*, 77.

[75] Ibid., 68–75 (esp. 74–5).

[76] Anne Marie Sweet, "A Religio-Historical Study of the Greek Life of Adam and Eve" (PhD diss., University of Notre Dame, 1992), 26.

[77] Johnson, "Life of Adam and Eve," 252.

[78] Jan Dochhorn, *Die Apokalypse des Mose* (Tübingen: Mohr Siebeck, 2005), 112–24, 152–72.

to the later end of the range that Tromp and de Jonge propose, placing the GLAE in the fourth to fifth centuries CE.[79] Thus, even if we date the GLAE to the earlier end of the proposed spectrum in the first century CE, if the Latin version is the latest stage of the development of the text, and dated substantially later, it is not at all clear that *Vita* 45:2 reflects a Jewish tradition that would have been current when Origen wrote his *Commentary on Matthew* in the mid-third century CE.[80] It is not impossible that late texts can transmit earlier traditions, but thus far, no attestation of the Mount Moriah burial tradition can be clearly or indisputably placed prior to or contemporary with Origen. This leads to the conclusion that it is not likely to have been known to him. At the very least, we cannot be certain that the Mount Moriah burial tradition antedates Origen. Moreover, it is certainly possible that multiple competing traditions can coexist, as shown by the existence of both the Moriah and Machpelah Adamic burial traditions in rabbinic literature. Even if the Moriah or Machpelah traditions were circulating in the third century CE, the coexistence of a Jewish tradition locating Adam's burial at Golgotha cannot be ruled out.

There are significant problems with the passages in the GLAE that some have argued present Temple imagery in connection with the place in which Adam was created and buried. The key passages are 5:3, which mentions a "house into which he [Adam] used to enter to pray to God," and 33:4, which mentions an altar. The narrative involving this altar is difficult to interpret and may describe an altar located at the place where the events of ch. 33 take place, or a visionary altar that Eve sees upon the death of Adam. The mention of the "prayer house" in 5:3 is a late addition to the text and was not included in the main text of the critical editions of the GLAE.[81] Given the range of possible dates of the original composition of the GLAE, it is unlikely that this late addition can be considered a witness to a tradition that would have been current in or prior to the third century CE. The altar mentioned in 33:4 is located at the place where Adam dies, but this is not where he is buried. The primordial humans are expelled from Paradise in chs. 28–29, and we are told in 29:6 that Adam "went out of Paradise." Then, in 38:3–4, the text describes the angels taking Adam's body from where it lay *into* Paradise. Thus, within the narrative of the GLAE, the altar mentioned by Eve in 33:4 is not located at the place where Adam is buried but at the place where he died, which is apparently not located in Paradise (cf. 29:6), where Adam is eventually buried (ch. 40).

Our search for the earliest Jewish tradition concerning the location of Adam's burial has, somewhat surprisingly, led us to circle back to Origen. No extant tradition about the burial of Adam in Jewish sources can be confidently placed prior to or

---

[79] Nir, "Aromatic Fragrances," 45. See, however, the counter argument of Peter-Ben Smit, "Incense Revisited: Reviewing the Evidence For Incense as a Clue to the Christian Provenance of the *Greek Life of Adam and Eve*," *Novum Testamentum* 46, no. 4 (2004): 369–75.

[80] On the date of Origen's *Commentary on Matthew*, see R. P. C. Hanson, *Origen's Doctrine of Tradition*, repr. (Eugene: Wipf and Stock, [1954] 2004), 16–17. Hanson places Origen's *Commentary on Matthew* in 246 CE.

[81] Tromp, *Critical Edition*, 126–7. Tromp and de Jonge note the point of contact between this mention of the "prayer house" and the Cave of Treasures tradition (*Life of Adam and Eve*, 33, 86). Likewise, see Dochhorn, *Die Apokalypse des Mose*, 219–20.

contemporary with Origen.[82] Taylor's suggestion that there may be polemic involved in the development of competing traditions is intriguing, though perhaps the polemic cut in the opposite direction. Given the later dates of its attestation, it is possible that the Mount Moriah tradition arose in Jewish circles in late antiquity in response to the Christian use of a tradition of Adamic burial at Golgotha, which had become well known in Palestine by the fourth century CE., and to the incorporation of Golgotha into the Church of the Holy Sepulchre.

It has sometimes been argued that Adam is buried at the site of Mount Moriah in GLAE because he is buried "in the place from which God had found the dust" (GLAE 40:6), that is, the place where he was created, since Jewish tradition locates the Temple mount as the place where Adam was formed.[83] However, GLAE does not indicate that Adam was formed from dust taken from Mount Moriah (or anywhere else in Jerusalem). Louis Ginzberg is aware of this problem and in response claims that Adam's grave is "erroneously placed in paradise," and thus "paradise" should not be taken literally but must instead mean Jerusalem,[84] which is not a convincing argument. Since there is no internal evidence in GLAE for the identification of the place of Adam's creation with Mount Moriah, the argument has to rely on other Jewish texts. However, the sources for this tradition are quite late,[85] probably later than the composition of GLAE,[86] and later than Origen. However, there is a potentially earlier source for this tradition in 2 En. 71:35-36:

> He, Melkisedek, will be priest and king in the place Akhuzan, that is to say, in the center of the earth, where Adam was created, and there will be his final grave. And in connection with that archpriest it is written how he also will be buried there, where the center of the earth is, just as Adam also buried his own son there—Abel.[87]

---

[82] An author's aside: this was certainly not the conclusion that I expected to reach at the outset of this research, but it is the one that emerged from consideration of the data.

[83] Isaiah Gafni, *Jews and Judaism in the Rabbinic Era: Image and Reality – History and Historiography*, TSAJ 173 (Tübingen: Mohr Siebeck, 2019), 37; cf. Johnson, "Life of Adam and Eve," 293 n. g; Louis Ginzberg, *The Legends of the Jews*, 2 vols., reissue ed., trans. Henrietta Szold and Paul Radin (Philadelphia: Jewish Publication Society of America, 2003), 1: 97–8 n. 137; Victor Apowitzer, "Les Elements Juifs dans la legend du Golgotha," *Revue des Études Juives* (1924): 145–62.

[84] Ginzberg, *Legends of the Jews*, 1: 98 n. 137.

[85] The key earlier sources are Gen. Rab. 14:8 and y. Nazir 7, 56b (attributed to Judah ben Pazi, a fourth-century sage). As Adiel Kadari has written, "The very claim, however, that Adam's burial in Jerusalem was a Jewish tradition that was prevalent in the Second Temple period lacks a sufficient basis," in Adiel Kadari, "Interreligious Aspects in the Burial of Adam in *Pirkei de-Rabbi Eliezer*," in *Religious Stories in Transformation: Conflict, Revision and Reception*, ed. Alberdina Houtman, Tamar Kadari, Marcel Poorthuis, and Vered Tohar, Jewish and Christian Perspectives 31 (Leiden: Brill, 2016), 82–103.

[86] On the range of proposed dates, see above. An early date might be in the early second century CE.

[87] Translation from F. I. Anderson, "2 (Slavonic Apocalypse of) Enoch," in *The Old Testament Pseudepigrapha*, 2 vols., ed. James J. Charlesworth (Peabody: Hendrickson, 1983), 1: 91–221. On the manuscripts of 2 Enoch, see Grant Macaskill, "2 Enoch: Manuscripts, Recensions, and Original Language," in *New Perspectives on 2 Enoch: No Longer Slavonic Only*, ed. Andrei A. Orlov and Gabriele Boccaccini, associate ed. Jason Zurawski, Studia Judaeoslavica 4 (Leiden: Brill, 2012), 83–101.

Although Moriah is not named here, it has been argued that the Jerusalem Temple mount is in mind here, since it is the center of the world in Jewish tradition.[88]

A fair case has been recently made for a Second Temple date for the original composition of 2 Enoch.[89] However, the tradition of Adam's creation and burial in 2 En. 71:35–36 is problematic and cannot be traced to the original composition. First of all, it is essential to recognize that 71:34–37 are late interpolations found only in one manuscript (R).[90] Moreover, it has been convincingly shown that this is part of a *Christian* interpolation.[91] Furthermore, it is questionable as to whether Akhuzan really is meant to be the Temple in Jerusalem. As Tromp writes,

> It is often assumed that Achuzan or Azuchan (mentioned in 2 En 64:2; 68:5; 70:17; 71:35) stands for the temple in Jerusalem, but to me, the evidence on which this assumption is based, seems weak. The text speaks about the altar erected by Enoch (64:2), not about the temple in Jerusalem … In 71:35–36 it is also regarded as the place where Adam was made and where he was buried (together with Abel), and it is designated there as the center of the earth. A second Melchizedek (71:34) will be priest and king at that place. This second Melchizedek is undoubtedly a reference to Christ, and the likeliest place where he is here regarded as having performed his office of priest and king is Golgotha, where Adam was buried according to a widespread tradition in Christianity.[92]

Thus, contrary to the notion that 2 En. 71:35–36 witnesses a Second Temple or pre-Christian Jewish tradition about the location of Adam's burial, it more likely belongs to the history of Christian interpretation and may in fact be a reference to the burial of Adam at Golgotha. If this segment of the text has a Christian origin, then the "center of the earth" may well be Golgotha, since in Christian tradition, "the central point of the

---

[88] Gafni, *Jews and Judaism*, 37 (esp. n. 31); cf. Ginzberg, *Legends of the Jews*, 1: 88 n. 109. On the concept of Jerusalem as the center of the world in general, see Philip S. Alexander, "Jerusalem as the *Omphalos* of the World: On the History of a Geographical Concept," *Judaism* 46, no. 2 (1997): 147–58.

[89] See Christfried Böttrich, "The 'Book of the Secrets of Enoch' (2 En): Between Jewish Origin and Christian Transmission," in *New Perspectives on 2 Enoch: No Longer Slavonic Only*, ed. Andrei A. Orlov and Gabriele Boccaccini, associate ed. Jason Zurawski, Studia Judaeoslavica 4 (Leiden: Brill, 2012), 37–67 (52–7); Andrei A. Orlov, "The Sacerdotal Traditions of 2 Enoch and the Date of the Text," in *New Perspectives on 2 Enoch: No Longer Slavonic Only*, ed. Andrei A. Orlov and Gabriele Boccaccini, associate ed. Jason Zurawski, Studia Judaeoslavica 4 (Leiden: Brill, 2012), 103–16.

[90] Anderson, "2 Enoch," 208 n. p.

[91] Christfried Böttrich, *Weltweisheit, Menschheitsethik, Urkult: Studien zum slavischen Henochbuch*, WUNT R.2, 50 (Tübingen: Mohr Siebeck, 1992), 118–25; cf. Böttrich, "'Book of the Secrets of Enoch,'" 42–3, 46–7; Charles A. Gleschen, "Enoch and Melchizedek: The Concern for Supra-Human Priestly Mediators in 2 Enoch," in *New Perspectives on 2 Enoch: No Longer Slavonic Only*, ed. Andrei A. Orlov and Gabriele Boccaccini, associate ed. Jason Zurawski, Studia Judaeoslavica 4 (Leiden: Brill, 2012), 369–85 (370); Harold W. Attridge, "Melchizedek in Some Early Christian Texts and 2 Enoch," in *New Perspectives on 2 Enoch: No Longer Slavonic Only*, ed. Andrei A. Orlov and Gabriele Boccaccini, associate ed. Jason Zurawski, Studia Judaeoslavica 4 (Leiden: Brill, 2012), 387–410 (esp. 397–405).

[92] Johannes Magliano-Tromp, "Adamic Traditions in 2 Enoch and in the Books of Adam and Eve," in *New Perspectives on 2 Enoch: No Longer Slavonic Only*, ed. Andrei A. Orlov and Gabriele Boccaccini, associate ed. Jason Zurawski, Studia Judaeoslavica 4 (Leiden: Brill, 2012), 283–304 (293 n. 39).

earth is Golgotha."[93] Moreover, the notion of Golgotha as the center of the world and burial site of Adam is strongly paralleled in Cave of Treasures 23:15–18, a late antique Christian text that also includes the investment of Melchizedek as priest at Golgotha (23:19–23).

Could Origen have transmitted a genuine Jewish tradition about Golgotha? Possibly. Origen's location in Palestine and his Alexandrian formation certainly put him into contact with Jews and Jewish traditions.[94] Recently, Ronald Heine has situated the *Commentary on Matthew* within the context of Origen's time in Caesarea.[95] Heine highlights the increased Jewish population of Caesarea in the third century and notes the breadth of Origen's interactions with the Jewish community there.[96]

Origen demonstrates some knowledge of Jewish Christians, such as the Ebionites (*Contra Celsus* 5.61, 65). Elsewhere, he mentions having received a Jewish exegetical tradition about the existence of two call narratives in Isaiah from a "man who, because he had come to believe in Christ and had abandoned the law for something higher, fled his native land and arrived where we were living" (*Hom. Jer.* 20.2).[97] This implies that Origen had received this particular tradition from a Palestinian Jew who had become a Christian and had left his home in Roman Palestine for Alexandria.[98]

Although there is little certainty to be had about the source of Origen's Golgotha tradition, it is plausible that it may have come to him from a Jewish source. Whether it is *probable* is a different matter altogether. It is curious that the tradition of Adam's burial at Golgotha does not appear in early Jewish sources, as it is unique to Christian sources and to Christian reworkings of Jewish sources, such as the Cave of Treasures. This is reasonable cause for suspicion, and I am of the opinion that the matter cannot be settled definitively. Furthermore, there is no evidence on which we might base an inference that the Adamic Golgotha tradition can be retrojected into the first century CE.[99] It is more prudent to view it as an interpretation of the site's nomenclature.

Given the general lack of interest in a placed called "Golgotha" (or anything similar to it) in extant non-Christian Jewish sources, it is likely that the tradition has its origin in a Christian context, since Christians, whether Jewish or Gentile, might have a vested interest in the place due to its prominence in the gospel narratives as the site of Jesus' crucifixion. Thus, the Adamic Golgotha tradition is an interpretation of the place that arose precisely *because* of the prominence of Golgotha in Christian memory of Jesus

---

[93] Cyril of Jerusalem, *Catechesis* 13.28, translation from Edward Yarnold, *Cyril of Jerusalem*, The Early Church Fathers (London: Routledge, 2000), 157.
[94] On this generally, see Joseph W. Trigg, *Origen*, The Early Church Fathers (New York: Routledge, 1998), 13–14, 24.
[95] Heine, *Origen on the Gospel of St. Matthew*, 4–7.
[96] Ibid., 4–5.
[97] Cf. Trigg, *Origen*, 14.
[98] On this particular figure, see Pierre Nautin, *Origène: sa vie et son œuvre* (Paris: Beauchesne, 1977), 132–3; cf. also Trigg, *Origen*, 14.
[99] Contra Bagatti, who speculates that Jesus' descent to Sheol to liberate Adam was already remembered in "some grotto" at Golgotha prior to 135 CE (*Church from the Gentiles*, 24). Although this is not strictly impossible, there is no clear evidence to support the connection between Golgotha and Adam prior to Origen.

and its function as a *lieu de mémoire* well before the time of Constantine and the advent of Christian pilgrimage to Jerusalem.

Whatever its roots may be, Origen's deployment of the "Hebraic" tradition of Adam's burial at Golgotha paves the way for further Adamic-Christological interpretation of the place. This, in turn, allows for a layer of theological interpretation to coalesce around the event and the historical person that the place had come to commemorate in the Christian community. The reception history of the Adamic Golgotha tradition helps us to better understand the connection of the reception history of the Adam-Christ typology to the site of Golgotha. As the continued presence and use of the Chapel of Adam in the modern Church of the Holy Sepulchre witnesses, this specific interpretation has become a fixed dimension of the commemoration of Jesus at this particular place.[100] Despite its tenuous relationship to first-century historical reality, it has become an integral and remarkably resilient facet of Jesus memory and Christian commemorative activity at Golgotha.

The Reception of the Adamic Golgotha Tradition in Fourth-Century Exegesis

The Adamic Golgotha tradition first witnessed by Origen is received and further elaborated in fourth-century Christian writings. It is discussed and remembered with much greater frequency in the fourth century than in the centuries preceding. That interest was likely stimulated by the excavations made by Constantine in preparation for the construction of the Church of the Holy Sepulchre and the restored visibility of the rock of Golgotha in the first decades of the fourth century. In this period, it was not only an idea, a place remembered, but also an actual place that could be seen and touched, bearing witness in the minds of the pious to the salvific events that they believed had transpired three centuries earlier on its spire. Special attention will be given in our examination to Palestinian sources.

Epiphanius mentions the Adamic Golgotha tradition in his polemical discussion of Tatian's belief that Adam cannot be saved.[101] The course of this polemic[102] leads Epiphanius to raise the Adamic Golgotha tradition in the theological context of his refutation of Tatian:

> And so we must be surprised at someone (like Tatian) who knows—as I too have found in the literature—that our Lord Jesus Christ was crucified on Golgotha, nowhere else than where Adam's body lay buried. For after leaving Paradise, living opposite it for a long time and growing old, Adam later came and died in this place, I mean Jerusalem, and was buried there, on the site of Golgotha. This is probably the way the place, which means "Place of a Skull," got its name, since the contour of

---

[100] On the reception of this tradition in the Byzantine period and beyond, see Bellarmino Bagatti, "Note sull'iconografia di Adamo sotto il Calvario," *Liber Annuus* 27 (1977): 5–32; cf. Ignazio Mancini, "Adamo sotto il Calvario," *Terra Santa* 41 (1965): 277–82.

[101] Concerning Tatian on the salvation of Adam, see William L. Peterson, "Tatian the Assyrian," in *A Companion to Second-Century Christian 'Heretics'*, ed. Antti Marjanen and Petri Luomanen (Leiden: Brill, 2008), 125–58 (142–52).

[102] In Epiphanius, *Pan.* 46.

the site bears no resemblance to a skull. Neither is it on some peak so that this can be interpreted as a skull, as we say of the head's position on a body. Nor is it on a height. And indeed, it is no higher than the other "places" either ... Why the name "Of the Skull" then, unless because the skull of the first-formed man had there and his remains were laid to rest there, and so it had been named "Of the Skull"? By being crucified above them our Lord Jesus Christ mystically showed our salvation, through the water and blood that flowed from him through his pierced side—at the beginning of the lump beginning to sprinkle our forefather's remains, to show us too the sprinkling of his blood for the cleansing of our defilement and that of any repentant soul; and to show, as an example of the leavening and cleansing of the filth our sins have left, the water which was poured out on the one who lay buried beneath him, for his hope and the hope of us his descendants. Thus the prophecy, "Awake thou that sleepest and arise from the dead, and Christ shall give thee light," was fulfilled here.[103]

This passage is rich and leads us to make some comments and observations about Epiphanius' reception and interpretation of Golgotha. His statement about Tatian's knowledge of Jesus' crucifixion on Golgotha, "where Adam's body lay buried" (46.5.1) is curious, since it may imply that Tatian, who lived in the second century, may have had knowledge of the Adamic Golgotha tradition. If so, this would push the earliest known instantiation of the connection between Golgotha and Adam back into the mid-second century. However, it is not clear whether Epiphanius means to say that Tatian knew of Adam's burial on Golgotha, presumably in reference to a text that is not extant, or simply that Tatian knew that Jesus was crucified at Golgotha (cf. *Diatessaron* 51.25). The former is more likely to be the case,[104] given Epiphanius' assertion that he too has found the same thing "in the literature,"[105] which probably refers to the Adamic tradition rather than to the fact of Jesus' crucifixion on Golgotha, which would almost certainly have been common knowledge in fourth-century Palestine, especially following the construction of the Church of the Holy Sepulchre, which had begun by 325 CE. Moreover, this suits the rhetorical logic of *Pan.* 46.5.1, as the point seems to be that Epiphanius is surprised at Tatian's stance on Adam given that Tatian knew that Adam was buried where Christ was crucified. However, even if Epiphanius did claim

---

[103] *Pan.* 46.5.1-9. Translation from Frank Williams (trans.), *The* Panarion *of Epiphanius of Salamis*, 2nd ed. (Leiden: Brill, 2009).

[104] It is important to note, however, that neither Eusebius nor Cyril of Jerusalem, who wrote in the first half of the fourth century, mentions the Adamic Golgotha tradition. This has led some to suggest that it developed in the mid-fourth century, since it does appear in the writings of Epiphanius and Jerome, who both wrote in the latter half of the century. Thus, its instantiation in Origen, *Comm. Matt.* 27:53, would need to be regarded as inauthentic. On this, see P. W. L. Walker, *Holy City, Holy Places?: Christian Attitudes to Jerusalem and the Holy Land in the Fourth Century*, Oxford Early Christian Studies (Oxford: Clarendon Press, 1990), 255, n. 58. Although not impossible, this constitutes an argument from silence, and it seems imprudent to base a judgment about the inauthenticity of Origen's witness to the tradition on such grounds. It is also further problematized by Epiphanius' implication that Tatian knew of this same tradition.

[105] It is possible, as Frank Williams suggests, that the source referred to here by Epiphanius may be Origen. See Williams, *The* Panarion, 379, n. 19.

that Tatian knew that Adam was supposedly buried at Golgotha, it is by no means certain that his claim is correct or reliable.[106] There is no firm basis here on which to push the earliest attestation of the Golgotha burial tradition from the third into the second century.

In Epiphanius' estimation, the name "Golgotha" cannot be explained by reference to the physical features of the place that was identified as Golgotha in the fourth century, and, thus, it must refer to an actual skull.[107] As mentioned above, this passage appears in the course of a refutation of Tatian's stance on the salvation of Adam.[108] The potential soteriological significance of the imagery of water and blood flowing from the side of the crucified Christ (5.7; cf. John 19:34; see also 1 John 5:6) at the very place where Adam lay buried is not lost on Epiphanius. Accordingly, he writes of the "sprinkling" of the water and blood poured out from Christ on "our forefather's remains" (5.8) as having "mystically showed our salvation" (5.7). Moreover, the water "poured out on the one who lay buried beneath" is "an example of the leavening and cleansing of the filth our sins have left" (5.8). It is worth noting that Epiphanius relies heavily upon the Johannine theological tradition of the New Testament in his interpretation and reception of Golgotha (John 19:34; cf. 1 John 5:6), while also making reference to the Pauline tradition (Eph 5:14; *Pan.* 5.9). This helps to develop the Adam-Christ typological interpretation of Golgotha in a new direction. Epiphanius, in whose day the rock of Golgotha was visible, granted literal theological significance as well as symbolic significance to the place of Golgotha as the site of the crucifixion as well as the place of the literal skull of Adam.

As a result of his interpretation of Golgotha as the place where Adam was buried and subsequently cleansed by the water and blood of Christ "for his hope and the hope of us his descendants" (5.9), Epiphanius considers Golgotha to be the place where the "prophecy" of Eph 5:14 ("Awake thou that sleepest and arise from the dead, and Christ shall give thee light"[109]) to be fulfilled. This imbues the memory of the place of Golgotha with further soteriological, eschatological, and prophetic significance. While Origen saw Golgotha's location as both the place of Adam's burial and Christ's crucifixion as fitting, its significance was mostly symbolic. For Epiphanius, by means of his reference to the Johannine water and blood tradition, the matter is more visceral. The water and blood shed from Christ's side were poured out on Adam's remains, exemplifying the

---

[106] Epiphanius' information on Tatian likely came primarily from other heresiological writings. See Williams, *The Panarion*, 376 n. 1.

[107] On this, see Andrew S. Jacobs, *Epiphanius of Cyprus: A Cultural Biography of Late Antiquity* (Oakland: University of California Press, 2016), 144.

[108] Jacobs argues that Epiphanius' point here is "the effect of the Bible as a site of antiquarian display," since "it is less clear how this biblically inspired geographic detail supports his heresiological point (that Adam was saved)" (Jacobs, *Epiphanius of Cyrpus*, 144). I would that this passage does indeed highlight the effect of the Bible as a site of antiquarian display, but this does not exclude the heresiological/soteriological point that Epiphanius makes through the use of this tradition. As Grypeou and Spurling write concerning the theological dimension of the Adamic Golgotha tradition, "Adam must be buried in the place where Jesus was crucified in order for him to receive direct salvation through Jesus' sacrifice" (*Genesis in Late Antiquity*, 73).

[109] Translation from Williams, *The Panarion*, 380.

redemptive effect of Christ's death for humanity and demonstrating, against Tatian, the salvation of Adam.

We turn now to Jerome. In Epistle 46, written *c.*386 CE by Jerome in the name of Paula and Eustochium to Marcella, he mentions the Adamic Golgotha tradition in a form that is remarkably similar to that known by Epiphanius. Jerome writes,

> Tradition has it that in this city, nay, more, on this very spot, Adam lived and died. The place where our Lord was crucified is called Calvary, because the skull of the primitive man was buried there. So it came to pass that the second Adam, that is the blood of Christ, as it dropped from the cross, washed away the sins of the buried protoplast, the first Adam, and thus the words of the apostle were fulfilled: "Awake, you that sleep, and arise from the dead, and Christ shall give you light."[110]

Here, Golgotha again serves as a geographical point of contact between the memory of Christ and the biblical conception of Adam, as the place where Christ was crucified and where Adam was buried. The similarities to Epiphanius' reception of Golgotha are notable. The notion of the blood of Christ falling on the remains of Adam and cleansing his sins and the fulfillment citation of Eph 5:14 are both present here. The similarities are such that it is seems possible that Epiphanius and Jerome shared a source, or perhaps that Jerome knew of the tradition from the *Panarion*. However, in his *Commentary on Ephesians*, he writes,

> I know that I have heard someone preaching about this passage in church. As a theatrical marvel he presented a model never before seen by the people so that it was pleasing. He said of this testimony, that it is said that Adam was buried at Calvary where the Lord was crucified. The place was called Calvary [i.e. skull], therefore, because the head of the ancient man was buried there. At the time when the Lord was crucified, therefore, he was hanging over Adam's grave and this prophecy was fulfilled which says, "Awake," Adam, "who are asleep and arise from the dead," and not as we read, πιφασει σοι Χριστος, that is, "Christ will rise like the sun on you," but πιψασει, that is, "Christ will touch you." That was because, of course, by the touch of his blood and hanging body Adam would be made alive and would arise. That type was also truly fulfilled at the time the dead Elisha awakened the dead. Whether these things are true or not I leave to the reader's decision. They were certainly pleasing at the time they were spoken among the people who received them with applause and by stamping their feet. I mention one thing which I know: that understanding does not fit with the interpretation and coherence of this passage.[111]

---

[110] Jerome, Epistle 46.3, translation from W. H. Fremantle, *St. Jerome: Letters and Select Works*, NPNF 2.6 (New York: Christian Literature Publishing, 1892), 61. On the date, see p. 60.

[111] Jerome, *Commentary on Ephesians*, 5:14, translation from Ronand E. Heine, *The Commentaries of Origen and Jerome on St. Paul's Epistle to the Ephesians* (Oxford: Oxford University Press, 2003).

This work is dated along with Jerome's other Pauline commentaries to 386–388 CE.[112] Thus, if there is a shift in Jerome's thinking on the Adamic Golgotha tradition and its interpretation here, it must have come about in a relatively short period of time.[113] This passage indicates that Jerome heard the Adamic Golgotha burial tradition along with the Eph 5:14 interpretation in a sermon in a church setting. This is significant in and of itself for the study of the transmission and reception of extra-biblical traditions in early Christianity. Common church gatherings and sermons could be settings for the popular oral transmission of traditions, both antiquarian and exegetical. Several elements in common with Epiphanius' reception and interpretation of Golgotha/Calvary are constant here: the notion that the name of Golgotha is related to its status as the burial place of Adam, the belief that Christ's blood was poured out on Adam's remains to salvific ends, and that this fulfilled the tradition cited in Eph 5:14. Given the similarity of this unnamed preacher's version of the Golgotha tradition to Epiphanius' discussion of the same tradition and to Jerome's own Ep. 46, it is reasonable to suggest that these common elements were a part of the form in which the tradition typically circulated in Palestine by the final quarter of the fourth century CE. This passage indicates the popularity of the tradition and its potential to spread within the local Christian communities of Palestine.[114] The memory of Golgotha as the place of Jesus' crucifixion had combined with Adam-Christ typology in Pauline fashion and with the eschatological hope for resurrection expressed in Eph 5:14.

There is a measure of skepticism in Jerome's discussion here that is not present in Ep. 46.[115] Jerome is skeptical of the exegesis of Eph 5:14 used to combine it with the Adamic Golgotha tradition. Moreover, he is at least ambivalent if not moderately skeptical about the whole tradition, leaving it up to the reader's discretion to decide whether it is true or not.

---

[112] Heine, *Commentaries*, 7. For specific discussions of the date of this epistle, see Pierre Nautin, "La Date des commentaires de Jérôme sur les épîtres pauliniennes," *Revue d'Histoire Ecclésiastique de Louvain* 74, no. 1 (1979): 5–12. John Norman Davidson Kelly, *Jerome: His Life, Writings, and Controversies* (New York: Duckworth, 1975), 145. Jerome himself comments on the composition of the commentary in *Commentary on Ephesians*, Preface, 1.539-40 (Heine, *Commentaries*, 76–7).

[113] Lipatov makes the intriguing suggestion that the unnamed preacher was John of Jerusalem or one of his followers and argues that the quick shift in Jerome's attitude is related to his falling out with John of Jerusalem. See Lipatov, "Early Christian Tradition," 173–4.

[114] Cf. Grypeou and Spurling, *Genesis in Late Antiquity*, 78–9.

[115] On this shift, see Krewson, *Jerome and the Jews*, 126–7; C. T. R. Hayward, *Jerome's Hebrew Questions on Genesis: Translated with an Introduction and Commentary*, Oxford Early Christian Studies (Oxford: Clarendon Press, 1995), 183. Lipatov-Chicherin ("Early Christian Tradition," 173–4) has made the intriguing suggestion that the unnamed preacher is in fact John II of Jerusalem, and that Jerome's rejection of the Adamic burial tradition is connected to his falling out with John and thus to the Origenist controversy. He points to Epiphanius' use of the same tradition as evidence supporting this, since Epiphanius also heard John preach in Jerusalem. This is certainly a possible explanation of the evidence, and one that the present author is open to, though it is by no means the only possible explanation. Epiphanius' knowledge of the tradition, for example, could have come from other local sources, we simply cannot be sure. Whatever the case may be, I suspect that the solution to the problem posed by the difference in attitude toward the Adam-Golgotha tradition in Epistle 46 and in *Commentary on Ephesians* needs to take the role of Paula and Eustochium in the authorship of Epistle 46 seriously, since it may well their thought expressed on the tradition in the letter to Marcella rather than that of Jerome.

Jerome's skepticism would become total rejection of the connection between Adam and Golgotha. In his *Commentary on Matthew*, Jerome writes,

> I have heard that someone has explained that "place of the skull" [Latin *Calvariae locus*] is the place where Adam is buried and that the reason it is so named is because the head of that ancient man is laid there. They relate this to what the apostle says: "Awake, you who sleep, and arise from the dead, and Christ shall enlighten you." This interpretation is attractive and soothing to the ear of the people, but it is not true. For outside the city and outside the gate there are places in which the heads of the condemned are cut off. This is where they took the name "of the skull" (Lat. *Calvariae*); that is, it refers to the skulls of the decapitated. But the reason the Lord was crucified there was so that where there was once a site of the condemned, there the banner of martyrdom would be raised ... But if anyone should wish to contend that the reason the Lord was crucified there was so that his blood might trickle own on Adam's tomb, we shall ask him why other thieves were also crucified in the same place ... in the book of Joshua the son of Nave we read that Adam was buried near Hebron and Arba.[116]

This passage further indicates the popularity of the tradition of Adam's burial at Golgotha, even as Jerome attempts to discredit it. As the theme of Adam's skull beneath the cross in later Christian art and the continued commemoration of Adam at the modern Church of the Holy Sepulchre demonstrates,[117] the popularity of this tradition has endured and remains a notable dimension of the memory of Golgotha and the scene of Jesus' crucifixion to this day.

Jerome's rejection of Golgotha as Adam's burial place is partly rooted in his linguistic exegesis. He understands the nomenclature of the site of crucifixion (Golgotha, Latin *Calvariae*) to mean, more literally, "place of the decapitated,"[118] thus referring to its status as an execution site. Moreover, his identification of the Cave of Machpelah at Kiryat Arba (Hebron) as Adam's burial place is based on his reading of the Hebrew biblical text.[119] The passage that Jerome refers to here is Josh 14:15. In the Vulgate, he renders the relevant portion of this verse as follows: "nomen Hebron antea vocabatur Cariatharbe Adam maximus ibi inter Enacim situs est" (Vulg. Josh 14:15).

The Douay-Rheims renders this:

> The name of Hebron before was called Cariath-Arbe: Adam the greatest among the Enacims was laid there (DRB Josh 14:15).

---

[116] Translation from Thomas O. Schenk (trans.), *St. Jerome: Commentary on Matthew*, The Fathers of the Church 117 (Washington, DC: Catholic University of America Press, 2008), 315–16.

[117] See, e.g., Bagatti, "Note sull'iconografia di Adamo"; Sigrid Esche, *Adam und Eva: Sündenfall und Erlösung* (Düsseldorf: L. Schwann, 1957), 38. On the Chapel of Adam in the Church of the Holy Sepulchre, see (e.g.) the classic studies of Joachim Jeremias, "Golgotha und der heilige Felsen," ΑΓΓΕΛΟΣ 2 (1926): 78; Jeremias, *Golgotha*.

[118] Cf. on this point, Andrew M. Bain, *Passion and Resurrection Narratives: Post-Nicene Latin Interpretations* (Eugene: Wipf and Stock, 2018), 49–50.

[119] Cf. Grypeou and Spurling, *Genesis in Late Antiquity*, 78–9.

However, the MT (BHQ) reads:

וְשֵׁם חֶבְרוֹן לְפָנִים קִרְיַת אַרְבַּע הָאָדָם הַגָּדוֹל בָּעֲנָקִים הוּא

In the RSV, this is rendered as:

> Now the name of Hebron formerly was Kiriath-arba; [this Arba was] the greatest man among the Anakim.

Jerome's reading of the passage results from his understandable misreading of הָאָדָם as "Adam," the proper name, rather than "man," a common noun. Although it is possible that the Jewish tradition of Adam's burial at Machpelah could have been circulating in Palestine in Jerome's day, he does not indicate any awareness of such a tradition. Rather, his belief that Adam was buried at Machpelah and thus not Golgotha is based, at least in his somewhat flawed estimation, on biblical authority. The burial of Adam at Kiryat Arba (Hebron, Machpelah) is repeated by Jerome in *lib. loc.* 75.23, *Qu. Heb. Gen.* 23:2, and Epistle 108. The phrase "great Adam" (mistranslated from Heb. הָאָדָם הַגָּדוֹל) is repeated in both Epistle 108 and *lib. loc.* 75.23, which points us back to Jerome's translation in Vulg. Josh 14:15.

In Epistle 108.11, Jerome calls Kiryat Arba the "City of Four Men" (Hebrew "Arba" = four), writing that the four men are "Abraham, Isaac, Jacob, and the great Adam whom the Hebrews suppose (from the book of Joshua the Son of Nun) to be buried there. But many are of opinion that Caleb is the fourth and a monument at one side is pointed out as his." From this, it is unclear whether Jerome is aware of a Jewish tradition about Adam's burial at Kiryat Arba that was circulating in his day that was based on or supported by Josh 14:15,[120] or if, by saying that "the Hebrews suppose (from the book of Joshua the Son of Nun)," he means to say that the Hebrews must think that this is so, since Jerome believed that the book of Joshua said that Adam was buried at Kiryat Arba. The idea that Kiryat Arba is named for the four great patriarchs buried there, and that one of them is Adam, is also found in late antique Jewish sources, particularly b. Erub. 53a and Gen. Rab. 58:4, 58:9.[121] While it is possible that Jerome and the sages came to the same exegetical conclusions based on the name "Arba" and perhaps also Josh 14:15, the similarity between these exegetical moves by Jerome and the Sages points toward shared tradition. That said, it is clear that Jerome believed himself to be invoking biblical authority rather than oral tradition to reject the Golgotha burial tradition.

Although Jerome's acceptance of Kiryat Arba as the burial place of Adam rather than Golgotha is usually taken to be a shift in his thought, Epistle 46 is the only source among Jerome's writings that upholds the Golgotha tradition. It is also the only source among Jerome's writings that discuss Adam's burial place that is written in the names of Paula and Eustochium. In my opinion, it is important to consider Paula and

---

[120] Cf. Taylor, *Christians and the Holy Places*, 130.
[121] On the burial of Adam at Kiryat Arba in early Judaism, see Grypeou and Spurling, *Genesis in Late Antiquity*, 50–4.

Eustochium as authors of Epistle 46, and to see Jerome as writing on their behalf.[122] Thus, the possibility that it better reflects Paula and Eustochium's opinion on the burial place of Adam than it does Jerome's must be considered.

Why, in contrast to other early Christian writers, does Jerome reject the Golgotha burial tradition in favor of Kiryat Arba? William Krewson has convincingly argued that it fits into a supersessionist program of shifting focus from Jerusalem to Bethlehem.[123] There is undoubtedly merit to Krewson's analysis, though we must note that the rationale that Jerome himself provides is biblical, based on his (mistaken) reading of the Hebrew text of Josh 14:15. Despite his rejection of it, Jerome's discussions of the Golgotha tradition in multiple places and his apparent need to refute it bear witness to the widespread association of the place of Golgotha with Adam Christology throughout the fourth century.

A few more examples of connections drawn between the commemoration of the event of Jesus' crucifixion on Golgotha and Adam's burial at the same place from the fourth century CE will serve to further illustrate just how widespread the tradition had become after Origen. A pseudonomyous text, *De passione et cruce Domini* (English "On the Passion and Cross of the Lord; Greek "ΕΙΣ ΤΟ ΠΑΘΟΣ ΤΟΥ ΚΥΡΙΟΥ ΚΑΙ ΕΙΣ ΤΟΝ ΣΤΑΥΡΟΝ") attributed to Athanasius of Alexandria dating to the second quarter of the fourth century (325–350 CE)[124] and perhaps originating from Palestine,[125] mentions the burial of Adam at Golgotha in connection with a second Adam typology:

> He did not suffer his Passion anywhere else nor was he crucified in any other place but in the place of the Skull, on which the Jewish teachers say that the grave of Adam is … Then the Lord who wanted to renew the first Adam, had to suffer in this place, in order to abolish his sin, so that it would be lifted from the entire humankind. (Ps. Athanasius, *De passione et cruce Domini*, in PG 28:208)[126]

Here, we note that the source of the Golgotha burial tradition is attributed to "Jewish teachers," which is reminiscent of Origen's claim about its "Hebraic" origin.

---

[122] Anni Maria Laato, "What Makes the Holy Land Holy? A Debate between Paula, Eustochium, and Marcella (Jerome, Ep. 46)," in Erkki Koskenniemi and J. Cornelis de Vos (eds.), *Holy Places and Cult*, Studies in the Reception History of the Bible 5 (Winona Lake: Eisenbrauns, 2014), 169–99 (174–8).

[123] Krewson, *Jerome and the Jews*, 127–35.

[124] On the date see Hubertus R. Drobner, 'Eine pseudo-athanasianische Osterpredigt (CPG II. 2247) über die Wahrheit Gottes und ihre Erfüllung', in *Christian Faith and Greek Philosophy in Late Antiquity*, ed. Lionel R. Wickham, Caroline P. Ammel, assisted by Erica C. D. Hunter (Leiden: Brill, 1993), 43–51 (44). According to Drobner, "Als Datum der Abfassung geht man aufgrund der betont nizanischen Theologie, die aber noch nicht die Entwicklung nach 356 zu kennen scheint, von den Jahren 325 bis 350 aus. Die vorliegende pseudo-athanasianische Osterpredigt muß danach jedenfalls vor 350 entstanden sein." Lipatov-Chicherin has suggested that the author of this text may in fact be John II of Jerusalem or one of his followers (see "Early Christian Tradition," 174).

[125] Concerning the possible Palestinian provenance of this text, see V. Hugger, "Mai's Lukaskommentar und der Traktat De passione athanasianisches Gut?," *Zeitschrift für katholische Theologie* 43 (1919): 732–41 (esp. 741); cf. Drobner, "pseudo-athanasianische Osterpredigt," 43.

[126] Translation adapted from Grypeou and Spurling, *Genesis in Late Antiquity*, 73.

The tradition of remembering the event of the crucifixion at Golgotha in light of Adamic Christology had made its way into the Syriac tradition by the mid-fourth century CE. Ephrem's *Hymn on Virginity* 16 includes the following:

> Very sad was the Tree of Life
> That saw Adam hidden from him
> Into the virgin earth he sank and was buried,
> but he arose and shone forth from Golgotha.[127]

This appears within the context of an anti-Arian hymn.[128] The setting and genre of this particular instantiation of the reception of the Golgotha tradition is notable. Ephrem's hymns were used in public liturgical settings,[129] and this would have provided an opportunity for the popular transmission of the Golgotha tradition, contributing to the crystallization of the Adam Christological typology over the memory of Golgotha in early Christianity. The parallelism that Ephrem draws between Adam, buried in the earth, and Christ, the Second Adam who arises and shines forth from the same place at Golgotha, is palpable.

A bit further afield from Palestine, other references to Adam's burial at Golgotha dated to the fourth century are found in the works of John Chrysostom[130] and Ambrose.[131] Notably, Ambrose identifies "the Hebrews" as the source of the Goglotha burial tradition, in agreement with Origen. The mere fact that this tradition is cited at all by these influential Christian thinkers based outside of Palestine speaks to how widespread it had become before the close of the fourth century.[132]

---

[127] Translation from Kathleen E. McVey (trans.), *Ephrem the Syrian: Hymns*, Classics of Western Spirituality (New York: Paulist Press, 1989).

[128] Ibid., 329.

[129] On the use and transmission of Ephrem's hymns in Syriac liturgy, see Sebastian P. Brock, "The Transmission of Ephrem's *madrashe* in the Syriac Liturgical Tradition," in *Studia Patristica* 33, ed. E. A. Livingstone (Leuven: Peeters, 1997), 490–505. Reference to the public performance of Ephrem's hymns by female singers found in Jacob of Serugh, *A Metrical Homily on Mar Ephrem*, 96–9, translation in Joseph P. Amar, *A Metrical Homily on Holy Mar Ephrem by Mar Jacob of Serugh* (Turnhout: Brepols, 1995). According to Jacob, the choirs were founded for the purpose of instructing right doctrine. See Susan A. Harvey, "Revisiting the Daughters of the Covenant: Women's Choirs and Sacred Song in Ancient Syriac Christianity," *Hugoye* 8, no. 2 (2005): n.p. Ephrem himself makes mention of choirs of "chaste women" in *Hymns on Nativity* 4.62–3 (translation from McVey, *Ephrem the Syrian*, 94).

[130] *Homiliae in Joannem* 85 on John 19:16–18.

[131] *Expositio Evangelii secundum Lucam* 10.114.

[132] It is worth mentioning that there are further references in Christian texts that are pseudepigraphical or misattributed to early Christian authors, but the difficulties of dating and situating these texts requires us to treat them with some caution. Perhaps the most interesting of these texts is Ps.-Tertullian, *Carmen adversus Marcionem*, 2.4, which mentions several facets of the traditional legend: Adam's burial at Golgotha ("Here, we have heard, the first man lay entombed"), the salvific power of Christ's blood upon Adam's remains ("Adam's dust, with blood of Christ commingled, by that saving flood might rise"), and Golgotha's status as the *axis mundi*. A fairly extensive (but incomplete) list of traditions concerning Golgotha is compiled in C. W. Wilson, *Golgotha and the Holy Sepulchre* (London: Palestine Exploration Fund, 1906), 159–66, from which the translations quoted above are drawn. *Carmen adversus Marcionem* is probably wrongly attributed to Tertullian, but its importance as an early Christian text should not be overlooked because of

One other instance of the Adamic Golgotha tradition is worth mentioning here. The *Commentary on Isaiah* attributed to Basil of Caesarea contains a number of extrabiblical traditions concerning Adam, including some discussion about the Place of the Skull (Golgotha). While the authorship of the text has been called into question in the past, Nikoai A. Lipatov has presented good rationale for the authenticity of its attribution to Basil,[133] leading to the acceptance of the attribution by some scholars.[134] In lieu of further discourse, I will tentatively treat the *Commentary on Isaiah* attributed to Basil of Caesarea as a genuine product of the fourth century CE and will refer to the author as Basil, though the measure of uncertainty concerning the authorship of the text should be acknowledged.

Here is the relevant passage:

> The following story has been preserved in the Church in an unwritten tradition, claiming that Judea had Adam as its first inhabitant, and that after being expelled from Paradise he was settled in it as a consolation for what he had lost. Thus it was first to receive a dead man too, since Adam completed his condemnation there. The sight of the bone of the head, as the flesh fell away on all sides, seemed to be novel to the men of the time and after depositing the skull in that place they named it Place of the Skull. It is probable that Noah, the ancestor of all men, was not unaware of the burial, so that after the Flood the story was passed on by him. For this reason the Lord having fathomed the source of human death accepted death in the place called Place of the Skull in order that the life of the kingdom of heaven should originate from the same place in which the corruption of men took its origin, and just as death gained its strength in Adam, so it became powerless in the death of Christ. (*Comm. Is.* 5.141).[135]

This provides additional data and insight into the interpretation and reception of Golgotha.[136] The legend of Adam's burial at Golgotha is identified as *unwritten* tradition,

---

this misattribution. Indeed, a persuasive case has recently been made that this text should not be forgotten simply because its author is unknown, noting its affinities with the Asian Pre-Nicene school of Patristic thought, in Roberto López Montero, "La antropología teológica del *Carmen Adversus Marcionem* del Pseudo-Tertuliano," *Salmanticensis* 60 (2013): 257–303. An attribution of the text to Commodian (third century CE) has been sometimes suggested, e.g., Hans Waitz, *Das Pseudotertullianische Gedicht Adversus Marcionem: ein Beitrag zur Geschichte der alchristlichen Litteratur sowie zur Quellenkritik des Marcionitisus* (Darmstadt: Johannes Waitz, 1901). However, Karla Pollmann has strongly argued in a modern study that the mostly likely date is in the first of the fifth century CE, specifically c.420–450. See Karla Pollman, *Das Carmen adversus Marcionitas. Einleitung, Text, Übersetzung und Kommentar* (Göttingen: Vandenhoeck & Ruprecht, 1991). As such, a fifth century date puts it outside of the scope of this project.

[133] Nikolai A. Lipatov, "The Problem of the Authorship of the Commentary on the Prophet Isaiah Attributed to St. Basil the Great," in Studia Patristica Vol. XXVII: Cappadocian Fathers, Greek Authors After Nicaea, Augustine, Donatism, and Pelagianism, ed. Elizabeth A. Livingstone (Leuven: Peeters, 1993), 42–8.

[134] Ilaria L. E. Ramelli, "Basil and Apokatastasis: New Findings," *Journal of Early Christian History* 4, no. 2 (2014): 116–36 (122); see also Steven A. McKinion (ed.), *Isaiah 1–39*, Ancient Christian Commentary on Scripture: Old Testament 10 (Downers Grove: InterVarsity, 2004), xviii.

[135] Translation from Nikolai A. Lipatov (trans.), *St. Basil the Great: Commentary on the Prophet Isaiah*, Texts and Studies in the History of Theology 7 (Mandelbachtal: Edition Cicero, 2001), 162.

[136] It is worth noting that Lipatov-Chicherin has demonstrated key similarities between Basil's version of the tradition and its instantiations in Jerome's Epistle 46 and Epiphanius' *Panarion*. He suggests

perhaps indicating that it came to Basil (or the otherwise unknown author) orally. This matches the situation presented by Jerome discussed above. Although Origen had already written some version of the Golgotha tradition down in his *Commentary on Matthew* in the third century, the spread of this interpretive legend in the collective memory of the early church was clearly driven by oral as well as written transmission.

Basil notes that the Greek toponym "Place of the Skull" is named specifically for Adam's skull, which was deposited there. Notably, the location of the rest of Adam's remains is not identified. Jeremias identifies this text as the earliest instantiation of the mention of Adam's skull specifically connected to Golgotha,[137] which may well be correct if the attribution to Basil is correct.[138] The burial of Adam's skull at Golgotha is vested with soteriological significance, but not due to the blood of Christ falling upon it as in the works of some of the authors with connections to Palestine discussed above. Instead, Basil claims that Jesus ("the Lord") knew of the burial of Adam's skull at Golgotha and "accepted death" in the very place that the source of human death, Adam—or at least his skull, was buried. Basil writes, "Just as death gained its strength in Adam, so it became powerless in the death of Christ." The point, then, seems solely to be typological parallelism rather than a literal image of the salvation of Adam and all humanity through the literal cleansing power of Christ's blood on the protoplast's remains.

Analysis of the Adamic Golgotha Tradition

The attachment of Adam to the collective memory and interpretation of the site of Golgotha can be traced from at least the mid-third century through the fourth century. Its origins are obscure, though it is quite clear, based on its earliest known appearance in Origen's *Commentary on Matthew*, that it predates the fourth century and thus the building of the church of the Holy Sepulchre and the display of Golgotha within its precincts. There is no evidence from Jewish sources prior to the third century that would corroborate Origen's claim about its "Hebraic" origins. However, there is no convincing evidence that would lead us to think that the claim is mere charlatanry.

In lieu of further evidence, the inference to the best explanation at this point is that the tradition of Adam's burial at Golgotha stemmed from Christ-believing Jews out of exegetical curiosity about the memorable toponym of the place of Jesus' execution, which is translated but goes otherwise unexplained in the canonical gospels. The lack of reference to Golgotha in early Jewish writings prior to the time of Origen makes it difficult to accept that it was a common tradition in mainstream Judaism, or that there was any interest in Golgotha in Jewish circles apart from Christ-believers. This

---

that Jerome based his version of the tradition on Basil's in *Comm. Is.* 5.141 and on that of Pseudo-Athanasius, and that Epiphanius also used the same two sources (Lipatov-Chicherin, "Early Christian Tradition," 169–70). The similarities are undeniable, so some sort of relationship does seem plausible, as Lipatoc-Chicherin suggests. This in no way speaks against the oral circulation of the tradition, which is also attested by Jerome. It is most likely that the tradition of Adam's burial at Golgotha circulated both orally and in written sources.

[137] Jeremias, *Golgotha*, 34.
[138] However, Epiphanius' *Panarion* dates prior to Basil's death.

is particularly acute in texts such as the Life of Adam and Eve or Jubilees, which narrate Adam's death but do not identify Golgotha as his burial place. Neither is it Mount Moriah, nor Kiryat Arba. Instead, both texts identify Paradise (Eden) as the burial place of the protoplast (GLAE 40:6; Jub. 4:29). In fact, Golgotha appears to be unknown in the corpus of currently extant non-Christian Jewish sources prior to the fourth century. It is also suspiciously convenient that Jesus would be crucified precisely where Second Temple tradition held that Adam was buried, especially given (1) the lack of any mention of such a tradition anywhere in the New Testament and (2) the Adamic typology expressed by Paul without recourse to such a tradition.[139]

It is much more likely that the connection between Adam and Golgotha arose from circles of followers of Jesus as a way to explain and interpret the mysterious references to the Aramaic toponym of the site of the crucifixion reported in the gospels. This much is fairly certain. If Origen's reference to the Hebraic origins of the tradition is correct, then we might tentatively infer that Jewish believers in Jesus explain the most evidence. However, we cannot rule out the possibility that Origen and the other ancient writers who agree with him are mistaken on this matter.

In light of collective memory, it is striking that Golgotha is so strongly remembered in the early Christian tradition in light of Paul, despite the fact that Golgotha is never mentioned in the Pauline texts of the New Testament. There are two ways in which the memory of Golgotha has been thoroughly colored by Paul in the early Christian tradition: first, through direct references to Pauline literature in Christian reception and interpretation of Golgotha,[140] and second, through the Christ-Adam typology in Pauline mode that infuses popular early Christian interpretation of Golgotha following Origen.

Several passages of Pauline literature are directly cited in connection with the interpretation of Golgotha and the Adam tradition. Origen cites 1 Cor 15:22 (*Comm. Matt.* 126): "as all die in Adam, so all will be made alive in Christ." This is a fitting quotation for explicating the theological impact of the Golgotha tradition, as it draws out the "second Adam" typology that lies at the heart of the Adamic interpretation of Golgotha. The point made by Origen through this citation is clear. There is a parallelism between Adam and Christ, as death came through the former death and life came through the latter, and this is demonstrated by the fact that the divine act of life-giving redemption took place where Adam was buried, and where Christ was raised so too will Adam be raised, since he is buried at the same location. We should note that this apparently draws on the tradition that the crucifixion and burial happened in the same place (cf. John 19:41?), which is followed by the traditional location of Golgotha and the tomb, contained within the same area in the Constantinian Church of the Holy Sepulchre.

The tradition of tying Adam to the memory of Golgotha is clearly inspired and influenced by Paul's Adam-Christ typology (1 Cor 15:21–22, 45–49; Rom 5:12–21). Curiously, by the late fourth century, Eph 5:14 had entered into the collective memory

---

[139] Cf. Taylor, *Christians and the Holy Places*, 127.
[140] By "Pauline," I mean to refer to not only the undisputed epistles but also the New Testament Pauline corpus in general, which were understood by the Church Fathers to be Pauline.

of Golgotha. Despite its lack of mention of either Adam or Golgotha, both the nomenclature of the place and the Adam-Christ tradition came to be interpreted in light of it. This, in my opinion, represents an evolution of the collective memory of the site that gained in popularity in the second half the fourth century, well after the traditional rock of Golgotha had been visibly incorporated into the precincts of the Church of the Holy Sepulchre. Eph 5:14 is mentioned in connection with Golgotha by Ps.-Athanasius, Epiphanius, Jerome, and Paula and Eustochium with him, and by the unnamed preacher discussed by Jerome in *Comm. Eph.* 5:14.

The use of Eph 5:14 in connection with Golgotha is curious, given that it mentions neither Adam nor Golgotha. It does not even mention the crucifixion. Its appeal is not entirely clear, although Jerome may provide some rationale in his suggestion in *Commentary on Ephesians* that it is related to reading πιψασει σοι Χριστος ("Christ will touch you") rather than πιφασει σοι Χριστος ("Christ will rise like the sun on you") in Eph 5:14. Whatever the case may be, the image is one of resurrection, and the "sleeper" is identified as Adam, whose remains lie at Golgotha, and is redeemed by the blood of Christ who is crucified in the same place, allowing for the hope of Adam's resurrection. The memory of Jesus at Golgotha is thus colored by the church's memory of Paul.

The interpretation of the toponym "Golgotha" (or "Place of the Skull") is somewhat varied, although there is some level of agreement in our sources that it has something to do with Adam. Origen connects it with Adam being the "head" of the human race, without any recourse to the notion that the "skull" has something to do with human remains. Ps.-Athanasius does not attempt to explain the toponym but observes the appropriateness of the place as Adam's resting place and the place of the cross. Likewise, Ephrem makes no attempt to explain the toponym of Golgotha. Basil offers a clear-cut explanation for the nomenclature, as it is called "Place of the Skull" after Adam's skull, which was buried there. He is specific about the *skull* being deposited at Golgotha, but apparently this was done apart from the rest of Adam's remains. Epiphanius takes a slightly different approach, arguing that Golgotha must be so named for Adam's body, as it *cannot* be named for its height not for its resemblance in appearance to a skull. Notably, Epiphanius makes reference to the *body* of Adam being buried there as a whole, not only his skull. The blood and water from Jesus' side fell not only on Adam's skull (κρανίον, as in Basil) but on his whole corpse (λείψανον). Jerome knows of the tradition that Golgotha is so named because Adam's skull is buried there. He appears to endorse this in the letter to Marcella on behalf of Paula and Eustochium (Epistle 46.3) and also attributes such a belief to the unnamed preacher discussed in his commentary on Eph 5:14. However, in his *Commentary on Matthew*, Jerome instead argues that the name of Golgotha (Latin *Calvariae*) refers to the skulls of the decapitated, as people who are condemned are brought outside the city to be beheaded. The variation in interpretation of Golgotha as a toponym is indicative of its enigmatic quality, which provides an opportunity for theological exegesis.

Resurrection from the dead, often connected with Adam, plays a central role in the memory of Golgotha, despite it being the place of Jesus' death rather than his resurrection. This can be explained by its proximity to the place of the resurrection, the tomb itself, in John 19:41 and at the traditional sites, as well as to the influence of Pauline teaching on the resurrection in connection to the Christ-Adam typology. The connection between Golgotha and the resurrection of the dead is another facet of the thoroughgoing theological lens through which the place is remembered and forms yet another crystalline layer of memory overtop of the crucifixion of Jesus of Nazareth.

Eusebius and Golgotha

Not all interpretations of Golgotha in early Christianity after Origen were Adamic. This is certainly true of the earliest examples. The canonical evangelists, for example, make no direct connections between Golgotha and Adam, and neither does Melito. Here, we will consider some other non-Adamic interpretations by two early Christian figures: Eusebius of Caesarea and Cyril of Jerusalem.

Eusebius includes Golgotha in his *Onomasticon*:

Γολγοθά, κρανίου τόπος, ἔνθα ὁ Χριστός ἐσταυρώθη, ὅς καὶ δείκνυται ἐν Αἰλίᾳ πρὸς τοῖς βορείοις τοῦ Σιὼν ὄρους.

Golgotha, "Place of a Skull," where Christ was crucified, which is also pointed out in Aelia to the north of Mount Zion.[141]
(*Onomasticon* 74.19-21)

The date of the *Onomasticon* is of some significance, since it was almost certainly written before the completion of the Constantinian churches, mentioning none of them. Taylor, for example, assigns it a date ranging between 313 and 325 CE, preferring a relatively early date.[142] Although this range falls after the Edict of Milan, it is prior to the Constantinian transformation of Palestine through the various imperial building projects that began in the second quarter of the fourth century. T. D. Barnes, followed by Jerome Murphy-O'Connor, makes a compelling case for an even earlier date in the 290s CE, based on the administrative boundaries of that time, which Barnes sees reflected in *Onomasticon*.[143] Certainty about the precise date is difficult to achieve, but for our purposes, it is sufficient to regard to *Onomasticon* as a composition of the late third century or first quarter of the fourth century CE at the very latest. We may thus regard it as functionally pre-Constantinian (if Taylor is correct) due to being written prior to Constantine's building projects in Palestine, or actually pre-Constantinian (if Barnes and Murphy-O'Connor are correct).

Unlike many of the other authors discussed above, Eusebius provides little in the way of interpretation of the nomenclature of Golgotha, providing only the exact Greek rendering of Golgotha found in Mark 15:22 and Matt 27:33 without further

---

[141] Translation is my own, though done with reference to G. S. P. Freeman-Grenville, Rupert L. Chapman III, and Joan E. Taylor (eds.), *The Onomasticon by Eusebius of Caesarea* (Jerusalem: Carta, 2003). Any subsequent translations are from Freeman-Grenville et al. unless otherwise indicated.
[142] Joan E. Taylor, "Introduction," in *The Onomasticon by Eusebius of Caesarea*, ed. G. S. P. Freeman-Grenville, Rupert L. Chapman III, and Joan E. Taylor (Jerusalem: Carta, 2003), 1–8 (3).
[143] T. D. Barnes, "The Composition of Eusebius' *Onomasticon*," *JTS* 26, no. 2 (1975): 412–15; Jerome Murphy-O'Connor, *Keys to Jerusalem: Collected Essays* (Oxford: Oxford University Press, 2012), 175.

comment.¹⁴⁴ Golgotha, for Eusebius, is simply where Christ was crucified, the precise role that it plays in the gospel narratives. The Adamic interpretation is notably missing here, despite having appeared already in Origen's *Commentary on Matthew*. This is curious, given Eusebius' knowledge of Origen's life (e.g., *Hist. eccl.* 6.2-3, 8, 16, 19, 23-26, 32) and works (*Hist. eccl.* 6.16, 24-25, 32, 36), to say nothing of his location in Caesarea, where Origen had been, and where Pamphilus had collected Christian writings.¹⁴⁵ Eusebius' own library included what Pamphilus and Origen themselves had left behind, including an extensive collection of Origen's works (*EH* 6.32).¹⁴⁶ Moreover, as discussed above, the Adamic tradition was widespread and demonstrably popular in the fourth century CE, though this popularity may admittedly have been triggered by the construction and dedication of the Church of the Holy Sepulchre, which came after Eusebius wrote his *Onomasticon*. Although it is impossible to be certain, it is plausible, perhaps even likely, that Eusebius was aware of the Adamic Golgotha tradition but omitted mention of it in *Onomasticon* as well as in his later writings.

For Eusebius, Golgotha was a tangible place, one that could be "pointed out" (Greek δείκνυται)¹⁴⁷ and located precisely within the Jerusalem of his day.¹⁴⁸ In *Onomasticon*, the physical site of the traditional location of Golgotha has merged with the gospel narrative of the crucifixion. Past and present elide, and the events of the gospels can be located in real space. The place that is "pointed out" north of Mount Zion *is* the place where Christ was crucified. This is particularly significant in light of the date of the *Onomasticon*, perhaps as early as the late third century, and certainly prior to the building of the Church of the Holy Sepulchre. Indeed, Murphy-O'Connor considers this passage to be evidence of pre-Constantinian interest in holy sites connected to the life of Jesus.¹⁴⁹ If the traditional site of Golgotha was known well enough to be "pointed out" prior to the construction of the Church of the Holy Sepulchre, and apparently located within the limits of the city,¹⁵⁰ then this may lend further support to the notion that Melito could have had the same place in mind in the second century CE. Whether or not the site is authentic is a different matter altogether,¹⁵¹ but it seems rather unlikely that the site was simply invented or "identified" when Constantine

---

¹⁴⁴ See also the discussion of the very similar Lukan and Johannine forms above. The Johannine form is only a difference in case (John 19:17 has the accusative "Τόπον"), while the Lukan form omits τόπος ("place").

¹⁴⁵ On Origen, Eusebius, and the library at Caesarea, see Anthony Grafton and Megan Williams, *Christianity and the Transformation of the Book: Origen, Eusebius and the Library of Caesarea* (Cambridge, MA: Harvard University Press, 2008), esp. 178–80.

¹⁴⁶ Ibid., 179–80.

¹⁴⁷ On Eusebius' use of this term, see John Wilkinson, "L'Apport de Saint Jérome a la Topographie," *Revue Biblique* 81, no. 2 (1974): 245–57 (251–2).

¹⁴⁸ On this, see Murphy-O'Connor, *Keys to Jerusalem*, 174–5.

¹⁴⁹ Ibid.

¹⁵⁰ Cf. ibid., 174.

¹⁵¹ Although I consider it unlikely, it is possible that the identification of the traditional location of Golgotha extends back to the second century CE but not to the first century CE. The authentic location of Jesus' crucifixion could possibly have been forgotten after the upheaval involved in the destruction that took place during the two Jewish revolts against Rome, and a new traditional site could have emerged amongst the Christian community in Aelia Capitolina in the second century after the rebuilding of the city. That said, possibility is not the same as hypothesis or probability, and so I regard this as a possible but unlikely scenario.

began his excavations in Jerusalem in preparation for the construction of the Church of the Holy Sepulchre.

This entry in the *Onomasticon* is the most that Eusebius writes anywhere about Golgotha in his extant works, as his only other mention of Golgotha is just a passing reference in a citation of a gospel passage (*Comm. in Ps.* 54.7–12).[152] It is particularly surprising that there is no mention of Golgotha in his lengthy discussion and description of the Church of the Holy Sepulchre in *Life of Constantine* 3.25–40.

P. W. L. Walker has convincingly argued that there is a theological motive lying behind Eusebius' silence on the place of the crucifixion.[153] He rightly observes that Eusebius focused on revelation rather than soteriology, and that the crucifixion was not "efficacious for salvation" in Eusebius' understanding.[154] Thus, Walker writes, "The Cross of Christ simply was not a vital part of his [Eusebius'] theology,"[155] and moreover, "Eusebius would never give to the rock of Golgotha a central place in his understanding of the Holy Sepulchre."[156]

Walker's analysis demonstrates how place and its reception can relate to interpretation and theology. Eusebius can thus write a lengthy oration on the Church of the Holy Sepulchre, "the blessed locality of our Savior's Resurrection" (*Life of Constantine* 3.25)[157] without ever directly mentioning the rock of Golgotha, which was located within the court between the Anastasis and the Martyrium.[158] Hence, as Walker writes, "theology clearly colored place."[159]

While Eusebius does not directly mention Golgotha, there are some indirect references to the place of crucifixion in relation to the site of the Church of the Holy Sepulchre contained within the discussion in *Life of Constantine* 3.25–40. Eusebius writes,

> On the very spot which witnessed the Saviour's sufferings, a new Jerusalem was constructed, over against the one so celebrated of old, which, since the foul stain

---

[152] As observed by Walker, there is just one other minor mention of Golgotha in Eusebius' extant writings, which is nothing more than a phrase from the gospels, "they led him to a place called Golgotha," offered without further comment, in Eusebius' *Comm. in Ps.*, 54.7-12 (Walker, *Holy City*, 255). Walker also notes that, although Eusebius discusses the crucifixion elsewhere (e.g., *Dem. ev.* 10; *De sollemnitate Paschali*), his references to Golgotha are limited just these two, from the *Onomasticon* and *Commentary in Psalms* (ibid., 255 [n. 60]).

[153] Ibid., 256–60.

[154] Ibid., 256.

[155] Ibid.

[156] Ibid. See also George Huntston Williams, "Christology and Church-State Relations in the Fourth Century," *Church History* 20, no. 3 (1951): 3–33 (17).

[157] Translation from Ernest Cushing Richardson (trans.), *Eusebius: Church History, Life of Constantine the Great, and Oration in Praise of Constantine*, ed. Philip Schaff and Henry Wace, vol. 1., A Select Library of the Nicene and Post-Nicene Fathers of the Christian Church, Second Series (New York: Christian Literature Company, 1890).

[158] Jean-Michel Spieser has argued that Eusebius omits mention of Golgotha because, while the rock of Calvary had already been identified in Eusebius' day, it did not include architectural framework until later. See Jean-Michel Spieser, "En Suivant Eusèbe Au Saint-Sépulcre," *Antiquité Tardive* 22 (2014): 95–103. This may account for why Eusebius does not mention the architectural features of the monument featuring Golgotha, but given that Eusebius clearly knew of the rock when he wrote *Onomasticon* and that the rock was in a fairly prominent location, the omission is still curious and requires further explanation.

[159] Walker, *Holy City*, 256.

of guilt brought on it by the murder of the Lord, had experienced the last extremity of desolation, the effect of Divine judgment on its impious people. It was opposite this city that the emperor now began to rear a monument to the Saviour's victory over death, with rich and lavish magnificence. (*Life of Constantine* 3.33)[160]

This is an important passage, and we will later consider its importance for understanding the Eusebian interpretation of the tomb of Christ. For the present, we will consider its relevance for the interpretation and commemoration of the place of crucifixion. Eusebius indirectly references Golgotha in describing the site of the church as "the very spot which witnessed the Savior's sufferings," which must refer to the crucifixion. Here, the purpose of the indirect reference to Golgotha is, unfortunately, anti-Jewish rhetoric. It is the spot where the "New Jerusalem," that is, the Constantinian monument of the Church of the Holy Sepulchre, is constructed, which is contrasted with "the one so celebrated of old," which is to say, the Jerusalem of Jesus' day.

Eusebius sees the "old" Jerusalem as being tinged with the "foul stain of guilt" that came as a result of the death of Jesus. He contrasts the "New Jerusalem," which he describes as "a monument to the Savior's victory over death," presumably referencing the Anastasis and focusing on the tomb as the site of the resurrection, with the "old" Jerusalem, which is associated with the Savior's sufferings and the guilt that came along with it, in order to serve his problematically anti-Jewish rhetoric. Thus, for Eusebius, the place of crucifixion is tied to old Jerusalem, the place of suffering, stained with guilt, while the Anastasis represents the New Jerusalem and Jesus' victory over death.[161] Given that this is the case, it is perhaps not surprising that Eusebius "robbed" Golgotha of its importance[162] and focused instead on the "New Jerusalem," represented by the Constantinian monument, particularly the Anastasis.

Cyril of Jerusalem on Golgotha

Cyril of Jerusalem's interpretation of Golgotha provides a striking counterpoint to that of Eusebius. In contrast to Eusebius, Cyril makes reference to Golgotha more frequently than to the Sepulchre,[163] with thirteen mentions of Golgotha in his *Catechetical Lectures*.[164] Hence, Edward Yarnold writes that, in contrast to Eusebius' "systematic refusal to speak of Golgotha," Cyril "takes every opportunity of drawing his listeners' attention to the rock."[165]

Cyril was writing in the mid-fourth century CE, after the Constantinian excavation in Jerusalem and subsequent construction of the Church of the Holy Sepulchre. As

---

[160] Translation from Richardson, *Life of Constantine*.
[161] This will be discussed in greater detail in a later chapter.
[162] My phraseology here echoes that of Williams, "Christology," 17.
[163] Cf. Alexis James Doval, *Cyril of Jerusalem, Mystagogue: The Authorship of the Mystagogic Catecheses*, Patristic Monograph Series 17 (Washington, DC: Catholic University of America Press, 2001), 182.
[164] As noted by both ibid., 182, and Jan Willem Drijvers, *Cyril of Jerusalem: Bishop and City*, Supplements to Vigiliae Christianae (Leiden: Brill, 2004), 156. The references include Cyril of Jerusalem, *Cat.* 1.1; 4.10, 14; 5.10; 10.19; 13.4, 22, 23, 26, 28, 39; 14.6; 16.4.
[165] Edward Yarnold, *Cyril of Jerusalem* (London: Routledge, 2000), 12.

mentioned above, Taylor has convincingly argued that Golgotha is best understood as an area, the rock quarry located underneath the Church of the Holy Sepulchre, rather than as a specific spot.[166] However, the rock spire currently located to the right of the entrance of the modern Church of the Holy Sepulchre would have protruded above the ground, and was thus visible, incorporated into the Constantinian complex. Even though he generally refers to Golgotha as an area,[167] Cyril can nevertheless write that Golgotha "rises above us here" (*Cat.* 10.19)[168] and can speak of being gathered beside it (*Cat.* 13.4), presumably in reference to the rock spire.[169] In *Cat.* 13.39, he writes that Golgotha "is still visible today and still shows how the rocks were split because of Christ that day." He elsewhere speaks of Golgotha as though it can be seen and even touched" (*Cat.* 13.13, 22). As such, Cyril's references are to a visible Golgotha, a place that could be experienced through the human senses, part of which was displayed in the complex of the Church of the Holy Sepulchre.

Golgotha frequently functions in Cyril's writing as a witness to the reality of the crucifixion. This occurs no less than four times in the *Catecheses*. In *Cat.* 4.10, Cyril writes, "He was truly crucified for our sins. For even if you would like to deny it, the place visibly refutes you, this blessed place of Golgotha where we are now congregated because of the one who was crucified here." Cyril appeals directly to the visibility of the place of Golgotha in order to demonstrate the reality of the crucifixion. We should recognize that Cyril likely delivered the catechetical lectures in the complex of the Church of the Holy Sepulchre sight of the rock spire of Golgotha (cf. *Cat.* 13.4),[170] which would have added rhetorical force to statements such as this one. Similarly, in *Cat.* 10.19, Cyril claims that "there are many true testimonies concerning Christ," and Golgotha is among them, writing that "Holy Golgotha, which rises above us here, bears witness." Here Golgotha is not just a witness to the reality of the crucifixion, but to Christ himself.

The two other instances are found in *Cat.* 13. In *Cat.* 13.4, Cyril writes, "He was crucified; we do not deny it, we boast of it. If I do deny it now, I am given the lie by Golgotha here, beside which we are now gathered." Again, Cyril uses Golgotha and its visible presence as a means of establishing the reality of the crucifixion. It is worth noting the mention of being gathered beside Golgotha. The physical place has become imbued with the theological significance of the belief in the reality of the crucifixion and all that the event had come to carry in the Christian tradition by the fourth century. Hence, Cyril can say that "while others can only hear, we can see and touch" (*Cat.* 13.22). Elsewhere in the same lecture, Golgotha's role as a witness is vested with

---

[166] Taylor, "Golgotha," 183–4. See also the study of Golgotha in Shimon Gibson and Joan E. Taylor, *Beneath the Church of the Holy Sepulchre, Jerusalem: The Archaeology and Early History of Traditional Golgotha* (London: Palestine Exploration Fund, 1994), 55–9.

[167] On this, see John Wilkinson, *Egeria's Travels*, 3rd ed. (Warminster: Aris & Philipps, 2002), 22; Drijvers, *Cyril of Jerusalem*, 14. Both Wilkinson and Drijvers note that Egeria likewise appears to refer to Golgotha as an area.

[168] Translations of Cyril's works are from Yarnold, *Cyril of Jerusalem*, unless stated otherwise.

[169] Cf. Wilkinson, *Egeria's Travels*, 22 n. 3.

[170] Cf. Walker, *Holy City*, 254. On this rock spire, see the study in Gibson and Taylor, *Beneath the Church*, 55.

eschatological significance. Cyril writes that Golgotha will "give the lie" on Judgement Day to anyone who denies the Crucified one (*Cat.* 13.38–39).

In Cyril's writings, Golgotha is a physical reality that can be experienced and that bears witness to the past. He does not write about it abstractly but has a specific place in mind. It is, to his mind, the center of the earth (*Cat.* 13.28).[171] The concept of the center of the world being located in Jerusalem can be traced back to Jewish literature of the Second Temple period.[172] Thus, Cyril appropriated and took over an existing Jewish tradition,[173] relocating it at Golgotha. This allowed him to apply the words of the LXX Psalmist, which he calls "the prophet" to his interpretation of the place (*Cat.* 13.28): "you have accomplished salvation in the center of the earth" (*Cat.* 13.28, citing Ps 73:12 LXX).[174] To Cyril, there is no question that it is the very place where Jesus was crucified, and thus the place where God's plan for salvation came to fruition. Moreover, as the place where salvation was accomplished and the center of the earth, Golgotha and the wood of the cross with it granted Jerusalem, over which Cyril was Bishop, a certain preeminence. This, no doubt, served Cyril's political aims, as he had struggled to claim primacy for Jerusalem over Caesarea.[175]

Cyril discusses the interpretation of the nomenclature of Golgotha in *Cat.* 13.23:

> "Golgotha" means "the Place of the Skull." Who were they then who gave such a prophetic name to this place Golgotha, where Christ the true Head endured the cross? As the Apostle says: "Who is the image of the unseen God" (Col 1:15); and a little later: "And he is the head of his body, the church" (Col 1:18); and again: "The head of every man is Christ" (1 Cor 11:3); and again: "Who is the head of every principality and power" (Col 2:10). The Head suffered in the Place of the Skull. A great and prophetic name! The very name seems to remind you, saying: Do not consider the Crucified to be a mere man: he is "the head of every principality and power." [176]

Like other early Christian authors, Cyril understands Golgotha in light of Pauline writings. It is Paul that enables him to explain the name, despite the fact that Golgotha is never referenced in the Pauline corpus. However, unlike the other Christian authors discussed above who employ Paul to interpret Golgotha, Adamic typology plays no role for Cyril's understanding of the meaning of Golgotha. There is, nevertheless, some parallel here between Cyril and Origen, as both understand "skull" (*kranion*) in terms of the theological use of "head" (*kephalē*) in the Pauline corpus to refer to Christ's primacy.

---

[171] On the concept of Jerusalem as the center of the world in early Judaism and Christianity, see Alexander, "Jerusalem as the *Omphalos*."

[172] As argued by ibid., 147–53. The earliest instantiation of this tradition is Jub. 8:19, wherein Zion is identified as the navel of the earth.

[173] Perhaps known to Cyril through the LXX. On Jerusalem as *omphalos* in the LXX, see ibid., 152–3.

[174] Note, however, that the LXX (following the MT) has the third-person singular as the subject ("he") rather than the second-person singular ("you"). See Yarnold, *Cyril of Jerusalem*, 201 n. 16.

[175] See Sozomen, *Hist. eccl.* 4.25.2 (NPNF II, 2: 707); Theodoret, *Hist. eccl.* 2.22 (NPNF II, 3: 194–5). Cf. Drijvers, *Cyril of Jerusalem*, 157.

[176] Trans from Yarnold, *Cyril of Jerusalem*.

For Cyril, the name of Golgotha is prophetic. It is not derived from earlier Jewish tradition, as some of the other others discussed above have claimed, but rather prophetically establishes the headship of Christ and speaks to his divinity. Thus, for Cyril, the name reminds the hearer that the Crucified is not a mere man but is the head of every principality and power (in accordance with Col 2:10).

Cyril's accentuation of Golgotha in his catechetical writings is almost certainly related to his theology of the cross.[177] Walker has called the cross the "apex" of Cyril's theological system.[178] His soteriological emphasis was on the crucifixion rather than on the resurrection.[179] According to Walker, for Cyril, the cross "was the foundation of faith (*Cat.* 13.38), the ground of salvation (*Cat.* 13.37), the end of sin (*Cat.* 13.9), a source of illumination and redemption (*Cat.* 13.1) and of life (*Cat.* 13.20), the 'crown' of Christ (*Cat.* 13.22), the glory of the Catholic Church (*Cat.* 13.1) and the sign of Christ's Second Coming in the future (*Cat.* 15.22)."[180] Moreover, for Cyril, the cross was not something that existed in the past, nor was it an abstract symbol.[181] Rather, the *lignum crucis* was, much like Golgotha, something tangible that could be experienced (e.g., *Cat.* 4.10). It is worth considering the wood of the cross to be a *lieu de mémoire* as well, one that had the advantage of being both physical and portable. The constant connection between the Cross and Golgotha[182] in Cyril's thought leads me to forward the possibility that the wood of the Cross could be considered an extension of the *lieu de mémoire* of Golgotha and vice versa, in which collective Christian memory of the event of the crucifixion was imbued.

Pilgrim Experiences of Golgotha (Bordeaux, Egeria, Breviarius)

Up to this point, we have primarily discussed the perspective of Christian scholars, churchmen, and bishops. This is, of course, due to the fact that it is mostly the writings of the elite that survive. However, it is important for us also consider the experiences of others, as much as we are able to do so. For that reason, we now turn to the experiences of fourth-century pilgrims, represented by the Pilgrim of Bordeaux, Egeria, and the earliest layer of the pilgrimage guide known as the Jerusalem Breviarius. In a later chapter we will also examine the archaeology and architecture of the Constantinian Church of the Holy Sepulchre, which will give us access to the site as it was experienced by all who visited it, regardless of status.

The Pilgrim of Bordeaux's visit to Palestine is dated to 333 CE, on the basis of the names of the consuls that are given in the text (*Itin. Burd.* 571).[183] Little can be known

---

[177] Cf. Walker, *Holy City*, 256; Drijvers, *Cyril of Jerusalem*, 156.
[178] Walker, *Holy City*, 256.
[179] Cf. Edward Yarnold, "Who Planned the Churches at the Christian Holy Places in the Holy Land?," in *Studia Patristica* 18.1, ed. E. A. Livingstone (Leuven: Peeters, 1989), 105–9.
[180] Walker, *Holy City*, 256–7.
[181] See also Drijvers, *Cyril of Jerusalem*, 156–7.
[182] Especially in *Cat.* 13, wherein the two are frequently discussed in tandem.
[183] Cf. Wilkinson, *Egeria's Travels*, 22.

about the pilgrim's identity, though as John Wilkinson has noted, they must have been of some importance, since they traveled in the coaches of the *cursus publicus*.[184] The gender of the pilgrim has been called into question in previous scholarship, as it has been suggested that they may have been female,[185] although this has been rejected on the basis of a lack of evidence.[186] I will proceed under the assumption that the pilgrim was a male of some social standing, though acknowledging that the possibility that the pilgrim was a woman has rightly been raised in the past.[187]

The Bordeaux Pilgrim mentions Golgotha only very briefly. It comes up in his itinerary after describing the valley where the traditional site of Pilate's house was located.[188] He then writes,

> On your left of the hillock Golgotha where the Lord was crucified, and about a stone's throw from it is the vault where they laid his body, and he rose again on the third day. By order of the Emperor Constantine there has now been built there a "basilica"—I mean a "place for the Lord (*dominicum*)"—which has beside it cisterns of remarkable beauty, and beside them a baptistery where children are baptized (*Itin. Burd.* 594).[189]

The Bordeaux Pilgrim is remarkably brief in his description of Golgotha. Apart from information pertaining to location, he informs us only that Golgotha is a hillock, probably in reference to the mound over the quarry on which the Constantinian Church of the Holy Sepulchre was built rather than to the rock spire,[190] and that it is the place where "the Lord was crucified."

The fact that the Bordeaux Pilgrim's interest in Golgotha, apart from giving directions to the place, is solely in its biblical relevance is curious. Noting the pilgrim's general lack interest in contemporary life, human or animal, as well as geographical formations, Blake Leyerle suggests that this may be because the presence of these things "would distract from the conveyed perception of a direct interaction with the biblical past instantiated in architectural shrines."[191] There is no doubt that the pilgrim's interest is almost entirely in the biblical past, particularly as it is instantiated in, or we might say *mediated* through, architecture. The notion of the biblical past mediated through imperial architecture is a matter that we shall return to at various points in this study. The wood of the cross is unmentioned by the pilgrim, an omission that is shared by Eusebius as well. This may be due to either a lack of interest in such an object

---

[184] Ibid.
[185] Laurie Douglass, "A New Look at the *Itinerarium Burdigalense*," *JECS* 4 (1996): 313–33; cf. Taylor, *Christians and the Holy Places*, 313.
[186] Susan Weingarten, "Was the Pilgrim from Bordeaux a Woman? A Reply to Laurie Douglass," *JECS* 7, no. 2 (1999): 291–7.
[187] Rightly raised because this is, at the very least, a hypothesis worth exploring even if (as demonstrated by Weingarten, cited above) there is no firm evidence to support it.
[188] Wilkinson identifies this as the valley "down which runs Valley Street" (*Egeria's Travels*, 31 n. 3).
[189] Translation from ibid., 31. All translations of *Itinerarium Burdigalense* here are from Wilkinson, unless otherwise noted.
[190] Cf. Gibson and Taylor, *Beneath the Church*, 59.
[191] Leyerle, "Landscape as Cartography," 119–43.

or perhaps to a deliberate omission,[192] although Vered Shalev-Hurvitz has recently advanced the possibility that the wood of the cross was only "discovered" sometime later, perhaps after the Pilgrim of Bordeaux had written.[193] Whatever the case may be, it is clear that, for the Pilgrim of Bordeaux, the sole significance of Golgotha lay in its connection to the biblical past.

The Jerusalem *Breviarius* is an early pilgrimage guide. Although the extant versions (A and B) of this text date to later centuries, it is clear that these are later recensions of an earlier text. Based on its content, this earlier text dates to the fourth century CE,[194] and Wilkinson has convincingly reconstructed it by subtracting the unique material added by both manuscript traditions (A and B), leaving only the base text, which is shared in common by the two.[195]

The *Breviarius* describes the area of Golgotha as it existed within the Church of the Holy Sepulchre complex (*Breviarius* 2). According to the author, "There Adam was formed. There the Lord was crucified."[196] This is a curious variation on the Adam-Christ Golgotha tradition, since it identifies Golgotha as the place where Adam was formed but does not mention Adam's burial at the same site, though it does explicitly draw a parallel between Adam's formation and Jesus' crucifixion on the same spot. Wilkinson suggests that the reference to Adam's formation at Golgotha is a function of the conception of Golgotha as the Temple of the New Israel, since there are Jewish traditions that identify the Temple Mount as the place where Adam was formed (Gen. Rab. 14.2; y. Naz. 7.56b).[197] This may have been a factor in the generation of the tradition of Golgotha as the place of Adam's formation, but this tradition needs to be understood and approached in light of the earlier tradition that Adam was buried where he was formed, in GLAE 38:4, 40:3–4, which explicitly states that Adam (and Abel along with him) was "buried according to the command of God in the regions of Paradise [Greek μέρη τοῦ παραδείσου] in the place from which God had found the dust."[198]

Once combined with the well-attested tradition already known in Christian circles by the third century that Adam was buried at Golgotha, one would naturally come to the conclusion that Adam must also have been formed at the same place. It is thus very likely that the tradition that Adam was formed at the traditional site of Golgotha, located in the fourth century in the inner courtyard of the Church of the Holy Sepulchre, which is witnessed here by the Jerusalem *Breviarius*, is a Christian reception and redeployment of the earlier Jewish tradition about Adam being buried where he was created. In my opinion, it is better understood as a Christian reception of a Jewish tradition and an instantiation of the way in which Christians could reuse

---

[192] However, on Eusebius' omission of the *lignum crucis* as a possible deliberate act stemming from theological and political rationale, see Walker, *Holy City*, 126–30, 258–60.

[193] Vered Shalev-Hurvitz, *Holy Sites Enircled: The Early Byzantine Concentric Churches of Jerusalem*, Oxford Studies in Byzantium (Oxford: Oxford University Press, 2015), 55.

[194] As argued effectively by John Wilkinson, *Jerusalem Pilgrims before the Crusades* (Warminster: Aris & Philipps, 2002), 3–4.

[195] Ibid., 4, 117–21.

[196] Translation from ibid., 93. All subsequent translations of the Jerusalem *Breviarius* are taken from this source unless otherwise stated.

[197] Ibid., 363.

[198] See the discussion of this tradition above.

Jewish traditions and combine them with their own, rather than as an intentional resiting of the Jewish Temple. That having been said, there is no doubt that the Church of the Holy Sepulchre was understood as a new and superior Jerusalem Temple, as indicated by Eusebius' designation of it as the "New Jerusalem." However, it is unlikely that this New Jerusalem theology underlies the designation of Golgotha as the place where Adam was formed in the *Breviarius*, as there is a simpler explanation provided in a tradition that can be dated prior to the fourth century with certaint, and which is found in a text that has a clear Christian reception and preservation history.

Egeria's pilgrimage likely took place during the 380s CE.[199] She provides valuable insight into the liturgy of Jerusalem, bringing the stones of the Christian holy places to life and allowing us to imagine how visitors would have experienced them. Egeria mentions Golgotha with some frequency in her description of the Jerusalem liturgy. Most frequently, she refers to Golgotha as the place upon which the Martyrium, or "the major church that Constantine built" (*Itin. Eger.* 25.1),[200] is constructed.[201] One possible exception is found in *Itin. Eger.* 37.1, where Egeria speaks of a chair for the bishop being placed "on Golgotha behind the Cross," where the bishop would sit while displaying the *lignum crucis* for the people to see and kiss (37.2).

Since the Martyrium was constructed over Golgotha, located "behind the Cross" (probably in reference to a crucifix set up at the rock spire), the liturgical functions that took place in the Martyrium took place at the site of the crucifixion. We cannot discuss all of the liturgical functions that Egeria describes here, nor is there need to do so. We need concern ourselves only with the most relevant material, that is, the commemoration of Jesus' passion. The public reading of the gospels naturally has a collective mnemonic function insofar as it recalls and disseminates canonical Jesus traditions. Egeria relates an account of a Good Friday liturgy that took place "before the Cross," that is, in the courtyard between the Marytrium and the Anastasis:

> A chair is placed for the bishop before the Cross and from the sixth to ninth hour nothing else is done except that readings are read thus, that is, first there are readings from the Psalms, wherever they speak of the passion; they are also readings from the Apostle, either from the letters of the Apostles or from the Acts, wherever they speak of the Lord's passion; and also passages from the gospels where he suffered are read; so they read from the prophets where they say that the Lord will suffer and then they read from the gospels where he speaks of his passion. (*Itin. Eger.* 37.5)[202]

---

[199] As argued by Paul Devos, "Le date due voyage d'Égérie," *Analecta Bollandiana* 85 (1967): 165–94. For a discussion and overview of the scholarship on the date of Egeria's pilgrimage, see Wilkinson, *Egeria's Travels*, 169–71; Anne McGowan and Paul F. Bradshaw, *The Pilgrimage of Egeria: A New Translation of the* Itinerarium Egeriae *with Introduction and Commentary*, Alcuin Club Collections 93 (Collegeville: Liturgical Press Academic, 2018), 22–7.

[200] McGowan and Bradshaw, *Pilgrimage of Egeria*, 154. Translations of the *Itererarium Egeriae* are from ibid., unless otherwise noted. However, as McGowan and Bradshaw do not include the segments of Egeria's writings preserved by Peter the Deacon, references to Peter the Deacon's *de locis sanctis* will be taken from Wilkinson, *Egeria's Travels*.

[201] *Itin. Eger.* 25.1, 6, 8, 10, 11, 27.3, 30.1.

[202] Translation from McGowan and Bradshaw, *Pilgrimage of Egeria*, 177.

> So, from the sixth hour to the ninth hour readings are read and hymns recited continually, to show all the people that whatever the prophets foretold concerning the Lord's passion is shown to have been done both from the gospels and also from the writings of the Apostles ... Prayers that are appropriate to the day are always interspersed. To each of the readings and prayers there is such emotion and lamentation from all the people that it is astonishing; for there is no one, either older or younger, who on that day in those three hours does not bewail more than can be reckoned that the Lord has suffered those things for us. After this, when the ninth hour has already begun to approach, that passage from the Gospel according to John is read where he gave up his spirit. When it has been read, a prayer and the dismissal are done. (*Itin. Eger.* 37.6–7)[203]

Here, Egeria gives us a fascinating look into the texts that were used to remember Jesus' passion at the site that functioned as the *lieu de mémoire* for that very event. She names the Psalms, the New Testament epistles, the Acts of the Apostles, the Prophets, and the gospels. It is worth noting that Egeria indicates that the gospel passages include both passion predictions as well as the passion narrative itself. The only specific passage that we are given is John 19:30, in which Jesus gives up his spirit while on the cross. Nevertheless, we can gain a fairly good sense of what was read over the course of that three-hour service.[204]

We can make a few observations by way of analysis of the service and readings. First, the readings incorporated readings from both Testaments. It is not surprising that readings from the Psalms and Prophets were used to interpret and remember Jesus' passion, as this was a regular feature of Christian exegesis going back as far as the New Testament itself.[205] The use of other New Testament texts is intriguing, fitting the pattern that we have seen above of using Pauline material to interpret the events that transpired at Golgotha in the gospel narratives. Egeria specifies that the foretelling of the passion in the prophets is shown to be fulfilled not only in the writings of the gospels but also in "the Apostles" (*Itin. Eger.* 37.6). Thus, the Jesus remembered at the fourth-century Cross at Golgotha is the canonical Jesus, drawn from various quarters all over the Christian scriptures.

In Egeria's account of the pilgrim's experience of Good Friday at Golgotha, we see the recognizable mark of official memory, memory "supported by cultural and political leaders with state power to promote individual and group interests that confirm the status quo."[206] It is clear that her experience of Golgotha was very much mediated by her experience of the architecture of the Church of the Holy Sepulchre, and, thus, by imperial architecture. It was also mediated by the bishop of Jerusalem, an ecclesiastical authority, who performed the reading. In light of this, it is worth noting that Egeria mentions no extracanonical traditions (such as the Adamic Golgotha tradition) in

---

[203] Translation from ibid., 178.
[204] On commemorative ritual and the Jesus tradition in general, see Alan Kirk, *Memory and the Jesus Tradition*, Reception of Jesus in the First Three Centuries 2 (London: T&T Clark, 2018), 234–5.
[205] E.g., Acts 2:25–28 (citing Ps 16:8–11), 4:25–26 (citing Ps 2:1–2), 8:32–33 (citing Isa 53:7–8).
[206] Pelak, "Institutionalizing Counter-Memories," 308. See also Bodnar, *Remaking America*, 13.

connection with the site or name of Golgotha. Scripture is marshalled in support of the reality and truth of the event that the Church of the Holy Sepulchre, which was as much a monument to Constantinian power as it was to the death and resurrection of Jesus, was built to commemorate. In the Jerusalem liturgy that Egeria describes, we see, to quote Jonathan Z. Smith, "a historical system of commemoration, memorialization, and recollection,"[207] all of which is determined by the institution, by the ecclesiastical authorities, and by the space provided by the imperial monument that was the Constantinian Church of the Holy Sepulchre.

The extreme emotional response of the crowd gathered at Golgotha to the public readings on Jesus' passion is significant. As recent research on affect and collective memory have shown, a shared emotional response can serve to align individuals with the collective through intense attachment.[208] This can be facilitated by what some researchers have called "sticky objects of emotion," objects saturated with affect.[209] In this case, the traditional place of Golgotha, including its monumental architecture, the rock spire, and the Cross, functions as such a "sticky object." Certainly, this was facilitated by the readings of the biblical texts, which give it its significance.

Conclusion

The very name of Golgotha, translated but not explained in the canonical New Testament, attracted exegetical interest. The memory of the death of Jesus was strongly attached to one particular tradition, which was facilitated by the nomenclature of the place where the crucifixion took place. By at least the third century, Golgotha was associated in Christian memory with the burial place of Adam. The Adamic Golgotha tradition was widely disseminated in the fourth century, likely invigorated by the construction of the Church of the Holy Sepulchre. Passages from Pauline epistles, naturally including the Adam-typology passages in 1 Cor 15:21–22, 45–49; and Rom 5:12–21, played an important role in the way that Jesus was remembered in connection with the tradition of Adam's burial at Golgotha. However, Eph 5:14 was widely attached to the Adamic burial tradition at Golgotha, for reasons that are not entirely clear. One possibility is that this passage was utilized in the liturgical readings associated with Golgotha or with the Passion narrative.[210] Egeria mentions that there were readings from the apostles that took place at the commemorative services at Golgotha (*Itin. Eger.* 37.5), so this is certainly a possible explanation for what is otherwise an enigmatic exegetical tradition.

The relationship of the tradition of Adam's burial at Golgotha to Jewish traditions about Adam's final resting is a complicated matter. Our review of the relevant Jewish

---

[207] Jonathan Z. Smith, *To Take Place: Toward Theory in Ritual* (Chicago: University of Chicago Press, 1987), 93.
[208] See Sara Ahmed, *The Cultural Politics of Emotion* (Edinburgh: Edinburgh University Press, 2004), esp. 12; Rumi Sakamoto, "Mobilizing Affect for Collective War Memory," *Cultural Studies* 29, no. 2 (2015): 158–84 (esp. 163–4).
[209] Ahmed, *Cultural Politics*, esp. 10–11.
[210] Thanks is due to Halvor Moxnes, who recently suggested this possibility to me in conversation after a talk on Golgotha that I gave at the University of Oslo.

sources has revealed no evidence that the connection between Adam and Golgotha predates the New Testament, nor the earliest Christian witness to the tradition in the third century. In fact, the earliest Jewish traditions seem to locate Adam's final repose in the regions of Paradise. However, later Jewish traditions place Adam's burial site at Mount Moriah or at Kiryat Arba. This development in the tradition comes after the construction of the Church of the Holy Sepulchre in the fourth century and the earliest witness to the Adam-Golgotha tradition in the third century. As a result, it is most likely that the later Jewish siting of Adam's burial at Mount Moriah or Kiryat Arba was a response to and rejection of the Christian claims about the connection between Jesus and Adam made through the Golgotha tradition. This highlights the way in which Golgotha played a noteworthy role in Jewish-Christian relations in antiquity, which began prior to the earliest attestations of the Adam tradition. As early as the second century, Melito leveraged memory of the site of Golgotha for supersessionist purposes.

As visitors to the modern Church of the Holy Sepulchre may attest, the traditional place of Jesus' crucifixion still retains its power to elicit strong affective responses from pilgrims. Although the affect is individually experienced, the emotional experience described by Egeria is collective and is tied to the publicly remembered past of the death of Jesus.[211] In the words of Smith, "In Jerusalem, story, ritual, and place could be one."[212]

---

[211] Cf. the findings of Sakamoto's study of collectively shared emotion experienced through a *kamikaze* exhibit at the controversial Yūshūkan shrine in contemporary Japan, which provides an interesting comparative case ("Mobilizing Affect," 164, 177–9). Sakamoto aims for this study to be a case study that can contribute more generally to thinking through the role of affect in collective war memory (158). Although we are not dealing with collective war memory in our study, her findings may also have relevance for collective religious memory.

[212] Smith, *To Take Place*, 86.

3

The Tomb of Jesus in Christian Memory and Interpretation

How did the place of Jesus' burial figure into early Christian collective memory? As with our investigation of Golgotha, our focus is not primarily upon the authenticity of the traditional site. I am not so much concerned with the memory of the *location* of the authentic tomb but rather with how the place of Jesus' burial was received and remembered in early Christian writings, what layers of interpretation it accumulated, and how was it understood once crystallized in the form of the *aedicule* and Anastasis in the age of Constantine, a little less than three centuries after the event of Jesus' burial. These concerns are the burden of this present chapter.

The Tomb of Jesus in the Gospels

Since it is in the gospels that we find our earliest memories of the tomb of Jesus, it is fitting that we should begin our conversation with them. Mark provides the earliest extant account of the tomb of Jesus.[1] There are a number of additional details that are preserved by Matthew and Luke that are missing from Mark. It is possible to view this as collective remembering in process.[2] What an author, any author, chooses to include or exclude in a narrative is a part of their interpretation of the past, and so the differences in details between Mark and the other canonical gospels deserve our attention. This does not speak to the accuracy or reliability of a text so much as it does to the intentional communication of an author's interpretation of the events that they have narrated.

A recent study by Daniel A. Smith has helpfully shed light on the space of Jesus' tomb in early Christian memory.[3] According to Smith, Mark's narrative does not

---

[1] Assuming Markan priority.
[2] As recently argued by Daniel A. Smith, "'Look, the Place Where They Put Him' (Mk 16:6): The Space of Jesus' Tomb in Early Christian Memory," *Harvard Theological Studies* 70, no. 1 (2014): 1–8. See also Smith's broader study on the empty tomb narratives, Daniel A. Smith, *Revisiting the Empty Tomb: The Early History of Easter* (Minneapolis: Fortress Press, 2010).
[3] Smith, "Jesus' Tomb," 1–8.

appear to present the empty tomb as sacred space.[4] In fact, he argues that Mark depicts Jesus as having received a dishonorable burial as an executed criminal.[5] Despite this, Mark 16:1–8 nevertheless presents the site of the empty tomb as a place where "the divine realm has broken through,"[6] indicated by the stone moved from the entrance of the tomb (v. 4), the presence of the "young man dressed in a white robe" (v. 5), and the missing body of Jesus (v. 6). However, as the celestial young man in white says, "He is not here." The site of the encounter with the risen Jesus will not be the tomb but will instead be Galilee (v. 7). The interior of the tomb is the site where Jesus was raised, but it is not where the risen Jesus is to be found. This is a point on which all of the canonical evangelists agree: the tomb is empty.

Smith observes several elements of the empty tomb narratives that appear in Matthew, Luke, and John, but not in Mark: additional witnesses at the tomb, mention of graveclothes at the tomb, adaptations of the angelophany, and the appearance of the risen Jesus at the tomb.[7] Mark's narrative appears to intentionally end abruptly with the women fleeing the empty tomb. However, all three of Matthew, Luke, and John mention additional witnesses at the tomb beyond the women mentioned in the Markan narrative. Luke and John both place Peter at the empty tomb (Luke 24:12; John 20:6), and John also places the Beloved Disciple there as well (20:2–4). Matthew's narrative includes hostile witnesses in mentioning the guards placed at the tomb and their report (Matt 27:62–66; 28:11). Smith argues that the presence of these witnesses not mentioned by Mark function to "confirm that this 'place' is the site of the resurrection,"[8] making the narrative more compelling.

Similarly, Smith argues that the discovery of the graveclothes in Luke 24:12 and John 20:5–7 speaks to the tangible bodily resurrection of Jesus.[9] Notably, Cyril of Jerusalem considered the graveclothes to be a "witness" to the resurrection.[10] The impact of the addition of the detail about the graveclothes on the spatial understanding of the tomb is notable, since, as Smith writes, "the empty tomb is no longer empty: it contains a sign now that the absent Jesus had been raised."[11] What we see here is a shift in the depiction of the space of the tomb as a place that has been vacated by Jesus, and that is fled from in terror (Mark 16:8), since he is no longer there. In the longer, more detailed

---

[4] Smith, "Jesus' Tomb," 3–4; cf. Helmut Koester, "On Heroes, Tombs, and Early Christianity: An Epilogue," in *Flavius Philostratus: Heroikos*, trans. Ellen Bradshaw Aitken and Jennifer K. Berenson MacLean, Society of Biblical Literature Writings from the Greco-Roman World 1 (Leiden: Brill, 2004), 259–64 (263); Hans Dieter Betz, "Hero Worship and Christian Beliefs: Observations from the History of Religion on Philostratus's Heroikos," in *Philostratus's Heroikos: Religion and Cultural Identity in the Third Century C.E.*, ed. Ellen Bradshaw Aitken and Jennifer K. Berenson MacLean, Society of Biblical Literature Writings from the Greco-Roman World 6 (Leiden: Brill, 2004), 25–47.

[5] Smith, "Jesus' Tomb," 2. On the dishonorable burial of Jesus, see Raymond E. Brown, "The Burial of Jesus (Mark 15:42–47)," *CBQ* 50, no. 2 (1988): 238–45; Byron R. McCane, *Roll Back the Stone: Death and Burial in the World of Jesus* (Harrisburg: Trinity Press International, 2003), 89–108; James F. McGrath, *The Burial of Jesus: History and Faith* (Englewood: Patheos Press, 2012), 61–98.

[6] Smith, *Revisiting the Empty Tomb*, 89.

[7] Smith, "Jesus' Tomb," 4.

[8] Ibid., 5.

[9] Ibid.

[10] *Cat.* 14.22.

[11] Smith, "Jesus' Tomb," 6.

narratives of Luke and John, it is revisited by witnesses and contains a physical artifact of the event of the resurrection in the graveclothes.

Both John 20:12 and Luke 24:4 mention two angels inside the tomb. The positioning of the angels in the Johannine narrative are of particular interest. According to John, when Mary bent over to look into the tomb, "she saw two angels in white, sitting where the body of Jesus had been lying, one at the head and the other at the feet" (20:12). As some scholars have noted, the positioning of the angels reflects the image of the two cherubim atop the mercy seat of the Ark of the Covenant described in Exod 25:18–22.[12] The instructions for the construction of the Ark specifically mentions two golden cherubim, "at the two ends of the mercy seat" (v. 18), who face one another (v. 20). According to Smith, "this allusion, because it correlates the missing (risen) body of Jesus with the space between the cherubim, which remained empty and yet was the site of the LORD's enthronement (1 Sam 4:4; Ps 80:1), creates a 'sacred space' within the tomb equivalent to the inner sanctum of the Temple."[13] Thus, he rightly argues that this is a "point in the trajectory from the 'place' of Mark's empty tomb to the 'sacred space' of the Church of the Resurrection."[14]

Matthew 28:9–10 and John 20:14–18 both narrate appearances of the risen Jesus at the tomb. Smith rightly observes that "the tomb is now not only the site of the resurrection, but also the site of a Christophany, and this further sacralises the place,"[15] noting that the site of a theophany was considered sacred ground in the Hebrew Bible (e.g., Exod 3:5).[16]

Smith's study has suggested a trend in the tradition toward drawing out the sacralization of the tomb of Jesus, which finds its beginning in the New Testament gospels themselves. This trend would reach its apex in the construction of the Church of the Holy Sepulchre, and especially the *aedicule*, almost three centuries after the life of Jesus. The sanctity of the place of Jesus' burial and subsequent resurrection in the narratives of Matthew, Luke, and John would naturally be transferred and applied to the Church of the Holy Sepulchre and the space of the *aedicule* itself.

The Gospel of John provides a few unique details of the site of Jesus' burial that deserve further discussion and comment.[17] John tells us directly that the place of crucifixion was "near the city" (19:20). Furthermore, according to John 19:41–42, "there was a garden in the place where he was crucified, and in the garden there was a new tomb in which no one had ever been laid. And so, because it was the Jewish day of Preparation, and the tomb was nearby, they laid Jesus there." The mention of the

---

[12] For discussion and defense of this allusion to the cherubim in Exod 25:18–22, see Christian Grappe, "Les deux anges de Jean 20:12: Signes de la presence mystérieuse du Logos (à la lumière du targum d'Ex 25:22)?" *Revue d'Histoire et de Philosophies Religieuses* 89 (2009): 169–77; cf. Smith, "Tomb of Jesus," 6; Nicholas P. Lunn, "Jesus, the Ark, and the Day of Atonement: Intertextual Echoes in John 19:38-20:18," *JETS* 52 (2009): 731–46.
[13] Smith, "Tomb of Jesus," 6.
[14] Ibid.
[15] Ibid., 7.
[16] Ibid.
[17] It is worth noting here that John lacks certain details that are included in the Synoptics. Most notably, John omits the description of the tomb as rock-cut. On this, see C. H. Dodd, *Historical Tradition in the Fourth Gospel* (Cambridge: Cambridge University Press, 1963), 138.

"garden" (*kēpos*) is unique to John, at least among the canonical evangelists. Moreover, the fact that the tomb is "nearby" and "in the place" (*en tō topō*) where Jesus was crucified is not directly conveyed by the Synoptics.[18]

According to Heb 13:12, Jesus "suffered outside the city gate in order to sanctify the people by his own blood." For the author of Hebrews, this is taken as a parallel to the burning of the bodies of animals "outside the camp" in v. 11. This generally coheres with what we find in the canonical gospels. According to Mark 15:20, the Roman soldiers led Jesus out (Greek ἐξάγουσιν) to crucify him. Likewise, the location of the crucifixion outside the city is also strongly implied by the use of ἐξέρχομαι ("to go out") in Matt 27:32 and John 19:17. There is some convergence here with both the Johannine (cf. John 19:20) and Synoptic traditions. In Matthew's narrative, some of the guards of the tomb of Jesus come into the city (*eis tēn polin*). If we combine this with the Johannine description of the tomb as being "in the place" where Jesus was crucified (John 19:41), then it stands to reason that the crucifixion and burial both took place outside of the city, at least according to the composite witness of the New Testament authors.

A few comments about the Johannine location of the site of the crucifixion and tomb in a "garden" (*kēpos*) are necessary at this point.[19] Some scholars have suggested that there is literary significance to John's location of the tomb in a garden, proposing that there is an intentional allusion or connection to the Eden narrative (Gen 2–3) in John's use of *kēpos* to describe Gethsemane (18:1, 26) and the site of Jesus' crucifixion and burial (19:41).[20] The idea that the place of the crucifixion and burial in some way alludes to Eden is certainly a part of the early reception history of the Johannine passion narrative, as there is a tradition in Patristic exegesis of drawing this same connection.[21] However, the connection to Eden is tenuous on the Johannine level. The word utilized in Gen 2–3 LXX for the "garden" of Eden is *paradeisos*. As Carlos Sosa Siliezar has noted, while there are some textual variants of Gen 2–3 that use *kēpos* to refer to Eden,[22] "it is impossible to know whether he [John] has access to such a reading. Extant evidence only allows us to assert that the great majority of extant Greek manuscripts of Gen 2–3 use παράδεισος in reference to the garden of Eden instead of κῆπος,"[23] and moreover, even if John did know of a reading of Jewish Scripture using *kēpos* to refer to

---

[18] Brown, however, regards the nearness of the tomb to the place of crucifixion to be implied by the Synoptics, since "none mentions carrying Jesus' body to the place of burial, an action that could not have traversed any distance granted the hour and oncoming Sabbath" (*Death of the Messiah*, 2: 1249 n. 21).

[19] It is important to recognize that the Greek term *kēpos* can refer generally to an agricultural area. Cf., e.g., C. K. Barrett, *The Gospel According to St. John*, 2nd ed. (Philadelphia: Westminster, 1978), 560; D. A. Carson, *The Gospel According to John*, PNTC (Grand Rapids: Eerdmans, 1991), 631; Andreas J. Köstenberger, *John*, BECNT (Grand Rapids: Baker, 2004), 556. E.g., in the LXX, see 2 Kgs 5:26; LXX Amos 9:14; LXX Eccl 2:5. On the use of *kēpos* in the LXX in general, see Carlos Raúl Sosa Siliezar, *Creation Imagery in the Gospel of John*, LNTS 546 (London: T&T Clark, 2015), 182.

[20] Examples include Nicolas Wyatt, "'Supposing Him to Be the Gardener' (John 20,15) A Study of the Paradise Motif in John," ZNW 81 (1990): 21–38; Klink, *John*, 819; Frederick Dale Bruner, *The Gospel of John: A Commentary* (Grand Rapids: Eerdmans, 2012), 841, 844; Jodi Magness, "Sweet Memory: Archaeological Evidence of Jesus in Jerusalem," in *Memory in Ancient Rome and Early Christianity*, ed. Karl Galinsky (Oxford: Oxford University Press, 2016), 324–43 (considered on 338).

[21] See the discussion that follows.

[22] Sosa Siliezar, *Creation Imagery*, 180–1.

[23] Ibid., 181.

the garden of Eden, "a direct link between Jn 18.1, 26; 19.41 and the garden of Eden is not straightforward, because the noun *kēpos* is used in various ways in the LXX."[24] At best, if John meant to allude to Eden, the attempt lacks enough specificity to make it impactful, certain, or clear.[25] C. K. Barrett is probably correct in his statement that "if John had intended an allusion to the Garden of Eden it is probable that he would have used the LXX word, παράδεισος."[26] In response to Barrett, Nicolas Wyatt argues that John's point was "to hint, to suggest, to lead the mind of the reader to this conclusion without spelling it out."[27] However, in my opinion, while not altogether impossible, this strains the limits of credulity and is difficult to prove, especially as the argument is based primarily on a single word, *kēpos*. The better explanation is that a connection to Eden imagery is not clear precisely because no such connection is intended.

While it is unlikely that John *intended* the description of the place of the crucifixion and burial of Jesus in 19:41 to be taken as Eden imagery, the potential to draw a parallel between the "garden" of Golgotha and the sepulcher to the garden of Eden was seized upon by early Christian interpreters. Thus, although John probably did not intend such a connection, Eden imagery quickly entered into the commemoration of Golgotha and the sepulcher in the reception history of the tradition.

Other scholars have argued that the mention of the garden at the tomb is a Johannine historical recollection of the topography of Jesus' burial place.[28] Nevertheless, this would not rule out the possibility that the mention of the garden has a literary function, or that the author's intentions were solely historical rather than interpretive or symbolic. No such distinction need be drawn between the "literary" and the "historical." All remembering is interpretive, and there is no memory without interpretation. Moreover, as Jan Fokkelman writes, "every word that the author allows to participate has a relation to his vision and themes."[29] Naturally, this is true regardless of whether or not the narrative intends to accurately represent the past. Perhaps the central insight of Hayden White's contributions to the philosophy of history in *Metahistory* is the notion that historical writing is a kind of narrative.[30] It is important to be wary of drawing too hard a line between "historical" and "literary" characteristics of the gospels. Thus, while the historical Jesus may have indeed been buried in a tomb located in a garden, the fact that John intentionally *chose* to mention this detail at all may have some significance for the Johannine author's vision and themes in his story of Jesus.[31]

---

[24] Ibid., 182.
[25] Compare, for example, Rev 22:2, in which the reference to Eden, through the "tree of life" (Gk. ξύλον ζωῆς; cf. Gen 2:9, "ξύλον τῆς ζωῆς") is abundantly clear.
[26] Barrett, *John*, 560. See also Brown, *Death of the Messiah*, 2: 1270.
[27] Wyatt, "Supposing Him to Be the Gardener," 37.
[28] E.g., Urban C. von Wahlde, *The Gospel and Letters of John*, 3 vols., Eerdmans Critical Commentary (Grand Rapids: Eerdmans, 2010), 832.
[29] Jan Fokkelman, *Reading Biblical Narrative: A Practical Guide* (Leiden: Deo, 1999), 76.
[30] Hayden White, *Metahistory: The Historical Imagination in Ninteenth-Century Europe*, 4th ed. (Maryland: Johns Hopkins University Press, [1973] 2014).
[31] Similarly, see Joachim Schaper, "The Messiah in the Garden: John 19.38-41, (Royal) Gardens, and Messianic Concepts," in *Paradise in Antiquity*, ed. Markus Bockmuehl and Guy G. Stroumsa (Cambridge: Cambridge University Press, 2010), 17-27 (27). Schaper speaks of a "false dichotomy between historical events and sites on the one hand and their potential theological symbolism on

In the LXX, gardens, denoted by the term *kēpos*, are sometimes the place of royal burials. At least two Judean kings are supposed to have been buried in gardens. According to 4 Kgdms 21:18, Manasseh is buried in "the garden of his house" ("ἐν τῷ κήπῳ τοῦ οἴκου αὐτοῦ"), which is also called the "garden of Oza." Amon, his son, is buried in the same place (21:26). However, the most significant datum for our purposes is a reference to the "garden of the grave of David" (κήπου τάφου Δαυιδ) in 2 Esd 13:16.[32] No mention of a "garden" is made in the equivalent Hebrew text of the MT (Neh 3:16). This suggests that David's burial place was known to be located in a garden in the later Second Temple period. We need not imagine a direct allusion or reference to 2 Esd 13:16 LXX in John 19:41. There is, we must note, a difference in vocabulary used for the burial places in these two passages. David's tomb is referred to in 2 Esd 13:16 using the word *taphos*, while the tomb of Jesus is referred to using the term *mnēmeion* in John 19:41. While we can remain open to the possibility, though it may be a slim one, of a direct allusion in John 19:41 to 2 Esd 13:16, it need not be the case. It is enough to recognize that the traditional location of David's tomb[33] was known to be located in a garden in the late Second Temple period.

A site considered to be David's tomb was apparently known in the late Second Temple period and perhaps also the years that directly followed. In Acts 2:29, Peter mentions that David "died and was buried, and his tomb is with us to this day." If the tomb was known at the time when Acts was written, it is certainly plausible that the author of the Fourth Gospel would have been familiar with it as well. Josephus, writing after the destruction of Jerusalem, relates an incident in which Herod the Great attempts to loot David's tomb (*Ant.* 16.179–83). Both 2 Esdras and Josephus apparently locate this tomb in the Jerusalem area. It is reasonable to think that the author of the Fourth Gospel, who is often thought to have knowledge of the Jerusalem area, intended to draw a parallel in John 19:41 to the famed tomb of David, which was similarly located in a garden near Jerusalem. The Fourth Gospel situates Jesus as "King of the Jews" in eyes of Roman characters in the passion narrative (John 18:33, 39; 19:3, 14–15, 19). More importantly, however, he is recognized as the "King of Israel" by Nathanael in John 1:49 (whom Jesus recognizes as a true "Israelite," cf. v. 47) and by the great crowd that had come for Passover in Jerusalem during the "triumphal entry" in John 12:13. That Jewish characters in John recognize Jesus as the King of *Israel* is noteworthy, especially given that the same title could be applied to David (2 Sam 6:20).

The tomb of David known in the late Second Temple period is a literal *lieu de mémoire*, a monument vested with historical significance in the collective memory of early Palestinian Judaism. That there are multiple references to it in the late Second Temple period by authors as diverse as Luke, Josephus, and the Septuagint translator

---

the other." Likewise, Sosa Siliezar notes that, while John could have used *kēpos* to denote that the location of the events in John 19:41 took place in a garden, "nevertheless, it is legitimate to ask whether John wanted to convey further meaning when he used κῆπος in John 18:1, 26; 19:41 by relating those verses to the OT" (*Creation Imagery*, 183).

[32] The mention of a garden is lacking in the Hebrew text of the MT.
[33] Whether or not the tomb associated with David in the Second Temple period actually *was* the authentic tomb of David is inconsequential for our purposes. What matters is simply that it was remembered as or recognized to be David's tomb by people in antiquity.

responsible for 2 Esdras speaks to its prominence and importance during this time. It is reasonable to think that the mention of the location of Jesus' tomb in a garden by the Fourth Evangelist could have drawn a natural comparison to the well-known garden tomb of the famed biblical king, which was located in the same city (Neh 3:16; cf. 1 Kgs 2:10).

The Fourth Gospel is not the only source to locate Jesus' burial in a garden. According to the Gospel of Peter, "And taking the Lord he washed and wrapped [him] in a linen cloth and brought [him] into his own tomb called 'Joseph's Garden' (Greek κῆπον Ἰωσήφ)" (Gos. Pet. 24).[34] Questions of literary dependence and hypothetical prior sources aside, the memory of the garden location of the tomb here is significant. While it is commonly thought that the Gospel of Peter displays knowledge of the synoptic gospels, its relationship to John is much less certain.[35] It is possible that the author of the Gospel of Peter had knowledge of the Gospel of John.[36] At the very least, it is a notable instance of the reception of the garden burial tradition in the second century CE.[37] This is all the more significant given the lack of clear evidence of a literary dependence of the Gospel of Peter on the Fourth Gospel, as the reference to the "Garden of Joseph" in Gos. Pet. 6.24 may indicate that the garden location of the burial had entered into the common memory of the passion. Brown presents a reasonable hypothesis that offers some explanation of the minor parallels in the Gospel of Peter to the Fourth Gospel. According to Brown, although it is doubtful that the author of the Gospel of Peter had a copy of the Gospel of John in front of him, "he had heard people speak who were familiar with" the Gospel of John.[38] The notion that the garden burial tradition was passed on orally, perhaps as a result of knowledge of the Johannine passion narrative, is reasonable and makes good sense of the data. It may thus be one of the earliest instantiations beyond the canonical gospels of the reception of the garden burial tradition.

Unlike the Fourth Gospel, the Gospel of Peter names the garden, calling it the "Garden of Joseph." There is, then, a "double association"[39] in the Gospel of Peter of the burial site with Joseph, as the tomb belongs to him and the garden is named for him.[40] It is difficult to know what to make of this nomenclature. It is possible that the

---

[34] Translation from Paul Foster, *The Gospel of Peter: Introduction, Critical Edition and Commentary*, TENT 4 (Leiden: Brill, 2010), 201.

[35] See, e.g., ibid., 115–47; Brown, *Death of the Messiah*, 2: 1317–47; Pheme Perkins, "Apocryphal Gospels and the Historical Jesus," in *Jesus Research: New Methodologies and Perceptions – The Second Princeton-Prague Symposium on Jesus Research*, ed. James H. Charlesworth with Brian Rhea and Petr Pokorný (Grand Rapids: Eerdmans, 2014), 663–90 (675).

[36] Paul Foster's cautious statement that "uncertainty about use of John means that it is probably best to state that the author of the Gospel of Peter knew the three synoptic accounts" (*Gospel of Peter*, 147) is judicious and reasonable. However, a good case for the knowledge and rewriting of a Johannine pericope in the Gospel of Peter has been made by Alan Kirk, "The Johannine Jesus in the Gospel of Peter," in *Jesus in Johannine Tradition*, ed. Robert Tomson Fortna and Tom Thatcher (Louisville: Westminster John Knox, 2001), 313–22.

[37] On the date of the Gospel of Peter, see the discussion in Foster, *Gospel of Peter*, 169–72. It is most likely dated to the latter half of the second century CE.

[38] Brown, *Death of the Messiah*, 2: 1335.

[39] Foster, *Gospel of Peter*, 347.

[40] It is worth mentioning that there is a garden connected to the passion belonging to another Joseph, that is, Joseph of Nazareth, mentioned in a tradition contained in Gos. Phil. 73:9–15. According to this tradition, attributed to Philip the Apostle, "Joseph the carpenter planted a garden because

garden in which Jesus was buried came to be known as the "Garden of Joseph."[41] It is also possible that the name came as a result of a combination of the traditions of Joseph's ownership of the tomb (Matt 27:60) and the location of the tomb in a garden (John 19:41). However, Joan Taylor rightly notes that the name is "new," insofar as it does not derive from the canonical gospels, and, moreover, that "if Joseph owned the tomb, he owned the garden outside it; the tomb had probably been newly cut in a plot of land he had purchased."[42]

Josephus mentions a gate called "Gennath" (*War* 5.146), which means "garden." This gate is usually thought to be in the general area in which the traditional sites of Jesus' crucifixion and burial are located.[43] Although it is not possible to be certain, a gate located in this area dated to the Hasmonean period discovered by Nahman Avigad is the best and only candidate for identification as the Gennath Gate.[44] It is possible, perhaps even likely, that this is the gate referred to in Heb 13:12. The reference to a garden in the nomenclature of this gate is intriguing, especially in light of the mention of the garden at the tomb in John 19:41 and in light of the agricultural layer from the Herodian period that has been identified as a garden located underneath the Church of the Redeemer,[45] which is near the Church of the Holy Sepulchre. Curiously, Cyril of Jerusalem mentions that "signs and remains" of the garden were still visible at his time in the fourth century (*Cat.* 14.5). When taken together, it is reasonable to interpret the evidence as pointing toward the existence of a literal garden at the place where Jesus was buried, particularly if we accept the traditional location of the Holy Sepulchre.

Although I have argued that the author of the Fourth Gospel did not intend to allude to Eden by mentioning the garden in which Jesus' tomb was located, there were certainly some early Christian authors who did see a parallel between Eden and the sepulchral garden. The essential background of this connection is, as with the Adamic Golgotha tradition, the Christ-Adam typology. According to Hanneke Reuling, "Already in the earliest Christian documents it is suggested that the ultimate significance of Christ can only be fully grasped against the background of the first creation. Christ is the *typos*, Adam the *anti-typos*,"[46] and thus, this paradigm informs Christian exegesis of the Eden narrative.[47]

---

he needed wood for his trade. It was he who made the cross from the trees which he planted. His own offspring hung on that which he planted. His offspring was Jesus and the planting was the cross" (translation by Wesley W. Isenberg, *The Nag Hammadi Library in English*, rev. ed., ed. James M. Robinson (Leiden: Brill, 1990), 139–60 [153]). However, it is unlikely that this tradition is related to the garden burial tradition found in the Gospel of Peter. It is much more likely that the Joseph of the "Garden of Joseph" is Joseph of Arimathea.

[41] See Brown, *Death of the Messiah*, 2:1269.
[42] Taylor, "Golgotha," 199.
[43] See, e.g., ibid., 186–7; Murphy-O'Connor, "Argument for the Holy Sepulchre," 81–3.
[44] Nahman Avigad, *Discovering Jerusalem* (Nashville: Nelson, 1983), 50, 66, 69. Cf. Taylor, "Golgotha," 186–7; Murphy-O'Connor, "Argument for the Holy Sepulchre," 82–3.
[45] Marcel Serr and Dieter Vieweger, Is the Holy Sepulchre Church Authentic?" *Biblical Archaeology Review* 42, no. 3 (2016): 28–9, 66.
[46] Hanneke Reuling, "The Christian and the Rabbinic Adam: Genesis Rabbah and Patristic Exegesis of Gen 3:17–19," in *The Exegetical Encounter Between Jews and Christians in Late Antiquity*, ed. Emmanouela Grypeou and Helen Spurling (Leiden: Brill, 2009), 63–74 (65).
[47] Ibid., 65.

In the Palestinian tradition, Cyril of Jerusalem connects the place of Jesus' burial in the Fourth Gospel with Eden.[48] He writes,

> And since we have touched on things connected with paradise, I am truly astonished at the truth of the types. In Paradise was the fall, and in a garden was our salvation. From the tree came sin, and until the tree, sin lasted. In the evening, when the Lord walked in the garden, they hid themselves. And in the evening the robber is brought by the Lord into paradise. (*Cat.* 13.19)[49]

Cyril draws a typological connection between the Garden of Eden, in which the fall of Adam and Eve took place, and the garden in which Jesus was crucified (*Cat.* 13.8), buried, and resurrected. This follows the same Adam-Christ typology discussed in a previous chapter that so thoroughly colored the memory of Jesus' passion in early Christian writings.

Cyril carries this typology further in his discussion of the place of Jesus' burial:

> But we are looking for a clear indication of the place of his burial … Give us, prophets, the precise facts about the grave: where is it, and where shall we look for it? They reply: "Look upon the solid rock which you have quarried" (LXX Isa 51:1), look upon it and see. You have in the gospels: "in a carved tomb" (Luke 23:53), where the rock had been quarried. And what happened? What was the door of the tomb like? Again, another prophet tells us: "They killed my life in the pit, and placed a stone over me" (LXX Lam 3:53). I, the chosen, precious corner-stone, I, the stone to trip up the Jews and bring salvation to believers, I lie for a short time within the stone (Isa 28:16; 8:14; 1 Pet 2:6, 8). Thus the tree of life was planted in the earth, so that the cursed earth might enjoy the blessed, and the dead be redeemed. (*Cat.* 13.35)[50]

This passage, as with the rest of the catechetical lectures, was probably delivered in the precinct of the Church of the Holy Sepulchre, the exact place where the tomb under discussion was located. The questions about the tomb would have had a rhetorical effect heightened by the proximity, perhaps even visibility of the actual rock-cut tomb nearby. The impact of Cyril's use of Isa 51:1 LXX would have likely been particularly forceful in light of the fact that the very rock in question had been re-quarried recently when Constantine had excavated the tomb. It is worth noting the combination of Mark 12:10 (citing Ps 118:22; cf. Matt 21:42, Luke 20:17) and its apparently Christological reference to "the stone [Greek *lithon*] that the builders rejected" with 1 Pet 2:7–8, which also cites Ps 118:22 along with Isa 8:14, and the designation of the cross as a "stumbling block to Jews" in 1 Cor 1:23, which Cyril

---

[48] Cf. Sosa Siliezar, *Creation Imagery*, 188–9.
[49] Translation from Edwin Hamilton Gifford, trans., "The Catechetical Lectures of S. Cyril, Archbishop of Jerusalem," in *Cyril of Jerusalem, Gregory Nazianzen*, ed. Philip Schaff, NPNF 2.7 (New York: Christian Literature, 1893), 195. Omitted in Yarnold, *Cyril of Jerusalem*.
[50] Translation from Yarnold, *Cyril of Jerusalem*, 160, including biblical references.

employs to anti-Jewish polemical effect. The function of the Holy Sepulchre in anti-Jewish polemic will be revisited when we discuss Eusebius' interpretation of the tomb below.

The final sentence of *Cat.* 13.35 identifies Jesus, who lay "within the stone," as the "Tree of Life," which was "planted in the earth." The purpose of this figurative "planting" is to undo the curse of Adam. This idea is paralleled in *Cat.* 14.11, where Cyril refers to Jesus' burial in the tomb as a vine planted in the garden, combining John 19:41 ("in the garden there was a new tomb") and John 15:1 ("I am the vine"), "in order that the curse that came because of Adam might be rooted out." The image of Jesus "planted" in the garden of his burial as the Tree of Life is a direct reference and typological parallel to the Garden of Eden in Gen 2–3.

The explicit exegetical connections that Cyril draws between the burial of Jesus in the garden and the Garden of Eden further demonstrates the persistence of the attachment of the Adam-Christ typology to the site of Jesus' crucifixion and burial in early Christian memory. Although I am not of the opinion that the author of the Fourth Gospel intended to allude or refer to Eden in referencing the garden location of Jesus' burial, the mention of the garden in John 19:41 certainly opened the door for that sort of interpretation in later exegesis.

Did the actual tomb of Jesus function as a *lieu de mémoire* as early as the first century CE? Did the place itself have a function in the early Christian commemoration of Jesus in the first decades following his lifetime? There is little certainty to be had here. Bellarmino Bagatti, following Emmanuel Testa, held that the tomb of Jesus was used as a "mystic grotto" by Jewish Christians as a place to carry out cultic acts.[51] This idea is derived from Eusebius' description of the sites on which the Constantinian commemorative churches in Palestine were built as "sacred caves."[52] Taylor, however, considers it unlikely that the tomb was venerated in the first century.[53] She notes that Paul does not mention the tomb at all, as well as the general silence in the earliest sources about veneration or visits to the tomb by members of the Jerusalem church. Taylor also argues that, although there was a practice in early Judaism of honoring the tombs of the righteous and of biblical figures, "the honour accorded these tombs was as a result of the corpses being interred within them."[54] Therefore, since Christians generally believed that Jesus was risen and that his body was thus not in the tomb, the empty tomb would not have been important. Both positions are possible, and yet, neither is verifiable. As a result, we are left only to draw inferences from the evidence at hand. We will return to this matter later when we consider the archaeological and architectural evidence.

---

[51] Bellarmino Bagatti, *The Church from the Circumcision: History and Archaeology of the Judaeo-Christians*, repr. ed., trans. Eugene Hoade (Jerusalem: Franciscan Printing Press, [1971] 2004), 133–6.

[52] Eusebius, *De laudibus Constantini* 9.17, English translation from H. A. Drake, *In Praise of Constantine: A Historical Study and New Translation of Eusebius' Tricennial Orations*, Classical Studies 15 (Berkeley: University of California Publications, 1976), 101.

[53] Taylor, *Christians and the Holy Places*, 136–7.

[54] Ibid., 136.

Between Easter and the Church of the Holy Sepulchre

The Tomb of Jesus in Gospel of Peter

Some insight into the interpretation and collective remembering of the tomb in the second century can be gleaned from extracanonical rewritings of the passion narrative. The Gospel of Peter presents a few notable details in its narrative of the empty tomb that speak to the trajectory of the ongoing interpretation and commemoration of the burial of Jesus, which will eventually find its apex in the construction of the Church of the Holy Sepulchre.

The Gospel of Peter presents the tomb as a place of dignity. Jesus' body is washed by Joseph of Arimathea (Gos. Pet. 6.23) in accordance with proper funerary customs (cf. *m. Sabb.* 23:5; see also Acts 9:37), a detail that is notably missing from the canonical accounts of the burial of Jesus.[55] The Gospel of Peter is also clear that Jesus is buried in Joseph's own tomb, called the "Garden of Joseph" (6.24), and the women come to the tomb explicitly to mourn (12.50–54), though they were unable to do so on the day that he was crucified. Thus, in the Gospel of Peter, Jesus' body is washed, he is buried in a family tomb, and his followers come to his tomb to mourn him. These details, which all speak to a dignified burial,[56] are lacking from the Markan narrative.[57]

According to the Gospel of Peter, Jesus' tomb was sealed with seven seals (8.33). This expands upon the mention of the sealing of the tomb in Matt 27:66.[58] Brown notes that the seven seals are particular to the Gospel of Peter and comments that "the number seven is commonly symbolic in the Bible, but it is difficult to be certain whether the seven is just part of the folkloric imagination or has special symbolism."[59] While Brown's caution is reasonable, it is worth observing that the seven seals (ἑπτὰ σφραγῖδας) on the tomb call to mind the seven seals (ἑπτὰ σφραγῖδας, Rev 5:5) on the scroll in Rev 5–8. The breaking of the seven seals of the scroll in Rev 5–8 sets eschatological events of significance in motion, as though the seals were holding them back. The breaking of a seal of eschatological significance is, in itself, reminiscent of the scroll that Daniel is instructed to keep sealed "until the time of the end" (Dan 12:4).

The seven seals on the tomb of Jesus are also reminiscent of the triangular seal placed on the tomb of Adam in GLAE 42:1. The triangular seal in GLAE is difficult to interpret, but some scholars have nevertheless noted the importance of the number three in GLAE.[60] Thus, much like the Gospel of Peter, the seal on Adam's tomb has numerical significance. Both seals are also broken by apparently supernatural, divine action (GLAE 42:1; Gos. Pet. 9.37). The possibility that both the GLAE and the Gospel of Peter are drawing on some tradition pertaining to the sealing of tombs is enticing. It is possible, as tentatively suggested by de Jonge and Tromp, that the triangular seal

---

[55] As observed by Brown, "Burial of Jesus," 242.
[56] Cf. Smith, "Jesus' Tomb," 3; Brown, "Burial of Jesus," 242–3; McCane, *Roll Back the Stone*, 101–4.
[57] Cf. Brown, "Burial of Jesus," 242–3; Smith, "Jesus' Tomb," 2–3.
[58] Foster, *Gospel of Peter*, 385.
[59] Brown, *Death of the Messiah*, 2: 1296. Brown is followed by Foster, *Gospel of Peter*, 385.
[60] Cf. de Jonge and Tromp, *Life of Adam and Eve*, 72; Sweet, "Religio-Historical Study," 193–4.

is meant to ward off evil powers that might disturb the dead.[61] Perhaps the seven seals on Jesus' tomb in the Gospel of Peter might also have been meant to be a sort of magic ward to prevent the disturbance of the body, though this admittedly seems to be a stretch. In my opinion, although the parallel is noteworthy, we should refrain from making too much of the similarities between the triangular seal of the GLAE and the seven seals of the Gospel of Peter given the lack of evidence and possible superficiality of those similarities.

One of the most striking and unique aspects of the resurrection account in the Gospel of Peter is the emergence of a mobile talking cross from the tomb of Jesus (9.39). Notably, this is the earliest extant mention of the presence of the cross at the tomb following the crucifixion. Since the cross is depicted exiting the tomb, following the angelic figures and the risen Jesus, it would appear as though the author of the Gospel of Peter imagined that it was buried in the tomb with Jesus. Although there is no clear archaeological or literary evidence from the early Roman period that victims of crucifixion were buried with the crosses on which they were crucified, Socrates Scholasticus' account of the legendary finding of the cross in the fourth century by Helena places the cross within Jesus' sepulcher (*Historia Ecclesiastica* I, 17). Other accounts, however, simply place the cross nearby the tomb.[62]

It would seem that there is a trajectory from the presence of the talking cross in the tomb to the legend of the discovery of the cross within the tomb as reported by Socrates. At the very least, it is clear that a connection between the cross and the place of the tomb had entered into the collective memory long before the time of Helena. In all likelihood, this was facilitated by the Johannine description of the tomb in John 19:41–42, which locates the tomb within a garden "in the place where he was crucified." The fact that the cross speaks and affirms that it has "preached to those who sleep" depicts the cross as a witness.

Origen on the Tomb of Jesus

In his *Commentary on Matthew*, Origen presents the tomb as a place of purity, newness, and cleanliness. This comes about in the context of his comments on Matt 27:59–60, which mentions both the "clean linen" in which Jesus' body was wrapped as well as the "new tomb" in which Jesus was buried. On this passage, Origen writes,

> Now I think that that linen possessed a greater cleanliness after the body of Christ was wrapped in it than before, for even when the body of Jesus is dead, it purifies whatever it touches as the body of Jesus. It made that new tomb that had been carved "in the rock" even newer. And do not think that it was written by accident and just happened to be said that "he wrapped" the body "in clean linen and placed it in a new tomb," and that that tomb had been carved "in the rock," a clean tomb

---

[61] de Jonge and Tromp, *Life of Adam and Eve*, 72.
[62] Ambrose, *De Obitus Theodosii* 43–8 (CSEL 81); Rufinus, *Hist. eccl.* 10.7–8 (ed. Theodor Mommsen, in E. Schwartz, ed., *Eusebius Werke*, 2.2 [Leipzig: J. C. Hinrich, 1908], 969–71); Sozomen, *Hist. eccl.* II, 1 (NPNF II. 2).

that was made cleaner by the body of Jesus than it was before the body of Jesus was placed in it. (*Commentary on Matthew*, 143)[63]

Origen considers Jesus' body to have a purifying effect, even in death. This is a reversal of both Jewish and Greco-Roman cultural conventions, as corpse impurity is discussed and attested in both Jewish and Greco-Roman legal texts from around Origen's time.[64] Recent research by Moshe Bildstein has illuminated the apparent rejection or lack of interest of death defilement practice in third-century Christianity,[65] highlighting Origen's explicit rejection of Jewish practices concerning death defilement.[66] Further, as Ramsay MacMullen has shown, early Christian worship in the third and fourth centuries was closely tied to the martyr cult and to what he refers to as "cemetery churches,"[67] which speaks to an attitude toward corpses that departed from typical Greco-Roman and Jewish conventions.

Elsewhere, in *Contra Celsum*, Origen writes further of the purity connected Jesus' body and tomb. Impressed by the fact that Matthew, Luke, and John all mention the newness of the tomb (or in Luke's case, the fact that no one had been laid in it prior to Jesus), Origen writes,

> For he who was unlike other dead men, but showed even as a corpse signs of life in the water and the blood, ought as a new dead man, so to speak, to be in a new and clean tomb. Thus, just as his birth was purer than all other births in that he was born not of sexual intercourse but of a virgin, so also his burial had the purity which was symbolically shown by the fact that his body was put away in a newly made tomb; this was not built of unhewn stones without any natural unity, but consisted of one rock all of one piece which was cut and hewn. (*Contra Celsum* II, 69)[68]

The tomb here is understood symbolically, as a signal of the purity of Jesus, by highlighting the evangelists' description of the tomb as new and hewn from the rock. In Origen's comments on the burial of Jesus, we see the complete transformation of the understanding of the tomb as a place of shame to a place of absolute purity, cleanliness, and newness. This is another point on the trajectory of the collective memory of Jesus' burial place in the tradition leading to the eventual designation of the place as the "holy" sepulcher, a nomenclature that persists to this day.

---

[63] Translation from Heine, *Origen on the Gospel of St. Matthew*, 762.
[64] In Greco-Roman law, see, e.g., Paulus, *Opinions* 1.21; in Jewish legal discussion of this period, see *m. Ohalot*. In the Torah, see Num 19:11–20.
[65] Moshe B. Bildstein, "Polemics against Death Defilement in Third-Century Christian Sources," in *Studia Patristica Vol. LXIII*, ed. Markus Vinzent (Leuven: Peeters, 2013), 373–84.
[66] Ibid., 380–2. See, in particular, Origen, *Homilies on Leviticus* III, 3.1, in Gary Wayne Barkley, trans., *Origen: Homilies on Leviticus*, The Fathers of the Church (Washington, DC: Catholic University of America Press, 1990), 55.
[67] Ramsay MacMullen, *The Second Church: Popular Christianity A.D. 200–400*, Writings from the Greco-Roman World Supplement Series 1 (Atlanta: Society of Biblical Literature, 2009), esp. 104–11.
[68] Translation from Henry Chadwick (trans.), *Origen: Contra Celsum* (Cambridge: Cambridge University Press, 1980), 119.

Perhaps the most significant concept for our purposes that we see in what Origen writes on the place of Jesus' burial is that the mere presence of Jesus, even his dead body, has the effect of renewal, purification, and cleansing on a place. It is important to recognize Origen's particular perspective on impurity, which he understands as the result of sin.[69] Origen does not consider the tomb to be purified and made new by being the location of the event of the resurrection. Rather, it is the presence of Jesus within it that grants these statuses. This is a step toward the establishment of Christian "holy places," a status granted to traditional sites because of the connection of the place to the events of the life of Jesus. For Christians living roughly three hundred years after the life of Jesus, it was the presence of Jesus at these places in the past that granted them their auspicious status as "holy sites" in the present. Origen goes so far as to say that everything that surrounds Jesus' body is "surpassingly great" (*Commentary on Matthew*, 143). Elsewhere, Origen writes that "it is absurd that some stones or buildings should be regarded as more pure or more impure than other stones or buildings because they have been built for the honor of God."[70] Thus, he understands that the purity of a place, its eminence, is not due to an inherent sanctity. While Origen does not refer to a *sanctity* of the tomb resulting from the presence of Jesus, the idea that the presence of Jesus renders a site or object clean, pure, and new is certainly a step toward the concept of the sanctity of sites where Jesus was present that would emerge in the fourth century.

Origen further interprets the tomb symbolically in light of the Pauline theology of baptism in Rom 6:4 in combination with the supremacy of Christ as the firstborn from the dead expressed in Col 1:18 (*Commentary on Matthew*, 143). Curiously, this leads Origen to claim that men and women were laid in the tomb after Jesus by combining citations of Rom 6:4, Col 1:18, and the evangelical references to the new tomb (Matt 27:60; John 19:41). He writes,

> Surely if no one had as yet been laid there, men and women were afterward laid there. For this is the meaning for those who consider carefully ... He who said, "We have been buried with Christ through baptism and have risen with him," has himself been after Christ buried together with Christ in a new and spiritual tomb hewn in the rock. It is the same for all who have been buried together with Christ in baptism so that they may rise with him from the new tomb of the firstborn from the dead who holds the preeminence in all things. (*Commentary on Matthew*, 143)[71]

Here again we see that the memory of Jesus' passion and the places associated with it have been strongly colored by Pauline memory and ideas. For Origen, the tomb of Christ has symbolic value as a sign of baptism and resurrection, and thus, followers

---

[69] Moshe B. Bildstein, *Purity, Community, and Ritual in Early Christianity*, Oxford Studies in the Abrahamic Religions (Oxford: Oxford University Press, 2017), 227.

[70] Origen, *Contra Celsum* IV, 59. Translation from Chadwick, *Origen: Contra Celsum*, 232.

[71] Translation from H. D. Smith, ed., *Ante-Nicene Exegesis of the Gospels*, 6 vols. (London: SPCK, 1925–9), 6: 101, reproduced in Joel C. Elowsky, ed., *John 11–21*, Ancient Christian Commentary on Scripture 4b (Downers Grove: InterVarsity Press, 2007), 335.

of Jesus can "buried" and "raised" with Jesus symbolically through baptism. On the basis of this symbolic value, Origen deduces that others were laid in the tomb after Jesus. While there is a certain historical likeliness to this idea, it is curious that the symbolic interpretation of Jesus' burial, derived primarily from Paul's thought in Rom 6:4, impacts Origen's interpretation of the actual space of the tomb. That having been said, Origen's point here is primarily theological and symbolic, and should not be pushed too far.

The Dura Europos Church Fresco

The baptistery in the third-century church at Dura Europos features a wall fresco depicting several (probably five) women carrying torches and proceeding, apparently through a door, to a large white structure. This has frequently been interpreted as a depiction of the women at the empty tomb.[72] The large white structure is interpreted as a sarcophagus. If this interpretation is correct, it is worthwhile to note that it would be a very early visual depiction and commemoration of the space of Jesus' tomb. The fact that a sarcophagus is depicted rather than the more historically and culturally accurate practice of laying the body on a burial bench prior to secondary burial of the bones in an ossuary is intriguing yet unsurprising, showing that Jesus was remembered in light of practices common in the time and culture of those doing the remembering. Moreover, this situation of the fresco within a baptistery, and thus in connection to the rite of baptism, is noteworthy, as it dovetails nicely with the image seen in Origen's writing discussed above of the parallelism between Jesus' burial and Christian baptism.

However, an alternative interpretation, which is that the fresco depicts the Parable of the Virgins, has also been proposed. Recently, proponents of this interpretation have effectively problematized the interpretation of the empty tomb interpretation of the fresco.[73] To quote Michael Peppard,

> How many women were represented originally, and how does that number line up with associated narratives? (There would have been room for one or two more figures on the northern wall.) What might the door represent, and how did they get inside? Should there not be guards or angels, or any other typical iconographic patterns of the empty tomb accounts? Why is the supposed sarcophagus so big—taller than the women? And if it is a sarcophagus, why does it still look closed if the tomb's door was already open? Isn't Christ risen and gone? Isn't that the point of a "resurrection sequence?"[74]

---

[72] E.g., William Seston, "L'Église et le baptistère de Doura-Europos," *Annales de l'École des Hautes Études de Gand* 1 (1937): 161–77; André Grabar, "La Fresque des saintes femmes au tombeau à Doura," *Cahiers Archéologiques* 8 (1956): 9–26; Carl H. Kraeling with C. Bradford Welles, *The Excavations at Dura-Europos, Final Report VIII, Part II: The Christian Building* (New Haven: Dura Europos Publications, 1967), esp. 80–8; Ann Perkins, *The Art of Dura-Europos* (Oxford: Clarendon Press, 1973).

[73] Michael Peppard, *The World's Oldest Church: Bible, Art, and Ritual at Dura-Europos, Syria*, Synkrisis (New Haven: Yale University Press, 2016), 114–154; Sanne Klaver, "The Brides of Christ: 'The Women in Procession' in the Baptistery of Dura-Europos," *Eastern Christian Art* 9 (2012–13): 63–78.

[74] Peppard, *World's Oldest Church*, 117–18.

Peppard further identifies the torches carried by the women in the fresco as the largest problem for the empty tomb interpretation, since the Synoptics depict the women arriving at dawn, while John has Mary of Magdala come to the tomb in the dark, but she does so alone.[75] Suffice it to say, the fresco of the women at Dura Europos imperfectly fits the narrative details of the Evangelists' story of the empty tomb. Peppard suggests that the "sarcophagus" may not be a sarcophagus at all and could actually be a depiction of a bridal chamber.[76] Regardless of whether or not we agree with the details of Peppard's interpretation of the fresco, we must nevertheless conclude that the empty tomb interpretation of the Dura-Europos fresco of the women in procession is problematic and should thus be treated with caution.

Interpretation of the Church of the Holy Sepulchre as Commemoration of the Burial and Resurrection of Jesus in Early Christian Writings

About three centuries after the crucifixion of Jesus, the Church of the Holy Sepulchre was consecrated. This event had a major impact on the ongoing commemoration and reception of the death, burial, and resurrection of Jesus. First, the construction of the Church *localized* the memory, anchoring it to a physical location in a way that has proven irreversible even until the present time. Second, the architecture crystallized the memory as a definitive *lieu de mémoire* and shaped it accordingly, communicating meaning and interpretation of the biblical narratives through its form. Its features became the features of the place of the death, burial, and resurrection described in the gospels. Third, it transformed what had essentially been local, vernacular memory into official, institutional memory, through the construction of an imperial monument on the place identified by local tradition as the place of the crucifixion and resurrection of Jesus, which embodied the confluence of the Easter tradition of a sect that had very recently been illicit.

In Eusebius, a high-ranking Palestinian churchman and a member of the pro-Constantinian imperial elite,[77] we have something as close to an "official" interpretation of the Church of the Holy Sepulchre from both an ecclesiastical and imperial perspective.[78] In fact, Eusebius claims to have given a discourse on the Holy Sepulchre before Constantine himself (*Life of Constantine*, 4.33) and to have spoken at the dedication of the Church of the Holy Sepulchre in Jerusalem (*Life of*

---

[75] Ibid., 118–19.
[76] Ibid., 146.
[77] Although Eusebius did not have many personal dealings with the emperor, he was apparently held in high imperial regard, so much so that he delivered the panegyric *De laudibus Constantini* at Constantine's tricennalia at the imperial palace "in the emperor's own presence" (Eusebius, *Life of Constantine*, 4.45.1). On this, see H. A. Drake, "When Was the 'De Laudibus Constantini' Delivered?" *Historia* 24, no. 2 (1975): 345–56; Cameron and Hall, *Life of Constantine*, 23, 33.
[78] On Eusebius' understanding of the relationship between the Church and the Constantinian empire in general, see James Corke-Webster, *Eusebius and Empire: Constructing Church and Rome in the Ecclesiastical History* (Cambridge: Cambridge University Press, 2019), particularly 291–301.

Constantine, 4.43–5). In Eusebius' own words, at this dedicatory celebration of the very building under discussion, he "partly explained by a written description the details of the imperial edifice, and partly endeavored to gather from the prophetic visions apt illustrations of the symbols it displayed" (*Life of Constantine*, 4.45).[79]

The speech that Eusebius delivered at the dedication of the Church of the Holy Sepulchre, *De Sepulchro Christi*, is preserved as chs. 11–18 of *De Laudibus Constantini*.[80] This auspicious event was convened by imperial order (*Life of Constantine*, 4.43), and the gathering consisted of high-ranking ecclesiastical authorities from far and wide,[81] together with an imperial escort and officers of trust from the imperial palace itself. This same assembly of church authorities (without the imperial personnel) came to Jerusalem directly from Tyre, where they were convened in council by imperial order.[82] All of this provided the original setting for the delivery of Eusebius' interpretation of the Church of the Holy Sepulchre in *De Sepulchro Christi*. We are thus justified in regarding it as an institutional interpretation, or at least, an instantiation of the official memory (in the Bodnarian sense) with which the Church of the Holy Sepulchre was imbued and which it was constructed to perpetuate and preserve in stone.

We will focus here on Eusebius' interpretation of the Church of the Holy Sepulchre and the Sepulchre itself rather than on the physical description of the architecture, since we will be discussing the architecture shortly. Eusebius had already commented on the Sepulchre of Jesus in his *Theophania*, sometime after 325 CE, shortly after the tomb had been revealed by Constantine's excavations but before the construction Church of the Holy Sepulchre had been completed.[83] In this earlier work, Eusebius writes, "It is astonishing to see even this rock, standing out erect and alone in a level land, and having only one cavern within it; lest, had there been many, the miracle of him who overcame death should have been obscured" (*Theoph.*, 3.61).[84] Here, Eusebius appears to be struck by the simplicity of the tomb, particularly its singular cavern.[85]

Eusebius' comments in the *Theophania* on the uncomplicated nature of the single-chambered tomb stand in stark contrast to his later understanding of this very same place seen in *De Sepulchro Christi* and *Life of Constantine*, both of which were composed shortly after the completion of the construction of the Constantinian church.[86] Both of these works provide valuable insight into the inside of the event of the building of the

---

[79] Translation from Richardson, *Life of Constantine*, 552.
[80] As argued and maintained throughout H. A. Drake, *In Praise of Constantine: A Historical Study and New Translation of Eusebius' Tricennial Orations*, Classical Studies 15 (Berkeley: University of California Publications, 1976). See also (e.g.) Drake, "When Was the 'De Laudibus Constantini' Delivered?" 346, 352; Johannes Quasten, *Patrology*, vol. 3 (Allen: Christian Classics, 1983), 326–7.
[81] In order to illustrate the breadth of geographical representation at this event, Eusebius specifically mentions ecclesiastical authorities from Macedonia, Pannonia, Moesia, Persia, Bithynia, Thrace, Cilicia, Cappadocia, Mesopotamia, Phoenicia, Arabia, Palestine, Egypt, Libya, and the Thebaid (*Life of Constantine*, 4.43).
[82] *Life of Constantine*, 4.41–2.
[83] Cf. Walker, *Holy City*, 273.
[84] Translation from Samuel Lee, *Eusebius on the Theophaneia* (Cambridge: Cambridge University Press, 1843).
[85] Cf. Walker, *Holy City*, 273.
[86] On the dates, see Averil Cameron and Stuart G. Hall, *Life of Constantine*, Clarendon Ancient History Series (Oxford: Clarendon Press, 1999), 9–12.

Church of the Holy Sepulchre and into the theological intentions that undergirded the laying of its stones.

In *De Sepulchro Christi*, Eusebius describes the Constantian complex of the Church of the Holy Sepulchre as "houses of prayer and hallowed temples" (προσευκτηρίων οἴκοις καὶ ναῶν ἀφιερώσασιν),[87] which Constantine has "raised as trophies of his [the Savior's] victory over death," "lofty and noble structures, imperial monuments of an imperial spirit, which thou hast erected in honor of the everlasting memory of the Savior's tomb" (*Laud. Const.* 11.2).[88] There is much to unpack in the words that Eusebius uses to designate the Church of the Holy Sepulchre here. We have a come a long way from his earlier description of the unadorned, freestanding burial "cave" discussed in *Theophania*, and further still from the apparently shameful burial of the Markan narrative. The place of Jesus' burial has been transformed into a complex of sacred buildings, the sanctity of which Eusebius clearly indicates by describing them as ναῶν ἀφιερώσασιν ("hallowed temples").

The purpose of these buildings is, first and foremost, explicitly commemorative. The complex is a "memorial" (μνῆμά, cf. *Laud. Const.* 9.16), meant as a *tropaion* ("trophies;" *Laud. Const.* 11.2; 18.1) to commemorate Jesus' victory over death. Walker has highlighted Eusebius' tendency to place emphasis on Jesus' resurrection rather than on his crucifixion, and thus on the Sepulchre rather than Golgotha,[89] and to understand the Sepulchre "not so much as the place of Christ's burial, but instead as the scene of the Resurrection, and as the particular place where the universal presence of Christ had been unleashed into the world and out own immortality assured."[90] Thus, as Eusebius conceived of it, the Church of the Holy Sepulchre was not so much a monument to the life of Jesus of Nazareth as it was to the risen Lord, the Savior through whom salvation was made possible. For Eusebius, the victory of the Easter event not only colors but also fully encompasses the collective memory of Jesus that had crystallized around the place of his burial. Thus, the Constantinian buildings at the site of Jesus' tomb are monuments of immortal life and his heavenly kingdom (*Laud. Const.* 18.1).[91]

In *De Sepulchro Christi*, Eusebius emphasizes the imperial nature of the Church of the Holy Sepulchre. He compares the construction of the commemorative buildings to ascribing victory and triumph to the Word of God "with imperial characters" (βασιλικοῖς χαρακτῆρσιν; *Laud. Const.* 18.1). They are "βασιλικῆς διανοίας βασιλικὰ μεγαλουργήματα" (*Laud. Const.* 11.2). Richardson renders this as "imperial monuments of an imperial spirit," which captures the emphasis that Eusebius places here on the fact that they are explicitly imperial constructions, conceived from the imperial mind, whose royal grandeur is underscored by his use of the term "μεγαλουργήματα," which indicates the incredible magnificence of the structures.

---

[87] Translation of these designations is my own. In NPNF, Richardson renders this "hallowed edifices and consecrated temples" (see the next note below for reference).
[88] Translation from Richardson, *Life of Constantine*, 595.
[89] Walker, *Holy City*, 252–7.
[90] Ibid., 281.
[91] Cf. Shalev-Hurvitz, *Holy Sites Encircled*, 61.

Given the explicitly imperial nature of the buildings and of the event of their dedication, it would seem as though the Church of the Holy Sepulchre was, in Eusebius' understanding, a monument to the saving power of the risen Lord, but it was also a testament to the greatness of the emperor who had built it and who had himself come to recognize the power of the one to whom the edifice was dedicated. It is not a coincidence that the dedication of the Church of the Holy Sepulchre coincided with the celebration of Constantine's tricennalia. As Eusebius informs us, Constantine "judged the festival of his tricennalia to be a fit occasion for thanksgiving to the Sovereign Lord of all, at the same time believing that the dedication of the church which his zealous magnificence had erected at Jerusalem might advantageously be performed" (*Life of Constantine*, 4.40.1).[92]

In his study of fourth-century martyr shrines, Nathaniel Morehouse demonstrates the importance of martyr shrines as locations where "powerful Christians exerted their control over the construction of Christian memory," observing that speech acts performed at such sites carried more weight and that the monumental nature of the shrines gave them and the builders of the shrines "tremendous authority, and the power to craft memory around these sites."[93] The Church of the Holy Sepulchre differed somewhat from typical martyr shrines insofar as (1) the body of Jesus was not located in his tomb, for "he is not here, he is risen" (Matt 28:6); and (2) as the divine son of God, Jesus was naturally much more significant to the early Christian mind than a typical martyr. That having been said, there is little doubt that what Morehouse says here about martyr shrines as places where the powerful, through the construction of monuments or through speech acts, could shape Christian memory of the past, could be applied to the Church of the Holy Sepulchre. Morehouse argues that Constantine was able to speak on behalf of the martyrs by crafting architecture around them, buildings that were erected "to elicit a specific response in those who were living when they were created, but also with an eye toward future generations who would come there to worship."[94] This granted Constantine great political and mnemonic power within the church. How much more could the same be said for the act of the construction of an imperial monument around the place where the divine savior of the world was resurrected, where death itself was defeated? There is a very real sense in which the Church of the Holy Sepulchre was as much a monument to Constantine's memory as it was to that of Jesus. Thus, in the Church of the Holy Sepulchre, the memory of Jesus is mediated and colored by the imperial power of Constantine.

In the Shadow of Nicaea

The literary and historical contexts of Eusebius' discussion of the Church of the Holy Sepulchre in *Life of Constantine* is important to consider. Eusebius places his discussion of the search for the tomb of Jesus and Constantine's order to construct

---

[92] Translation from Richardson, *Life of Constantine*, 550.
[93] Nathaniel J. Morehouse, *Death's Dominion: Power, Identity, and Memory at the Fourth-Century Martyr Shrine*, Studies in Ancient Religion and Culture (Sheffield: Equinox, 2016), 54–5.
[94] Ibid., 55.

the Church of the Holy Sepulchre immediately after his discussion of the Council of Nicaea.[95] This order likely reflects the progress of historical events, since the Council of Nicaea took place in 325, and the work on the traditional site of Jesus' burial began shortly after, beginning with the destruction of the Temple of Venus that lay on the site, in 325–6.[96] It is also worth observing that the Council of Nicaea, itself called by the emperor, as well as the beginning of the work toward the construction of the Church of the Holy Sepulchre shortly thereafter, coincide with Constantine's vicennalia in 325, which is all the more interesting given that the dedication of the Church of the Holy Sepulchre coincides directly with his tricennalia celebration in 335. Thus, there are major imperial events that bookend and mark the process of the construction of what would become Palestine's premiere Christian holy site for centuries to come.

It is probably not mere coincidence that the Church of the Holy Sepulchre, the first of the commemorative churches in Roman Palestine dedicated to the memory of the events of the life of Jesus, was commissioned and constructed following the Council of Nicaea. Shalev-Hurvitz has pointed to several issues discussed at Nicaea that likely influenced or inspired an interest in sites connected to the life of Jesus: (1) the discussion of nature of Jesus, including his death, resurrection, and ascension; (2) the fixing of the date of Easter; and (3) the recognition in Canon 7 of the special honors granted to the see of Jerusalem (Aelia).[97] Moreover, given that the Nicene Creed of 325 also includes statements of belief in the incarnation and ascension, it is perhaps no surprise that the Holy Sepulchre was shortly followed by the Church of the Nativity and the Eleona on the Mount of Olives.[98] The Church of the Holy Sepulchre, which enshrines in a sacred space of worship and divine liturgy the places of Jesus' crucifixion and resurrection, the sites of his suffering as well as his victory, can be understood as a physical, visual, architectural crystallization of the premises of Nicene Christianity.

The Interpretation of the Church of the Holy Sepulchre in Eusebius' Life of Constantine

Eusebius writes that Constantine "gave orders for a place of worship to be constructed, conceiving this idea not without God, but with his spirit moved by the Savior himself" (*Life of Constantine*, 3.25).[99] Eusebius considered the conception of the Church of the Holy Sepulchre to be divinely inspired.[100] We should note that this is comparable, though admittedly not identical, to his understanding of the inspiration of prophetic Scripture by the Spirit, either delivered plainly or communicated through symbols and

---

[95] As noted by Shalev-Hurvitz, *Holy Sites Encircled*, 50.
[96] See, e.g., Charles Coüasnon, *The Church of the Holy Sepulchre in Jerusalem*, trans. John-Paul Beverley and Claude Ross (New York: Oxford University Press, 1974), 14; Gibson and Taylor, *Beneath the Church*, 73; Murphy-O'Connor, *Keys to Jerusalem*, 162. O'Connor thinks it likely that work at the site began *before* Helena's journey in 326–7.
[97] Shalev Hurvitz, *Holy Sites Encircled*, 51.
[98] As per discussion of the Eleona elsewhere in this work, I am convinced by the hypothesis advanced by Shalev-Hurvitz that the Eleona is connected to the Imbomon and thus by association to the commemoration of Jesus' ascension (ibid., 101–2).
[99] Translation from Cameron and Hall, *Life of Constantine*, 132.
[100] Cf. ibid., 275.

circumstances to the human author.[101] To Eusebius, the Church of the Holy Sepulchre went beyond being sacred space. It was divinely inspired sacred space, an instantiation of the confluence of the wills of God and the emperor.

The aim of the church, in Eusebius' understanding, is to make the "blessed site" of "the Savior's resurrection" universally famous and renowned. The architecture of the church was a divinely inspired sign bearing witness to the identity of Jesus as the Savior and to the truth of his resurrection. Robert L. Wilken compares Eusebius' discussion of the life-of-Jesus commemorative churches built by Constantine to the book of signs in the Fourth Gospel, though he writes that "unlike the signs in the Gospel of John, which were miracles, those in Eusebius' book are *places*."[102]

Eusebius views the excavation and recovery of the tomb as a representation of the Savior's resurrection (*Life of Constantine*, 3.28), and this "resurrection" of the tomb is accomplished by Constantine's demolition and clearing away of the temple of Venus (Aphrodite). The excavation of the tomb thus not only reflects the resurrection of Jesus but also symbolizes the ultimate triumph of Christianity over paganism. Eusebius claims that the temple of Venus was intentionally built on top of the place of Jesus' burial in order to "hide the truth" (*Life of Constantine*, 3.26.2), which they accomplished by burying the tomb under "foul pollutions" (*Life of Constantine*, 3.26.3).

It is important to note the language of impurity present in Eusebius' discussion of the temple of Venus.[103] The aspects of impurity and purification in his account appear to be mostly rhetorical. Since the Hadrianic temple to Venus was impure, tantamount to "foul pollutions," Eusebius claims that Constantine had the remains removed far away. The rationale for this was, according to Eusebius, explicitly related to purity, and was determined by Constantine "under divine inspiration" (*Life of Constantine* 3.27). However, this claim cannot be entirely true, since archaeological investigation has determined that Hadrianic elements were reused in the Constantinian building.[104] One of the central premises of social memory theory is that the past is remembered in light of the present. This is certainly operative here. Eusebius presents the building of the Church of the Holy Sepulchre, a monument dedicated to the memory of the death and resurrection of Jesus, in light of the triumph of Christianity over paganism. Thus, just as Jesus triumphed over death by rising from the rock-cut tomb, so too does the Holy Sepulchre triumph over paganism by rising from the "tomb of souls" of the pagan temple.

Eusebius understood the Sepulchre itself, meaning the remains of the rock-cut tomb identified as the tomb of Jesus, to be a witness (Greek *martyrion*),[105] "testifying by facts louder than any voice to the resurrection of the Savior" (*Life of Constantine*, 3.28). This

---

[101] See the opening preface of Eusebius, *Commentary on Isaiah*. On Eusebius' concept of prophetic inspiration, see Jonathan J. Armstrong, "Translator's Introduction," in *Eusebius of Caesarea: Commentary on Isaiah*, ed. Joel C. Elowsky, Ancient Christian Texts (Downers Grove: IVP Academic, 2013), xxvii–xxix.

[102] Robert L. Wilken, *The Land Called Holy: Palestine in Christian History and Thought* (New Haven: Yale University Press, 1992), 90.

[103] Cf. the observations of ibid., 89; Cameron and Hall, *Life of Constantine*, 275.

[104] Gibson and Taylor, *Beneath the Church*, 67–8; cf. Cameron and Hall, *Life of Constantine*, 279.

[105] The use of *martyrion* here should be taken to refer to the function of the tomb as a "witness," not as a reference to the architectural form of a *martyrium*. Cf. Cameron and Hall, *Life of Constantine*, 281.

is a remarkably strong statement to the effect that the tomb is the strongest possible witness to the resurrection of Jesus. Presumably, this is because, unlike testimony that can be received through oral delivery or text, the tomb could be experienced through the senses, a remnant of the biblical past that could be seen and touched in the present. However, this "witness" would only be able to "testify" when combined with the gospel narratives of the passion events. Hence, we are reminded of Egeria's description of the Scripture readings, including gospel passages from the passion narrative, which took place in the courtyard between the Cross and the Anastasis (where the tomb was located) in the Church of the Holy Sepulchre.[106] Thus, it is through the scriptural narratives that the commemorative site was given meaning.

Because Eusebius does not explain why he considers the tomb to be testimony (Greek *martyrion*) to the resurrection, it is sometimes suggested that there was something about the tomb that could have been taken as proof of its authenticity, such as graffiti.[107] While it is not unlikely that the tomb contained graffiti, recourse to a hypothetical explanation is unnecessary. The simple fact that an authentic Jewish rock-cut tomb from the first century emerged from the ground precisely where Constantine's workmen had been directed to dig, in the vicinity of the place where Eusebius knew that Golgotha was located (*Onomasticon*, 74), combined with his belief that Constantine was guided by the Holy Spirit was probably enough to convince him of the site's authenticity.

Notably, in the letter from Constantine to Macarius that Eusebius includes in *Life of Constantine* (3.30-2), Constantine refers to the tomb as "evidence [Greek *gnorisma*] of [Jesus'] most sacred passion" (3.30.1). Whether or not this letter actually comes from the pen of Constantine, it is clear in both passages that the rock-cut tomb itself was considered to be proof of the gospel events. However, while Eusebius presents the tomb as a witness of Jesus' resurrection, the letter from Constantine to Macarius regards it as evidence of Jesus' passion. As discussed above, Eusebius may have had some aversion to speaking of the crucifixion, preferring to comment on the resurrection.[108] This, however, appears to have been particular to Eusebius' theology, and so we should imagine that the tomb functioned for most Christians who experienced it as a *lieu de mémoire* of the passion in general, including both the death and resurrection of Jesus. Indeed, as Taylor writes, "there is good reason to believe that Eusebius' emphasis on the tomb gives an unbalanced picture of what Constantine considered important on Golgotha."[109] This stands to reason since, as a tomb, it was place of the burial of Jesus' body as well as of his resurrection as per the canonical gospel accounts.

---

[106] *Itin. Eger.* 37.4–7.
[107] E.g., Rainer Riesner, "Golgota und die Archäologie," *Bible und Kirche* 40 (1985): 21–6; Biddle, *Tomb of Christ*, 66; Murphy-O'Connor, *Keys to Jerusalem*, 176. Although it is not mentioned and probably not accepted by Eusebius, others suggest that the discovery of the True Cross at the site of the tomb may have strengthened this identification of the site. See, e.g., Ze'ev Rubin, "The Church of the Holy Sepulchre and the Conflict between the Sees of Caesarea and Jerusalem," in *The Jerusalem Cathedra*, ed. Lee Levine (Jerusalem: Yad Izhak Ben-Zvi, 1982), 79–99; Walker, *Holy City*, 244–6.
[108] Cf. Walker, *Holy City*, 251–60.
[109] Taylor, *Christians and the Holy Places*, 137.

Eusebius ascribes a high level of sanctity to the tomb itself, not just to the monumental church constructed around it. It was, in his eyes, a truly holy site. Consider his interpretation of the event of the finding of the tomb in 325 CE: "at last against all expectation the revered and all-hallowed Testimony (*martyrion*) of the Savior's resurrection was itself revealed, and the cave, the holy of holies, took on the appearance of a representation of the Savior's return to life" (*Life of Constantine*, 3.28). The Jesus remembered here was, for Eusebius, the Christ of faith, the resurrected Lord, the divine Son of God. Thus, the place is holy in itself, as people, the Church, and Scripture had been called holy prior to the discovery of this site.[110] It is holy not only because it is where Jesus was raised but also because it bears witness to the truth of the gospel accounts by virtue of the fact that the rock-cut tomb discovered in the Constantinian excavations was understood to be the very same place described in the gospels, and thus the place was itself a participant in the canonical narrative of the life of Jesus. Thus, the place of a dishonorable burial had become the new Holy of Holies.

The idea of the tomb as the Holy of Holies should be understood in relation to the conception of Jerusalem and its temple as the center of the world, with the city itself being divided into concentric circles of increasing holiness radiating out from the Holy of Holies and the various courts of the temple complex.[111] That Eusebius should identify the tomb of Jesus as the Holy of Holies resites and reorients this tradition. If the tomb of Jesus is the new Holy of Holies, then the complex of the Church of the Holy Sepulchre would be the new temple courts. The supersessionist ideology that lies behind this reorientation cannot be overlooked, as it fits in with the Christianization of Jerusalem and its Jewish heritage in the fourth century.[112] Indeed, by the time that the Madaba Map was created in the sixth century CE, the temple mount had been so overshadowed by the Christian monumental architecture of Jerusalem in the minds of local Christians that it is conspicuously absent from the map despite its obvious topographical prominence within the city and its historical significance for both the Jewish and Christian traditions.[113] Indeed, the temple mount would remain unadorned by monumental commemorative architecture until the Islamic conquest,[114] perhaps conspicuously so given its prominence in the gospel narratives and in broader biblical history.

---

[110] Cf. Robert L Wilken, "Eusebius and the Christian Holy Land," in *Eusebius, Christianity, and Judaism*, ed. Harold W. Attridge and Gohei Hata (Detroit: Wayne State University Press, 1992), 736–55 (743).

[111] Cf. ibid., 748–9. On Jerusalem as the center of the world in early Judaism and early Christianity, see Alexander, "Jerusalem as the *Omphalos*," 147–53.

[112] See, e.g., Oded Irshai, "The Christian Appropriation of Jerusalem in the Fourth Century: The Case of the Bordeaux Pilgrim," *Jewish Quarterly Review* 99, no. 4 (2009): 465–86; Andrew S. Jacobs, *The Remains of the Jews: The Holy Land and Christian Empire* (Stanford: Stanford University Press, 2004), 139–99; Ora Limor, "Reading Sacred Space: Egeria, Paula,and the Christian Holy Land," in *De Sion exibit lex et verbum domini de Hierusalem*: *Essays on Medieval Law, Liturgy, and Literature in Honour of Amnon Linder*, ed. Yitzhak Hen, Cultural Encounters in Late Antiquity and the Middle Ages 1 (Turnhout: Brepols, 2001), 1–15.

[113] Cf. Jacob, *Remains of the Jews*, 140–1.

[114] On this and on the relationship of the Dome of the Rock to the early Christian commemorative churches, see Shalev-Hurvitz, *Holy Sites Encircled*, 297–300, 303–7.

Immediately prior to describing the monument that Constantine built at the tomb, Eusebius describes the tomb itself: "a tomb full of agelong memory, comprising the trophies of the great Savior's defeat of death, a tomb of divine presence, where once an angel, radiant with light, proclaimed to all the good news of the rebirth demonstrated by the Savior" (*Life of Constantine*, 3.33.3).[115] Eusebius himself regards the tomb as a place imbued with memory of Jesus, though not in the same manner as modern historians. To him, the memory of Jesus presented by the tomb was thoroughly colored by the theology and Christology of the Church.

Three theological concepts are present in this interpretation of the tomb. First, the concept of the defeat of death that the tomb represents. This concept is not explicit in the gospel narratives of the Easter event but is a feature of Paul's discussion of resurrection (1 Cor 15:12–57, esp. vv. 54–57). Again, we see that the Easter event, including both the death of Jesus and the empty tomb, was remembered through the lens of Pauline literature. Second, the concept of the divine presence within the tomb. Eusebius understands the tomb as a place where a theophany occurred, apparently not because of the presumed presence of the risen Lord within it, but because of the angelic apparition at the tomb narrated in the gospels (Mark 16:5–7; Matt 28:2–7; Luke 24:4–7; John 20:12–13). Whether or not Eusebius is strictly correct in equating an angelic apparition with the divine presence, the imagery of the tomb as being filled with the divine presence is striking and certainly furthers and supports his designation of the tomb as the Holy of Holies. Third, Eusebius expresses the idea that the Savior's resurrection demonstrates "the good news of the rebirth," that is, the general resurrection. This concept, that Jesus' resurrection signifies or demonstrates the general resurrection, comes from Pauline literature (1 Cor 15:12–23; 1 Thess 4:14; Rom 8:11; cf. Col 1:18). Again, we see Pauline literature coloring the memory of the Easter event as it was instantiated in the place of the traditional site of Jesus' tomb.

We move now from Eusebius' understanding of the actual rock-cut tomb to his interpretation of the monument built by imperial decree around it and upon the traditional site of Golgotha. We will treat the architecture and the meaning conveyed by it in the next chapter. For now, we will focus on how Eusebius interpreted the imperial monument which was dedicated to the memory of Jesus of Nazareth about three centuries after his crucifixion.

Eusebius interprets the monumental church prior to describing it. He writes,

> New Jerusalem was built at the very Testimony to the Savior, facing the famous Jerusalem of old, which after the bloody murder of the Lord had been overthrown in utter devastation, and paid the penalty of its wicked inhabitants. Opposite this then the Emperor erected the victory of the Savior over death with rich and abundant munificence, this being perhaps that fresh new Jerusalem proclaimed in

---

[115] The referent of μνῆμα (translated here as "tomb" by Cameron and Hall) is not entirely clear. I take it to refer to the rock-cut tomb itself, not to the Constantinian monument (the edicule) constructed upon it, though my interpretation of Eusebius does not depend on this one way or the other. See, however, Cameron and Hall, *Life of Constantine*, 289. On the rock-cut tomb and how it was contained within the Constantinian edicule, see Biddle, *Tomb of Christ*, 65–71.

prophetic oracles, about which long speeches recite innumerable praises as they utter words of divine inspiration. (*Life of Constantine*, 3.33.1–2)

This is an extraordinary interpretation of the Church of the Holy Sepulchre and provides us with insight into the meaning and rhetorical function that the commemorative site of Jesus' death and resurrection was imbued with. We have already discussed above how the Church of the Holy Sepulchre replaced a pagan temple and could have thus been interpreted as a sign of the victory of Christianity over paganism. Here, Eusebius envisions it in opposition to the Jerusalem of old, which is to say, Jewish Jerusalem and particularly its temple. The Church of the Holy Sepulchre faced the Temple Mount and was literally opposite the Temple Mount, as Eusebius writes.[116] According to Shalev-Hurvitz, "The New Jerusalem took over the site of the Temple of Venus but remained in clear opposition, topographically and ideologically, to the Jewish Temple."[117]

Both Egeria and Eusebius describe the Constantinian Church of the Holy Sepulchre as an astoundingly lavish building. Both describe gold, silver, and marble involved in the construction. To take just one excerpt from Eusebius' lush description of the structure, "Its interior was covered with slabs of varied marble ... the interior of the structure was fitted with carved coffers and like a vast sea spread out by a series of joints binding to each other through the whole royal house, and being beautified throughout with brilliant gold made the whole shrine glitter with beams of light" (*Life of Constantine*, 3.36). Similarly, Egeria describes the architectural decoration of the building as "adorned with gold, mosaic, and precious marble" (*Itin. Eger.* 25.9). Moreover, she comments on the lavish material adornment of the spaces of the Holy Sepulchre complex as well as the Church of the Nativity on a festival day: "you see there nothing other than gold and jewels and silk ... All kinds of vessels of gold and jewels are brought out that day" (*Itin. Eger.* 25.8). Both Eusebius and Egeria describe the Church of the Holy Sepulchre in language befitting a temple, calling to mind the biblical descriptions of the Jerusalem Temple (e.g., 1 Kgs 6–7). This comparison is clearly intended by Eusebius, with his designation of the tomb of Jesus as the "holy of holies" and of the whole complex as the "new Jerusalem."

According to Margaret Baker, the construction of the new Christian temple, the Church of the Holy Sepulchre, "was a conscious attempt to restore the original temple, not to replace the temple destroyed by the Romans."[118] The notion that the Church of the Holy Sepulchre may have been a conscious attempt to restore the original temple is astute, but if I may make a friendly amendment, Eusebius at least seems to have understood this new building as a supersession and ideological opponent of the ruined Second Temple. It is doubtful, however, that Constantine himself understood it this way, since, as E. D. Hunt has shown, Constantine's "new Jerusalem" owed its existence to the political and religious ideology of the new Christian government rather than

---

[116] On this, see Shalev-Hurvitz, *Holy Sites Encircled*, 62.
[117] Ibid.
[118] Margaret Baker, "Jerusalem the Golden: Vision and Memory of the Church," *Journal for the Study of the Christian Church* 5, no. 1 (2005): 1–10 (8).

to anti-Jewish polemic.[119] Constantine seems to have been sensitive enough to Jewish concerns to have refrained from any known Christian building projects on the Temple Mount, although the image of the barren Temple Mount was itself a powerful symbol that could be leveraged for anti-Jewish purposes. However, in the mind of Eusebius, not only had Christianity inherited Rome, but it had also inherited Jerusalem.

It is likely that by drawing explicit parallels to the Jerusalem Temple, Eusebius was drawing out something that was intended in the construction of the Church of the Holy Sepulchre. As Wilkinson's studies of its floor plan have demonstrated, the Constantinian Church of the Holy Sepulchre and the other Constantinian commemorative churches dedicated to the life of Jesus at the Mount of Olives and Bethlehem were built on the plan of Ezekiel's vision of the heavenly temple described in Ezek 40.[120] This is a significant instance of reception in itself. For the place where Jesus was crucified and buried to become the focal point of a new Christian temple built on the biblical plan of the heavenly temple communicates, in semiotic fashion through the iconography of its architecture, Jesus' giving of himself as sacrifice in the heavenly temple. That is to say, the Church of the Holy Sepulchre instantiates the tradition of Jesus as the Great High Priest of the heavenly Temple from Heb 9:1–10:18 in architectural form.

According to the author of Hebrews, the heavenly temple is superior to the earthly temple in Jerusalem, insofar as the earthly temple is "a sanctuary made by human hands, a mere copy of the true one" (Heb 9:24). This New Testament concept of the superiority of the heavenly temple over the Jerusalem Temple is invoked by Eusebius in his comparison of the "New" and "Old" Jerusalems. In his *Commentary on Isaiah*, which was probably written after the dedication of the Church of the Holy Sepulchre,[121] Eusebius frequently discusses the concept of the heavenly Jerusalem in relation to Heb 12:22, which is the most cited biblical verse in that commentary.[122] It is thus clear that Eusebius was well aware of the presentation and understanding of Jerusalem and its relation to the Christian faith in Hebrews. It is not a stretch to think that this scriptural tradition may have informed his own presentation of the Church of the Holy Sepulchre as the "New Jerusalem."

There is an unmistakable measure of anti-Judaism in Eusebius' presentation of the Church of the Holy Sepulchre as the "New Jerusalem." The point of his polemic appears to be that, as Cameron and Hall put the matter, "a 'new' Christian 'Jerusalem' had now been built to excel the old Jerusalem, the city of the Jews, which had been destroyed,"[123] a common point in Christian polemic probably made for the first time here.[124] Moreover,

---

[119] E. D. Hunt, "Constantine and Jerusalem," *Journal of Ecclesiastical History* 48, no. 3 (1997): 405–24 (423).

[120] John Wilkinson, "Constantinian Churches in Palestine," in *Ancient Churches Revealed*, ed. Yoram Tsafrir (Jerusalem: Israel Exploration, 1993), 23–7; Wilkinson, *Egeria's Travels*, 62–4. Baker states, "The proportions of the Church of the Resurrection were those of the temple" ("Jerusalem the Golden," 8) in reference to the First Temple, citing Wilkinson, but this is not quite correct. It is the heavenly temple, not the Jerusalem temple that was the inspiration for the Constantinian commemorative churches.

[121] On the date of this text, see Armstrong, "Translator's Introduction," xxi–xxv.

[122] Cf. M. J. Hollerich, *Eusebius of Caesarea's Commentary on Isaiah*, Oxford Early Christian Studies (Oxford: Clarendon Press, 1999), 174.

[123] Cameron and Hall, *Life of Constantine*, 284.

[124] Cf. ibid.

Eusebius presents the destruction of "old" Jerusalem as a penalty paid by its "wicked inhabitants" for the "bloody murder" of Jesus (*Life of Constantine*, 3.33.1). Notably but unsurprisingly, Eusebius makes no mention of the Roman involvement in the death of Jesus. The memory of the death of Jesus and its commemoration instantiated in the Church of the Holy Sepulchre are thus employed in service of anti-Judaism conjoined with a pro-Constantinianism. There may be some significance to this for the study of Jewish-Christian relations in antiquity, insofar as a genuine Jewish burial site that may have been the final resting of Jesus or other first-century Jews had been appropriated as the focal point of a Christian monument, which was interpreted as a sign of the triumph of Christianity over Judaism.

Eusebius claims an eschatological significance for the newly constructed Church of the Holy Sepulchre. It is not merely *like* the eschatological New Jerusalem described in Christian Scripture. Eusebius suggests that it *is* the eschatological New Jerusalem, the very one "proclaimed in prophetic oracles" (*Life of Constantine*, 3.33.2). The Church of the Holy Sepulchre was thus an eschatological reality, realized in his own day.[125]

The irony of the dishonorable burial place of a man executed by Roman imperial power being transformed into an imperial monument dedicated on the occasion of an emperor's tricennalia is palpable. Prior to Constantine's involvement with the site, the area of Golgotha, including the tomb, were *lieux de mémoire* of the vernacular variety, both in the collective conception of the place and in the actual, physical site itself. The fact that the identification of the place itself prior to Constantine and the origins of the traditions attached to it are so obscure is, in my opinion, an indication of the vernacular character of the early Christian memory associated with these places. These memories are certainly non-state, and although they come down to us from church elites, the discussion in the previous chapter has certainly shown that the church elites who preserved these memories in writing appear to be reporting common traditions rather than imposing official narratives on the collective memory. Writing as early as the final decade of the third century, Eusebius' description in his *Onomasticon* of Golgotha, a place imbued with the memory of a man crucified by imperial soldiers able to be pointed out in Roman Aelia Capitolina in the precincts of an imperial temple dedicated to the Roman deity Venus, is an antithesis of official memory. Yet, just a few decades later, the same place had been thoroughly absorbed into an imperial monument.

Eusebius was certainly not blindly pro-imperial, but rather, he aimed to show that Christians were the heirs of the Roman Empire, and best suited to run it.[126] Nor was Eusebius "Constantine's man."[127] However, the Church of the Holy Sepulchre was Constantine's building, and Eusebius' interpretation of it reflects this. So closely was it attached to Constantine's memory as it to that of Jesus that, decades after Constantine had died, Egeria refers to the buildings of the complex as the church that Constantine built (*Itin. Eger.* 25.1, 6, 9).[128] The memory of Constantine's connection to the place of

---

[125] Cf. Hollerich, *Commentary on Isaiah*, 196–7.
[126] Cf. Corke-Webster, *Eusebius and Empire*, 292. On Eusebius' nuanced attitude toward Rome in general, see especially pp. 249–79 of the same work.
[127] Cf. ibid., 291.
[128] On this, see Shalev-Hurvitz, *Holy Sites Encircled*, 70–1.

Jesus' crucifixion and burial would become firmly fixed in Christian collective memory for centuries to come.[129]

Memory of Jesus in Pilgrim Experiences of the Space of the Holy Sepulchre

Authors such as Eusebius and Cyril present us with visions of the *lieu de mémoire* of Jesus' tomb that stem from the upper echelons of the religious and political elite. However, it is just as important to consider the experiences of the common pilgrims and faithful who would have encountered this same site of memory. In order to complete our picture of the memory instantiated at this place, we may consider the earliest accounts of pilgrimage to the Church of the Holy Sepulchre from the fourth century CE. The texts that are preserved are, most likely by virtue of the privilege of literacy or proximity to an author of significance, mostly the products of privilege in one sense or another: the Bordeaux Pilgrim was respected enough to travel in the official coaches of the *cursus publicus*,[130] and Paula was a noble from a senatorial family in Rome.[131] Egeria is a different matter. Though she is able to afford travel, as well as to read and write, there are no clear indications in her writings that she had a particularly high socioeconomic status,[132] and she writes with a level of Latin that likely represents the education of a middle-class person rather than an aristocrat.[133] Regardless of the status of these figures, their experiences reflect those of the faithful who have come to experience the holy sites, and we may extrapolate what common experiences of these places were like from these recorded experiences. Certainly, they are unlike the theological and rhetorical works of Eusebius and Cyril in that they simply reflect the genuine religious experiences of fourth-century pilgrims. We will focus here on their experiences of the Anastasis and Aedicule.

A detailed account of the typical weekly liturgy on the Lord's day at the Anastasis comes from Egeria (*Itin. Eger.* 24.1–12). Egeria tells us that the service begins with the bishop going into the tomb. After three psalms and prayers, just before a gospel account of the resurrection is read by the bishop at the tomb, "censers are brought into the cave of the Anastasis [the aedicule], so that the whole Anastasis basilica is filled with the smell" (*Itin. Eger.* 24.10). Notably, this is among the earliest attestations of the use of incense in Christian worship. Given that Egeria does not mention the

---

[129] E.g., in sources prior to the Crusades: Eucherius, *Letter to Faustus the Island Presbyter*, 5–6 (in Wilkinson, *Jerusalem Pilgrims*, 94); Adomnan, *Holy Places*, 1.6.1 (in Wilkinson, *Jerusalem Pilgrims*, 173–4); Epiphanius the Monk, *The Holy City and the Holy Places*, 3–4 (in Wilkinson, *Jerusalem Pilgrims*, 208); Bede, *On the Holy Places*, 2.1 (in Wilkinson, *Jerusalem Pilgrims*, 217); Bernard the Monk, *A Journey to the Holy Places and Babylon*, 314 (in Wilkinson, *Jerusalem Pilgrims*, 266).
[130] Cf. Wilkinson, *Egeria's Travels*, 22.
[131] Jerome, *Epist.* 108.1. On Paula's status and early life, see Andrew Cain, *Jerome's Epitaph on Paula: A Commentary on the Epitaphum Sanctae Paulae*, Oxford Early Christian Texts (Oxford: Oxford University Press, 2013), 1–4.
[132] Cf. McGowan and Bradshaw, *Pilgrimage of Egeria*, 12.
[133] Cf. Higath Sivan, "Who Was Egeria? Piety and Pilgrimage in the Age of Gratian," *Harvard Theological Review* 81 (1988): 59–72 (66–7); McGowan and Bradshaw, *Pilgrimage of Egeria*, 13.

use of incense in connection with any other time or place,[134] its connection with the site of Jesus' burial and with the public reading of the resurrection account is curious. It has been suggested that this practice is meant to be a representation of the spices brought by the women at the tomb with which to anoint Jesus' body (Mark 16:1; Luke 23:56, 24:1),[135] though others have been skeptical of this interpretation.[136] Although Egeria does not make a connection to the spices for anointing explicit, it is clear from later artistic and literary evidence that the use of incense at the Aedicule explicitly came to be understood in this way.[137] Ally Kateusz notes depictions from the sixth to the seventh centuries especially common on pewter pilgrim ampules of two women, identified as the two Marys, carrying a censer and walking toward the Aedicule, "as if about to enter the shrine and cense the tomb with incense,"[138] and that the Typikon (ninth to tenth century CE) specified that it was women who performed the censing at the Aedicule.[139] Closer in time to Egeria's day, the fifth-century palimpsest text of the "Six Books" Dormitian apocryphon depicts Mary carrying and using a censer at the tomb of Jesus for the spices that she had brought, which Kateusz reasonably suggests may reflect the practice of the use of censers by women at the Aedicule in Jerusalem, and that Egeria may provide an early witness to this tradition.[140] Although the gender of the people carrying the censers is not explicit, the fact that later tradition casts them as women suggests but does not prove that this may have been the case in the fourth century as well. If the people responsible for censing at the Aedicule were women, it is all the more reasonable to see this ritual as a representative, mimetic performance of the memory of the women coming to the tomb with spices to anoint Jesus' body.

Ultimately, it is not possible to be certain that the use of incense in the liturgy at the Aedicule necessarily represented the spices brought by the women to the tomb in the Markan and Lukan narratives. However, it is a good inference and the best available explanation.[141] In my opinion, the best evidence in favor of this hypothesis are the facts that in Egeria's account, incense is only used at this Sunday service at the tomb itself and that this ritual was immediately followed by the reading of the gospel narrative of the resurrection, which also took place at the tomb and which seems to have been the signature element of this particular service. From this, we may infer that the incense ritual was in some way connected to the commemoration of the resurrection. Even though the evidence for explicit connections to the women at the tomb is later, it

---

[134] Cf. McGowan and Bradshaw, *Pilgrimage of Egeria*, 153.
[135] Originally proposed by Juan Mateos, "La vigile cathédrale chez Egérie," *OCP* 27 (1961): 281–312 (292). See also McGowan and Bradshaw, *Pilgrimage of Egeria*, 153; Ally Kateusz, *Mary and Early Christian Women: Hidden Leadership* (Cham: Palgrave Macmillan, 2019), 37–9.
[136] Paul F. Bradshaw, *Daily Prayer in the Early Church: A Study of the Origin and Early Development of the Divine Office*, repr. ed. (Eugene: Wipf and Stock, 1981), 87; Clemens Leonhard, *The Jewish Pesach and the Origins of the Christian Easter: Open Questions in Current Research* (Berlin: De Gruyter, 2006), 297 n. 482. Note, however, the more positive comments on this hypothesis by Bradshaw and his coauthor (McGowan), in Bradshaw and McGowan, *Pilgrimage of Egeria*, 153.
[137] See Kateusz, *Mary and Early Christian Women*, 37; cf. Bradshaw and McGowan, *Pilgrimage of Egeria*, 153.
[138] Kateusz, *Mary and Early Christian Women*, 37.
[139] Ibid.
[140] Ibid.
[141] Cf. McGowan and Bradshaw, *Pilgrimage of Egeria*, 153.

indicates at the very least that this ritual was eventually understood in this way. The use of the incense at the tomb is thus best understood as a performative reception and a commemoration of the gospel narrative of the discovery of the empty tomb, which accompanied the public reading of that very tradition.

As mentioned above, the incense ritual was followed by a reading of the resurrection account from "the gospel" at the enclosure of the tomb by the bishop (*Itin. Eger.* 24.10). It is not clear which resurrection account was read. Indeed, the gospel read may have varied from week to week. However, if the use of incense within the tomb represented the spices brought by the women at the tomb to anoint Jesus' body, it is most likely that the resurrection reading likely included either Mark 16:1–8 or Luke 24:1–12, since the spices brought to anoint Jesus' body only appear in Mark (16:1) and Luke (23:56, 24:1). It is also worth noting that the old Armenian Lectionary lists Mark 15:42–16:8 as the gospel reading for Easter Sunday, which is the only resurrection account read specifically on a Sunday in the Armenian Lectionary (AL; the Lukan account is read on the Monday following Easter Sunday).[142]

According to Egeria, the congregants responded to the reading with moaning, groaning, and tears because "the Lord had undergone such things for us" (*Itin. Eger.* 24.10). This would be a curious response to the resurrection narrative on its own, so it seems likely that the reading included the passion narrative as well. Bradshaw and McGowan observe that Egeria records similar responses to certain gospel readings during Holy Week as well (*Itin. Eger.* 34, 36.3, 37.7)[143] and ask whether there may have been "a cultural expectation that accounts of suffering should receive this response."[144] The fact that this response was apparently expected weekly is significant. It is difficult to know whether such a cultural expectation existed, but it certainly appears as though this response was an expected performative element of the public reading ritual.

We have already discussed the significance of emotional responses for collective memory in the previous chapter, and our observations there apply here as well. The Aedicule itself, as well as the passion narrative, were "sticky objects" that facilitated the alignment of the participants in the ritual with the collective. In the fourth century, this likely served to strengthen identity formation in a city and site that was transitioning from pagan control to Christian control in a very rapid fashion, just as it had transitioned from Jewish to pagan control a few centuries earlier. This performance of public memory would help to align individuals with the emergent official Christological memory of the orthodox Nicene church and its imperial benefactors.

In the emotional responses to the public reading of the passion and resurrection narratives in conjunction with the ritual of the liturgy and the place of the Aedicule, a space positively dripping with sticky affect and thoroughly imbued with the church's memory of the crucified and risen Jesus, we can identify affective memory. Affective memory "manifests a group's moral and emotional involvement with its past" and "has to do with why *this* event, *this* person means so much to us and proves to be

---

[142] AL 45; Wilkinson, *Egeria's Travels*, 188.
[143] As discussed in the previous chapter.
[144] McGowan and Bradshaw, *Pilgrimage of Egeria*, 153.

determinative for our corporate existence."[145] This, too, serves to further identity formation and to align the experiences and memory of the individual with the collective.

The weekly Sunday ritual at the Anastasis that Egeria describes is clearly a commemorative ritual,[146] commemorating the death, burial, and resurrection of Jesus. Commemorative rituals are sites of social memory in which "a community is reminded of its identity as represented by and told by a master narrative."[147] Thus, the Sunday resurrection service would have served to strengthen the identity of congregants, Jerusalemites and pilgrims alike, as specifically represented by the master Christological narrative of the canonical passion narrative (possibly in Markan form as per the discussion above). In this ritual, sensory experience, space, the presence of a *lieu de mémoire*, narrative, affect, mimesis, and performance come together in the forum of public memory to present and fortify the official memory of the orthodox Nicene church. The historical context of the construction of the Church of the Holy Sepulchre, in the shadow of Nicaea and both the bicennalial and tricennalial celebrations of Constantine's reign, is surely significant, since it presents us with a direct line of sight from the official memory presented at and by the Anastasis to the state and church powers that sponsored and ran it, and thus, to the inside of the event of its construction. Moreover, reading the narrative of the resurrection at the tomb, complete with performative aspects such as the use of incense in the tomb and the apparently expected emotional response of grief by the congregants to the text served to solidify the connection between the place of the Aedicule and the remembered events of the life of Jesus.

Analysis and Conclusions

In this chapter, we have examined the memory and interpretation of Jesus' place of burial over three centuries. The course that we have plotted draws a line from the earliest extant depiction of Jesus' tomb in Mark to the speech given by Eusebius at the dedication of the Church of the Holy Sepulchre and his account and interpretation of the place in *Life of Constantine*.

Over the course of the development of the memory of the tomb of Jesus from the first to the fourth centuries CE, we see a shift in the mode of experience of this *lieu de mémoire* from a site that, though it must have existed physically prior to the Hadrianic era, was remembered primarily through narrative in the form of the gospel traditions, to a site that was commemorated and filtered through a monumental ecclesiastical

---

[145] Georgia Masters Keightley, "Christian Collective Memory and Paul's Knowledge of Jesus," in *Memory, Tradition, and Text: Uses of the Past in Early Christianity*, ed. Alan Kirk and Tom Thatcher, Semeia 52 (Atlanta: Society of Biblical Literature, 2005), 129–50 (136); following Iwona Irwin-Zarecka, *Frames of Remembrance: The Dynamics of Collective Memory* (New Brunswick: Transaction, 1994), 60.

[146] On commemorative rituals, see Paul Connerton, *How Societies Remember* (Cambridge: Cambridge University Press, 1989), 41–71.

[147] Ibid., 70.

structure built by the emperor. As the weekly public reading ritual at the Anastasis demonstrates, the memory in the narrative form of the canonical gospel texts continued to inform the commemoration of Jesus at the site. At the same time, the narrative memory of the gospel account of the passion and resurrection was incorporated into the official commemoration activity of the Anastasis.

Our exploration of the data has shown a progressive sacralization of the site of Jesus' burial, both as it exists conceptually in literary form and in physical space. This is true in the religious sense[148] but also in the political sense as a site originally remembered as the dishonorable burial place of a man crucified by Roman soldiers would become a place of the performative commemoration of Constantine's reign in the form of his tricennalial celebration in Jerusalem at the dedication of the Church of the Holy Sepulchre.

As with the site of crucifixion, the place of Jesus' burial was remembered by early Christians in light of Pauline Christology. While this is perhaps not entirely surprising, it is worth noting the prominence of Pauline theological concepts and passages in connection with Jesus' tomb and site of crucifixion in our sources. The Jesus who was remembered there was as much the Jesus known from Paul's proclamation as he was the Jesus proclaimed by the evangelists.

We have also seen how the site of Jesus' burial would be used in Christian identity formation, particularly in opposition to Judaism and paganism. The site, which began as a typical Jewish rock-cut tomb, would come to represent the triumph of Christianity over Judaism as well as paganism. The counterparts of the Church of the Holy Sepulchre in Eusebius' imagination were the Temple of Venus that it literally replaced, and the Jewish Temple, which Eusebius believed that it had figuratively and eschatologically replaced.

The power dynamics of memory at play that begin in the gospels and carry through to the Constantinian age are significant. As discussed both here and in the introductory chapter, "control of a society's memory largely conditions the hierarchy of power,"[149] and commemoration serves to bring the memory of individuals in line with the collective memory of the group. The tomb of Jesus, both as a literary construction and as an actual place, is a site of public memory. While we have largely focused on the Church of the Holy Sepulchre and its emergence as a site of official memory, we should not overlook the place of vernacular memory here. It is important to recall that public memory emerges from the intersection of official and vernacular memory,[150] and that the two are not necessarily in opposition to one another.

Vernacular memory, we should recall, is the product of small-scale communities.[151] The gospel narratives of Jesus' crucifixion, burial, and empty tomb are themselves the product of vernacular memory. Those narratives, and thus the vernacular memory that undergirds them, are the very bedrock that constitutes the *lieu de mémoire* of Jesus' tomb. The products of official culture that constitute the Constantinian Church of the

---

[148] Cf. the findings of Smith, "Jesus' Tomb."
[149] Connerton, *How Societies Remember*, 1.
[150] Cf. Bodnar, *Remaking America*, 15.
[151] Ibid., 14.

Holy Sepulchre and its rituals could only be meaningful for early Christians insofar as they enshrine the evangelical passion narratives that are embedded within them, which are themselves the products of vernacular culture.

Another manner in which we have seen the influence of vernacular memory is through the persistence and transmission of the Adamic Golgotha tradition, beginning at least with Origen if not earlier. This particular tradition attached itself to the site of the passion events with such resilience that it was eventually incorporated into the architecture of the Church of the Holy Sepulchre in the form of the Tomb of Adam as late as the seventh century CE,[152] despite having no canonical basis and in spite of its elusive and questionable origins. It probably owes this longevity and eventual fixture in architecture to its popularity with the common people. We may recall that Jerome went so far as to dismiss this tradition as popular and "soothing to the ear of the people," though it was not true.

The tomb of Jesus, which represented the central events of the Christian tradition, was thus a major site of public memory for the early church. The memory that accrued there played a major role in Christology and identity formation.

---

[152] See Taylor, *Christians the Holy Places*, 132–4; Gibson and Taylor, *Beneath the Church*, 59, 83.

4

Locating a Memory: The Architecture of the Constantinian Church of the Holy Sepulchre as Jesus-Memory

Meaning in Architecture

Architecture conveys meaning.[1] So too can it convey and contain memory.[2] The Church of the Holy Sepulchre was explicitly understood as a *monument*, and thereby as commemorative architecture. The Church of the Holy Sepulchre, as with the other commemorative churches for which it is the prototype, is crystallized memory that occupies a physical space. It thereby performs a function that I will call "locating memory." There are some narrative traditions or memories that are ostensibly set within space and time but whose actual spatial setting, including geography and topography, is obscure, unrecorded, or has been forgotten. The construction of a physical monument can locate that memory in actual space.

Such localizations of memory are common fare for Christian holy sites in antiquity and in contemporary society. The modern pilgrim can ostensibly touch the very spot where Jesus was born, see the very shore where the resurrected Jesus instructed Peter to feed his sheep, and see the very place where Jesus ascended to heaven. Such places need not necessarily be the actual place where the remembered event happened, nor do the events themselves need to have actually happened at all. This is the case with the "Inn of the Good Samaritan," where a commemorative church was built in the sixth century CE to mark the traditional location of the inn mentioned in Luke 10:34–35, a parable that was not intended by the author of Luke nor by the historical Jesus to be taken to be a historical story. These places need only be where these events, whether they be literally historical or otherwise, are remembered. By locating the event, an individual's encounter with the memory being commemorated will be colored and impacted by their experience of the monument and its location in the present.

---

[1] See the discussion of the iconography of architecture in Chapter 1.
[2] For a brief overview of scholarship on memory and monuments, see Stephen Hoelscher and Derek H. Alderman, "Memory and Place: Geographies of a Critical Relationship," *Social and Cultural Geography* 5, no. 3 (2004): 347–55 (350).

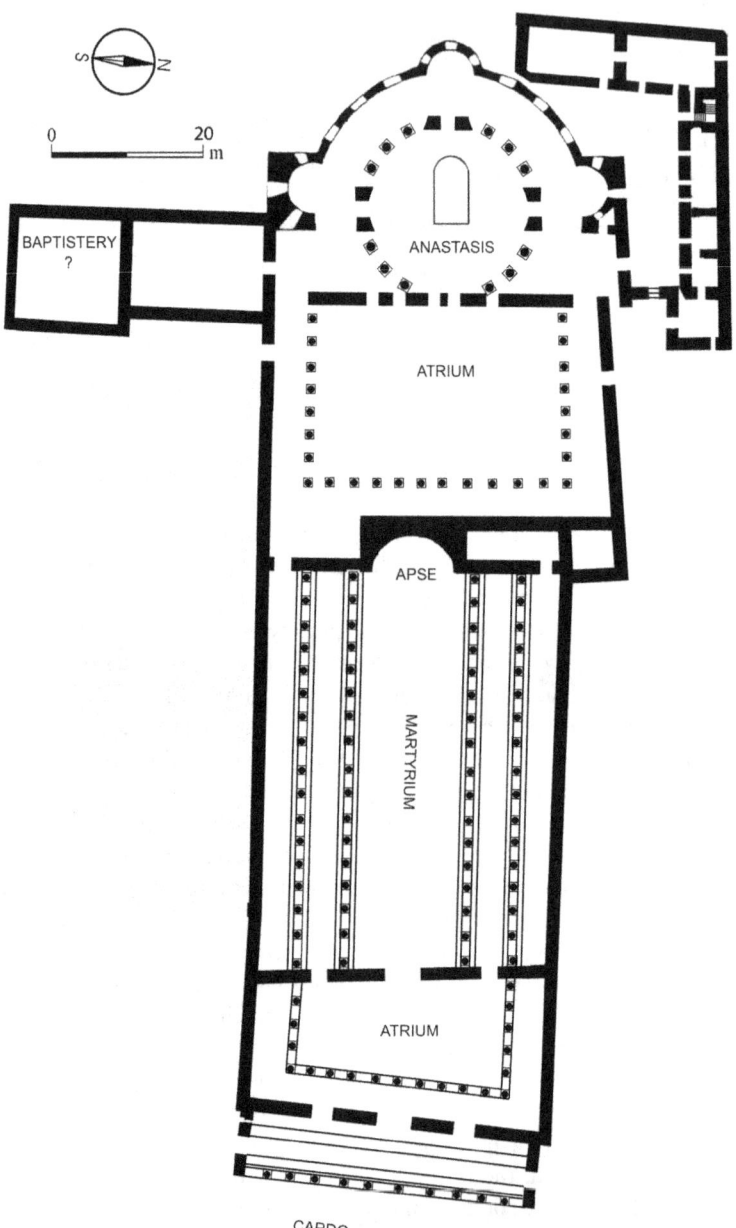

Figure 1 Floor plan of the Constantinian Church of the Holy Sepulchre.

Source: Vered Shalev-Hurvitz, *Holy Sites Encircled: The Early Byzantine Concentric Church of Jerusalem*, Oxford Studies in Byzantium (Oxford: Oxford University Press, 2015), fig. 1. Courtesy of Vered Shalev-Hurvitz and Oxford University Press.

In Chapter 1, we introduced the concept of the iconography of architecture. Its basic principle is that any structure, particularly any public structure such as a church,[3] "was meant to convey a meaning which transcends the visual pattern of the structure."[4] Thus, "the study of a building's symbolic content is as important as the study of its formal or technical elements."[5] In this chapter, our aim is to explore the symbolic content of the Constantinian Church of the Holy Sepulchre in order to interpret and grasp the meaning that its architecture would have conveyed to those who first experienced it almost three centuries after the crucifixion and burial of Jesus took place, ostensibly on the very ground that the complex occupied. In so doing, the goal is to further illuminate the "inside of the event," the intention behind the action, of the construction of the first commemorative church in Palestine.

The Church of the Holy Sepulchre is monumental commemorative architecture. Its location in the Jerusalem of its day within premiere public space is fortuitous, given the preexisting tradition that sited the events of the crucifixion and burial of Jesus at this spot, granting the ecclesiastical and imperial authorities an opportunity to shape that space to convey desired lessons,[6] both theological and political.

As products of human imagination, intention, and thought, monuments are packed with meaning. A structure like the Church of the Holy Sepulchre, the first true monument erected by a state power in commemoration of Jesus of Nazareth, requires interpretation in order to unpack that meaning. Janet Donohoe has recently elaborated a hermeneutic of monuments,[7] which will be helpful in this endeavor. According to Donohoe, "Monuments are places of intensified meaning that construct our world and preserve and produce collective memories and traditions."[8] They both embody and generate memory and tradition, focused on a particular place. By embodying and generating memory and tradition, monuments also shape them, and in so doing, shape the contemporary world through their presentation of the past. The present investigation aims to illuminate that collective memory and tradition, as it is preserved, produced, and shaped. In the case of the Church of the Holy Sepulchre, the significance of its place lies in the fact that tradition identifies it as the actual place where the crucifixion and burial of Jesus of Nazareth took place, as well as in the way that the architecture shapes that story and applies it to the experiences of the Christian community in fourth-century Jerusalem and in the Roman empire as a whole.

By their very nature, monuments interpret the past, presenting a specific vision of it. It would be naïve to assume that they are concerned primarily with the preservation

---

[3] Indeed, the concept of the iconography of architecture was originally developed within the study of medieval churches, particularly medieval copies of the Church of the Holy Sepulchre. See Krautheimer, "Iconography," 3.
[4] Krautheimer, "Iconography," 20.
[5] Valdez del Álamo, "Iconography of Architecture," 377.
[6] As Sanford Levinson has shown, "those with political power within a given society organize public space to convey (and thus to teach the public) desired political lessons," in *Written in Stone: Public Monuments in Changing Societies*, 2nd ed. (Durham: Duke University Press, 2018), 7. This citation articulates the central premise of Levinson's book.
[7] Janet Donohoe, *Remembering Places: A Phenomenological Study of the Relationship between Memory and Place* (Lanham: Lexington, 2014), 91–138.
[8] Ibid., 93.

of the bare facts of the past devoid of agenda or ideology. Certainly, a monument is open to multiple interpretations, insofar as not all who behold it will understand or experience it in the same way. Nevertheless, even though we may perceive it differently, we all perceive the same monument, which represents the same thing to its viewers.[9] Donohoe's recent work on monuments and memory provides some helpful orientation for our present discussion. According to Donohoe, monuments are "places of intensified meaning where the transference of cultural values and traditions can take place."[10] They are selective in their construction, presenting a version of events that is definitive or "closed."[11] As such, they not only preserve the past but also apply it to their society's present. The architecture of the Church of the Holy Sepulchre, constructed by imperial order (Eusebius, *Life of Constantine*, 3.30-2), is a product of official memory, though it certainly incorporates and co-opts vernacular memory. As such, it intends to present certain elite church and imperial ideologies in the way that it shapes and utilizes the canonical passion narratives.

Monuments call us to reflect on the past and, in so doing, to relate that past to our present, to the world around us. According to Donohoe, "The intensification of meaning, which the monument effects, calls us to reflect upon a moment or moments of the past and to relate those moments to our sense of who we are and what our community values."[12] As such, monuments are a conduit between the remembered past and the experienced present.

In their presentations of the past, and in calling us to remember, monuments tell stories. They are "narratives written in stone."[13] In the case of the earliest commemorative churches dedicated to the memory of Jesus in Palestine, each church tells its own individual narrative, and the collection of them together tells a broader narrative that could be charted and experienced by pilgrims as they encountered each site in their travels. In our consideration of the Church of the Holy Sepulchre, it will be necessary to ask what narrative or narratives it told, how it told them, and what the intention behind the narrative might have been. As much as they are narratives, monuments are also a form of testimony,[14] bearing witness to the events of the past insofar they keep the past alive through remembered narrative, symbol, and place.[15] This does not mean that authentic historical truth is necessarily communicated through them any more so than any other form of collective memory. Essentially, monuments replace the testimony of a witness with contemporary collective memory of the event or individual being commemorated.

This theoretical framework for considering monuments, along with the methodological considerations that were laid out in the introductory chapter, will provide some orientation as we consider the place that came to embody the memory

---

[9] Ibid., 111–12.
[10] Ibid., 97.
[11] Ibid.
[12] Ibid., 108.
[13] Ibid., 121.
[14] Ibid., 125.
[15] Ibid.; cf. Annette Wieviorka, *The Era of the Witness*, trans. Jared Stark (Ithaca: Cornell University Press, 2006), esp. ix–xv.

of the crucifixion and burial of Jesus of Nazareth. In the sections to follow, we will examine the history of the site itself, including the rock-cut tomb that was and is remembered as the place of Jesus' burial, and the commemorative church that was built on the site in the fourth century. Once this is accomplished, we will be prepared to analyze the Constantinian Church of the Holy Sepulchre as a site of memory and reception.

The Archaeology and History of the Traditional Site of the Tomb of Jesus

During the early first century CE, the traditional site of Jesus' crucifixion and burial was located in an area that had been used as a quarry up until the first century BCE.[16] The toponym "Golgotha" likely refers to an area rather than to a specific locus.[17] As Joan Taylor has argued, the name "Golgotha" likely referred to the whole (200 m × 150 m) area of the quarry rather than to the specific rock spire that came to be known as the "rock of Calvary."[18] Excavations under the nearby Church of the Redeemer have revealed that at least some area of the quarry was converted and used as an agricultural area that might be described as a garden during the Herodian period.[19] This fits well with the description of the place of the crucifixion and burial in the Gospel of John (19:41), as well as with the Gennath ("garden") gate mentioned by Josephus (*War*, 5.4.2), which is mostly to be identified with a Hasmonean gate discovered in this area.[20]

Cyril of Jerusalem makes the claim that the "signs and remains of" this garden were still present in his day (*Cat.* 14.5), but this seems incredible. It is more likely that the Johannine passion account was well known to Cyril and that he interpreted his surroundings in the Church of the Holy Sepulchre in his own day through the lens of that narrative. Cyril's claim indicates only that the Johannine tradition of Jesus' burial in a garden persisted and was connected directly to this place.

The traditional site of the crucifixion, the "rock of Calvary," was a rocky outcropping of the quarry rising above the ground. Gibson and Taylor rightly observe that its size would not have allowed for three individuals to be crucified on this spot, which they consider to be evidence against the authenticity of the site.[21] While the observation

---

[16] Cf. Virgilio Corbo, "A proposito di presunti scavi stratigrafici al S. Sepolcro," *Liber Annuus* 34 (1984): 409–16 (412); Gibson and Taylor, *Beneath the Church*, 56; Dieter Vieweger and Gabriele Förder-Hoff, *The Archaeological Park under the Church of the Redeemer in Jerusalem* (Jerusalem: German Protestant Institute of Archaeology, 2013), 34–5. On this quarry and its history, see also Kathleen Kenyon, *Digging Up Jerusalem* (New York: Praeger, 1974), 226–35.

[17] As convincingly argued by Taylor, "Golgotha," 182–6.

[18] Ibid., 184. For the dimensions of the quarry, see Gibson and Taylor, *Beneath the Church*, 59.

[19] Vieweger and Förder-Hoff, *Church of the Redeemer*, 27; cf. Dieter Viewger, "Archaeological Park & Museum: Durch die Zeiten," *Bible and Interpretation* (2013): n.p.; Serr and Vieweger, "Is the Holy Sepulchre Church Authentic?," 28–30 (29). See also the earlier study, Karel Vriezen, *Die Ausgrabungen unter der Erlöserkirche im Muristan, Jerusalem (1970-1974)*, Abhandlungen des Deutschen Palästina-Vereins 19 (Wiesbaden: Harrassowitz, 1994), 297.

[20] Avigad, *Discovering Jerusalem*, 50, 66, 69; cf. Taylor, "Golgotha," 186–7; Murphy-O'Connor, 82–3.

[21] Gibson and Taylor, *Beneath the Church*, 57.

is certainly correct, we cannot rule out the possibility, whether it is likely or not, that one person could have been crucified on the spire, and the others on the ground below on either side. Whatever the case may be, it is extremely difficult to verify the authenticity of the precise traditional location with any certainty. Whether it is truly the place where Jesus was crucified or not, the visible prominence of the outcropping would have drawn attention, and due to its proximity to the tomb, this may have drawn passion narrative traditions to crystallize around it. It may well have been the place where Jesus was crucified, but if it was not, it may have been destined to be the place where the crucifixion was remembered.

The traditional site of Jesus' burial was a rock-cut Jewish tomb.[22] Indeed, it was one of several Jewish burial places that have been discovered in the vicinity of the Holy Sepulchre complex.[23] The shape and structure of the tomb was impacted heavily by the Constantinian construction, and the tomb was later heavily damaged in 1009 by order of Caliph al-Hakim bi-Amr Allah, though it was not completely destroyed.[24] In fact, recent archaeological studies have confirmed that at least two sections of the rock-cut tomb have indeed survived and are embedded within the modern Aedicule.[25] As a result of these dramatic alterations, although the present Aedicule preserves the remains of the first-century rock-cut tomb, its original form is not immediately apparent and can be difficult to discern. That said, the history of the tomb's use and incorporation into the Church of the Holy Sepulchre in the fourth century CE is itself a kind of reception of Jesus tradition, a reception not just of place but also of space connected to Jesus. For that reason, it serves the aims of this study to briefly discuss scholarly reconstructions of the space of the tomb that has been traditionally identified as the place of Jesus' burial.

Martin Biddle's influential study of the Aedicule[26] provides us with the foundation for a reconstruction of the original rock-cut tomb that can be supplemented with the work of other scholars and updated with the results of the recent archaeological investigations carried out during the restoration work on the Aedicule that began in 2016.[27] The combination of these studies allows us to reasonably infer the form

---

[22] For a brief overview and discussion, see the recent work of Justin L. Kelley, *The Church of the Holy Sepulchre in Text and Archaeology: A Survey and Analysis of Past Excavations with a Collection of Principal Historical Sources* (Oxford: Archaeopress, 2019), 73–87.

[23] See Louis-Hugues Vincent and Félix-Marie Abel, *Jérusalem Nouvelle*, Book II of *Jérusalem: Recherches de topographie, d'aechéologie et d'histoire* (Paris: Gabalda, 1922), 192–94; Virgilio Corbo, *Il Santo sepolcro di Gerusalemme*, 3 vols. (Jerusalem: Franciscan Printing Press, 1981–2), plate 52, photo 4; Conrad Schick, "Notes from Jerusalem," *PEFQS* (1887): 156–70. See also Gibson and Taylor, *Beneath the Church*, 52–3. The quarries in Jerusalem are often related to rock-cut tombs. On this, see Amos Kloner and Boaz Zissu, *The Necropolis of Jerusalem in the Second Temple Period* (Leuven: Peeters, 2007), 15–16.

[24] On the survival of portions of the rock-cut tomb, see Biddle, *Tomb of Christ*, 72, 114–16.

[25] A. Georgopoulos, E. Lambrou, G. Pantazis, P. Agrafiotis, A. Papadaki, L. Kotoula, K. Lampropoulos, E. Delegou, M. Apostolopoulou, M. Alexakis, and A. Moropoulou, "Merging Geometric Documentation with Materials Characterization and Analysis of the History of the Holy Aedicule in the Church of the Holy Sepulchre in Jerusalem," *The International Archives of the Photogrammetry, Remote Sensing and Spatial Information Sciences* 42, no. 5 (2017): 487–94 (493).

[26] Biddle, *Tomb of Christ*, esp. 109–19.

[27] Kyriakos C. Lampropoulos, Antonia Moropoulou, and Manolis Korres, "Ground Penetrating Radar Prospection of the Construction Phases of the Holy Aedicula of the Holy Sepulchre in Correlation with Architectural Analysis," *Construction and Building Materials* 155 (2017): 307–22; Antonia

of the first-century rock-cut tomb, which in turn enables us to later explore how it was transformed by and incorporated into the Constantinian building project three centuries later.

In his influential study, Biddle proposed several conclusions about the rock-cut tomb: (1) it consisted of two components: a forecourt that was either unroofed or partly covered and an enclosed tomb chamber, both of which were cut from the rock; (2) the tomb chamber was sealed with a large stone, though there is no evidence that it was a perfectly round disc; (3) the tomb chamber probably had burial benches cut from the rock on two or three sides; (4) the ceiling of the chamber was flat, and there is no evidence that the burial bench presently preserved in the modern Aedicule was originally set in an arched arcosolium; (5) the burial chamber was a quadrilateral room with a flat roof and burial benches on the sides, and a standing pit in the central area, which allowed visitors and attendants to stand upright in the tomb; (6) the forecourt was 3–4 m wide and 3–4 m long, while the tomb chamber was 2.8 m^2 and 2 m high.[28]

Murphy O'Connor has proposed several reasonable amendments to Biddle's conclusions that may provide us with a more period accurate reconstruction. He rightly observes that the basic form of the tomb as conceived by Biddle is essentially an Iron Age configuration that was long abandoned by the Early Roman period.[29] Indeed, *kokhim* (or "loculi"), burial shafts or slots cut horizontally into the rock into which bodies or ossuaries could be deposited, are lacking from Biddle's reconstruction, which are a regular feature of Jerusalem rock-cut tombs of this time.[30] *Kokhim* were receptacles that first appeared in the first century BCE, which were originally used for primary burial, but in later times (around the first century CE) could also be utilized as space for bone collection in ossuaries and repositories.[31]

Murphy-O'Connor proposes that the rock-cut tomb identified as Jesus' burial place originally featured *kokhim*,[32] which would have been carved into the walls of the tomb, radiating outward. Given the period appropriateness and the existence of *kokh* tombs just steps away, those identified in modern tradition as the tombs of Nicodemus and Joseph of Arimathea just off the Syrian Chapel, Murphy-O'Connor's suggestion is reasonable. However, the recent studies of the Aedicule during its restoration that have been published to date have not confirmed the existence of *kokhim* shafts.[33] The recently published results of the ground-penetrating radar (GPR) study of the Aedicule

---

Moropoulou, Calliope Maria Farmakidi, Kyriakos Lampropoulos, and Maria Apostolopoulou, "Interdisciplinary Planning and Scientific Support to Rehabilitate and Preserve the Values of the Holy Aedicule of the Holy Sepulchre in Interrelation with Social Accessibility," *Sociology and Anthropology* 6, no. 6 (2018): 534–46; Georgopoulos et al, "Merging Geometric Documentation"; A. Moropoulou, N. Zacharias, E.T. Delegou, M. Apostolopoulou, E. Palamara, and A. Kolaiti, "OSL Mortar Dating to Elucidate the Construction History of the Tomb Chamber of the Holy Aedicule of the Holy Sepulchre in Jerusalem," *Journal of Archaeological Science: Reports* 19 (2018): 80–91.

[28] Biddle, *Tomb of Christ*, 116–18.
[29] Murphy-O'Connor, *Keys to Jerusalem*, 188. Cf. Kloner and Zissu, *Necropolis*, 87.
[30] Rachel Hachlili, *Jewish Funerary Customs, Practices and Rites in the Second Temple Period*, JSJSupp 94 (Leiden: Brill, 2005), 450–7.
[31] Ibid., 57.
[32] Murphy-O'Connor, *Keys to Jerusalem*, 188–9.
[33] See the diagram in Lampropoulos et al., "Ground Penetrating Radar," 316; cf. the reconstruction of the tomb chamber rock on p. 313. See also Kelley, *Church of the Holy Sepulchre*, 86.

show two blocks of living rock (called the "Holy Rock" by the authors) belonging to the walls of the original rock-cut tomb.[34] Given the poor preservation state of the rock of the original tomb and the difficulties involved in studying it, we might not rule out the possibility that they existed in the tomb chamber altogether, but as of yet there is no clear direct archaeological evidence for their existence. It is thus rather unlikely that *kokhim* existed in the tomb chamber.[35]

The recent investigations of the Aedicule during its restoration in 2016–17 have produced some results that are of note for the reconstruction of the rock-cut tomb. In particular, the study revealed two main blocks of living rock that would have been part of the original tomb, one on the north side of the burial chamber, and the other on the south side.[36] A bedrock shelf was also confirmed to exist beneath the marble slab covering the traditional resting place.[37] This generally fits with what was reported in 1809 by the monk Maximos Simaios when he saw the remains of the rock-cut tomb when the Aedicule was dismantled following a fire in 1808.[38] Assuming that the north and south blocks represent the walls of the tomb, this leaves no room in the central area for a burial bench on the south side that Biddle had included in his reconstruction.[39] Indeed, the wall of the south block rises to a height over 130 cm, whereas the bedrock of the traditional "burial bench" (for lack of a better designation) on the north side is much lower at just 45 cm.[40]

No remains of the living rock on the west side of the tomb were discovered,[41] which leaves us with further questions. It is possible, for instance, that the western side of the tomb could have featured *kokhim*, an arcosolium, or both. We should also be willing to consider the possibility, contrary to Biddle's reconstruction, that the tomb may have continued and featured further chambers which were cut away during the Constantinian construction phase. The notion that part of the tomb has been lost dovetails with an inference that Biddle draws in considering the dimensions of the tomb as reported by Maximos Simaios in 1809 when the Aedicule was dismantled following a devastating fire. Biddle observes that there seems to be something missing at one end or the other of the rock, since the length that Maximos Simaios provides converts to 1.57 meters, which seems short.[42] As it stands, all that we can identify of the

---

[34] Lampropoulos et al., "Ground Penetrating Radar," 313–19. See especially the diagram on p. 316, which shows the form and extent of the north and south blocks of the living rock of the original tomb.
[35] A similar conclusion has recently been reached independently by Kelley. As he writes, "The biblical Tomb of Jesus could have been a typical tomb chamber, with or without loculi, that had three burial brenches in a U-shape, and that was blocked with a square blocking stone" (*Church of the Holy Sepulchre*, 86). Notably, Kelley observes that the shape of the tomb contained within the Aedicule does not correspond to the typical shape of a first-century tomb chamber, since the recent studies show that the structure in the Aedicule was a chamber with a burial shelf on the north side, and suggests that the tomb may have been altered in antiquity. This is an interesting suggestion, and one worth considering in future research.
[36] Lampropoulos et al., "Ground Penetrating Radar," 313–19.
[37] See the diagram showing the heights of sections of rock in ibid., 317 (fig. 9).
[38] Vincent and Abel, *Jérusalem Nouvelle*, 300. Summarizing Maximos, they write, "Les parois de roc n'existaient plus qu'au nord et au midi" ("the rock walls existed only to the north and south").
[39] See the drawing with meter scale in Georgopoulos et al., "Merging Geometric Documentation," 493 (fig. 14).
[40] Lampropoulos et al., "Ground Penetrating Radar," 317 (incl. fig. 9).
[41] Ibid., 317.
[42] Biddle, *Tomb of Christ*, 115.

rock-cut tomb with certainty are the walls constituted by the north and south blocks, and the rock shelf, which Biddle identifies as a burial bench, but which the team that recently studied the Aedicule identifies as an arcosolium,[43] or which might also be a quadrosolium. Although arcosolia (and quadrosolia) are often located further in,[44] this is not always the case, and there is no rule that prevents an arcosolium from being located in the first chamber of a tomb, or in a tomb with only one chamber. In fact, a tomb discovered on Mount Scopus in Jerusalem has a chamber with an arcosolium and two *kokhim* in a room (designated "Chamber A" by the excavators) just off a forecourt.[45]

Arcosolia were typically used as shelves to store ossuaries,[46] so it is unlikely that this was the only funerary element of that original tomb. Although it is debated as to whether or not arcosolia were used for primary burials,[47] this matter is tangential for our study, since it is enough for our purposes that a Jewish tomb of any sort and any form was incorporated into a Constantinian monumental church.

So far as historical authenticity goes, the matter is also only of minor relevance, since Mark describes a burial that is apparently dishonorable and hasty, as there is not even time given to wash and anoint the body (15:45–46).[48] Indeed, the women went to the tomb for the purpose of anointing the body with spices (16:1). Jesus' body could well have been laid on an arcosolium temporarily.[49] This would be possible in a new tomb in which no one had ever been laid (Luke 23:53; John 19:41; cf. Matt 27:60, which mentions only that the tomb is new), since there would be no ossuaries to occupy the arcosolium. Furthermore, Mark mentions the angelic young man "sitting on the right side" inside the tomb (16:5), which presumes that there is something for him to sit on the right side of the tomb. An arcosolium, perhaps like the rock shelf located to the right of the entrance of the Aedicule, would provide precisely such a seat.

The findings of the GPR study show that nothing of the rock-cut tomb remains in the contemporary Chapel of the Angel, which lies east of the tomb chamber, at least not in the form of walls.[50] However, Maximos observed in 1809 that the earth underneath both the Sepulchre and the Chapel of the Angel were composed of natural rock.[51] Biddle's suggestion that the tomb had a forecourt remains plausible, even though no

---

[43] Lampropoulos et al., "Ground Penetrating Radar," 312, 317.
[44] Cf. Murphy-O'Connor, *Keys to Jerusalem*, 201 n. 29; see also Kloner and Zissu, *Necropolis*, 84–6.
[45] Amos Kloner and Sherry Whetstone, "A Burial Complex of the Second Temple Period on Mount Scopus, Jerusalem," in *Viewing Ancient Jewish Art and Archaeology: Vehinnei Rachel, Essays in Honor of Rachel Hachlili*, ed. Ann E. Killebrew and Gabriele Faßbeck, JSJSupp 172 (Leiden: Brill, 2016), 193–217 (194–6, incl. figs. 10.1 and 10.2).
[46] See Kloner and Zissu, *Necropolis*, 83–4; followed by Murphy-O'Connor, *Keys to Jerusalem*, 187. This at least goes for the type without a trough for the body, as noted by Murphy-O'Connor. Maximos Simaios describes a trough.
[47] See Hachlili, *Jewish Funerary Customs*, 71.
[48] Compare, however, John 19:39–40.
[49] Perhaps once they had anointed the body the women may have planned to move him into a *kokh*, though this is admittedly speculative and not mentioned by the text.
[50] Lampropoulos et al., "Ground Penetrating Radar," 317.
[51] Vincent and Abel, *Jérusalem Nouvelle*, 300 ("Quant au sol, il était formé par le rocher naturel tant dans le Sépulcre et que dans le Chapelle de l'Ange").

clear evidence of its existence has turned up in the recent studies by the restoration team. His reconstruction in this instance is supported both by literary testimony drawn from Cyril of Jerusalem and by comparative archaeological material, since there are innumerable examples of tombs of the early Roman period with forecourts in the Jerusalem area.[52]

Cyril connects portions of Cant. 2:10 LXX ("Arise, come, my kinswoman") and v. 14 ("in the shelter of the rock") to the resurrection of Jesus and to his interpretation of the space of the tomb itself. His use of this passage appears to be triggered by the combination of "Ἀνάστα" ("arise") in v. 10 and the phrase "σκέπη τῆς πέτρας" in v. 14 ("shelter of the rock"), calling to mind the resurrection (ἀνάστασις) and the form of the rock-cut tomb, which he may plausibly have seen in his youth before it was altered.[53] He writes,

> The phrase "shelter of the rock" refers to the shelter which at that time stood in front of the door to the Savior's tomb, and had been hollowed from the very rock in the way that was customary here in front of tombs. It is no longer visible because the front chamber was then cut away to give the tomb the decoration it had today. (*Cat.* 14.9)

It is interesting that Cyril refers to this area as a "chamber," as this has led some scholars to conclude that there was another roofed chamber before (directly east) the chamber preserved in the Aedicule.[54] This is a tantalizing possibility, because it would allow for the possibility that the preserved chamber is actually an arcosolium room, while the *kokhim* and standing pit may have been in the now missing chamber before it. However, on the basis of the description given by Cyril, it is most likely that he is referring to a forecourt with an overhanging "shelter."[55] However, it is also possible, perhaps even probable, that Cyril's description of the "shelter" is conditioned by his exegesis of Cant 2:14 LXX, and the use of the term "shelter" (Greek σκέπη) is merely derived from the passage and imperfectly described the actual "chamber." Although I lean toward the position that Cyril here describes a forecourt, it is important not to rely too heavily on a description that is clearly conditioned by the wording of a Septuagint passage. Perhaps it is best to leave the matter open unless further evidence or argumentation leads us toward a clearer conclusion.

Although some of the details remain obscure, such as precisely what lay to the east and west of the preserved elements, current research has enabled us to draw some conclusions about the traditional tomb of Jesus that was incorporated into the Constantinian complex of the Holy Sepulchre in the fourth century CE. Based on the archaeological evidence, it is fairly certain that the cave that was incorporated into

---

[52] See, e.g., Hachlili, *Jewish Funerary Customs*, 10–11, with examples described on (e.g.) pp. 34, 36, 43–4, 49, 61.
[53] Cf. Biddle, *Tomb of Christ*, 65; Walker, *Holy City*, 272.
[54] Vincent and Abel, *Jérusalem Nouvelle*, 96 (fig. 53); Corbo, *Santo Sepolcro*, pl. 67. See also Gibson and Taylor, *Beneath the Church*, 62.
[55] As per Biddle, *Tomb of Christ*, 116.

the Aedicule was a rock-cut Jewish tomb, though its only funerary feature that remains is the rock shelf,[56] which is most likely an arcosolium or a quadrosolium.

In the second century CE, Jerusalem underwent major changes as Hadrian rebuilt the city as Aelia Capitolina following the events of the Bar Kochba Revolt. As part of this transformation, Hadrian constructed a temple dedicated to Venus adjoining a forum on the location of the quarry in which the traditional tomb of Jesus was located.[57] In order to do this, massive amounts of earth were brought in to fill and level the quarry. As a result, the traditional tomb of Jesus was buried and covered by the earth underneath the temple of Venus in the construction process. According to Eusebius,

> It was this very cave of the Savior that some godless and wicked people had planned to make invisible to mankind, thinking in their stupidity that they could in this way hide the truth ... above the ground they constructed a terrible and truly genuine tomb, one for souls, for dead idols, and built a gloomy sanctuary to the impure demon of Aphrodite; then they offered foul sacrifices there upon defiled and polluted altars. (*Life of Constantine*, 3.26.2–3)

Our interest here is in the description of the construction of the temple over top of the area where the traditional tomb was located, and in Eusebius' claims concerning the motivation for the construction of the temple.

Some archaeological evidence pertaining to the Hadrianic construction has survived, showing the large rectangular platform of the *temenos*.[58] It appears as though the "Rock of Calvary" was incorporated into the Hadrianic temple complex and was enclosed within its own platform.[59] According to Jerome, a statue of Jupiter was set up over the traditional place of the resurrection (the tomb), and a statue of Venus was set upon the site of the crucifixion (*Ep.* 58.3). For various reasons that we need not discuss here, Jerome's statement about the statue of Jupiter is not confirmed by other sources and is considered to be misunderstood, suspect, or mistaken by some scholars.[60] However, it is quite likely that Jerome's report that a statue of Venus stood on the place of crucifixion is accurate, or at least that a statue of Venus stood on the "Rock of Calvary," which in his day was understood to be the place of the crucifixion, since the sources generally agree that the Hadrianic temple in question was dedicated to Venus.[61]

---

[56] Biddle suggests quite rightly that the shelf looked something like the rock couch that is visible and venerated in the Tomb of Mary in the Kidron (*Tomb of Christ*, 116).
[57] For a brief, recent overview of the archaeological evidence pertaining to Hadrian's temple, see Kelley, *Church of the Holy Sepulchre*, 87–94.
[58] The archaeological evidence is summarized succinctly in Gibson and Taylor, *Beneath the Church*, 65–8.
[59] Ibid., 65–7.
[60] See ibid., 68–9. Gibson and Taylor view Jerome's statement about the statue of Jupiter to be a use of the literary technique of parallelism and meant to refer to the area more generally rather than to the precise location over Jesus' tomb. Alternatively, see Murphy-O'Connor, *Keys to Jerusalem*, 148–55.
[61] Eusebius, *Life of Constantine*, 3.26; Socrates Scholasticus, *Hist. Ecc.* 1.17; Sozomen, *Hist. Ecc.* 2.1; Rufinus, *Hist. Ecc.* 9.6. See also Gibson and Taylor, *Beneath the Church*, 68.

Christian sources written after the destruction of the temple to Venus (circa 324) generally presume that Hadrian intentionally built the temple on the traditional site of Jesus' death and resurrection as a means of obscuring the Christian site.[62] It is unlikely in my opinion that Hadrian specifically chose this same site as the location of the temple of Venus in order to hide or co-opt the Christian holy place.[63] At least, the notion seems farfetched. How would the Roman authorities have known that the place was important or sacred to Christians? Would Hadrian have had a particular reason to try to co-opt or suppress the localized memory of the Christian community in Jerusalem? So far as we know, it was not marked with any commemorative architecture, and even if (as is likely) some graffiti were present that would identify it, it is unlikely that the imperial authorities would have been looking for it.

It is much more likely that the location fit into Hadrian's city planning, as it was located in the central area of Aelia Capitolina, in the area at the intersection of the Decumanus Maximus and Cardo Maximus.[64] The odd geological formation of the "Rock of Calvary" would naturally have attracted attention and made for a good platform for a statue. Thus, the location of the temple of Venus over the traditional site of Jesus' crucifixion and burial is probably a coincidence. That having been said, the burial of the site underneath a pagan temple may have helped preserve the memory of the place for the local Christian community despite being covered by the Hadrianic construction, since the temple provided a clear marker.[65]

More significant for our purposes is the fact that the Christian community in Palestine apparently remembered the construction of the temple to Venus on the traditional site of Jesus' crucifixion and burial as a deliberate attempt by imperial authorities to conceal the place where the most important Christological events of the New Testament narrative had occurred. According to Eusebius, the earliest author to present this perspective, wicked people and "the whole tribe of demons with them" had desired to "consign to darkness and oblivion that divine monument to immortality," and intended to make the tomb "invisible," thinking that this would allow them to "hide the truth" of the resurrection (*Life of Constantine*, 3.26.1-2).[66] This memory would in turn impact the memory of the construction of the Church of the Holy Sepulchre by Constantine, which necessarily involved the destruction of the Hadrianic temple to Venus and would also be interpreted and remembered through the lens of religious competition.

---

[62] Eusebius, *Life of Constantine*, 3.26.1-3; Jerome, *Ep.* 58.3; Socrates Scholasticus, *Hist. Ecc.* 1.17.
[63] Cf., e.g., Coüasnon, *Church of the Holy Sepulchre*, 11; Brown, *Death of the Messiah*, 2: 1281-2.
[64] On the location of the temple of Venus and its attached forum at this intersection, see Taylor, "Golgotha," 189-1, esp. fig. 4.
[65] Cf. Georg Krestchmar, "Kreuz und Auferstehung Jesu Christi. Das Zeugnis der Heiligen Stätten," *Erbe und Auftrag* 54 (1978): 423-431; 55 (1979): 12-26 (424); Brown, *Death of the Messiah*, 2: 1281-2.
[66] Note that Hadrian is not specifically mentioned. This is likely a tactful move on Eusebius' part in order to avoid any direct insults to one of Constantine's imperial predecessors (cf. Walker, *Holy City*, 244 n. 15).

Establishing the Architecture

In order to analyze the architecture of the Constantinian Church of the Holy Sepulchre, we will need to first establish its form. In this section, we will briefly describe and review the church as it has been reconstructed in scholarship on the basis of archaeological and historical evidence. However, the structure has undergone many changes in form over the centuries due to destructions, rebuildings, and renovations. It has also been virtually in continual use since the advent of the modern science of archaeology, making sustained and complete archaeological investigations and excavations difficult and rare.[67] As a result, there has been some disagreement in scholarship over the architectural form of the complex.[68] This matter will need to be addressed, and so we will be attentive to it as we proceed in our review of the architectural form of the Constantinian Church of the Holy Sepulchre.

The Church of the Holy Sepulchre is roughly oriented east-west. As depicted in the Madaba Map,[69] its primary entrance was on its eastern end, along the Cardo Maximus in the heart of the city.[70] Indeed, as the *Breviarius* states, "In the center of the city is the Basilica of Constantine" (1).[71] Pilgrim itineraries often reflect movement from the

---

[67] Despite this, there have been several opportunities for archaeological excavation, which have resulted in some important publications, e.g., Virgilio Corbo, "Gli edifici della Santa Anastasi a Gerusalemme," *Liber Annuus* 12 (1962): 221–316; Corbo, *Santo sepolcro*; Bellarmino Bagatti, *The Church from the Gentiles in Palestine: History and Archaeology*, repr. ed., trans. Eugene Hoade, SBF Collectio Minor 4 (Jerusalem: Franciscan Printing Press, [1970] 1984), 163–75; Coüasnon, *Church of the Holy Sepulchre*; Magen Broshi and Gabriel Barkay, "Excavations in the Chapel of St. Vartan in the Church of the Holy Sepulchre," *IEJ* 35, no. 2 (1985): 108–28; Gibson and Taylor, *Beneath the Church*; Kyriakos C. Lampropoulos, Antonia Moropoulou, and Manolis Korres, "Ground Penetrating Radar," 307–22; M. Apostolopoulou, E.T. Delegou, Emm. Alexakis, M. Kalofonou, K.C. Lampropoulos, E. Aggelakopoulou, A. Bakolas, and A. Moropoulou, "Study of the Historical Mortars of the Holy Aedicule as a Basis for the Design, Application and Assessment of Repair Mortars: A Multispectral Approach Applied on the Holy Aedicule," *Construction & Building Materials* 181 (2018): 618–37. For an overview and history of excavations, see Joseph Patrich, "An Overview of the Archaeological Work in the Church of the Holy Sepulchre," in *The Archaeology and History of the Church of the Redeemer and the Muristan in Jerusalem*, ed. Dieter Vieweger and Shimon Gibson (Oxford: Archaeopress, 2016), 139–61. Extensive studies have also been recently published in Grazia Tucci (ed.), *Jerusalem – The Holy Sepulchre: Research and Investigations (2007–2011)* (Florence: Altralinea Edizioni, 2019). For a review of archaeological studies, see Alessandra Angeloni and Carmelo Pappalardo, "The Archaeological and Historical Context of the Basilica of the Holy Sepulchre in Jerusalem," in *Jerusalem – The Holy Sepulchre: Research and Investigations (2007–2011)*, ed. Grazia Tucci (Florence: Altralinea Edizioni, 2019), 25–45 (25–32). A philological review of the historical and archaeological material has also been published by Osvaldo Garbarino, "Il Santo Sepolcro di Gerusalemme. Appunti di ricercar storico-architettonica," *Liber Annuus* 55 (2005): 239–314. A helpful, brief guide to the archaeological excavations can be found in Kelley, *Church of the Holy Sepulchre*, 38–64.

[68] On the difficulties of discerning the remains of the various phases of the Church of the Holy Sepulchre, Bagatti writes, "The plan of the Holy Sepulchre as it is today with an agglomeration of different types of walls, where with difficulty one succeeds in discerning the lines of the different epochs" (*Church from the Gentiles*, 163).

[69] On the route of the Cardo Maximus in the Madaba Map and its accuracy, see Herbert Donner, *The Mosaic Map of Madaba: An Introductory Guide*, Palaestina Antiqua 7 (Kampen: Pharos, 1992), 89–90.

[70] See Coüasnon, *Church of the Holy Sepulchre*, pl. 8.

[71] Both recensions of the *Breviarius* identify its location as the "center of the city," though only recension A mentions Constantine. Compare translation from Wilkinson, *Jerusalem Pilgrims*, 117.

easternmost structures to the westernmost, likely reflecting the fact that most visitors probably entered from the Cardo.[72] In our review of the structure, we will move from east to west, beginning at the easternmost section and ending with the westernmost. In this way, we can experience the building through the historical imagination in the same order that early pilgrims, entering from the Cardo, would have experienced it.

Coming from the Cardo, a visitor would first encounter the propylaeum, and just beyond it, an atrium.[73] Such an atrium would become common in Byzantine church design. Eusebius, our most important source for the architecture of the earliest phase of the church, describes an open space in front of the church: "Arcades stood there on either hand, a first court and colonnades beyond, and finally the gates of the court. Beyond these, right in the middle of the open square, the porticoes forming the entrance to the whole" (*Life of Constantine*, 3.39). Eusebius here describes the imperial grandeur of the entrance and atrium to the Church of the Holy Sepulchre. The monumental stairs and triple entrance are visible on the Madaba Map. Because the façade of the basilica (discussed below) and the Cardo were not aligned, as they slanted in opposite directions from one another, the shape of the atrium was irregular, described by Coüasnon as "an isosceles trapezium."[74]

Remains of the entrance have been uncovered, including the central and southern doorways and some elements of the stairs, in the modern Church of St. Alexander Nevsky and Zalatimo's bakery.[75] The atrium provided public space, accessible to all, whether or not they were baptized, catechumans, or non-Christians.[76] In general, church atria were places for gathering and for reflection,[77] and resembled the public peristyles of Roman temples in both form and function.[78] The Christian atrium was also an intentional display of architectural grandeur, as indicated by Eusebius' description of both this atrium and that of the Basilica at Tyre (*Hist. Ecc.* 10.4).[79] The location of this particular atrium along the Cardo, with its prominent propylaeum, steps, and entryway made it well suited for public space and assembly.

From the atrium, visitors would next enter through a set of triple doors into the Martyrium basilica. It appears as though the basilica was formally or popularly known

---

[72] E.g., *Breviarius* 1; Eucherius, *Letter to Faustus*, 5–6 (in Wilkinson, *Jerusalem Pilgrims*, 94; CSL 175); *Itin. Burd.* 594. Eusebius, however, moves from west to east in his description, but this is an architectural description rather than an itinerary per se, though his description does imagine a person walking through the structure from west to east. This may result from his desire to give primacy to the tomb of Christ as the place of the resurrection.

[73] See Coüasnon, *Church of the Holy Sepulchre*, 44–6; Joseph Patrich, "The Early Church of the Holy Sepulchre in the Light of Excavations and Restoration," in *Ancient Churches Revealed*, ed. Yoram Tsafrir (Jerusalem: Israel Exploration Society, 1993), 112; Gibson and Taylor, *Beneath the Church*, 74.

[74] Coüasnon, *Church of the Holy Sepulchre*, 43.

[75] See ibid., 46; Patrich, "Early Church of the Holy Sepulchre," 112; Gibson and Taylor, *Beneath the Church*, 74.

[76] Cf. Krautheimer, *Early Christian and Byzantine Architecture*, 40.

[77] Jennifer L. Gibson and Rabun M. Taylor, "Atrium," in *Eerdmans Encyclopedia of Early Christian Art*, ed. Paul Corby Finnery, 3 vols. (Grand Rapids: Eerdmans, 2016), 1:142–3.

[78] Sible de Blaauw, "The Church Atrium as a Ritual Space: The Cathedral of Tyre and St Peter's in Rome," in *Ritual and Space in the Middle Ages*, ed. Frances Andrews, Harlaxton Medieval Studies 21 (Lincolnshire: Paul Watkins, 2011), 30–43 (33).

[79] Cf. ibid., 40.

as the Martyrium (Greek *Martyrion*), as it appears by this name in some sources.[80] It is evident that this is apparently a name and not a designation of its architectural type, since it does not have the form of typical Christian martyria, which generally have central plans.[81] According to Egeria, "It is called the Martyrium for the reason that it is on Golgotha, that is, behind the Cross where the Lord suffered, and hence the Martyrium" (*Itin. Eger.* 30.1). We will further discuss the meaning of the name of the basilica when we present our analysis below.

Christian basilicas in Palestine[82] were rectangular structures, oriented lengthwise,[83] with an interior divided into an odd number of aisles (in Palestine, usually three) by rows of columns. Typically, they featured a clerestory roof, which was raised with a row of windows above the central aisle, or nave, supported by the columns on either side of the nave. The clerestory provided light for the basilica. They had a central apse, located at the far end of the building from the entrance where the nave terminated, which provided orientation for the building and space for the bema. Some basilicas (especially in later times) could have more than one apse, but the central apse was a common feature of Christian basilical architecture in Palestine. We will discuss the iconography of the basilical form below when we engage in our interpretation of the meaning of the architecture.

The basic form of the Constantinian Martyrium is known to us through archaeological evidence and through the architectural description of the structure provided by Eusebius (*Life of Constantine*, 3.36–38). Archaeological investigations have brought to light the apse of the Martyrium beneath the present-day Katholikon,[84] which has helped to determine the orientation of the building. Other portions of the walls have been discovered or are extant,[85] which has also helped to reveal the form of the building, such that its basic contours can be reconstructed with some confidence.[86]

---

[80] The basilica receives this designation in a number of sources. E.g., *Itin. Eger.* 30.1; Cyril of Jerusalem, *Cat.* 14.6; Eucherius, *Letter to Faustus*, 5–6. See Rubin, "Church of the Holy Sepulchre," 79–105 (82); Walker, *Holy City*, 266, 268 n. 115.

[81] On this form in general, see Yoram Tsafrir, "The Development of Ecclesiastical Architecture in Palestine," in *Ancient Churches Revealed*, ed. Yoram Tsafrir (Jerusalem: Israel Exploration Society, 1993), 5–6; David L. Eastman, "Martyria," in *The Oxford Handbook of Early Christian Archaeology*, ed. David K. Pettigrew, William R. Caraher, and Thomas W. Davis (Oxford: Oxford University Press, 2019), 89–104.

The form of the marthyrium is more relevant to our discussion of the Anastasis than the Martyrium basilica. We will distinguish between "martyrium," referring to the architectural form, and "Martyrium," referring to the proper name of the Constantinian basilica of the Church of the Holy Sepulchre, through capitalization.

[82] For other general descriptions or definitions of Christian basilicas in general, see Krautheimer, *Early Christian and Byzantine Architecture*, 41–3; Tsafrir, "Development of Ecclesiastical Architecture," 2–3; Charles Anthony Stewart, "Churches," in *The Oxford Handbook of Early Christian Archaeology*, ed. David K. Pettigrew, William R. Caraher, and Thomas W. Davis (Oxford: Oxford University Press, 2019), 127–46 (136).

[83] As opposed to a "broad house," which was oriented widthwise, as some ancient synagogues in Roman and Byzantine Palestine were (e.g., at Nabratein).

[84] Corbo, *Santo Sepolcro*, 104–7; Coüasnon, *Church of the Holy Sepulchre*, 41, cf. pl. 20b.

[85] Helpfully summarized in Gibson and Taylor, *Beneath the Church*, 74–6. See also Coüasnon, *Church of the Holy Sepulchre*, 42–3.

[86] See the more recent floor plans in Gibson and Taylor, *Beneath the Church*, 75 fig. 45; Shalev-Hurvitz, *Holy Sites Encircled*, 389 fig. 1.

The section of the façade discovered in the Church of St. Alexander Nevsky is slightly offline to the lateral walls of the Martyrium, resulting in a slightly trapezoidal shape.[87]

The Martyium basilica was unusually large, boasting five aisles including the nave (Eusebius, *Life of Constantine*, 3.37),[88] a number that was only matched in Palestine by the Church of the Nativity, which was also Constantinian. However, Eusebius informs us that the Martyrium had two storeys (*Life of Constantine*, 3.37), which the Church of the Nativity did not. It was by far the most impressive Christian commemorative structure in the eastern Roman Empire in the fourth century CE. Based on the extant discoveries, the size of the basilica was 58.50 m in length and 40.50 m in width.[89] Coüasnon estimates the height of the building above the nave (thus, at the clerestory) at 22 m.[90] This would have been an extraordinarily imposing basilica of uncommon size. By comparison, the Eleona, a Constantinian sister building to the Church of the Holy Sepulchre whose basic form has been reconstructed on its original site on the Mount of Olives, measured 25.50 m in length and 18 m in width.[91] The Martyrium was thus more than twice the size of the Eleona. A comparison with another well-known church in Palestine may further help the reader to fully conceive of the size of the Martyrium. The basilica at Kursi, a fifth-century construction that lies outside the scope of our investigation due to its date, is in such a good state of preservation that modern visitors can get a sense of its grandeur. The basilica at Kursi measures 45 m in length and 25 m in width.[92] Though impressive, it would have been dwarfed by the Martyrium.

The apse itself was oriented west, and points the building in the general direction of the Aedicule, though it is slightly offset to the south.[93] Eusebius describes a "hemisphere" at the head of the basilica, apparently referring to the apse.[94] He writes, "Facing these [the doors] as the chief point of the whole was the hemisphere attached to the highest part of the royal house, ringed with twelve columns to match the number of the Apostles of the Savior, their tops decorated with great bowls made of silver" (*Life of Constantine*, 3.38). What exactly is being described here is unclear, though it has been suggested that the columns described here supported a dome over the apse.[95] It is admittedly difficult to reconstruct precisely what sort of structure Eusebius is describing here, leading Megan Boomer and Robert Ousterhout to write that "Eusebius's text, and the difficulty of situating twelve columns in an apse with a diameter of 8.2 meters, has

---

[87] Patrich, "Early Church of the Holy Sepulchre," 112.

[88] On the unusual number of aisles, see the comments of Coüasnon, *Church of the Holy Sepulchre*, 42; MacMullen, *Second Church*, 121; and Bagatti, *Church from the Circumcision*, 191. The Constantinian St. Peter's Church in Rome also featured five aisles. Of all known Christian basilicas from the fourth century CE, only these three are known to have five aisles.

[89] Gibson and Taylor, *Beneath the Church*, 76; Patrich, "Early Church of the Holy Sepulchre," 111; following the dimensions of Corbo's reconstruction (see *Santa Sepolcro*, 226–7 pl. 31).

[90] Coüasnon, *Church of the Holy Sepulchre*, 44.

[91] Vincent and Abel, *Jérusalem Nouvelle*, 337–60; cf. also Shalev-Hurvitz, *Holy Sites Encircled*, 86.

[92] Vassilios Tzaferis, "The Early Christian Monastery at Kursi," in *Ancient Churches Revealed*, ed. Yoram Tsafrir (Jerusalem: Israel Exploration Society, 1993), 77–9 (78).

[93] Cf. Patrich, "Early Church of the Holy Sepulchre," 111; Gibson and Taylor, *Beneath the Church*, 74.

[94] See Wilkinson, *Egeria's Travels*, 20 n. 4. Cf. also Coüasnon, *Church of the Holy Sepulchre*, 44.

[95] Cf. Gibson and Taylor, *Beneath the Church*, 74. See, however, Cameron and Hall, *Life of Constantine*, 290; see also the cautious discussion in Shalev-Hurvitz, *Holy Sites Encircled*, 58–60.

led to a variety of fanciful reconstructions by scholars—highlighting the difficulties of using text to re-envision architecture in the absence of material evidence."[96]

The decoration of the interior was grand. According to Eusebius, the Martyrium was faced on the interior with marble slabs, and the ceiling was fitted with coffers plated with gold (*Life of Constantine*, 3.36). Marble and gold are also mentioned in Constantine's letter to Macarius ordering the building's construction (*Life of Constantine*, 3.31–2). Egeria also mentions the marble and gold in Constantine's structure, as well as mosaics (*Itin. Eger.* 25.9), not only in the basilica but also in the Anastasis and "at the Cross." Although the marble is now gone, some evidence of its presence remains in other parts of the church. Revetment holes for marble facing are still visible in some areas of the modern Anastasis (in the apses, for example).[97] Moreover, the recent studies of the Aedicule uncovered the grey Constantinian marble cladding of the burial shelf in the Aedicule[98] and found that it was Proconnesian marble, which was commonly used for Roman monumental architecture.[99] The marbles of the Martyrium and of the rest of the complex may thus have looked something like the grey Proconnesian marbles that were famously used in the Hagia Sophia two centuries later.

Although the Constantinian mosaic floors of the Church of the Holy Sepulchre complex have not survived, excavations at Bethlehem have uncovered mosaic floors dating to the fourth century in the Church of the Nativity below the present floors.[100] These fourth-century[101] Bethlehem mosaics feature complex geometric designs, meander patterns, as well as figurative panels depicting birds and vegetation.[102] Since the Church of the Nativity is also a Constantinian construction, and something of a sibling to the Church of the Holy Sepulchre, the mosaics of the Holy Sepulchre complex were probably comparable to what has been discovered at Bethlehem. Thus, while little of the décor of the Constantian Church of the Holy Sepulchre has survived, it may nevertheless be imagined.

Recent excavations have revealed a large square structure dated to the fourth century to the north of the basilica, whose walls are bonded to the church. The excavators suggest that this may have been the baptistery of the Church of the Holy Sepulchre. The baptistery is mentioned by the Bordeaux Pilgrim (*Itin. Burd.* 594), so its existence is attested in the earliest layer of the literary evidence. In his address to the newly baptized, Cyril describes a ritual in the outer hall of the baptistery in which the newly baptized would stand in the outer hall of the baptistery facing west, stretch

---

[96] Megan Boomer and Robert G. Ousterhout, "The Church of the Holy Sepulchre," in *Routledge Handbook on Jerusalem*, ed. Suleiman A. Mourad, Naomi Koltun-Fromm, and Bedross Der Matossian (New York: Routledge, 2018), 169–84 (171).

[97] See Bagatti, *Church from the Gentiles*, 166.

[98] Antonia Moropoulou, Ekaterini T. Delegou, Maria Apostolopoulou, Aikaterini Kolaiti, Christos Papatrechas, George Economou, and Constantinos Mavrogonatos, "The White Marbles of the Tomb of Christ in Jerusalem: Characterization and Provenance," *Sustainability* 11 (2019): 1–32; Moropolou et al., "OSL Mortar Dating," 88.

[99] Moropoulou et al., "White Marbles," esp. 27.

[100] William Harvey, "The Early Basilica at Bethlehem," *PEQ* 68, no. 1 (1936): 28–33 (28–31). See also Michele Bacci, *The Mystic Cave: A History of the Nativity Church in Bethlehem*, Conviva 1 (Viella: Masaryk University, 2017), 46–51.

[101] On the date of these mosaics, see Bacci, *Mystic Cave*, 49–51.

[102] Ibid., 46–9.

out one's hand, and "renounce Satan as though he stood before you" (*Myst. Cat.* 1.2). Cyril's interpretation of this ritual, which took place in this baptistery, is notable. He explains the "symbolic meaning" of the ritual in connection to the Passover story and to the Exodus narrative of Moses parting the Red Sea (Exod 14). When the Egyptian army pursued the Israelites, God instructed Moses, "Stretch out your hand over the sea, so that the water may come back upon the Egyptians, upon their chariots and chariot drivers and the subsequent drowning of Pharaoh's army" (v. 26), thus saving the Israelites from their pursuers (vv. 27–31).

Cyril connects the Exodus narrative, in turn, with Christ (*Myst. Cat.* 1.3). He then parallels Red Sea narrative with baptism, saying,

> Of old the tyrant pursued the people into the sea; in your case this headstrong, shameless demon, who is the origin of all evil, followed you even into the springs of salvation. The earlier tyrant was drowned in the sea; here the tyrant disappears in the water of salvation.[103]

The renunciation of Satan that took place at the baptistery of the Church of the Holy Sepulchre was thus a ritual, symbolic reenactment of Moses' act of stretching out his hand to bring the waters of the Red Sea back over the Egyptians. The parallels between the Exodus narrative of the escape from Egypt and the life of Jesus allow for a Christological reinterpretation of the Exodus event, which bridges the gap between Moses and the newly baptized in fourth-century Jerusalem. Thus, the drowning of Pharaoh in the Red Sea[104] symbolizes the drowning of Satan in the waters of baptism, made possible by the blood of Christ, the new Passover lamb (*Myst. Cat.* 1.3).

To the west of the Martyrium was an inner courtyard, a triportico that stood between the Martyrium and the Anastasis.[105] Significant remains of this triportico exist today in the Arches of the Virgin in the modern Church of the Holy Sepulchre.[106] It was in this courtyard that the Rock of Calvary was featured, in the southeast corner. At some point, a cross was erected on the rock.[107] Eusebius describes "a very large space wide open to the fresh air, which was decorated with a pavement of light-colored stone on the ground, and enclosed on three sides by long surrounding colonnades" (*Life of Constantine*, 3.35). Curiously, Eusebius neglects to mention the single most important feature of the inner courtyard, which was the Rock of Calvary.[108] However, it is mentioned frequently by Egeria, who refers to it as the place "before the Cross," as a location within the Church of the Holy Sepulchre complex at which liturgical

---

[103] *Myst. Cat.* 1.3. Translation from Yarnold, *Cyril of Jerusalem*, 170.
[104] As understood by Cyril in *Myst. Cat.* 1.2, though not specifically mentioned in Exod 14:27–29.
[105] See Corbo, *Santo Sepolcro*, 225; cf. also discussion in Coüasnon, *Church of the Holy Sepulchre*, 38–40; Patrich, "Early Church of the Holy Sepulchre," 108; Gibson and Taylor, *Beneath the Church*, 77; Alessandra Angeloni, "The Interpretation of Wall Stratigraphy of the North Transept of the Holy Sepulchre in Jerusalem," in *Jerusalem – The Holy Sepulchre: Research and Investigations (2007–2011)*, ed. Grazia Tucci (Florence: Altralinea Edizioni, 2019), 47–67 (esp. 51–2).
[106] See the stratigraphical study by ibid., esp. 51–2.
[107] See *Itin. Eger.* (e.g.) 24.7, 25.8, 27.2, 37.4–5; Jerome, Epistle. 108, 9.2; *Breviarius* 2.
[108] See the previous discussion on Eusebius and his avoidance of the topic of Golgotha above. Cf. Walker, *Holy City*, 252–75.

functions take place.[109] She describes the atrium "before the Cross" as outdoors, "like a rather large and quite beautiful court which is between the Cross and the Anastasis," which was one of the main gathering areas in the complex (*Itin. Eger.* 37.4). It was in this space that the Good Friday public reading of the passion narrative took place, along with readings from the Psalms, Prophets, and New Testament Epistles that were understood to refer to the passion (*Itin. Eger.* 37.4–7), as discussed in Chapter 2. Ordinarily, the weekly reading of the passion narrative took place at the Aedicule, except on Good Friday.

The fourth-century version of the *Breviarius* designates this whole inner courtyard as Golgotha, "a great court where the Lord was crucified," and describes "a silver screen round this Mount, where the Cross of the Lord has been displayed, adorned with gold and gems and a dome above" (2). Gibson and Taylor suggest that the slot hole on top of the Rock of Calvary that is venerated as the spot where Jesus' cross was fixed was actually the slot for the golden cross that was placed here in the fourth century,[110] which makes good sense of the material and literary evidence. If this is the case, then there is some archaeological evidence for this golden cross and its placement on the Rock of Calvary. As previously discussed above, the author of the *Breviarius* identifies Golgotha as the place where Adam was formed, which indicates that the popular Adamic Golgotha traditions were probably commemorated at this place, and combined with the commemoration of Jesus on the vernacular level. There are no indications that this was done on an official level in the liturgy, and no architecture dedicated to Adam appeared here until the time of Modestus, after the Persian invasion in the seventh century.[111]

There is some debate as to what lay to the west beyond the inner courtyard in the age of Constantine. There is wide agreement that, at some point, the Aedicule was housed in a rotunda, called the Anastasis ("Resurrection"). However, some scholars have argued that it was constructed later in the fourth century[112] and was not a part of Constantine's original construction, while others maintain that it was indeed a part of the original Constantinian complex.[113]

The issue primarily revolves around the interpretation of the literary evidence.[114] There is wide agreement that Egeria mentions that Anastasis rotunda in her *Itinerarium* (p. 24). However, some scholars have maintained that Eusebius (in *Life of Constantine*,

---

[109] E.g., *Itin. Eger.* 37.4–5.
[110] Gibson and Taylor, *Beneath the Church*, 60.
[111] Taylor, *Christians and the Holy Places*, 132–4; Coüasnon, *Church of the Holy Sepulchre*, 50. See discussion in Kelley, *Church of the Holy Sepulchre*, 104–5. Kelley rightly notes that the evidence for a later date is circumstantial.
[112] E.g., Coüasnon, *Church of the Holy Sepulchre*, 14–17, 21–3; Gibson and Taylor, *Beneath the Church*, 77; E. D. Hunt, *Holy Land Pilgrimage in the Later Roman Empire AD 312–460* (Oxford: Clarendon Press, 2002), 11.
[113] André Grabar, *Martyrium: Recherches sur le culte des reliques et l'art chrétien antique*, 2 vols. (Paris: Les Éditions d'art et histoire, 1943–6), 257; Bagatti, *Church from the Gentiles*, 165–175; Corbo, *Santa Sepolcro*; Shalev-Hurvitz, *Holy Sites Encircled*, 62–71.
[114] See, however, the disagreement between Corbo and Coüasnon about the dating of the wall in the transept of the present day Magdalene chapel (wall "G"). Corbo, *Santa Sepolcro*, iii (photo 35); Coüasnon, *Church of the Holy Sepulchre*, 23. However, as Shalev-Hurvitz notes, both interpretations are based on each respective scholar's reading of the literary evidence (*Holy Sites Encircled*, 64).

c.335 CE) and the Bordeaux Pilgrim (c.333 CE) do not make mention of the rotunda, leading to the conclusion that the rotunda was constructed at a later time than the rest of the Constantinian complex.[115] If this is correct, then the Aedicule would have stood in an open-air courtyard until the Anastasis rotunda was built later in the fourth century.

It must be noted that this reconstruction rests primarily upon an argument from silence in the literary evidence. The archaeological evidence has not settled this matter as of yet.[116] Recently, Shalev-Hurvitz has called the hypothesis of the later date of the Anastasis into serious question. She notes that the earliest unambiguous reference to the Anastasis as a building comes from Cyril of Jerusalem (c.350 CE), who identifies Constantine as its builder (*Cat.* 14.14, 22).[117] Moreover, Shalev-Hurvitz argues that Eusebius does discuss the rotunda in *Life of Constantine*. It is likely that Eusebius is in fact talking about the rotunda when he describes Constantine's decoration of the tomb of Jesus "like the head of the whole," particularly when he mentions the "superb columns" (*Life of Constantine*, 3.34), since the function of the columns would otherwise be puzzling.[118] Further, Eusebius indicates that the complex was built "around the Saviour's tomb" (*Life of Constantine*, 4.47). To add to this, Shalev-Hurvitz also observes that Egeria attributes the construction of the Anastasis to Constantine (*Itin. Eger.* 25.9) and that she also states that both the Anastasis and the Martyrium were consecrated on the same day (*Itin. Eger.* 48.1–2), which would necessitate them both being Constantinian.[119]

Shalev-Hurvitz's arguments convincingly show that the Anastasis was remembered as being Constantinian in the decades that followed its consecration, first by Cyril, who wrote in relatively close temporal proximity to the building's construction, and then by Egeria. Moreover, Eusebius' description is unclear, but he mentions some features that are best understood as references to the Anastasis rotunda. There is also no direct or clear evidence to the contrary. As a result, in lieu of further archaeological evidence, the best hypothesis is that the rotunda was part of the original Constantinian construction.

The Constantinian Anastasis is well preserved in comparison to the other areas of the fourth-century complex, and its form has been largely preserved in the form of the modern rotunda. It has an interior wall that is semicircular, which creates a

---

[115] E.g., Coüasnon, *Church of the Holy Sepulchre*, 14–17; Gibson and Taylor, *Beneath the Church*, 77; Hunt, *Holy Land Pilgrimage*, 11; Walker, *Holy City*, 251; Krautheimer, *Early Christian and Byzantine Architecture*, 462–3 n. 45. Notably, Coüasnon held that the Anastasis was part of the original Constantinian plan but was completed at a later date. The other scholars cited in this note do not ascribe the planning of the rotunda to Constantine.

[116] Cf. Shalev-Hurvitz, *Holy Sites Encircled*, 63–4. See, however, Angeloni, "Interpretation of the Wall Stratigraphy," 53, who notes a "clear hiatus" between the Constantinian constructions and those of Modestus. Angeloni is speaking specifically about the North Transept, but her construction phases (table 1, on p. 48) attribute the rotunda as well as the transept of the Crusader church and the Arches of the Virgin to Constantine, apparently regarding the North Transept and the rotunda as a single construction from the same period.

[117] Shalev-Hurvitz, *Holy Sites Encircled*, 62–3. Contra Gibson and Taylor, who claim that Cyril never mentioned the Anastasis (*Beneath the Church*, 77).

[118] Shalev-Hurvitz, *Holy Sites Encircled*, 59.

[119] Ibid., 70.

round ambulatory space around the central focus of the interior space, which is the Aedicule. The outer walls, which are preserved to a height between 11 and 12 m,[120] are polygonal rather than semicircular, forming half of a 24-sided polygon.[121] The rotunda has three relatively small apses, on the south, north, and west sides. The Aedicule lay at the intersection of the axis of the north-south apses and the western apse. The Anastasis was crowned with a dome, which is depicted in the Madaba map.[122] The dome was supported by a circle of four pairs of piers, one pair each on the north, south, east, and west sides, and twelve columns in groups of three between each pair of piers surrounding the Aedicule.[123] The façade of the rotunda was rectilineal, measuring 46 m in length.[124]

The Aedicule was the central focus of the Anastasis. As discussed above, it enclosed the rock-cut tomb and was probably faced with the same grey marble that was recently found covering the burial bench. According to Eusebius, it was lavishly decorated (*Life of Constantine*, 3.33–4). Its basic form is depicted on pewter pilgrim ampullae and in the marble Narbonne model, which may date to the fifth century.[125] This has allowed scholars to reasonably determine its appearance.[126] According to Biddle, who has produced the most detailed study of the Aedicule to date,

> the Edicule consisted of two parts. In front was a porch of four columns with a pediment and a gabled roof. Behind was the Tomb Chamber, freed on all sides from the living rock, rounded or polygonal outside, covered with marble, decorated by five columns with semi-detached bases and capitals, and surmounted by a conical roof of tapering panels, topped with a cross.[127]

Interpreting the Monument

Now that we have reviewed the history of the site and its architecture, we are primed to interpret the Constantinian Church of the Holy Sepulchre as a site of Jesus-memory. As we have discussed above, monuments convey narratives written in stone. What sort of narratives were conveyed by the Constantinian Church of the Holy Sepulchre, how were they conveyed, and why?

On the surface, the Church of the Holy Sepulchre presents testimony to the crucifixion, burial, and subsequent resurrection of Jesus of Nazareth. This is what we might designate as the primary narrative that it tells. The site is bifocal, featuring both the Anastasis and the Martyrium, which are essentially two separate churches contained within the same complex. The actual proper sites of memory, the places that

---

[120] Coüasnon, *Church of the Holy Sepulchre*, 26; Bagatti, *Church from the Gentiles*, 166.
[121] Shalev-Hurvitz, *Holy Sites Encircled*, 44.
[122] Cf. ibid., 45 n. 11, 58–59; contra Gibson and Taylor, *Beneath the Church*, 77.
[123] See Coüasnon, *Church of the Holy Sepulchre*, 27–32; cf. also Shalev-Hurvitz, *Holy Sites Encircled*, 44.
[124] Coüasnon, *Church of the Holy Sepulchre*, 32–5; Murphy-O'Connor, *Keys to Jerusalem*, 204.
[125] Biddle, *Tomb of Christ*, 21–3.
[126] See, e.g., ibid., 68–9; Wilkinson, *Egeria's Travels*, 173–5.
[127] Biddle, *Tomb of Christ*, 69.

positively drip with commemoration and tradition, are the Aedicule and the Rock of Calvary with its cross.

The entire structure is oriented towards the Aedicule. Everything points to it and leads to it. The apse of the Martyrium points toward it, and it lies at the intersection of the axes of the three apses of the Anastasis. By moving through the structure beginning from its monumental eastern entrance off of the cardo on the eastern end, one's journey would come to its completion at the Aedicule. Much like Solomon's Temple, which progressed in increasing sanctity from the outer court, to the inner court, then to the sanctuary, and finally to the Holy of Holies, so too do the structures of the Holy Sepulchre progress in sanctity. From the outer court, one would move into the Martyrium, and then into the inner court, where the Rock of Calvary and the cross were featured, then into the Anastasis, then into the Aedicule, and finally into the new Holy of Holies of the new high priest, the tomb chamber.

The Aedicule commemorates the event of the resurrection. To the faithful who visited it, it was not just the site of Jesus' burial but also the place where he was raised from the dead. To this effect, the Aedicule and the Anastasis differed from other similar architectural structures that housed the body of a deceased person of importance, such as the Mausoleum of Diocletian in Split, insofar as there was no body at rest within it. It is a literal, demonstrative presentation of the gospel narrative of the empty tomb. Much like the Markan version of the narrative, in which the risen Jesus does not appear, the visitor is invited to ponder and consider the meaning of the empty space. As mentioned above, monuments invite visitors to reflect on the narrative that they present. In the Aedicule, there is no body to venerate, and that is the point. It communicates the powerful, shocking ending of the canonical gospel narratives in space and architecture by presenting the visitor with an empty tomb.

By enshrining the empty tomb, decorating it with imperial splendor, housing it within the rotunda of the Anastasis, and having the whole grand complex oriented toward what was once a simple rock-cut tomb, the Church of the Holy Sepulchre communicated the victory of the risen Christ over death. Hence, Coüasnon writes, that the Anastasis "expresses an idea of Triumph … a monument to the glory of Christ the Conqueror,"[128] and further, "in Constantine's thoughts, the Rotunda was the triumphal mausoleum erected to the memory of the Risen One, the founder of the Church."[129] It is important to remember that at the time when the Church of the Holy Sepulchre was first constructed, no Christian architecture of that size, grandeur, or scale existed anywhere in the Eastern empire. Thus, its appearance must have been impressive indeed, a fitting monument to the risen Lord.

As discussed above, the apse of the Martyrium is oriented toward the tomb, though slightly offset. It also features twelve columns. While much of the scholarly discourse has centered upon what practical architectural function the columns served, I suggest that it might be helpful to consider the potential symbolic value of the architecture. The number twelve has clear symbolic value in the Christian tradition, in literature, art, and architecture, typically representing the Twelve Apostles. In this case, Eusebius

---

[128] Coüasnon, *Church of the Holy Sepulchre*, 35.
[129] Ibid.

specifically connects the number of pillars in the apse of the Martyrium with the number of Jesus' Apostles (*Life of Constantine*, 3.38). The columns in the apse, pointing toward the Aedicule, symbolically represent the Twelve bearing witness to the empty tomb. Hence, it is an architectural interpretation of Jesus' words to the Eleven (the Twelve less Judas), "you will be my witnesses [Greek *martyres*] in Jerusalem, in all Judea and Samaria, and to the ends of the earth" (Acts 1:8b), with particular emphasis placed on Jerusalem. Indeed, in the narrative of Acts, the Twelve bear witness to the resurrection (Greek *anastasis*) in Jerusalem (2:29–36). Furthermore, the imagery of the Apostles in Jerusalem as "pillars" may also allude to Paul's designation of Peter, James the Just, and John as "pillars" in Gal 2:9. In light of this, it seems likely that the nomenclature of the basilica, the "Martyrium," is related at least in part to the fact that it, in pointing toward the Aedicule, bears witness to the empty tomb just as the Apostles, represented by the columns in its apse, once did. It thus symbolically continued their witness.

The twelve pillars surrounding the tomb in the Anastasis also have symbolic value. The very fact that the number of pillars in both the Anastasis[130] and in the apse of the Martyrium[131] was counted and recorded by visitors shows that this symbolic relevance was not lost on pilgrims. It is possible that they also represent the Apostles' witness to the empty tomb. However, given the New Jerusalem ideology of the Church of the Holy Sepulchre, it is also possible that the twelve pillars reflect the architectural repetition of the number twelve in the description of the heavenly Jerusalem in Rev 21:10–14, 21. In particular, the "twelve foundations" with the names of the twelve apostles in v. 14 might have influenced the architectural design in its representation of the Twelve through the pillars of the Anastasis.

Through a monument, writes Donohoe, "someone is attempting to say something to someone about something."[132] The Church of the Holy Sepulchre shapes the canonical passion narrative and the history that underlies it into monumental architecture. It is bifocal, combining two architectural forms, the rotunda and the basilica. In order to better grasp the meaning conveyed by the Church of the Holy Sepulchre, it is necessary to consider the iconography of that architecture.

The interpretation of the iconography of the Martyrion as a basilica is bound up with the matter of the Christian adoption of the basilica form in general. The Martyrion was one of the earliest Christian basilicas, but it was not the first, nor even the first in the region. In the East, it was preceded by the basilica at Tyre.[133] It is, however, the first basilical life-of-Jesus commemorative church built in Palestine. Thus, it provides a sort of blueprint that would be emulated by later commemorative churches. Much has already been written on the origins of the Christian basilica, and there is no need to review all of those matters here, save for the broad contours.[134] The basilica form was adopted for Christian use from Roman civic architecture.[135] In Roman usage, a

---

[130] By Arculf, in Adomnan, *The Holy Places*, 2.4.
[131] By Eusebius, *Life of Constantine*, 3.38.
[132] Donohow, *Remembering Places*, 142.
[133] Eusebius, *Hist. Ecc.* 10.4.
[134] For a good recent summary of the state of the question on this issue, see Stewart, "Churches," 134–41.
[135] On this, see Krautheimer, *Early Christian and Byzantine Architecture*, 41–3.

"basilica" was, as Krautheimer writes, "but a large meeting hall."[136] In fact, just over a decade earlier, in the year 312, Constantine had himself completed the construction of one such civic basilica, the Basilica of Maxentius and Constantine in Rome. This particular basilica's similarity to Christian basilicas is immediately identifiable, as it features a nave terminating in an apse with two aisles. The form was thus recognizable as coming from the world of civic, official, public architecture. The Marytrion would have been instantly recognizable as a gathering place to those who saw it in the fourth century. At the same time, there was a clear architectural distinction between Christian basilicas and pagan temples.[137] However, this does not mean that Roman basilicas had no religious associations. For example, the emperor's divine image would have been fixed in the apse of Roman forum basilicas.[138] Famously, a colossal statue of Constantine himself was housed in the apse of the Basilica of Maxentius and Constantine.

It is tempting to identify the basilical form of the Martyrion with imperial ideology. Krautheimer, for example, has drawn attention to the parallels between early Christian basilicas and the form of the imperial palace basilica, in which the emperor's divine majesty sat enthroned in the apse.[139] However, basilical churches were frequently built without imperial funding, as is the case with the basilica at Tyre, which preceded the Martyrion. Moreover, it is hard to imagine Christians readily adopting elements of the symbolism and ideology of the imperial cult.[140] Thus, as Charles Anthony Stewart writes, "a better explanation it would seem, is that Christians adopted the basilica at least in part because it conveyed *royal* splendor rather than *imperial* ideology."[141] When applied to the Martyrion, we can imagine how that royal splendor, represented in the architectural form as well as in its lavish decoration, might have been directed primarily toward the Risen Lord who the building commemorates and secondarily reflected the emperor who constructed and adorned it.

The apse of a basilica provides orientation for the building. As mentioned above, the apse of the Martyrion points generally toward the Anastasis. Thus, the royal splendor of the basilica is thereby quite literally directed toward the place where the Risen Lord Jesus was commemorated. There is a sort of royal Christology expressed in this, one made all the more apparent by Constantine's instruction that the Martyrion be "a basilica superior to those in all other places … such that all the excellences of every city are surpassed by this foundation."[142] The Jesus remembered by the Martyrion is thus a royal Jesus, one for whom a monument greater than any other in the Roman world would be fit. Based on our discussion, we may conclude that the purposes and meaning of the adoption of basilical architecture for the Martyrion include the orientation provided by the apse and its twelve columns toward the Anastasis, representing the witness borne by the Twelve to the resurrection, the communication of royal splendor

---

[136] Ibid., 42.
[137] Cf. ibid., 41; Stewart, "Churches," 338.
[138] Cf. Krautheimer, *Early Christian and Byzantine Architecture*, 42.
[139] Ibid.
[140] Cf. Stewart, "Churches," 138.
[141] Ibid. Emphases original.
[142] Eusebius, *Life of Constantine*, 31.1.

through an architectural form associated with official and imperial purposes, and identity formation through a form that drew upon Roman architecture.

Although it was not the only concentric church, as the earliest concentric church, the Anastasis functioned as a prototype to be emulated by later concentric churches.[143] Thus, some discussion of this form is most appropriate here. Our understanding of the architectural iconography of the Anastasis rotunda has been greatly advanced as a result of Shalev-Hurvitz's recent study of the concentric churches of Jerusalem.[144] As Shalev-Hurvitz has astutely observed, all four of the concentric churches in Jerusalem (the Anastasis, the Church of the Ascension, the Tomb of Mary, and the Kathisma) were built over holy sites related to events in the lives of Jesus or Mary.[145] Although concentric churches unrelated to life-of-Jesus holy sites would eventually be constructed in Palestine, such as those at Caesarea and Scythopolis, the fact that so many major commemorative sites in Palestine, including those beyond Jerusalem at Bethlehem and Capernaum, espoused some form of concentric church in the fourth and fifth centuries speaks to the utility of the form for commemoration.

The concentric form naturally allows for the focus of the building to be placed over a particular point in the structure's very center. While it is not the only form that creates such a focal point,[146] it is nevertheless an effective way to do so. Moreover, it allows for that point to be accessible and seen from all sides, and for circumambulation around it.[147] The liturgy in the Anastasis was, as discussed earlier, performed from that venerated focal point in the center rather than from an apse as would be the case in a basilica. The form thus places focus on what is unique about the Anastasis and what cannot be reproduced anywhere other than the place where it stood—the traditional tomb of Jesus.

As previous scholarship has demonstrated, the natural architectural context in which to view the Anastasis is that of Roman mausolea or domed *heroa*.[148] It is important to consider what this architectural iconography would have signaled about the person and event that the Anastasis commemorated. Taylor has argued that the similarity between the Anastasis rotunda and imperial mausolea problematizes its Constantinian date, since mausolea were meant as reminders of those whose remains were buried within them.[149] Thus, "surrounding the Edicule with a ring of columns

---

[143] Cf. Shalev-Hurvitz, *Holy Sites Encircled*, 183.
[144] Ibid.
[145] Ibid., 184.
[146] Consider, for instance, the cruciform church at Jacob's Well, with the well at the intersection of the arms.
[147] Cf. Jordan Pickett and Oliver Nicholson, "Octagonal Buildings," in *The Oxford Dictionary of Late Antiquity*, ed. Oliver Nicholson (Oxford: Oxford University Press, 2018), 1095.
[148] Cf. Krautheimer, *Early Christian and Byzantine Architecture*, 74; Shalev-Hurvitz, *Holy Sites Encircled*, 173–6; see also Joan E. Taylor, "Christian Archaeology in Palestine," in *The Oxford Handbook of Early Christian Archaeology*, ed. David K. Pettegrew, William R. Caraher, and Thomas W. Davis (Oxford: Oxford University Press, 2019), 369–89 (374). On the architecture of domed Roman mausolea in our period, see Mark J. Johnson, *The Imperial Mausoleum in Late Antiquity* (Cambridge: Cambridge University Press, 2014), esp. 58–109 and 110–28. For an in-depth study of a late Republican mausoleum, see Henrik Gerding, "The Tomb of Caecilia Metella: Tumulus, Tropaeum and Thymele," PhD diss., Lund University, Lund, 2010.
[149] Taylor, "Christian Archaeology in Palestine," 374.

without a roof would have avoided any simple analogy with the imperial mausolea and would signal Christ's tomb as an empty one, without bodily remains. Opening the roof to heaven above would have architecturally proclaimed Christ's resurrection."[150] This is an intriguing suggestion, and one that takes the iconography of the architecture seriously. However, the problem remains that the rotunda was indeed built by *somebody* at some time and attributing to Constantius II rather than to Constantine kicks the can down the road. Whether it was Constantine and his architects or Constantius II and his, somebody endowed the tomb of Jesus with a rotunda resembling an imperial mausoleum, and it is essential to attempt to understand the ideology behind this deployment of architectural iconography before we can determine who would or would not subscribe to such an ideology.

Recent scholarship on Roman imperial mausolea has drawn attention to their function as cultic sites with religious functions and meaning.[151] As Mark Johnson has argued, imperial mausolea were tombs for semidivine people, monuments "meant to project an image of majesty and importance for all others to see, for these were, in fact, *sepulcra divorum*, tombs of the *divi*, or demigods, an honor reserved for emperors."[152] As a result, mausolea were sacred spaces and used for worship. Even Christian imperial mausolea were understood as places of worship, as the *divi* buried within them "entered the realm of sainthood on a popular if not always an official level."[153] The form of the rotunda, a common element of imperial monumental tombs, symbolized the cosmos,[154] with the dome symbolizing heaven.[155] Moreover, Johnson has noted some distinctions between pagan and Christian imperial mausolea and pagan imperial mausolea: Christian mausolea were typically attached to churches and did not feature crypts.[156]

How, then, should we understand the use of this architectural form for the Anastasis? We must observe that the Church of the Holy Sepulchre is distinguished in form from pagan imperial mausolea in the same way that Christian mausolea were distinguished from their pagan counterparts. The Anastasis is attached (though through a shared courtyard) to a basilical church, the Martyrion, and features the Aedicule rather than an underground crypt. Thus, while the Anastasis incorporates the basic design of pagan imperial mausolea, it is not entirely identical to them and should be seen within the tradition of the Christian adaptation of the form. The fact that the imperial mausoleum form was reserved for imperial royalty[157] speaks to the

---

[150] Ibid.
[151] Cf. Johnson, *Imperial Mausoleum*, esp. 1; Penelope J. E. Davies, *Death and the Emperor: Roman Imperial Funerary Monuments from Augustus to Marcus Aurelius* (Austin: University of Texas Press, 2004), esp. 86.
[152] Johnson, *Imperial Mausoleum*, 1.
[153] Ibid., 197.
[154] Ibid., 182.
[155] Ibid., 183. See Cassius Dio, *Roman History*, 53.27.2-4, in Earnest Cary, trans., *Dio Cassius: Roman History*, 9 vols., Loeb Classical Library (New York: Macmillan, 1914-27), 6: 265; Maurus Servius Honoratus, *Commentary on the Aeneid of Virgil*, 1.505, in Georgius Thilo and Hermannus Hagen, eds., *In Vergilii carmina comentarii. Servii Grammatici qui feruntur in Vergilii carmina commentarii* (Leipzig: B. G. Teubner, 1881), 157–8.
[156] Johnson, *Imperial Mausoleum*, 196 (see also 110–79).
[157] As Shalev-Hurvitz has noted, the mausoleum of Helena was contemporary with the Church of the Holy Sepulchre, constructed sometime between 324 and 330 (*Holy Sites Encircled*, 174–5). Thus, at

fact that the person commemorated by the Anastasis, Jesus of Nazareth, was someone who should be recognized as royalty as an emperor might be. Thus, we see in the form itself a reception in architectural form of the early Christian tradition of the kingship of Jesus.[158]

The cultic function of imperial mausolea, as a place commemorating deceased emperors as divine persons is also a significant dimension of the architectural iconography of the Anastasis. Granted, the title and concept of the deceased emperor as *divus*, a human who attained apotheosis and became divine,[159] is not an exact fit for the Jesus of the Nicene Creed, who is "very God of very God" and "of one substance with the Father." However, the ideology need not be identical, as it is clearly a Christian *adaptation* of a pagan architectural tradition associated with royal human beings who were considered divine. Taylor, as mentioned above, is correct to highlight the most important distinction between imperial mausolea and the Anastasis, which is that the Anastasis, despite commemorating a burial place, did not contain the body of Jesus of Nazareth. The recreation of the experience of the empty tomb in the form of the empty Aedicule, combined with the narrative of the resurrection expressed by the performative passion liturgy and the teaching about the resurrection that took place in the complex[160] ensured that there would be no simple identification of the Anastasis with a typical imperial mausoleum. The empty tomb and the experience of it was thus one major way in which the Anastasis was differentiated from an imperial mausoleum. The iconography called to mind the concept of a divine, royal person, but the experience of the place, including its very name, and the use of text and teaching within its precincts ensured that it proclaimed the resurrected Jesus, not the buried Jesus. In this way, he was unlike the emperors, and even unlike Constantine, who designed his own mausoleum as a rotunda that he planned to fill with the relics of the Apostles surrounding him, apparently to invoke a Christological comparison, for Constantine laid within his tomb and Jesus did not. The architectural iconography of the imperial mausoleum was thus utilized, in conjunction with the visitor's experience of the space, as a means of communicating the understanding of Jesus as both royal and divine.

The space that the Holy Sepulchre complex occupied is surely significant. As discussed above, it was situated within the premiere public space of fourth-century Jerusalem. While the selection of this space was likely related to the traditional location of the tomb of Jesus, it demands interpretation nonetheless.[161] Moreover, the simple fact that the complex laid claim to being constructed on the very place where the evangelical narrative of the crucifixion, burial, and resurrection was thought to

---

least by this time, we can say that imperial mausolea were constructed for members of the imperial family and not just for the emperor himself.

[158] E.g., as "King of the Jews" or "King of Israel" (Mark 15:2 and parallels, cf. 15:32 and parallels; Matt 2:2; John 18:33, 39, 19:2, 12, 14, 19, 21), but also as cosmic king (e.g., Rev 1:5, 17:14, 19:16).

[159] As opposed to *deus*. See the discussion and translation of Servius, *Commentary on the Aeneid of Virgil*, 5.45 in Gwynaeth McIntyre, *Imperial Cult* (Leiden: Brill, 2019), 7–9.

[160] See, e.g., Cyril of Jerusalem, *Cat.* 14.

[161] Cf. the notion of the power of space and the reshaping of it involved in the construction of imperial funerary monuments. See Davies, *Death and the Emperor*, 136–7.

have taken place is significant in and of itself. As Penelope Davies has demonstrated in her work on Roman imperial funerary monuments, topographical associations were powerful in the Roman world.[162] She points to a particularly illuminating quotation from Piso in Cicero's *De finibus* that speaks to this poignantly: "Is it our nature or our fantasy, I wonder, on seeing those places that tradition records to have been the favorite haunts of distinguished men, we are more moved than when we hear of their deeds or read something they have written?"[163] The fact that the complex was located in Jerusalem, where Jesus was crucified and buried, and with all of the religious and eschatological associations that come with the city itself, naturally makes it a monument of more particular significance in the Christian tradition than any other dedicated to the memory of Jesus' death and resurrection anywhere else in the world.

A Biblical Iconography of Architecture

While the physical architectural iconography of the Holy Sepulchre complex has highlighted certain associations that visitors to the place would have made based on visual identification with other contemporary structures in the Roman world, it is also important to consider the architectural iconography of the biblical associations and parallels that the structure would have called to mind. This is admittedly a departure from the sort of iconographical analysis of architecture that we have engaged in above, but it is no less valid. The Christian faithful who would have experienced the site, not to mention those who planned and constructed it, would likely have been just as influenced in their worldview by the literary world of the Bible as by their own cultural experiences.

The manner in which a visitor would have experienced the building draws attention to the symbolic significance of its layout. A visitor would have entered from moving from the monumental gate on the east end through to the atrium, then into the Martyrion, then the inner courtyard, then the rotunda, then the forecourt of the Aedicule, and finally into the Aedicule itself. We may make several observations here. First, much like the Jerusalem temples, both the First and the Second, the layout implies an experience of increasing sanctity as one progresses through the building.[164] The city of Jerusalem itself was holy, and from its main artery, one would enter through the gates of the Church of the Holy Sepulchre into something even more sacred. The monumental entrance, notable for its grandeur, set the space apart from the rest of the city, as one scholar has described it, "a gate of heaven in the sense that in this holy place earth meets heaven and one may pass between."[165] From there, one came to the atrium, which would have been experienced by a first-time visitor as a place of preparation that was separated by the "celestial" monumental gate from the rest of the ordinary world.[166] While the atrium would have also had practical functions for the

---

[162] Ibid., 136.
[163] Cicero, *De finibus*, 5.1.2. Cited in Davies, *Death and the Emperor*, 136.
[164] In this, Wilkinson's discussion of the similarities between Ezekiel's temple and the Constantinian commemorative churches of Palestine is instructive, in *Egeria's Travels*, 60–4.
[165] Gregory T. Armstrong, "Constantine's Churches: Symbol and Structure," *Journal of the Society of Architectural Historians* 33, no. 1 (1974): 5–16.
[166] Cf. ibid., 16.

local worshipping community as a gathering place, as per the usual function of atria in ancient churches, its semiotic role for pilgrims as a place between the gates and the basilica should also be recognized.

One would then move into the basilica, the place of congregational assembly and worship, decorated as it was in heavenly fashion. The Roman basilica is not the only relevant iconographical referent for the Martyrion. It is important to consider its relationship to biblical architecture as well. As we have already discussed, the basilical plans of the Constantinian commemorative churches were built according to the layout and dimensions of Ezekiel's vision of the heavenly temple (Ezek 40–42).[167] This too must be considered in our discussion about the iconography of the architecture of the Martyrion, particularly in light of the fact that the Holy Sepulchre complex stood facing the Temple Mount. The New Jerusalem ideology is thus a part of the architectural iconography of the Martyrion. In the Martyrion, we thus see a combination and appropriation of architectural traditions familiar to both Jewish (through the Hebrew Bible) and Roman architectural iconography. That it is specifically the heavenly, eschatological temple as Eusebius calls it, and not the Solomonic Temple nor the Tabernacle that provides the blueprint for the plan of Martyrion is surely significant. This in itself is an appropriation and deployment of narrative in monumental form.[168] Hence, it is architecturally vested with eschatological significance to the point that Eusebius is able to deem it the "New Jerusalem" (*Life of Constantine*, 3.33) in a direct allusion to the visionary New Jerusalem of Rev 21:2. In Ezek 43:1–5, the glory of the God of Israel returns to the heavenly Temple, entering by the eastern gate. Notably, the Martyrion is roughly oriented on an east-west axis, with its monumental entrance and staircase located on the eastern side. It is tempting to consider this to be a reception and reflection of that tradition, though it is difficult to say so with any certainty.

It is important also to see how this location opposite the Temple Mount at the heart of the "new" Jerusalem is a reception of the Jesus tradition. As discussed previously, Eusebius wrote that the "New Jerusalem" faced the Jerusalem of old, "which after the murder of the Lord had been overthrown in utter devastation, and paid the penalty of its wicked inhabitants" (*Life of Constantine*, 3.33). This anti-Jewish vitriol is an unfortunate instantiation of the reception of the New Testament passages that appear to place the blame for Jesus' death upon the Jewish inhabitants of Jerusalem,[169] combined with Jesus' prediction of the destruction of the Temple.[170] The implication was, moreover, that the Church of the Holy Sepulchre was the *successor* to the Jewish Temple. This "New Jerusalem" ideology was not peculiar to Eusebius. Rather, it was an intentional ideology that belonged to the very founding of the site. The date of the dedication of the Church of the Holy Sepulchre was the very same as the biblical date of Solomon's dedication of the original Jerusalem Temple (1 Kgs 8, esp. vv. 1–2).[171]

---

[167] Wilkinson, "Constantinian Churches in Palestine," 23–7; Wilkinson, *Egeria's Travels*, 62–4.
[168] On this, see Donohow, *Remembering Places*, 142.
[169] E.g., esp. Matt 27:25, but also Mark 15:9–15; Matt 27:20–23; Luke 13:21; John 18:28b–40, 20:19. See also 1 Thess 2:14–15.
[170] Mark 13:1–2; Matt 24:1–2; Luke 21:5–6.
[171] As also noted by Ari Finkelstein, *The Specter of the Jews: Emperor Julian and the Rhetoric of Ethnicity in Syrian Antioch* (Oakland: University of California Press, 2018), 102.

The selection of this particular date situated the Church of the Holy Sepulchre as the successor to the Temple[172] and, thus, the church as the true heir to Jerusalem's legacy.

Given our discussion of its grand décor above, the Martyrion would have been experienced as celestial space, space that is beyond the usual realm of human experience. It is abundantly clear from their descriptions that the decoration of the space of the basilica made an impact on both Eusebius and Egeria.[173] Both mention the gold used in the decoration of the basilica. Eusebius' description of the gold coffers is especially memorable.[174] The extensive use of gold calls to mind the imagery of the description of the Solomonic Temple (1 Kgs 6:21), whose interior was similarly overlaid with gold. The curtains and veils mentioned by Egeria (*Itin. Eger.* 25.8) also evoke sacred Temple space. The precious stones used in the decoration of the Holy Sepulchre complex (Eusebius, *Life of Constantine*, 3.40) are also of some potential significance, since precious stones appear in the decoration of the New Jerusalem in Rev 21:19.[175]

From the basilica, one would come to the inner courtyard, where the rock of Golgotha was located. Just beyond it lay the Anastasis and the Aedicule within it. The location of this open-air area before entering into the Anastasis separates the Anastasis from the Martyrion and calls to mind the biblical iconography of the altar, the place of sacrifice, located in an open air court before the sanctuary. Like the biblical First and Second Temples, the Holy Sepulchre was a place of sacrifice in the Christian theological tradition, insofar as it was the place of Jesus' crucifixion. In this way, the Holy Sepulchre is the space in which that sacrifice was offered. It was thus an architectural instantiation or image of the heavenly Temple of Heb 9–10 in which Jesus, in the mode of High Priest, offered a sacrifice of himself and entered into the Holy Place "once for all" (Heb 9:11–12). Semiotically speaking, if one were to consider this biblical image and transpose it onto the space of the Holy Sepulchre complex as the place where Jesus died and thus gave the sacrifice of himself, the Holy Place into which he would have entered would have been the Aedicule, that is, the tomb itself. This creates a striking parallel between the "Holy Place" of the heavenly temple of Hebrews, entered by Jesus the High Priest with his own blood (Heb 9:12), and the tomb enshrined as the central sacred place of the Holy Sepulchre complex, into which Jesus literally entered after his crucifixion when he was buried.

The Anastasis held the Aedicule. This was the primary sacred space enshrined by the complex, as marked by the concentric structure of the rotunda around it. As the "Holy Place" of the complex, the Aedicule was the place where the human and the divine symbolically met, much like the Holy of Holies in the Tabernacle and Jerusalem Temples. In light of this, it is significant that Egeria describes the bishop as the highest-ranking ecclesial figure, entering alone into the sacred space of the "cave" (the Aedicule)

---

[172] Similarly, see Robert Ousterhout, "New Temples and New Solomons: The Rhetoric of Byzantine Architecture," in *The Old Testament in Byzantium*, edited by Paul Magdalino and Robert Nelson, Dumbarton Oaks Byzantine Symposia and Colloquia (Washington, DC: Dumbarton Oaks, 2010), 223–53 (233–9).
[173] Eusebius, *Life of Constantine*, 3.34–40; *Itin. Eger.* 25.8–9.
[174] *Life of Constantine*, 3.36.
[175] E.g., 4Q554 Frag. 3 Col. 2.15.

during the Sunday commemorative ritual to commune with the divine through prayer (*Itin. Eger.* 24.3, 9). This strongly parallels the entrance of the High Priest alone into the Holy of Holies in Israelite and Jewish practice as well as in biblical tradition (Lev 16; Heb 9:7).

The Monument as Witness and Narrative

According to Donohoe, "Monuments function as testimony in recording the experience, in giving image or shape to something … and in making that memory available to the community as a whole. They serve as living reminders that appeal to us to remember."[176] Furthermore, monuments bear witness to the past by preserving it in the present, but also illuminate and shape the meaning of the past for the beholder.[177]

Above all, the Holy Sepulchre complex functioned as a witness to the biblical proclamation of the Easter story. It communicates the salient details of the canonical Easter narrative in architectural form to its visitors. The name *martyrion* itself directly communicates this function. The details of the Aedicule primarily reflect what is mentioned in the biblical text, including the mention of the angel seated on the right of the chamber, indicating the location of the bench on that side. Whether or not the tomb was the actual tomb in which Jesus was buried, the fact that the tomb that was selected had a bench on the right side reflects a reception of the Markan narrative. That the rest of the tomb was cut away is surely significant, as all that was left was what reflected the canonical Easter narratives.

This function of the Church of the Holy Sepulchre as a "witness" relates to its commemorative function and to the geography of memory. It was (and is) understood to be the very site of the events of the death, burial, and resurrection of Jesus. Similar to other historic sites, such as battlefields, the Church of the Holy Sepulchre was (and still is) dedicated to the reproduction of its evangelical, dominical past.[178] Naturally, it was a particular vision of the past and of the person of Jesus that the building constructed. According to Foote and Azaryahu, for sites like this, "the location itself, as the scene of past events, together with any available physical remains, can be used to create a sense of authenticity … remains of the past serve as both 'witnesses' and 'evidence.' In this symbolic capacity, they are instrumental in rendering the version of history presented at and by the site credible."[179] In this manner, the Church of the Holy Sepulchre created a sense of the authenticity of the events that it commemorated through its constructed witness and evidence; it was in itself a kind of history writing, advancing a particular vision of the authentic past, which we will discuss further below.

In light of the manner in which the Church of the Holy Sepulchre is engaged in this reproduction of the past, it is significant to observe that the fourth-century *Breviarius*[180] mentions a number of artifacts that were displayed in the Holy Sepulchre

---

[176] Donohoe, *Remembering Places*, 122.
[177] Ibid.
[178] Cf. the language of Foote and Azaryahu, "Geography of Memory," 127.
[179] Ibid., 128.
[180] As reasonably reconstructed in Wilkinson, *Jerusalem Pilgrims*, 93, cf. 3–4.

complex (*Brev.* 1–2). These included "the Lance with which they pierced the Lord," which was displayed in the center of the Martyrion basilica, the plate on which John the Baptist's head was carried, and the horn with which David was anointed, both of which were located in the court where the rock spire of Golgotha was visible, which was also where the cross was on display. These exhibits provided broader interpretive and historical contexts for visitors to the Church in combination with the site itself and its architecture.[181] All three—artifacts, site, and architecture—complemented one another "in propagating [the] official story"[182] told by the complex. Although these artifacts were all open to interpretation in the eyes of the beholder, we might at least say that the lance suggests further witness to the reality and suffering of Jesus. The plate testifies to the authenticity of the witness of John the Baptist, who also suffered a martyrdom of his own. The horn of anointing, presented within the context of Golgotha, clearly suggests a connection between Jesus and David, and along with that connection, the conception of Jesus' kingship and identity as the Anointed One, the Messiah.

The Church of the Holy Sepulchre receives the evangelical narrative of the passion and Resurrection, presents it in material form, and calls attention to it through its very existence. It would have dominated the prime public space of fourth-century Jerusalem in its royal splendor, making it impossible to ignore its witness to the death and resurrection of Jesus of Nazareth. This witness was reinforced by the weekly reading of the Easter narrative within the space of the complex. That it was also an imperial monument, commissioned by the emperor and dedicated in imperial fashion, granted that witness the air of officiality, communicating a sense of imperial approval of the story that it enshrined. It is also important to consider how that narrative would have been experienced by someone visiting the church and entering through the monumental eastern entrance, and making their way through the complex. The general progression through the building is narrated by the *Brev.* 1–2, which mentions in order the Basilica (Martyrion), Golgotha (the courtyard between the Martyrion and Anastasis), then the Holy Resurrection (Anastasis), and finally the Tomb of the Lord (the Aedicule). By progressing through this space in this order, the general outline of the Easter narrative would have been told, culminating in the Aedicule, which bore witness to the resurrection through its emptiness.

Monuments are place-embedded narratives that generate memory and history.[183] As we have seen, the primary narrative told by the Constantinian Church of the Holy Sepulchre is that of the victory of Christ in his resurrection. However, it also presses that narrative into service in order to express the stories of two other victories: the victory of Christianity over paganism and Judaism, and the victory of Constantine over his political rivals. Commemoration is a site of the construction of public memory, which has a clear political dimension insofar as the past can be controlled and represented "to express hegemonic relations of power and authority."[184] Likewise, we should naturally

---

[181] Cf. Foote and Azaryahu, "Geography of Memory," 128.
[182] Adapted from ibid.
[183] Donohoe, *Remembering Places*, 122.
[184] Cf. Foote and Azaryahu, "Geography of Memory," 129.

recognize that there was a political dimension to the commemorative activity of the Constantinian Church of the Holy Sepulchre.

The narrative of the victory of Christianity over paganism and Judaism is expressed in the location of the complex, built on the spot where a pagan temple once stood, facing the temple mount where the Jewish Temple once stood. The "New Jerusalem" ideology attached to the place, discussed above, clearly reflects this same narrative. The religious competition that existed in Palestine during the late Roman and early Byzantine periods is thus embodied in architectural form in the Church of the Holy Sepulchre. This embodiment of religious competition, combined with the incorporation of architectural traditions coming from the Roman world (in the form of the basilica and rotunda) as well as from the Jewish world (in the form of the inclusion of a rock-cut tomb as well as the shared biblical tradition of the heavenly Temple) would have contributed to the identity formation of the Christian community in Jerusalem.

The connection to the narrative of Constantine's victory is not overtly reflected in the architecture. Nevertheless, the fact that the Church of the Holy Sepulchre's construction coincides with Constantine's bicennalia, and its dedication coincides with his tricennalia, as discussed above, cannot be ignored. In Constantine's letter to Macarius, the connection between the discovery of the tomb and the defeat of Constantine's political opponents is attributed to the emperor himself. He claims that the tomb lay hidden "until through the removal of the enemy of the whole republic it was ready to be revealed, once they were set free, to his servants, truly surpasses all marvels" (Eusebius, *Life of Constantine*, 30.1). The "enemy of the whole republic" that Constantine refers to here is Licinius.[185] The implication of this passage is that the tomb of Jesus, hidden since the time of Hadrian, was made ready to be revealed through Constantine's defeat of Licinius, presumably insofar as it could only be revealed once the people were "set free" by this military victory, and insofar as it could only have happened once Constantine had sole rulership over the empire. Thus, in Constantine's mind (or at least the mind of Constantine as represented by this letter, whether it is authentic or otherwise), the event of his victory is what allowed for the discovery of the tomb of Jesus, which itself represents another royal victory, that of the Lord Jesus Christ over death, a victory that had just been affirmed by the Council of Nicaea in the same year that Constantine ordered work on the Church of the Holy Sepulchre to begin. The construction of a monument of such scale and royal splendor as the Church of the Holy Sepulchre and at a site of such significance to the Christian tradition ensured that Constantine's memory would live through it. It is thus probably no mere coincidence that the name of Constantine was frequently attached to the place in the literary descriptions of the Church of the Holy Sepulchre for many years to come.[186] His name and connection to the monument was certainly not quickly forgotten.

---

[185] Cf. Cameron and Hall, *Life of Constantine*, 283.
[186] As discussed in the last chapter. See, e.g., Eucherius, *Letter to Faustus*, 5–6; *Breviarius* A, 1 (in Wilkinson, *Jerusalem Pilgrims*, 117); Piacenza Pilgrim, *Travels*, 19 (in Wilkinson, *Jerusalem Pilgrims*, 139); Bede, *On the Holy Places*, 2.1 (in Wilkinson, *Jerusalem Pilgrims*, 217–18; Bernard the Monk, *A Journey to the Holy Places and Babylon*, 11 (in Wilkinson, *Jerusalem Pilgrims*, 266); Jachintus the Presbyter, *Pilgrimage*, 10 (in Wilkinson, *Jerusalem Pilgrims*, 271).

Not all of the narratives commemorated by the Church of the Holy Sepulchre were intended. The role of vernacular memory is important to consider here. At least one particular tradition, that of Adam's burial at Golgotha, was apparently preserved and developed unintentionally by the construction of the Church of the Holy Sepulchre. None of the official architecture or space in the church was dedicated to Adam in the fourth century. As mentioned above, official Adamic commemorative space, in the form of the Chapel of Adam, probably first appeared at the time of Modestus in the seventh century CE. Thus, so far as the *architecture* is concerned, the Adamic tradition is a late addition to the narrative. However, the Adam-Golgotha tradition saw a rapid increase in popularity in the fourth century, which is almost certainly due to the renewed interest in Golgotha resulting from the construction of the Church of the Holy Sepulchre. The preservation and further generation of Christological Adamic traditions connected to Golgotha was thus an unintended consequence of its construction, eventually resulting in the fixing of the tradition in the official memory of the site through the construction of the Chapel of Adam in late antiquity. The preservation of the Adamic Golgotha tradition had an impact in turn on how the significance of Jesus' crucifixion was understood, since by locating Adam's burial at the place where Jesus was crucified, early Christian authors were able to draw certain soteriological conclusions about the propitiatory symbolism and impact of the dripping of Jesus' blood upon the skull of Adam.

We have already mentioned that Shalev-Hurvitz has drawn attention to the Council of Nicaea as the historical background for the construction of the Church of the Holy Sepulchre. In its architecture, we see some of the confessions of the Nicene Creed reflected, specifically Jesus' passion and resurrection. When it is combined with the two other Constantinian commemorative churches dedicated to Jesus-memory, the Eleona and the Basilica of the Nativity, they together represent three central Christological events of the life of Jesus: the incarnation, the passion and resurrection, and the ascension. These three comprise the biographical details of the life of Jesus explicitly expressed by the Creed,[187] which is perhaps why these three sites (the Sepulchre, the nativity cave, and the Mount of Olives) were selected to be the first sites of commemorative churches dedicated to Jesus. This cannot be a coincidence. Together, they are expressions of the biography of Jesus according to the Nicene Creed written in stone upon the face of the land that Jesus walked. It is thus the Jesus of the Nicene Creed and the narrative of his life that it tells that is embedded, remembered, and represented at the Church of the Holy Sepulchre.

Conclusion

The architecture of the Constantinian Church of the Holy Sepulchre was both a receptacle for Jesus tradition as well as a vehicle for the transmission of particular ideological interpretations of that tradition and the person that it commemorated. It

---

[187] Cf. Shalev-Hurvitz, *Holy Sites Encircled*, 191–2.

made use of the iconography of existing architectural traditions, that of the basilica and the imperial mausoleum, to express ideas about Jesus' identity, particularly his royalty and divinity. The entire complex was designed to preserve the narrative of the passion and to facilitate the telling of that narrative within its grounds. Through its location and positioning, it also employs the narrative of Jesus' victory in the resurrection in the service of the narrative of the victory of Christianity over paganism and Judaism, as well as that of Constantine's victory over his opponents. The architecture thus deployed its reception and interpretation of Jesus to further the causes of religious competition and political currency in fourth-century Jerusalem. The concept of the complex as the "New Jerusalem" also vested it with eschatological significance, thus representing the biblical New Jerusalem of the cosmic Christ the Lamb in Rev 21–22. It is also important to consider what is notably missing, specifically commemorative architecture devoted to Adam, which did not appear until the time of Modestus, despite the popularity of the Adamic Golgotha tradition in the third and fourth centuries CE. This indicates that the architecture could also unintentionally preserve, develop, and generate tradition, most likely as a function of the fusion of vernacular and official memory that constitutes monuments such as the Church of the Holy Sepulchre.

5

Bethlehem and the Mount of Olives

The construction of the Church of the Holy Sepulchre was followed by the construction of two more Constantinian commemorative churches in the Jerusalem area dedicated to events in the life of Jesus, one at Bethlehem and the other on the Mount of Olives.[1] This chapter will focus on the commemoration of the birthplace of Jesus in Bethlehem, culminating in the construction of the Church of the Nativity; and the memory of Jesus on the Mount of Olives, culminating in the construction of the Eleona and the Church of the Ascension. We will begin with the earliest presentations of Jesus' birthplace in Matthew and Luke, and then move from there to discuss the second- and third-century reception of the place of Jesus' birth before turning to the crystallization of the memory in the form of the Constantinian Church of the Nativity.

The earliest accounts of the birthplace of Jesus are found in the canonical gospels, in Matt 2:1–6 and Luke 2:1–7, 15–16. As with the places of Jesus' crucifixion and burial, it is necessary to begin with the gospel accounts in order to establish the earliest interpretations of Jesus' place of birth, and to then track how the tradition is received, supplemented, and further interpreted in subsequent centuries. As such, my aim in this section is not to present an original reading of the gospel nativity narratives but instead to present the central issues as they have been understood in scholarship. Both Matthew and Luke identify the town of Jesus' birth as Bethlehem of Judea (Matt 2:5–6; Luke 2:4). Although the historicity of Jesus' birth in Bethlehem has been questioned by some scholars,[2] there is no direct testimony to a competing traditional location for Jesus' birth in the gospels or elsewhere in the New Testament. What matters most for our purposes is that Bethlehem alone was remembered as Jesus' birthplace.[3] As such,

---

[1] See Eusebius, *Life of Constantine*, 3.41–3.
[2] For summaries of the issues, see, e.g., Steve Mason, "O Little Town of … Nazareth?" *Bible Review* 16, no. 1 (2000): 32–9, 51–3; Raymond E. Brown, *The Birth of the Messiah: A Commentary on the Infancy Narratives in Matthew and Luke* (Garden City: Image, 1979), 513–16. Conversely, see the strong argumentation in favor of Bethlehem as the birthplace of Jesus in the response to Mason by Jerome Murphy-O'Connor, "Bethlehem… Of Course," *Bible Review* 16, no. 1 (2000): 40–5. See also William Mitchell Ramsay, *Was Christ Born at Bethlehem: A Study on the Credibility of St. Luke* (New York: Putnam, 1898).
[3] It is sometimes suggested that Jesus may have been born at Nazareth (see e.g., Mason, "Nazareth?") and that the passages identifying Nazareth as the *patris* of Jesus (Mark 6:1, 4, and parallels) could be taken as evidence that Nazareth was his place of birth (see also Brown, *Birth of the Messiah*, 515). However, *patris* has a wide range of meaning and potential referents even within the Jesus tradition.

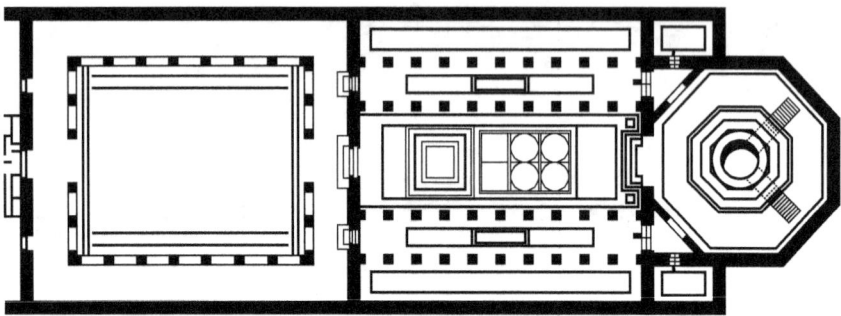

Figure 2 Floor plan of the Church of the Nativity.

Source: Redrawn after Ernest T. Richmond, "Basilica of the Nativity, Discovery of the Remains of an Earlier Church," *Quarterly of the Department of Antiquities in Palestine* 5 (1936): 75–81; 6 (1937): 63–72 (66).

Bethlehem must be the starting point for the present project, since Jesus' birthplace in reception history is firmly tied to Bethlehem and to no other place.

In these first narratives of the birth of Jesus, the setting in Bethlehem was already interpreted through the lens of the Davidic tradition and the messianic, royal overtones that come with it.[4] For both Matthew and Luke, the memory of Jesus' birth in Bethlehem is intertwined with the memory of Bethlehem as the town of David's origin and with the tradition of Jesus' Davidic lineage. The birthplace of Jesus is thus bound up in the canonical narratives with the concept of Davidic Messianism. Both canonical genealogies (Matt 1:1–17; Luke 3:23–38) firmly establish David as Jesus' ancestor in the mind of the intended reader, and both acknowledge David's ties to Bethlehem, albeit in very different ways. Luke explicitly draws attention to the Davidic association with Bethlehem, referring to it as "the city of David" (2:4, 11), and combines this with the tradition of Jesus' Davidic lineage through Joseph, writing that Joseph had to travel to Bethlehem "because he was descended from the house and family of David" (2:4). Likewise, the angel that appears at the shepherds' field[5] refers to the birthplace of Jesus, identified here as "a Savior, who is the Messiah, the Lord," as "the city of David" (2:11). This angelic pronouncement to the shepherds links Jesus, David, the Messiah, and

---

Luke and Matthew both call Nazareth Jesus' *patris* but also narrate Jesus' birth in Bethlehem, as though the two are not contradictory (Luke 4:16; Matt 13:54). On the referents and meaning of *patris* in the gospels, see John W. Pryor, "John 4:44 and the *Patris* of Jesus," *CBQ* 49, no. 2 (1987): 254–63. Since no narrative of Jesus' birth in Nazareth is known in the earliest tradition, and since Bethlehem is widely recognized as Jesus' birthplace (following the Lukan and Matthean narratives) in reception history, the notion of Nazareth as Jesus' place of birth is a nonstarter for the present study.

[4] This is a widespread view; for a helpful overview, see the classic work on this subject by Brown, *Birth of the Messiah*, 179–81, 421.

[5] The traditional site of this field is located just to the southeast of Bethlehem, and featured a commemorative in the Byzantine period by at least the fifth century, though there is also some evidence for mosaics paving the venerated spot, which is a cave. See Vassilios Tzaferis, "The Archaeological Excavation at Shepherds' Field," *Liber Annuus* 25 (1975), 5–52; cf. Tzaferis, "The Early Christian Holy Site at Shepherds' Field," in *Ancient Churches Revealed*, ed. Yoram Tsafrir (Jerusalem: Israel Exploration Society, 1993), 204–6.

Bethlehem all in one single verse. It may well be that the term "City of David" finds a more traditional referent in Jerusalem,[6] but it is clearly meant to refer to Bethlehem here and to call to mind the Davidic association with that locale,[7] since Luke has already identified it as Bethlehem in v. 4, and moreover, the shepherds correctly take "the City of David" to be Bethlehem without any explanation from the angel nor any confusion in v. 15. Bethlehem is thus established in Luke's narrative as David's city.

Fitzmyer suggests that the story of the shepherds is included by Luke because of the association of Bethlehem with David, who is shown performing the duties of a shepherd at Bethlehem in 1 Sam 16:11 (cf. also 17:14–15, 20, 28, 34).[8] Whether or not this is the reason for the inclusion of the shepherds in the story, the association of David and Bethlehem (Luke 2:11, 15) with shepherding, the activity that David was performing when he is first encountered in the Hebrew Bible narrative, is striking. The Lukan nativity story is certainly steeped in the legacy of David.

Matthew draws upon the Jewish scriptural tradition in order to illuminate the messianic significance of Jesus' birthplace, using a citation of Mic 5:2 combined with 2 Sam 5:2 to provide the lens through which the reader is meant to understand Jesus' birth in Bethlehem (Matt 2:5–6). Matthew cites Mic 5:2, which indicates that a "ruler" shall come from "Bethlehem, in the land of Judah," in order to demonstrate the royal connotations of Bethlehem as a birthplace for someone like Jesus, who has already by this point been established thrice as a member of the Davidic line by the author. This is accomplished first by the author's proclamation that Jesus is "the Son of David" in the opening verse of the First Gospel (1:1), then again through Jesus' genealogy (1:6), and then a third time through the angel's address to Joseph, Jesus' human father, as "son of David" (1:20). Although David is not explicitly connected to Bethlehem by Matthew, the addition of a line from 2 Sam 5:2, identifying the ruler of Mic 5:2 as one "who is to shepherd my people Israel," subtly cements the Davidic association of the ruler from Bethlehem with the Davidic legacy.[9] Within the literary context of 2 Sam 5:2, the tribes of Israel address David and tell him that Adonai has said to him, "It is you who shall be shepherd of my people Israel." Matthew has reapplied this appellation addressed to David to Jesus, the new ruler from Bethlehem. The image of the ruler as a "shepherd" is also appropriate, since David is depicted as a shepherd in the tradition (discussed above), and moreover, Bethlehem's topography associates it with the "natural environment of shepherds."[10] Moreover, it is made explicit that this new David from Bethlehem is the Messiah,[11] since the composite citation is given

---

[6] As argued by James R. Edwards, *The Gospel According to Luke*, PNTC (Grand Rapids: Eerdmans, 2015), 75–6.
[7] Contra ibid.
[8] Fitzmyer, *Luke*, 1: 395.
[9] Cf. Brown, *Birth of the Messiah*, 184–7.
[10] Paul H. Wright, "The Birthplace of Jesus and the Journeys of His First Visitors," in *Lexham Geographic Commentary on the Gospels*, ed. Barry J. Beitzel (Bellingham: Lexham Press, 2016, 2017), 1–9 (2).
[11] On the association between Bethlehem and the Davidic Messiah in early Judaism, see, e.g., the brief summary in Benjamin A. Foreman, "Matthew's Birth Narrative," in *Lexham Geographic Commentary on the Gospels*, ed. Barry J. Beitzel (Bellingham: Lexham Press, [2016] 2017), 19–29 (21–2).

by the chief priests and scribes of the people to Herod when he inquires where the Messiah is to be born (2:4).

Bethlehem thus becomes the site of conflict between the Davidic line and the progenitor of the Herodian dynasty. Unlike Luke, the author of the First Gospel does not explicitly identify Bethlehem as the "city of David." However, as established above, David's legacy is clearly in view throughout the Matthean account of the nativity. Ultimately, Herod resorts to atrocity, ordering the death of the children under the age of 2 in Bethlehem and its environs (2:16) in order to deal with the perceived threat of the ruler from Bethlehem. This, too, is interpreted through the citation of Jewish scripture, Jer 31:15: "A voice was heard in Ramah, wailing and loud lamentation, Rachel weeping for her children; she refused to be consoled, because they are no more" (Matt 2:18). The application of this passage, which explicitly mentions Ramah, to Bethlehem is curious. However, it is important to recognize that Bethlehem has some association with Rachel, insofar as Rachel was buried "on the way to Ephrath, that is, Bethlehem" (Gen 35:19). The memory of Rachel's burial near Bethlehem persisted, and was commemorated by a physical memorial site as early as the fourth century CE.[12] This connection to Rachel further demonstrates that the presentation of Bethlehem in Matthew's narrative is viewed through the lens of its history within the narrative of Jewish scripture. We will return to this link between Rachel and Bethlehem below when we consider the reception of Matthew's citation of Jer 31:15 in later Christian interpretation of Jesus' birthplace.

Luke provides further specificity about Jesus' birthplace, or at least about the place where Mary laid him, writing, "She [Mary] gave birth to her firstborn son and wrapped him in bands of cloth, and laid him in a manger because there was no place for them in the inn" (2:7). The word rendered in the NRSV as "inn" is *katalyma*, which is better understood as a "guest room," a room in the house typically utilized for hospitality.[13] The mention of the "manger" (Greek *phatnē*) is an indication that Jesus was laid in a place where animals were kept, and the reader is apparently also meant to infer that he was born there. Space for animals was not uncommon in first-century homes in the Land, such as in underground stables.[14]

The details about the lack of room in the guest room and Jesus being laid in a manger have been interpreted in various ways. For example, some scholars[15] see an allusion to Isa 1:3 LXX, which reads, "The ox knows its owner; and the donkey knows the manger (*phatnē*) of its lord; but Israel has not known me; my people has not understood

---

[12] See *Itin. Burd.*, 598.
[13] Cf., e.g., Rainer Riesner, "Archaeology and Geography," in *Dictionary of Jesus and the Gospels*, 2nd ed., ed. Joel B. Green, Jeannine K. Brown, and Nicholas Perrin (Downers Grove: IVP Academic, 2013), 45–59 (45); Wright, "Birthplace of Jesus," 3; Benjamin A. Foreman, "Luke's Birth Narrative: Reconstructing the Real Story," in *Lexham Geographic Commentary on the Gospels*, ed. Barry J. Beitzel (Bellingham: Lexham, 2016, 2017), 10–18 (13–14).
[14] See, e.g., David A. Fiensy, "The Galilean House in the Late Second Temple and Mishnaic Periods," in *Galilee in the Late Second Temple and Mishnaic Periods*, vol. 1, *Life, Culture, and Society*, ed. David A. Fiensy and James Riley Strange (Minneapolis: Fortress, 2014), 216–41 (229); Edwards, *Luke*, 73.
[15] Charles Homer Giblin, "Reflections on the Sign of the Manger," *CBQ* 29 (1967): 87–101; Fitzmyer, *Luke*, 1: 394–5; Brown, *Birth of the Messiah*, 419–20.

me," seeing a repeal of this dictum indicated by the Lukan narrative.[16] These same scholars also see a connection to Jer 14:8, which is addressed to the Lord, the Savior of Israel: "Why are you like an alien in the land, like a traveler who stays in lodgings (*katalyma*)?"[17] This suggests that the fact that Jesus is not born in "lodgings" (or a "guest room") is an indication that he is not an alien to the land.[18] Other interpreters see these details pertaining to the "guest room" and manger as indications of the humble status of Jesus' birth[19] or as foreshadowing his later rejection (e.g., Luke 4:16–30).[20] Perhaps, as Levine and Witherington have suggested, the significance of the manger is that "Jesus, who will give his body as food for his followers, is already found in the place where food is provided."[21] Whatever the case may be, the humble or ordinary[22] image of the circumstances Jesus' birth presented in Luke 2:7 is in stark contrast to the royal overtones of the narrative as a whole. As we will see below, the mention of a space that housed animals in Luke 2:7 will be relevant to the later interpretation and traditioning of the place of Jesus' birth in the centuries to follow.

Already in the first century, Bethlehem functioned as a *lieu de mémoire* within the Jesus tradition. It was a place in both space and literature in which memories of Jesus were mixed together with memories of David and all of the messianic valences that came with those memories, taking shape and crystallizing into an image of Jesus as the Jewish Messiah and heir to David's legacy. The influence of this *lieu de mémoire* would continue to resonate throughout antiquity with a remarkable resilience that continues to this day. The memory of Jesus' birth at Bethlehem, whether or not it corresponds to historical reality, became a fixed aspect of the memory of Jesus and solidified the Davidic facets of that memory. Within the memory of the church, the Bethlehemite Jesus is, almost by necessity, the Son of David.[23]

The Birthplace of Jesus in the Second and Third Centuries CE

In the second century CE, the memory and interpretation of Jesus' place of birth begins to accrue new traditional material. Justin Martyr, a Gentile Palestinian Christian hailing from Neapolis (Nablus), writing circa 155–161 recalling a debate that took

---

[16] Giblin, "Reflections," 99; Brown, *Birth of the Messiah*, 419; Fitzmyer, *Luke* 1: 394. Translation from Brown, *Birth of the Messiah*, 419.
[17] Brown, *Birth of the Messiah*, 419.
[18] Giblin, "Reflections," 100; Brown, *Birth of the Messiah*, 420.
[19] E.g., Joel B. Green, *The Gospel of Luke*, NICNT (Grand Rapids: Eerdmans, 1997), 135; Amy-Jill Levine and Ben Witherington III, *The Gospel of Luke*, NCBC (Cambridge: Cambridge University Press, 2018), 58;
[20] E.g., John T. Carroll, *Luke: A Commentary*, NTL (Louisville: Westminster John Knox, 2012), 67.
[21] Levine and Witherington, *Luke*, 58.
[22] Wright draws attention to traditional birthing practices in places such as Bethlehem, wherein the expectant mother would go to the place where animals were kept to give birth ("Birthplace of Jesus," 4–5).
[23] Cf. esp. Matt 1:1, 6, 20, 12:23, 21:9, 15; Luke 1:32, 3:31. See also Mark 10:47–48 and parallels, though Mark contains no memory of the birth of Jesus in Bethlehem. Notably, David's name appears no less than six times in the first chapter of Matthew alone.

place shortly after the Bar Kokhba revolt,[24] retells and interprets the story of Jesus' birth in his *Dialogue with Trypho*:

> Now, concerning the birth of the Child in Bethlehem, [you should know that] when Joseph could find no lodging place in the village, he went to a cave nearby, and there Mary gave birth to the child and laid him in a manger, and there the Arabian Magi found him. I have already quoted the words of Isaiah in which he foretold the symbol of the cave, but, for the benefit of those who have joined you today I will repeat the passage. Then I repeated the words of Isaiah which I have written above, and added that by these words the priests who performed the mysteries of Mithras were urged by the Devil to declare that they were initiated by Mithras himself in a place they call a cave. (Justin Martyr, *Dial.*, 78.5–6)[25]

There are some elements of Justin's telling of the birth of Jesus that are not found in the canonical gospels, namely, that Jesus was born in a cave located nearby the village, which is where the Magi, who came from Arabia, found him. The "words of Isaiah" pertaining to the "symbol of the cave" that Justin references here are almost certainly from Isaiah 33:16 LXX, which he cites in *Dial.* 70.2. The interpretive application of this Isaianic passage to the place of Jesus' birth is also novel and not derived from the canonical narrative.

It is difficult to determine the origin of these details, the most significant of which for our purposes is the identification of the place where Jesus was born as a cave. The fact that multiple novel details are found in Justin's version of the nativity may indicate there is some extracanonical tradition that underlies Justin's telling of the story,[26] since, as Taylor notes, these details are "more than romantic additions."[27] Taylor raises the intriguing suggestion that Justin could have introduced the cave setting into the tradition as a result of his knowledge of Palestinian stables, which were frequently caves.[28] This is attractive because it provides some reasonable explanation for the emergence of the nativity cave tradition and because it takes Justin's Palestinian context seriously. However, it is just as easy to imagine the cave tradition originating with anyone in Palestine prior to Justin, since anyone familiar with Palestinian stables could have connected the "manger" (*phatnē*) to a stable, and thus to a cave.[29] Taylor's point about the Palestinian tradition of using caves as stables is a good one, though

---

[24] On the date of *Dialogue with Trypho*, see Craig D. Allert, *Revelation, Truth, Canon and Interpretation: Studies in Justin Martyr's Dialogue with Trypho*, Supplements to Vigilae Christianae 64 (Leiden: Brill, 2002), 32–4.

[25] Translation from Thomas B. Falls (trans.), Saint Justin Martyr: The First Apology, The Second Apology, Dialogue with Trypho, Exhortation to the Greeks, Discourse to the Greeks, The Monarchy or the Rule of God, The Fathers of the Church 6, repr. ed. (Washington, DC: Catholic University of America, [1948] 2008), 272. All subsequent translations of this text are taken from this edition unless otherwise noted.

[26] Cf. Hugues Vincent and Félix-Marie Abel, *Bethléem, le sanctuaire de la nativité* (Paris: Gabalda, 1914), 16.

[27] Taylor, *Christians and the Holy Places*, 100.

[28] Ibid.; cf. Gustaf Dalman, *Arbeit und Sitte in Palästina*. Band VI. Zeltleben, Vieh- und Milchwirtshaft, Jagd, Fischfang (Hildesheim: Olms, [1939] 1987), 276–87.

[29] Cf. Bacci, *Mystic Cave*, 28.

it points us in the direction of a Palestinian origin in general rather than to Justin specifically. A scenario in which Justin knew of a tradition that Jesus was born in a cave, or that he knew that caves were typically used as stables in Palestine in his own day, and then interpreted that tradition in light of a Septuagint passage that he took to be messianic mentioning a cave is a plausible solution. It is more parsimonious than a scenario in which Justin first knows of the Isaianic passage involving a cave around which he then generates new elements of the nativity story in order to employ the Isaianic passage involving the cave. It is most likely that the details come from a local tradition that was current in Palestine by the middle of the second century CE, though anything beyond that, including whether it would have been encountered by Justin in written or oral form, is beyond our ability to determine.

The introduction of the cave into the nativity narrative plays a significant role in Justin's Christological interpretation of Jesus' birth.[30] By mentioning the cave (Greek *spēlaion*), Justin is able to connect the birth of Jesus to what he calls "the symbol of the cave" (*Dial.* 78.6; Greek τοῦ συμβόλου τοῦ κατὰ τὸ σπήλαιον), in Isa 33:16a LXX, which was included in a quotation of Isa 33:13–19 LXX earlier on in his discussion (*Dial.*, 70.2). The passage that Justin has in mind reads, "this one [Greek *houtos*] will live in the high cave [*spēlaion*] of a strong rock" (Isa 33:16 LXX, NETS). Within the context of Isa 33 LXX, the figure referred to in this passage is "one walking in righteousness" (v. 15), who will announce a coming judgment upon the lawless and impious and declare that "a fire is burning" and declare "the everlasting place" (v. 14),[31] "a king with glory" (v. 19). Justin clearly takes this passage to refer to the Messiah, and, thus, to Jesus.

Whether or not the cave tradition originates with Justin, and I am inclined to think that it does not, the messianic interpretation of cave tradition in light of Isa 33:16 LXX is an innovation, and an ingenious one at that. Justin emulates Matthew's use of Jewish scripture in order to interpret an extracanonical detail of the site of the nativity. We see here a progressive scripturalization of the site of Jesus' birth. Justin interprets the extracanonical cave tradition in relation to Jewish scripture in much the same way as other elements of the place where Jesus was born were interpreted through other passages of Jewish scripture by Matthew (2:6, 18).

Justin utilizes the cave tradition in order to make a polemical point against Mithraism. The basis of the polemic is Justin's claim that the Mithraic practice of initiating members in a cave, along with the belief that Mithras was "born of a rock," are imitations of the sayings of the biblical prophets, specifically in reference to Isa 33:13–19, as well as Dan 2:34. We need not presume that the cave tradition is dependent on or inspired by Mithraic practice,[32] since this is neither suggested nor implied by Justin's

---

[30] For another influential perspective on this tradition, see esp. the discussions in Vincent and Abel, *Bethléem*, 1–18.
[31] See, e.g., Ronald L. Troxel, *LXX-Isaiah as Translation and Interpretation: The Strategies of the Translator of the Septuagint of Isaiah*, JSJSupp 124 (Leiden: Brill, 2008), 114–16; John W. Olley, '*Righteousness' in the Septuagint of Isaiah: A Contextual Study* (Ann Arbor: Society of Biblical Literature, 1979), 80.
[32] On this, see Michael Gervers, "The Iconography of the Cave in Christian and Mithraic Tradition," in *Mysteria Mithrae*, ed. Ugo Bianchi, Études préliminaires aux religions orientales dans l'Empire romain 80 (Leiden: Brill, 1979), 579–99.

claim to the priority of the Judeo-Christian tradition of the birth of the Messiah in a cave.[33] Rather, the cave tradition and, moreover, the connection that Justin is able to draw from it to Isa 33:16 allows him the opportunity to claim priority, and thus superiority, for Christian tradition over Mithraic practice. I am thus in agreement with Craig Keener's statement that the echoes of their own traditions that practitioners of Mithraism and other pagans may have heard in the cave tradition "were not so pervasive and locally relevant that they need account for the rise of the cave tradition early in its history. They may, however, account for much of the appreciation for the story in subsequent times."[34]

Within its earliest appearance here in Justin's *Dialogue with Trypho*, the cave tradition thus contributes to the matrix of messianic memory that accrued around the birthplace of Jesus over the first three centuries. Although Justin does not directly mention David's association with Bethlehem, he does broadly associate Bethlehem with the birthplace of the Messiah, citing the Mic 5:2 tradition, following Matt 2:5–6 (*Dial.* 78.1).

Another innovation found in Justin's account of the nativity is the siting of Jesus' birth *nearby* (Greek Σύνεγγυς τῆς κώμης) Bethlehem (*Dial.* 78.5) rather than *in* Bethlehem as per Matthew's account (Matt 2:1, Greek ἐν Βηθλέεμ). This is a curious detail, and one worth examining, since it contradicts the canonical account. This shows that, although the narratives of the canonical gospels typically form the primary superstructure of developing *lieux de mémoire*, there are occasions where later layers of commemorative tradition may disagree with or shift earlier established elements of the remembered narrative to varying degrees of success. We recognize in this interpretive remembering the process of "memory distortion" or "refraction."[35] Since Justin is clearly aware of and drawing upon Matthew in his account of the nativity, this difference, this instance of refraction, requires explanation.

Why resite the birth of Jesus *near* Bethlehem rather than *in* Bethlehem? By shifting the location of Jesus' birth to the environs of Bethlehem, Justin might have been able to draw a subtle connection between Matthew's citation of Jer 31:15 ("A voice was heard in Ramah ... Rachel weeping for her children ...") and the location of Rachel's tomb "on the way" (Greek ἐν τῇ ὁδῷ) to Bethlehem (Gen 35:19–20 LXX). However, when Justin mentions Rachel's burial place, he does not clearly indicate that her burial place was outside of the village but instead says that the "place" (Greek *topos*) where she is buried is Bethlehem (*Dial.* 78.8).[36] If Justin intended to make the link between Rachel's burial and Jesus' place of birth direct and explicit through their locations

---

[33] Cf. also Craig S. Keener, "The Nativity Cave and Gentile Myths," *Journal of Greco-Roman Christianity and Judaism* 7 (2010): 59–67 (61–2), "Later generations may have connected the grotto of Jesus' birth with the Mithraic cave, but the tradition of Jesus' birth, and certainly Bethlehem's caves, predates the primary spread of Mithraism in the Roman world in the second century."

[34] Ibid., 67.

[35] For a brief discussion of this concept directly applied to Jesus memory, see Anthony Le Donne, *The Historiographical Jesus: Memory, Typology, and the Son of David* (Waco: Baylor, 2009), 85–6; cf. Le Donne, "Theological Memory Distortion in the Jesus Tradition: A Study in Social Memory Theory," in *Memory in the Bible and Antiquity*, ed. Loren T. Stuckenbruck, Stephen C. Barton, and Benjamin G. Wold, WUNT 212 (Tübingen: Mohr Siebeck, 2007), 163–77.

[36] As noted by Taylor, *Christians and the Holy Places*, 100–1.

just outside Bethlehem, then it stands to reason that he would have mentioned the fact that Rachel's burial was located near but not within Bethlehem. It is important to remember that while there was no monolithic concept of the Christian "canon" of the New Testament in the mid-second century,[37] it is nevertheless clear that the Gospels of Matthew, Mark, Luke, and John were cited with more far more frequency in the writings of the early church from the Apostolic Fathers on than gospels that would not come to be considered part of what would come to be the canonical New Testament.[38] This indicates, at the very least, that these were the most influential gospel texts, and so even if we eschew the language of "canonical" for the second century CE as anachronism, it is still curious that Justin differs from Matthew's narrative on this count. This is made even more curious by the fact that he is clearly dependent on Matthew (as well as Luke) for much of his knowledge and understanding of the nativity story, as though it were an authoritative source of information on the matter.

As it stands, the rationale behind the resiting of Jesus' birth in *Dialogue With Trypho* is obscure. Moreover, we cannot be certain about the source of Justin's information about the birthplace of Jesus, including whether to attribute it to Justin himself or to earlier tradition.[39] Even though the reason for and source of the resiting is unknown, the fact that it occurs at all is important to note. In this particular instance, the resiting of Jesus' place of birth would eventually be rejected in public and official memory, as the Church of the Nativity (which we will discuss below) was located within Bethlehem, not outside of it.

It was not always the case that the canonical topography could resist resiting within Christian collective memory. According to Luke's account of the feeding of the five thousand (Luke 9:10–17), the location of the miracle was at Bethsaida (9:10). John situates it "across the sea" from Capernaum, while Mark and Matthew set the narrative at a "deserted place" (NRSV; Greek *erēmos*) near the shore (Mark 6:32–35; Matt 14:13). However, the fourth-century commemorative church at Tabgha,[40] where the feeding of the five thousand is remembered, is located on the western shore of the Sea of Galilee, less than 3 km down the shoreline to the southwest from Capernaum. This reflects neither Luke nor John's location. These two examples show that it is certainly possible for later memory to disagree with or compete with the topographical locations of

---

[37] As raised by George Themelis Zervos, *The Protevangelium of James*, 2 vols. (London: T&T Clark, 2019), 1: 211.

[38] Cf. John Barton, *Holy Writings, Sacred Text: The Canon in Early Christianity* (Louisville: Westminster John Knox, 1997), 16–18.

[39] It is possible that, as Zervos suggests, Justin has received the cave tradition from The Protevangelium of James, in which the cave is apparently located a mile and a half outside of Bethlehem (*Prot. Jas.* 17:6–18:1; cf. Zervos, *Protevangelium*, 1: 143–4). However, this requires the acceptance of Zervos's hypothesis of Justin's knowledge of the Protevangelium and his particular understanding of its composition history.

[40] On this site, see Alfons M. Schneider, *The Church of the Multiplying of the Loaves and Fishes at Tabgha on the Lake of Gennesaret and its Mosaics*, ed. Archibald Alexander Gordon (London: Ouseley, 1937); Stanislao Loffreda, *Scavi di et-Tabgha*, Collectio Minor 7 (Jerusalem: Franciscan Printing Press, 1970); Renate Rosenthal and Malka Hershkovitz, "Tabgha," *IEJ* 30 (1980): 207; Bargil Pixner, *Paths of the Messiah and Sites of the Early Church from Galilee to Jerusalem: Jesus and Jewish Christianity in Light of Archaeological Discoveries*, ed. Rainer Riesner, trans. Keith Myrick, Sam Randall, and Miriam Randall (San Francisco: Ignatius Press, [1991] 2010), 102–14.

events in the life of Jesus in the canonical gospels, and that the competing location can sometimes even replace the canonical location in both official and public memory.

The Birthplace of Jesus in the Protevangelium of James

The Protevangelium of James represents further reception and development of the memory of Jesus' birthplace, including some tradition elements that are also found in Justin's *Dialogue with Trypho*. This, among other matters, has raised questions about the literary relationship between the two, and arguments have been made for dependency in both directions.[41] The fact that arguments can be made for dependency in both directions, and, moreover, that the level of verbatim agreement is not high enough to make any firm conclusions, leads to the inevitable conclusion that, while some sort of literary relationship is possible, the available evidence is not sufficient to make a clear judgment apart from hypothetical reconstructions of the composition history of these texts, nor is it necessary to do so for our present purposes.[42] Furthermore, even if the dependence of one on the other could be demonstrated beyond reasonable doubt, we would nevertheless not be able to then conclude that any of the shared elements contained in these texts originated with the earlier one, since either one or both could draw on earlier tradition.

For our purposes, since we are not concerned with the particular composition history of either of these texts, a worthy endeavor though that may be, it is preferable to regard both the Protevangelium of James and Justin's *Dialogue with Trypho* as instantiations of reception of similar traditions about Jesus' birthplace. The Protevangelium of James is typically dated to the late second to early third centuries CE.[43] The plausibility of this date has been convincingly demonstrated by Lily Vuong's reading of the text within the context of Syria during this period.[44]

The Protevangelium of James narrates the journey of Joseph and Mary to Bethlehem (17:1-11). Jesus is not born within Bethlehem but, rather, on the way to Bethlehem, a mile and a half away.[45] The journey begins with the familiar Lukan scenario of a census ordered by Augustus (*Prot. Jas.* 17:1, cf. Luke 2:1), but there are several notable

---

[41] The dependence of the Protevangelium of James on Justin's *Dialogue with Trypho* has been argued by Émile de Strycker, *La forme la plus ancienne du Protévangile de Jacques*, Subsidia Hagiographica 33 (Bruxelles: Société des Bollandists, 1961), 414. Conversely, the argument for Justin's dependence on the Protevangelium of James has been made by George Themelis Zervos, "Dating the Protevangelium of James: The Justin Martyr Connection," in *Society of Biblical Literature 1994 Seminar Papers*, ed. E. Lovering (Atlanta: Scholars Press, 1994), 415-34; cf. Zervos, *Protevangelium*, e.g. 143-4, 211.

[42] Similarly, see the conclusions of Eric M. Vanden Eykel, *"But Their Faces Were All Looking Up": Author and Reader in the Protevangelium of James*, The Reception of Jesus in the First Three Centuries 1 (London: T&T Clark, 2016), 138.

[43] See the informative robust discussion of scholarship on the date of the Protevangelium of James in Lily C. Vuong, *Gender and Purity in the Protevangelium of James*, WUNT 2. Reihe 358 (Tübingen: Mohr Siebeck, 2013), 32-9; cf. Lily C. Vuong, *The Protevangelium of James*, Early Christian Apocrypha 7 (Eugene: Cascade, 2019), 14-16.

[44] Vuong, *Gender and Purity*, 193-239.

[45] It is worth noting that Zervos suggests that this detail may be connected to the proximity of this location to Rachel's tomb (Protevangelium of James, 134, 143, 157). However, we must also observe that the Matthean citation of Jer 31:15 (in Matt 2:18) is omitted by the Protevangelium of James, though the slaughter of the infants is included (Prot. Jas. 22:1-2).

differences. The census is not for "all the world" (Luke 2:1) but, rather, for "everyone in Bethlehem of Judea" (Prot. Jas. 17:1).[46] Furthermore, it is not clear, as in Luke, that Mary and Joseph are traveling from Nazareth (2:4), since the narrative in the chapters preceding Prot. Jas. 17 is apparently set in Jerusalem.[47]

When Mary and Joseph are a mile and a half away from Bethlehem,[48] they are forced to stop their journey so that Mary can give birth, since the child is "pressing his weight on [her] to come forth" (17:10). Since they are in the wilderness, Joseph is compelled to find a place to hide Mary's "shameful nakedness"[49] and finds a cave there (18:10; Greek ἐκεῖ σπήλαιον). It is in this cave that Mary gives birth to Jesus (as implied by 19:16).

The identification of Jesus' birthplace as a cave near Bethlehem in the Protevangelium of James is strikingly parallel to Justin's version of the nativity in *Dial.* 78.5–6, which is indicative of some level of shared tradition. However, the interpretation of the meaning of the cave as the location of the birth of Jesus differs substantially in these two texts. While Isa 33:16 LXX is instrumental for Justin's understanding of "the symbol of the cave," no such Isaian reference to a cave is employed by the author of the Protevangelium of James. Instead, the significance of the cave is implied through the narrative of miraculous circumstances surrounding Jesus' birth (19:12–15; see also 18:3–11). This suggests that, although Justin and the author of the Protevangelium of James may draw on shared traditional elements, their respective interpretations of the significance of the tradition of Jesus' birth in a cave are most likely their own.

The cave is the site of a miraculous event (19:13–15) following the birth of Jesus, which serves to hint at how the author of the Protevangelium of James presents its significance for the reader. After taking Mary inside the cave, Joseph leaves it in order to find a "Hebrew midwife in the area around Bethlehem" (18:2). This reference to a "Hebrew midwife" echoes the account of the faithfulness of the Hebrew midwives in the Exodus narrative (Exod 1:15–21; 2:7–10).[50] Following Matthew, the Protevangelium of James depicts Bethlehem as the site of a repetition of elements of the account of Moses' birth narrative, including the massacre of infants (*Prot. Jas.* 22:2; Matt 2:16; Exod 1:15–22). The introduction of the "Hebrew midwife" (Greek *maian Hebraian*; cf. Exod 1:15 LXX), which is not found in Matthew, further cements this parallel. While Joseph is searching for the Hebrew midwife, time is suddenly suspended, signifying the moment when Jesus is born.[51]

---

[46] Translation from Vuong, *Protevangelium*, 91. All further translations of this text are from this same edition unless otherwise noted.

[47] The narrative in Prot. Jas. 15–16 is apparently set in Jerusalem. See esp. 15:2, where the Temple setting is made explicit. However, we are told in 16:3 that Joseph and Mary "returned home," though it is unclear what that home is understood to be.

[48] Specifically, we are told that they are at the "halfway point" (17:10) from "the third mile" (17:6).

[49] According to Vuong, the idea is to provide Mary with privacy and protection (*Protevangelium*, 93; cf. Vuong, *Gender and Purity*, 183).

[50] Cf. Vuong, *Protevangelium*, 94.

[51] In-depth discussion of this significant event in the narrative of the Protevangelium of James is beyond the purview of the present project, particularly since it has been discussed and interpreted at length by other scholars. On the interpretation and significance of the suspension of time in 18:3–11, see, e.g., Harm R. Smid, *Protevangelium Jacobi: A Commentary*, trans. G. E. Van Baaren-Pape, Apocrypha Novi Testamenti 1 (Assen: Van Gorcum, 1965), 128–130; François Bovon, "The Suspension of Time in Chapter 18 of the Protevangleium of Jacobi," in *The Future of Early Christianity: Essays in Honour of Helmut Koester*, ed. Birger A. Pearson (Minneapolis: Fortress, 1991), 393–405; Ronald F. Hock,

When time resumes (18:11), and once Joseph has found a midwife, he returns with the midwife to the cave (19:1–12). What happens upon their arrival at the cave is significant for understanding the symbolism and meaning of the cave within the Protevangelium of James:

> And they stood in front of the cave. And a dark cloud overshadowed the cave. And the midwife said, "My soul has been magnified today because my eyes have seen an incredible sign; for salvation has been born to Israel." And immediately the cloud contracted from the cave and a great light appeared within the cave so that their eyes could not bear it. A little time afterwards that light began to contract until an infant could be seen. (Prot. Jas. 19:13–16a)[52]

The miraculous appearance of the dark cloud and great light has clear symbolic value. According to Vincent and Abel,

> Le Christ naissant dans une grotte obscure, c'est la lumière éclatant soudain dans les ténèbres du monde. Le Christ naissant dans une grotte isolée, sans secours humain, c'est la manifestation de la puissance divine et de la virginité de Marie. L'univers suspend son cours, les créatures demeurent immobiles, et ce silence indique l'accomplissement d'un grand mystère. Toute cette mise en scène aurait pour but de caractériser le coté mystérieux de la naissance du Sauveur.[53]

For Vincent and Abel, the events surrounding the cave in the Protevangelium of James speak to the characterization of the event of the birth of the Savior as a great cosmic mystery. The birth of Jesus, the Messiah, in a dark (French "obscure") cave represents the light bursting suddenly into the darkness of the world, which is represented by the great light that shines through the dark cloud (*Prot. Jas.* 19:15), a light that eventually contracts around the infant Jesus (19:16). The birth of Jesus in a cave, as a place of safety and protection,[54] without any human help is also a manifestation of and testament to the virginity of Mary, which is immediately proven and demonstrated at length by the narrative of the Protevangelium of James (19:18–20:12). The miraculous birth, the stopping of time, and the presence of the light cutting through the cloud are all indications of the great cosmic mystery that occurs within the cave.

The imagery of the cloud and the light is theophanic.[55] The language of the darkness and the light that cuts through it is reminiscent of the dualism of John 1:1–5, in which "the light shines in the darkness." However, the cloud itself, though potentially representing the darkness of the world in Johannine mode (John 1:5, 3:19, 8:12, 12:35, 46) as suggested by Vincent and Abel, may also have theophanic value in itself insofar as

---

the Infancy Gospels of James and Thomas, The Scholar's Bible 2 (Santa Rosa: Polebridge, 1995), 65; Vanden Eykel, *Looking Up*, 138–44; Vuong, *Protevangelium*, 95–6.

[52] Trans. from Vuong, *Protevangelium*, 97–8.
[53] Vincent and Abel, *Bethléem*, 9.
[54] Cf. Vuong, *Protevangelium*, 93.
[55] See Hock, *Infancy Gospels*, 67; Vuong, *Protevangelium*, 97; Smid, *Protevenagelium Jacobi*, 134–8; Vanden Eykel, *Looking Up*, 144–5.

it parallels the divine manifestation in the form of a cloud in Exodus (13:21–22; 14:19, 24; 16:10; 33:9–10; cf. Num 16:42), particularly the "dark cloud" (νεφέλη γνοφώδης) in Exod 19:16 LXX.[56] The appearance of the great light marking the entry of Jesus into the world in Prot. Jas. 19:15–16 draws on theophanic imagery that is already present and applied to Jesus in the canonical gospels (John 1:1–9, 8:12, 9:5, 11:9, 12:28–36, 46; cf. Matt 4:16; Luke 1:79, 2:32). The cave is thus the place where the divine presence of God, manifest in the infant Jesus, breaks into the darkness of the world.

The accent in the unique material of the nativity account in the Protevangelium of James dealing with Jesus' birthplace is heavily upon the divinity of Jesus and the cosmic mystery of his birth. While the Davidic messianic association with Bethlehem is also present in the Protevangelium of James, it is only found in material that is directly drawn from Matthew (*Prot. Jas.* 21:4–8; following Matt 2:3–6). Notably, the Matthean citation of Mic 5:2 with 2 Sam 5:2 in Matt 2:6 is omitted by the Protevangelium of James, which otherwise follows Matthew fairly closely in its narrative of Herod and the Magi in Prot. Jas. 21:2–9 (cf. Matt 2:1–8). Moreover, Bethlehem's association with David is not made explicit by the author of the Protevangelium of James, an issue made acute by the omission of the Matthean citation of Mic 5:2 with 2 Sam 5:2,[57] though they do demonstrate Jesus' Davidic lineage elsewhere in the text (10:3–4).[58] It does seem as though, while the author does not deny the Davidic heritage of Jesus, the significance of the association of Jesus' birth in Bethlehem with David is eclipsed by the theophanic symbolism of the cave.

The novel detail of the appearance of the star *within* the cave, over the head of the infant Jesus (Prot. Jas. 21:10) certainly places a messianic symbol (cf. Num 24:17) directly within the place of Jesus' birth, but the oracle of Balaam from which this symbology derives is not explicitly Davidic in its original context. Nor can we be certain that the author of the Protevangelium of James knows the source of the messianic star tradition, since they derive this detail from the Matthean narrative and not directly from Num 24:17.

Eric Vanden Eykel has recently drawn attention to the connection between Jesus' birth in a cave in the Protevangelium of James and his burial in the canonical passion narratives.[59] He rightly observes that in Greek and Roman literature, caves are often the birthplaces of gods and heroes, which may have been taken by the reader as an indication of Jesus' divine or special status, while in the Hebrew Bible and LXX, caves are "places of scandal, havens for refugees, and tombs."[60] Vanden Eykel sees the cave as pointing the reader beyond the narrative of the Protevangelium of James toward the burial place of Jesus.[61] Although the canonical evangelists use different language

---

[56] As observed by Hock, *Infancy Gospels*, 67; Vuong, *Protevangelium*, 97. We should note, however, that while these are important parallels, the adjective γνοφώδης ("dark") used in Exod 19:16 LXX to describe the cloud differs from that used in *Prot. Jas.* 19:13, which is σκοτεινή ("dark"). At the least, this probably means that the Protevangelium of James is not directly borrowing the language of the LXX here, though it may be drawing on the same imagery nonetheless.
[57] See the discussion of the Davidic association with this composite citation above.
[58] On this passage and the association of Mary with the "tribe of David" in the Protevagelium of James, see Vanden Eykel, *Looking Up*, 105–6.
[59] Ibid., 135–66.
[60] Ibid., 135, 150–8.
[61] For a summary, see ibid., 169.

to identify Jesus' burial place (*mnēma* rather than *spēlaion*, which designates the birth cave in the Protevangelium of James), "the implication for the reader is the same: Jesus' earthly life begins and ends in a cave-like space."[62]

Although it is difficult to be completely certain as to whether the author intended the reader to look beyond the narrative to the accounts of Jesus' burial elsewhere in the tradition, Vanden Eykel has a point. It is certainly true that a connection would be drawn between the location of Jesus' birth in a cave and the place of his burial,[63] since there is an undeniable parallel regardless of the particular term used to describe these places in the traditional literature.

Strikingly, after his discussion of the Church of the Holy Sepulchre, Eusebius presents the second and third Constantinian commemorative Jesus-churches in Palestine, built at the place of Jesus' birth and ascension, as "other sites venerated for their mystic caves" (*Life of Constantine*, 41.1), as though the three Constantinian commemorative churches together were connected by virtue of the fact that they all enshrined "mystic caves" connected to the events of Jesus' life.[64] This commonality would have naturally drawn attention to the parallels between the three events that they commemorated.

Origen and the Birthplace of Jesus

Writing in the mid-third century CE, Origen comments at some length on the birthplace of Jesus in his *Contra Celsum* (1.51). Origen begins this discussion by citing Mic 5:2 as evidence that "the ruler shall come from Bethlehem." He then writes,

> This prophecy would not fit any of those who are in ecstasy and go about begging and saying that they have come from above, as Celsus' Jew says, unless it is quite clear that the man was born in Bethlehem, or as some one else might say, came from Bethlehem to rule the people. If anyone wants further proof to convince him that Jesus was born in Bethlehem besides the prophecy of Micah and the story recorded in the gospels by Jesus' disciples, he may observe that, in agreement with the story in the gospel about his birth, the cave at Bethlehem is shown where he was born and the manger in the cave where he was wrapped in swaddling-clothes. What is shown there is famous in these parts even among people alien to the faith, since it was in this cave that the Jesus who is worshipped and admired by Christians was born.[65]

For Origen, the primary significance of Jesus' birthplace is its location in Bethlehem, which he connects to the messianic prophecy, following Matt 2:5–6 in its citation of Mic 5:2. Notably, he omits the reference to 2 Sam 5:2, which is used in the Matthean narrative to draw attention to Bethlehem's significance of David's hometown. However, even without the use of 2 Sam 5:2, in Origen's understanding the Messiah born in

---

[62] Vanden Eykel, *Looking Up*, 136.
[63] E.g., Gregory of Nyssa, *Nativ.* 1141.43, as cited by Vanden Eykel, *Looking Up*, 136.
[64] On this, see Bagatti, *Church from the Circumcision*, 133–6.
[65] Origen, *Contra Celsum*, 1.51. Translation from Chadwick, *Origen: Contra Celsum*, 47–8.

Bethlehem is the Davidic Messiah, as he goes on to identify Bethlehem of Judea as the place "whence David was" (*Contra Celsum*, 1.51).

Origen's deployment of the cave tradition is done in support of his primary point that Jesus was born in Bethlehem in fulfillment of messianic prophecy. According to *Contra Celsum*, the cave is located *in* rather than *near* Bethlehem.[66] This differs from what Justin and the author of the Protevangelium of James write about the location of the cave. Furthermore, Origen is clearly referring to a *specific* cave rather than to a general tradition that Jesus was born in a cave. Origen's language of a cave being "shown" (Greek δείκνυται) implies that it is a place known to the local populace, which is identified for visitors.[67] This is also what is further implied by Origen's claim that the place is "famous in these parts," as it is known even to "people alien to the faith" as the place where "the Jesus who is worshipped and admired by Christians was born." As Michele Bacci writes,

> Origen's passage seems to state in rather unequivocal terms that, in the third century, a form of memorialization of the Nativity event was already developed and connected with a material site that was offered for the inspection of pious believers. This implies that the cave was associated with some forms of cultic practice, or with pilgrimage at its embryonic stage.[68]

Taylor interprets this passage differently, arguing that Origen preserves the words of the local population, who would have told people that "he who is worshipped and admired by Christians" was born in the cave.[69] Since Jerome indicates that Tammuz-Adonis was worshipped in this Bethlehem cave (Jerome, *Ep.* 58.3), Taylor argues that Origen is saying that the pagan people of Bethlehem ("people alien to our faith") believed that Jesus was born in this cave and that "the probability is that the pagans arrived at this notion by an identification of Jesus with Adonis."[70]

Although this is not an impossible scenario, it is difficult to accept. It requires us first to accept Jerome's statement over a century later that the cave was used for the worship of Tammuz and that this practice was current in Origen's time, despite Origen's omission of this information. Moreover, as Wilkinson point out, "Jerome also said that before Adonis was worshipped, Christ had been born there,"[71] which at least implies the priority of a Christian claim to the site. In light of this, it is relevant that the cave tradition existed in at least some form in the Palestinian tradition as evidenced by Justin's witness to it. When Justin, the Protevangelium of James, and Origen's witnesses are combined, as Wilkinson argues, "Surely all this mutually supporting evidence could be interpreted in line with the general meaning of the documents."[72] Nevertheless,

---

[66] As noted by Taylor, *Christians and the Holy Places*, 103. Taylor considers it the "first piece of evidence for the existence of a specific cave actually *in* Bethlehem."
[67] On this language, see Bagatti, *Church from the Circumcision*, 15; Taylor, *Christians and the Holy Places*, 105–6. On this term as used by Eubseius, see also Wilkinson, "L'Apport de Saint Jérome," 251–2.
[68] Bacci, *Mystic Cave*, 31.
[69] Taylor, *Christians and the Holy Places*, 104.
[70] Ibid.
[71] John Wilkinson, "Review of Joan E. Taylor, *Christians and the Holy Places*," *JTS* 45, no. 1 (1994): 304.
[72] Ibid.

Taylor's work here is instructive. It is essential to take a balanced approach to the data as she does and not to assume that Origen's statement in *Contra Celsum* 1.51 warrants the existence of a Christian cultic site or "sacred grotto" at Bethlehem in the third century.[73] However, we must acknowledge that the evidence points toward a *lieu de mémoire* commemorating Jesus' birth that had developed within Bethlehem by Origen's time. Thus, it is perhaps most prudent to conclude that a site where Jesus' birth was remembered existed in a cave in Bethlehem in the mid-third century but that we cannot be certain as to whether or what sort of Christian activity went on at that place apart from remembering. This implies an "embryonic" form of pilgrimage as Bacci rightly suggests, but what that may have looked like is lost to the mists of time.

Origen's purpose in raising the existence of the cave tradition is to firmly locate Jesus' birth within Bethlehem, which he considers to be proof of Jesus' identity as the messianic ruler, since the ruler is supposed to hail from Bethlehem. The symbol of the cave is thereby directly incorporated into the matrix of Bethlehem's association with the Messiah. This is accomplished by referencing an actual cave located in Bethlehem where Jesus' birthplace was remembered in Origen's day.

Eusebius on Bethlehem (before the Constantinian Church of the Nativity)

Writing prior to the construction of the Church of the Nativity,[74] Eusebius mentions Bethlehem several times in his *Demonstratio Evangelica*. According to Eusebius, it is so famous that people "still hasten from the ends of the earth to see it" (1.1.4).[75] Like Origen, Eusebius mentions the cave in order to demonstrate that Jesus was indeed born in Bethlehem: "Now all agree that Jesus Christ was born in Bethlehem, and a cave is shewn there by the inhabitants to those who come from abroad to see it" (*Dem. Evang.* 3.2.97) This comes after a citation of Mic 5:2 (combined with 2 Sam 5:2, following Matt 2:6). The cave is meant to provide evidence of the fact of Jesus' birth in Bethlehem, which then illuminates and bolsters the claim made by Matt 2:6 that the birth of Jesus in Bethlehem demonstrates his messianic identity.

Eusebius cites this same prophecy again later in *Dem. Evang.* 6.13.275,[76] this time without 2 Sam 5:2. Here, he claims that the prophecy must apply to Jesus, since he is "the only person after the date of this prophecy who came forth thence and attained to fame." This allows Eusebius to make a Christological point. Mic 5:2 portrays the "goings-forth" of this figure from Bethlehem as being "from the beginning of the days of eternity."[77] Thus, Eusebius is able to conclude that, since this figure can only be Jesus, the prophet "shews the pre-existence and essential origin of Him that is to come forth from Bethlehem," and thus Jesus, "our Lord and Savior who came from Bethlehem, was

---

[73] As argued by, e.g., Bagatti, *Church From the Circumcision*, 133–6.
[74] On the date of this text, see W. J. Ferrar (trans.), *The Proof of the Gospel*, 2 vols. (Eugene: Wipf and Stock, [1920] 2001), 1: xii–xiii.
[75] Translation from ibid., 1: 3. All further translations are from this same source unless otherwise indicated.
[76] Cf. also *Dem. Evang.* 7.2.341, where many of the same points are repeated.
[77] Following Ferrar's translation of Eusebius (*Proof of the Gospel*, 2:17).

shewn to be the ruler of the spiritual Israel," as opposed to "the Jewish nation" upon which "the woes that were foretold fell."

For Eusebius, the significance of Jesus' birth in Bethlehem is heavily tied to the prophecy of the ruler from Bethlehem in Mic 5:2.[78] He uses this passage not only to make a claim about Jesus' identity as the Messiah but also to make a higher Christological point about his preexistence. This serves his unfortunate anti-Jewish polemic, as in Eusebius' view, Jesus the ruler from Bethlehem is the preexistent ruler of "spiritual Israel," as opposed to the ruler of the Jewish nation. This interpretation of Mic 5:2 develops the Christological significance of the site of Jesus' birth in a new direction, one that emphasizes a high Christology and a movement away from the depiction of Jesus as Jewish Messiah, the rightful king of Israel, which is so emphasized by Matthew's nativity story. Although Eusebius cites the same passage as Matthew in order to draw out the significance of the memory of Jesus' birth at Bethlehem, his interpretation of the passage results in novel Christological conclusions.

The role that Eusebius gives to the traditional cave[79] in this Christological interpretation of Jesus' birthplace in Bethlehem is, again, to confirm the truth of the location of Jesus' birth. When, in *Dem. Evang.* 7.2.341–4, he reiterates the Christological points that he made earlier concerning Mic 5:2, Eusebius writes that "to this day the inhabitants of the place [Bethlehem] who have received the tradition from their fathers, confirm the truth of the story by shewing to those who visit Bethlehem because of its history the cave in which the Virgin bare and laid her infant." We see here the language of site-specific commemoration and remembering, and may infer from Eusebius' witness that, before the age of Constantinian church building, a traditional site associated with Jesus' birth had already developed and was being visited by outsiders. It is a reasonable inference to assume that this is the same cave that would eventually be enshrined within the Church of the Nativity.

As Taylor has pointed out, it is difficult to determine the religious affiliation of these Bethlehemites who showed the cave to visitors, and we cannot necessarily assume that they were Christians.[80] However, a place does not have to be venerated nor serve as ritual space in order for it to function as a *lieu de mémoire*, nor for it to be remembered in local tradition or to take on layers of interpretive significance as it is remembered. While the Constantinian project of commemorative church building may have later legitimated the Bethlehem cave, it did not generate the commemorative activity or early formation of crystalline memory that had already taken root at that spot, as witnessed by Eusebius and by Origen.

Eusebius further interprets Jesus' birthplace in light of Ps 131 LXX (MT Ps 132; *Dem. Evang.* 7.2.346–9). This is a curious interpretive move, since Ps 131 LXX is primarily concerned with Zion and the Jerusalem Temple. Eusebius draws attention to the desire expressed to find "a place for the Lord, and a tabernacle for the God of Jacob" (*Dem. Evang.* 7.2.347) in v. 5. Directly following this, the first line of v. 6, reads, "Look,

---

[78] See also *Dem. Evang.* 7.2.341.
[79] As per the discussion above, by Origen's time, it would be appropriate to speak of "the traditional cave," the actual cave which was identified as Jesus' birthplace, as opposed to "the cave tradition" in general.
[80] Taylor, *Christians and the Holy Places*, 106–7.

we heard of it in Ephratha," which opens the door to Eusebius' application of this text to Bethlehem.[81] Eusebius takes v. 6 to be "an oracle which cried 'Bethlehem', that being the place of the Lord, and the tabernacle of the God of Jacob" (*Dem. Evang.* 7.2.347), which he duly connects to his previous discussion of Mic 5:2 and its application to Jesus, who was born at Bethlehem (348). This in turn leads Eusebius to conclude that Jesus is the subject of the "prophecy" of the psalm, thus identifying Jesus as "the human tabernacle" and Bethlehem as the place where the God of Jacob would come to dwell among humanity (348). This is a further development of the interpretation of Jesus' birthplace, adding yet another to the memory of Jesus at Bethlehem that continued to crystallize and grow throughout the centuries. The concept of Bethlehem as a dwelling place for God, though applied here to Jesus' birth, is surely relevant for what was to come in Eusebius' own lifetime: the construction of the Church of the Nativity.

The Church of the Nativity

The Church of the Nativity, built over the traditional site of the birthplace of Jesus in commemoration of that event, was first constructed shortly after work began on the Church of the Holy Sepulchre.[82] Its construction is associated with Constantine (Eusebius, *Life of Constantine*, 3.41; *Itin. Burd.* 598), as well as with his mother, Helena (Eusebius, *Life of Constantine*, 4.43). The construction work must have begun sometime between Helena's trip to Palestine (Eusebius, *Life of Constantine*, 3.42) in 327/328 and the earliest mention of a church on the site by the Bordeaux Pilgrim (*Itin. Burd.* 598).[83]

Eusebius narrates the construction of the Church of the Nativity along with the Church of the Acension by Constantine following his description of the Church of the Holy Sepulchre. He writes, "He [Constantine] took in hand here two other sites venerated for their two mystic caves, and he adorned these also with rich artwork" (*Life of Constantine*, 3.41.1). Thus, we are told, perpetuated the memory of his mother, Helena, who Eusebius tells us had traveled to "the wondrous land" (3.42.1), and according to Eusebius,

> as she accorded suitable adoration to the footsteps of the Savior, following the prophetic word which says, "Let us adore in the place where his feet have stood," she forthwith bequeathed to her successors also the fruit of her personal piety. She immediately consecrated to the God she adored two shrines, one by the cave of his birth, the other on the mountain of the Ascension ... the most devout Empress beautified the Godbearer's pregnancy with wonderful monuments, in various ways embellishing the sacred cave there. The Emperor himself shortly afterwards

---

[81] Note that Eusebius knows that Ephratha is Bethlehem on the basis of the narrative of Rachel's burial there in Gen 35:19 (*Dem. Evang.* 7.2.347).
[82] Cf. Eusebius, *Life of Constantine*, 3.41–3.
[83] As rightly pointed out by Bacci, *Mystic Cave*, 35.

honored this too with imperial decorations, supplementing his mother's works of art with treasures of silver and gold and embroidered curtains.[84]

Eusebius is not particularly clear in all instances as to what can be attributed to the Empress and what can be attributed to the Emperor. However, it is abundantly clear that the nativity cave was the object of imperial endowment through construction projects, artwork, and decoration.

The description of Helena's decoration of the nativity cave as a beautification of "the Godbearer's pregnancy with wonderful monuments" is poignant. As Bacci writes, "That a material, geographically determined entity may be used as a metonymical surrogate for a temporal category indicates that, by Helena's and Eusebius' times, the cave had come to be regarded as a material concretization of the historical event of Jesus' birth."[85] Indeed, it had already served as evidence of the memory of Jesus' birth in Bethlehem well before Helena's visit, as indicated by Origen's testimony to the cave discussed above. Regardless of what the origin of the association of this particular cave with the birth of Jesus might be, obscure as it is within the mists of time, it was undoubtedly the place where Jesus' birth was remembered. By the fourth century, it had *become* the place where Jesus was born, irrespective of the literal "authenticity" of the site.

Eusebius cites Ps 131:7 LXX ("Let us adore in the place where his feet have stood") in his narrative of Helena's patronage to the holy sites. We should recall at this point that Eusebius understood LXX Ps 131 to refer specifically to Bethlehem,[86] so its citation here is particularly pointed. Bethlehem is the place where the God of Jacob had come to dwell, and the citation of this Psalm that Eusebius takes to refer to the "human tabernacle" of Jesus is significant precisely because it envisions "a place for the Lord" (Ps 131:5). Just as the Temple followed the tabernacle as a "place for the Lord," so too did this new Temple at Bethlehem dedicated to the "God with us" (*Life of Constantine*, 3.43.1) follow the human tabernacle that was that "God with us," who was born on the very spot where it stood.

The form of the present-day Church of the Nativity more closely reflects the rebuilding of the structure during the reign of Justinian,[87] and much of the décor dates to later periods.[88] However, the state of preservation of the building is remarkable,[89]

---

[84] Eusebius, *Life of Constantine*, 3.42.2–43.2. Translation from Cameron and Hall, *Life of Constantine*, 137.
[85] Bacci, *Mystic Cave*, 36.
[86] Cf. Cameron and Hall, *Life of Constantine*, 293.
[87] See esp. Harvey, "The Early Basilica at Bethlehem," 28–33. The recent dendochronological analysis of the church's timber structure has identified certain cedar lintels resting on the colonnades of the nave and aisles as well as on the masonry wall that date as early as the mid-sixth century CE, in Mauro Bernabei and Jarno Bontadi, "Dendrochronological Analysis of the Timber Structure of the Church of the Nativity in Bethlehem," *Journal of Cultural Heritage* 13 (2012): 54–60 (esp. 58–9, 60).
[88] For an excellent overview of the medieval decoration, see Bacci, *Mystic Cave*, 124–203.
[89] See, e.g., Bernabei and Bontadi, "Dendochronological Analysis," 60, which identifies timbers that date as early as the sixth century CE.

and much work has been done to accurately recover the form of the Constantinian phase of the edifice.[90]

The present-day Church of the Nativity, which essentially maintains the form of the sixth-century rebuild of the structure under Justinian, is a basilica terminating in a triconch apse.[91] The building is entered from the west side, and the orienting apse faces east. The other two apses, located where the nave and aisles end, are oriented north and south, respectively, forming a transept. The archaeological work conducted at the site has shown that the basilica itself, the nave and aisles, were rebuilt after a destruction,[92] as a mosaic floor belonging to an earlier form of the church was discovered about 75 cm below the present day floor, which belonged to the Constantinian phase of the church.[93] This lower floor provided the basic plan of the area of nave of the basilica, which coincides with the present sidewalls and eastern end of the nave, as well as the division of the nave into five aisles.[94] Although recent investigations have shown that the entire structure of the basilica as it now stands dates to the sixth-century rebuilding of the church,[95] the basic plan of the nave in terms of size appears to be relatively similar to that of the Constantinian church, whose floor lies below the present church. However, the triconch apse, the sanctuary area, dates to the time of Justinian and was of a completely different form in the Constantinian period.[96]

The Constantinian Church of the Nativity consisted of a basilica, with a nave divided into five aisles and paved with an intricate mosaic floor, which terminated in a polygonal structure that lay over the cave that was remembered as the place where Jesus was born. It was entered from the west through a vestibule leading into an atrium located in roughly the same place as the present-day courtyard.[97]

---

[90] See, in particular, Vincent and Abel, *Bethléem*, 73–106; Louis-Hugues Vincent, "Le sanctuaire de la Nativité d'après les fouilles récentes," *Revue Biblique* 45 (1936-7): 544–74, 46 (1936-7): 93–121; Harvey, "Early Basilica," 28–33; Ernest T. Richmond, "Basilica of the Nativity, Discovery of the Remains of an Earlier Church," *Quarterly of the Department of Antiquities in Palestine* 5 (1936): 75–81, 6 (1937): 63–72; Bellarmino Bagatti, *Gli antichi edifice sacri di Betlemme in seguito agli scavi e restauri practicati dalla Custodia di Terra Santa (1948-1951)* (Jerusalem: Franciscan Printing Press, 1952); Bagatti, *Church From the Gentiles*, 175–84; see the review of scholarship in Michele Bacci, Giovanna Bianchi, Stefano Campana, and Giuseppe Fichera, "Historical and Archaeological nalysis of the Church of the Nativity," *Journal of Cultural Heritage* 13 (2012): 5–26 (8–11).

[91] See the plan of the basilica in this form in, e.g., Bagatti, *Church from the Circumcision*, 176; or Vincent and Abel, *Bethléem*, pl. 2.

[92] Harvey suggests that this destruction was the Samaritan sack of Bethlehem c.525 CE ("Early Basilica," 31).

[93] Reported in Harvey, "Early Basilica," 28–31; see also Bacci et al., "Historical and Archaeological Analysis," 9; Bagatti, *Church from the Gentiles*, 176.

[94] Harvey, "Early Basilica," 30.

[95] Bacci et al., "Historical and Archaeological Analysis," 24–5.

[96] As shown especially by Harvey in his investigations, summarized in "Early Basilica," see also William Harvey, *Structural Survey of the Church of the Nativity, Bethlehem* (Oxford: Oxford University Press, 1935) for his full structural survey. However, the idea that the eastern portion of the church (the triconch sanctuary) dated to Justinian's time and did not reflect the Constantinian plan predates Harvey's study, as it was already proposed by Vincent and Abel, *Bethléem*, 118–23, recounting the rebuilding of church under Justinian). On the unitary construction of the present form of the basilica, see Bacci et al., "Historical and Archaeological Analysis," 24.

[97] Cf. Bacci, *Mystic Cave*, 39–40; R. W. Hamilton, "Excavations in the Atrium of the Church of the Nativity," *Quarterly of the Department of Antiquities in Palestine* 3 (1934): 1–8.

The polygonal structure at the eastern portion of the church was the focal point of the edifice, enshrining the cave that was the traditional site of Jesus' birth beneath it. This area of the church was accessed by means of stairs leading up from the nave,[98] which served to delineate the space of the nave from the presbytery. The precise form of the polygonal structure has been a matter of some dispute and discussion in scholarship.[99] Two pertinent issues pertaining to the form of this structure are, first, whether the structure was a full octagon attached to the building or a polygonal apse (roughly half of an octagon) protruding from it,[100] and second, whether visitors or congregants could view or interact directly with the enshrined cave below the structure, and if so, how?[101]

The exact form of the polygonal structure is difficult to determine. Bagatti has rightly pointed out that the northwestern wall of the octagon is missing, although there is an empty space in the mosaic flooring where it would be, which Bagatti notes could simply be where a transenna was located,[102] and not evidence of a wall at all. Whether or not the structure could be identified as a full octagon at floor level, the mosaic pavement and remains of an interior octagonal base nevertheless show that, even if this area were an apse (structurally speaking), it was nevertheless organized on a central plan around its middle point. This point was spatially located above the cave that was commemorated as the birthplace of Jesus. For our present purposes, this is what matters most—the central plan of the eastern end of the church, marking the spot of commemoration, the beating heart of the *lieu de mémoire* that was Jesus' birthplace.

The form of the Constantinian Church of the Nativity combines a central plan structure with a basilica, which draws a natural comparison with the Constantinian Church of the Holy Sepulchre. However, it is also clearly distinct in a major respect from the Church of the Holy Sepulchre. The Church of the Holy Sepulchre was bifocal, and the Anastasis rotunda was an independent structure distinct from the Martyrion basilica, whereas the octagon of the Church of the Nativity was attached to the eastern end of its basilica.[103] This arrangement had the effect of combining the primary space used for congregational gathering and worship with the venerated sacred space of the cave, and, thus, in the words of Bacci, "the sanctuary platform was a structural device instrumental to the pilgrims' worship of the holy cave."[104] Given the lack of an ambulatory in the Church of the Nativity,[105] the combination of venerated space with space used for congregational gathering allowed for the cave to have an ongoing symbolic role in worship. Although it would not have been visible to those gathered

---

[98] Cf. Bacci, *Mystic Cave*, 40.
[99] See the summary of the various views in Bacci et al., "Historical and Archaeological Analysis," 9–10; see also the summary of some of the key issues in Bagatti, *Church from the Gentiles*, 180.
[100] Compare, e.g., Harvey, "Early Basilica," 19–20, cf. pl. 1; and R. W. Hamilton, *The Church of the Nativity, Bethlehem: A Guide* (Jerusalem: Government of Palestine Department of Antiquities, 1947), 13–16; with Bagatti, *Church from the Gentiles*, 180, which efficiently summarizes the problems.
[101] See the summaries in Bagatti, *Church from the Gentiles*, 180–3; Bacci et al., "Historical and Archaeological Analysis," 9–10; Bacci, *Mystic Cave*, 42–4.
[102] Bagatti, *Church from the Gentiles*, 180.
[103] Cf. Shalev-Hurvitz, *Holy Sites Encircled*, 192.
[104] Bacci, *Mystic Cave*, 43.
[105] As noted by Shalev-Hurvitz, *Holy Sites Encircled*, 192.

in the aisle and naves during a service, the unusual central plan marked the vertical relationship between the cave and the presbytery,[106] and would have been a constant reminder of its presence among the gathered worshippers.

The presence of the central planned area marking the birth cave within the same building and space as the basilica where the congregation gathered is unusual, and differs from its siblings, the Eleona-Imbomon and the Holy Sepulchre, where the central planned area was a structure that was independent from their related basilicas.[107] In my opinion, this difference is best explained by considering the specific event that the Church of the Nativity commemorated. The cave enshrined by the octagon in Bethlehem was the place where Jesus was born, but moreover, to use the language of the Creed that sparked the construction of the life-of-Jesus commemorative churches, it was the place where Jesus was *incarnated*. The presence of the birth cave, marked by octagonal space above it, within the same space as the congregational area would have highlighted the presence of the incarnated Jesus with the faithful. It was a spatial representation, whether intended or otherwise, of the Word made flesh and dwelling among us (John 1:14), of Emmanuel, "God with us" (Matt 1:23), through the visible presence of the place where the incarnate Word came into the world among and before the worshippers.

The construction of the Church of the Nativity provided legitimation of the tradition of Jesus' birth at Bethlehem, and perhaps more surprisingly, of the Bethlehem cave tradition in the realm of official memory. Despite the fact that the cave tradition was extracanonical, whatever that would have meant in the fourth century, it became a fixed element of the tradition from thereon. Even Jerome, who we should recall from our earlier discussion was skeptical of the Adamic Golgotha tradition, appeared to accept the cave tradition without reservation.[108]

The iconography of the architecture of the Church of the Nativity is a trickier matter than that of the Church of the Holy Sepulchre. As we have already discussed, the central plan of the Holy Sepulchre evokes the iconography of imperial mausolea.[109] The octagonal form of the eastern end of the Church of the Nativity similarly calls the same architectural iconography to mind, as it is reminiscent of polygonal imperial mausolea, such as those associated with Galerius,[110] Maximian,[111] and perhaps most famously, Diocletian.[112] However, while there is a natural point of comparison between the Anastasis at the Church of the Holy Sepulchre and the domed rotundas of the imperial mausolea, since the Anastasis also enshrined a burial place, the enshrined cave in Bethlehem was not a tomb, but a birthplace. The closest analog within Christian architecture at the time of the construction of the Church of the Nativity was

---

[106] Cf. Bacci, *Mystic Cave*, 43.
[107] As noted by Shalev-Hurvitz, *Holy Sites Encircled*, 192.
[108] Jerome, *Ep.* 58.3.
[109] See also Hemming Winfeld-Hansen, "Centrally Planned Structures," in *The Eerdmans Encyclopedia of Early Christian Art and Archaeology*, ed. Paul Corbey Finney (Grand Rapids: Eerdmans, 2017), 289-93.
[110] Johnson, *Imperial Mausoleum*, 74-82.
[111] Ibid., 70-4.
[112] Ibid., 59-70.

the Church of the Holy Sepulchre, which also featured a basilica aligned with central-planned commemorative space. Thus, the Church of the Nativity's architecture, with its five-aisled basilica and rotunda, would have called to mind the iconography of the Church of the Holy Sepulchre, which was located just a few miles away from Bethlehem in Jerusalem.

Although it was not a tomb, the Church of the Nativity was a place where an important event in the life of Jesus was commemorated. It thus partakes of the iconography of *Christian commemorative architecture* that had been just previously established in the form of the Church of the Holy Sepulchre, through the combination of a richly decorated monumental basilica with a centrally planned rotunda. That is not to say that we should ignore the parallels to polygonal imperial mausolea. Like those mausolea, the Church of the Nativity commemorated the life of a divine royal figure, though it enshrined his birthplace rather than his tomb.

This use of architectural iconography typically associated with funerary monuments to make the place of Jesus' birth represents a development in Christian commemorative architecture, through the use of the central plan to mark a specific spot of significance and not just a place of burial. The use of a circular or polygonal structure to mark a spot other than a final resting place would be influential for Christian commemorative architecture in Palestine and would be found at the Mount of Olives, as well as at other major commemorative sites,[113] such as the Kathisma and the rotunda of "St. Peter's House" at Capernaum.[114] The use of a central-planned form marked the site as commemorative space, just as similar octagonal-shaped structures functioned as commemorative space for deceased emperors.[115] The iconography of the architecture of the Church of the Nativity thus signified commemorative space, but rather than marking a royal burial place, it marked a royal birthplace. The symbolism of the central plan form, in this case octagonal, as a representation of the cosmos[116] constructed around a cave marked this grotto as a place where the cosmic met the terrestrial in the form of Jesus, the incarnate Son of God according to Nicene theology.

The Church of the Nativity needs to be understood not in isolation but within a network of commemoration that developed around Bethlehem. No commemorative space dedicated to David was located within the Church of the Holy Sepulchre. However, in his *Onomasticon*, which is generally thought to predate the construction of the Constantinian commemorative churches,[117] Eusebius writes that tombs attributed to Jesse and David were "pointed out" in Bethlehem.[118] The Bordeaux Pilgrim, writing circa 333 CE,[119] provides further evidence through their Bethlehem itinerary:

---

[113] See, e.g., Winfeld-Hansen, "Centrally Planned," 290–1.
[114] See Shalev-Hurvitz, *Holy Sites Encircled*, 117–40; 267–73.
[115] On commemoration of emperors at their centrally planned mausolea, see Johnson, *Imperial Mausoleum*, 191–2.
[116] Ibid., 182.
[117] As discussed above.
[118] Eusebius, *Onomasticon*, Bethleem [II].
[119] See Wilkinson, *Egeria's Travels*, 22.

> Four miles from Jerusalem, on the way to Bethlehem, on the right of the road, is the tomb in which was laid Jacob's wife Rachel. Two miles further on, on the left, is Bethlehem, where the Lord Jesus Christ was born, and where a basilica has been built by command of Constantine. Not far away is the tomb of Ezekiel, Asaph, Job, Jesse, David, and Solomon. Their names are written in Hebrew characters low down on the wall as you go down into the vault. (*Itin. Burd.* 598)[120]

The pilgrim's visit to the Church of the Nativity is sandwiched between two tombs. The pilgrim's mention of Rachel's burial place makes good sense, as she and her burial place were already a fixed part of tradition surrounding Bethlehem in Jewish and Christian memory, as seen in our discussions of the traditions concerning Rachel and Bethlehem above. The second tomb was apparently a single burial location for a curious collection of figures from the Hebrew Bible. The core of the commemorative activity represented by this tomb is, in my opinion, clearly centered upon David. Eusebius' earlier witness mentions only that there were tombs of David and Jesse at Bethlehem, which is understandable since both were residents of Bethlehem. The addition of Solomon is almost to be expected, since according to 1 Kgs 11:43, Solomon "slept with his ancestors and was buried in the city of his father David." This could be taken to imply that Solomon was buried in a family tomb with his ancestors in Bethlehem, so the inclusion of Solomon within this Davidic tomb is unsurprising and likely represents a reception of 1 Kgs 11:43. Asaph is loosely connected to the Davidic tradition through the Psalms of Asaph (Pss 50, 73–83). The connections to Ezekiel and Job are, however, much more difficult to understand, and all the more so given that Egeria tells us of another site that was identified as Job's tomb in Syria (*Itin. Eger.* 16.5–6).

Apart from Ezekiel and Job, all of the other figures associated with this tomb are closely associated with David, and it is clear that this tomb primarily recalled Davidic memory. Its association with David is consistently mentioned by all our sources from Eusebius on. Jerome, like Eusebius, mentions only the tombs of Jesse and David at Bethlehem,[121] again indicating that the emphasis was on the memory of David as a Bethlehemite. The Piacenza Pilgrim writes of separate tombs of David and Solomon at Bethlehem, which by then had been incorporated into a church called "At Saint David" (*Itin. Piac.* 29). Adomnan only mentions a tomb of David at Bethlehem, which had by his time was housed in a commemorative church (*de loc. sanct.* 4.4). Note that only the Bordeaux Pilgrim mentions figures outside of the Davidic triad of David, Jesse, and Solomon, who all have a clear connection to Bethlehem. We are thus justified in inferring that the core of the memory attached to this site is very much centered upon David and that the site may have also attracted other memories that attached themselves to varying degrees of longevity to the site. It seems clear that the non-Davidic memories attached to this tomb appear to have dissipated already by the fifth century.

It is important to recall, as we have discussed in Chapter 3, that there was a site identified as David's tomb in Jerusalem during the Second Temple period (Josephus,

---

[120] Translation from ibid., 33.
[121] Jerome, *Onomasticon*, Bethlehem [I].

Ant. 7.392).[122] The Bethlehem tomb is thus clearly a "secondary" site, a resiting of an early place of commemoration. That David's tomb was resited sometime after either 70 or 135 CE makes a good deal of sense, and as a place closely associated with David, Bethlehem is an appropriate place for the memory of David to take hold. It was thus natural that commemorative activity associated with David had shifted from Jerusalem to Bethlehem by the dawn of the age of Constantinian church building in Palestine. In lieu of further evidence,[123] it is not possible to be certain whether the Bethlehemite tomb of David was a Jewish or Christian commemorative site, or whether it is even possible to determine between what constitutes one or the other in this period. The "Hebrew characters" in the tomb mentioned by the Bordeaux Pilgrim might seem to point toward a Jewish origin, but the use of Hebrew characters in the tomb does not exclude the Jewish believers in Jesus, nor other possible scenarios such as the Christian repurposing of an earlier tomb unrelated to David that had a Hebrew inscription that was incorrectly interpreted by non-Hebrew readers as the names of biblical figures.[124]

For our purposes, it is less important to determine who resited the Davidic tomb than it is to simply acknowledge that it was resited and thus became part of the pilgrim itinerary in Bethlehem, linking it to the Church of the Nativity. The fact that this tomb was visited by Christian pilgrims following their visit to the Church of the Nativity highlights the importance of the connection of Jesus to David within Christian memory and the messianic claims that come with that connection, symbolized and realized by these two monuments.

The Mount of Olives

The Mount of Olives plays a significant role in the narratives of the canonical gospels as the setting for several memorable episodes. It is the place from which Jesus comes as he enters Jerusalem (Mark 11:1 and Luke 19:37; cf. Matt 21:1 and Luke 19:29) for his final Passover. It is remembered as a place where Jesus would spend the night while in the Jerusalem area in Luke 21:37, and it is mentioned as the place where Jesus stays prior to the episode recounted in the addition to the Gospel of John known as the Pericope Adulterae (John 7:53–8:11[8:1]).[125] It is the place where Jesus predicts the desertion of his disciples and Peter's denial (Mark 14:26–31). Gethsemane is located on the lower slopes of the Mount of Olives (compare Mark 14:32 and Luke 22:39),[126]

---

[122] Cf. Wilkinson, *Egeria's Travels*, 33.
[123] Archaeological evidence for this site is lacking. However, it is worth noting that Bagatti proposed with some good reason that this tomb site would have been located near Biyar Da'ud, in Bellarmino Bagatti, "Recenti Scavi a Betlemme," *Liber Annuus* 18 (1968): 181–237.
[124] Although this scenario is imagined and merely hypothetical, it does have some precedent. To take one well-known example, the Tomb of Benei Hezir in Jerusalem was identified in the fourth century as the burial place of James. See Murphy-O'Connor, *Keys to Jerusalem*, 135–43.
[125] Although this episode is not found in the earliest manuscripts of the Gospel of John, it is nevertheless a very old tradition. For a thorough review of the history of this pericope, see Chris Keith, *The Pericope Adulterae, the Gospel of John, and the Literacy of Jesus* (Leiden: Brill, 2009), esp. 203–56.
[126] On the location of this site, see Taylor, *Christians and the Holy Places*, 192–201.

which is the site of Jesus' arrest (Mark 14:32; cf. Matt 26:36 and Luke 22:39). Bethany, and the events that took place there, including the anointing of Jesus (Mark 14:3–7 and parallels) and the raising of Lazarus (John 11:1–44), were also located on the Mount of Olives.[127] Furthermore, the Mount of Olives provides the setting for Jesus' eschatological discourse in Matthew and Mark (Matt 24:3–25:36; cf. Mark 13:3–36),[128] as well as the site of Jesus' ascension in the narratives of Luke and Acts (Luke 24:50; Acts 1:12).

The longer ending of Mark also includes Jesus' ascension (Mark 16:19). Although this ending is unlikely to be part of the original text of the Second Gospel, it does bear witness to the reception of the ascension tradition in the second century and beyond.[129] However, the longer ending of Mark does not set the ascension on the Mount of Olives. Instead, the scene is set in Mark 16:14 as a time when the Eleven were "sitting at table," implying an indoor setting. Then, according to v. 19, "So then the Lord Jesus, after he had spoken to them, was taken up into heaven and sat down at the right hand of God." Since there is no change of location, it would seem as though Jesus ascended from the place where he appeared and spoke to the Eleven. Even though the pseudo-Markan version of the ascension is not set on the Mount of Olives, it is worth noting its existence, since it contributes to the reception and interpretation history of the ascension, an event that is tied to the Mount of Olives in the broader tradition. Moreover, the possibility that the version of the ascension in the longer ending of Mark could have impacted the memory of that event as it was remembered at the Mount of Olives should not be excluded.

The Mount of Olives, or the mountain to the east of Jerusalem, appears in several narrative episodes in the Davidic and Solomonic cycles in the Hebrew Bible.[130] However, it is in the prophetic tradition that we find the material that is likely most relevant to the setting of the events of the life of Jesus in the canonical gospels. In Ezek 11:23, the "mountain east of the city" is the place where Yahweh's glory stands after rising from the city. Notably, it later returns from the east, presumably from the place where it stood, in Ezek 43:1–2. Moreover, Zech 14:1–5 envisions an eschatological scenario in which God will gather the nations to do battle against Jerusalem, and in which God "will go forth and fight against those nations" (v. 3). When this happens, "his [God's] feet shall stand on the Mount of Olives, which lies before Jerusalem on the east" (v. 4). This vests the site with eschatological significance, which is important to consider given that Matthew and Mark identify it as the location where Jesus pronounced his own eschatological teachings, and the place where he was taken up by a cloud (Acts 1:9), which is the same mode of transport as the eschatological figure of the Son of Man

---

[127] This may possibly also include the episode at the home of Martha and Mary (Luke 10:38–42), although this is somewhat tendentious. Luke does not explicitly set that episode at Bethany, and its location within the Lukan travel narrative would seem to imply that it took place further away from Jerusalem.

[128] See also Luke 21:7–36, although Luke sets this discourse in the Temple.

[129] On the date of the longer ending in the second century, see James A. Kelhoffer, *Miracle and Mission. The Authentication of Missionaries and Their Message in the Longer Ending of Mark*, WUNT 2/112 (Tübingen: Mohr Siebeck, 2000), 169–77.

[130] 2 Sam 15:30; 1 Kgs 11:7; 2 Kgs 23:13–14. See John Briggs Curtis, "An Investigation of the Mount of Olives in the Judaeo-Christian Tradition," *Hebrew Union College Annual* 28 (1957): 137–10.

in Dan 7:13–14 when he comes before the Ancient of Days and is given everlasting dominion, glory, and kingship (v. 14).

By the fourth century, the commemorative enterprise of the Jesus tradition was well underway at the Mount of Olives. As we have already mentioned above, Eusebius describes a Constantinian commemorative church on the Mount of Olives being commissioned by Helena. According to him, on the Mount of Olives, Helena raised a

> monument to the journey into heaven of the Saviour of the Universe in lofty buildings ... she raised the sacred house of the church, and constructed just there a shrine for prayer to the Saviour who chose to spend his time on that spot, since just there a true report maintains that in that cave the Saviour of the Universe initiated the members of his guild in ineffable mysteries. (*Life of Constantine*, 43.3)[131]

We note here that there are *two* events being commemorated by this construction: the ascension, and Jesus' teaching. On the basis of the canonical tradition, we might be naturally inclined to identify the teaching that Eusebius refers to as the eschatological discourse depicted in the synoptic tradition (Mark 13:3–36; Matt 24:3–25:46). However, the mention of this teaching taking place is a cave is curious, since this detail does not appear in the canonical tradition. It may be that, as with the Nativity cave, the teaching cave is an extracanonical siting of the canonical event.[132] Alternatively, the cave mentioned by Eusebius might be connected to some other tradition about Jesus teaching in a cave on the Mount of Olives that does not appear in the canonical gospels.

There may be evidence for the emergence of the Mount of Olives teaching cave in the early Christian apocrypha. The *Acts of John*, a text typically dated to the second or third centuries,[133] includes an episode in which, during Jesus' crucifixion, John flees to a cave located on the Mount of Olives and weeps in response to the tragic event that has taken place (*Acts of John* 97–102). There, Jesus appears to him, lighting up the cave, and teaches John, saying, "I put into your mind to come up to this mountain so that you may hear what a disciple should learn from his teacher and a man from God" (*Acts of John* 97).[134] The Mount of Olives is thus an intentional location for John to receive Jesus' teaching.

---

[131] Translation from Cameron and Hall, *Life of Constantine*, 137–8.
[132] Cf., e.g., Walker, *Holy City*, 203–4.
[133] On the problem of the date of the *Acts of John*, see the relatively recent work of István Czachesz, *Commission Narratives: A Comparative Study of the Canonical and Apocryphal Acts*, Studies on Early Christian Apocrypha 8 (Leuven: Peeters, 2007), 120–2, and his review of opinions in scholarship on the date of the *Acts of John* on p. 92 n. 1. Czachesz dates the initial composition of the *Acts of John* to the second century and a revision of the text to the third century. See also Knut Schäferdiek, "The Acts of John," in *New Testament Apocrypha*, ed. Wilhelm Schneemelcher, trans. Robert McLachlan Wilson, 2 vols. (Philadelphia: Westminster, 1964), 2: 188–215 (214–15). As Schäferdiek rightly notes, although the date is uncertain, the text must predate its earliest attestations in the early fourth century.
[134] Translation from Schneemelcher, *New Testament Apocrypha*, 215–59 (232). All subsequent translations are also drawn from this same source unless otherwise indicated.

The teaching that John receives in the cave on the Mount of Olives revolves primarily around the "Cross of Light," which is the Logos, that is, Jesus himself (see esp. *Acts of John* 98, 101). According to the teaching discourse in *Acts of John* 97–102, Jesus did not suffer (101) and is not the man who is on the (wooden) cross (99), which evinces a clearly docetic Christology. The teaching also emphasizes the importance of knowledge that has been secretly shown to John that he might know Jesus as he truly is (101). This episode belongs to a complex section of the *Acts of John* (94–102) that is often identified as Gnostic,[135] an issue that is complicated by the fact that it may not be authored by the same person who wrote the rest of the text.[136] According to Knut Schäferdiek, "Christ's revelation-discourse, cc. 97ff., teaches the Gnostic to recognize that he may know himself to be akin to the Revealer, who as such is the Redeemer; and that the redemption introduces him into a cosmic process which fulfills itself in and through the Cross of Light (98–100); it is this that is symbolically represented by the earthly event of the Passion of Jesus, which thereby ceases to have any independent significance (c. 99 and 102)."[137]

Gnosticism is a notoriously slippery category, and whether or not we identify this text as "Gnostic" will naturally depend a great deal on how we define "Gnosticism." That said, it certainly features elements that we might identify as heterodox, not the least of which are its docetic teachings. As Taylor has observed, the Mount of Olives functioned as the setting for the teaching of secret mysteries in several Christian texts broadly identified as "Gnostic."[138] We need not review all of them here, but a few examples will suffice. In the *Letter of Peter to Philip*, dated between the end of the second century or the beginning of the third,[139] the disciples go to "the mountain which is called 'the (mount) olives,' the place where they used to gather with the blessed Christ when he was in the body" (133.14–17).[140] Here, they pray, and Jesus appears to them in a great light, which makes the mountain shine (134.10–18). Jesus speaks out of the light and reveals cosmic knowledge to them (135.5–138.3) that is consistent with cosmological myth typical of texts identified with the "gnosis" movement in early Christianity.[141]

---

[135] See, e.g., Pieter J. Lalleman, *The Acts of John: A Two-Stage Initiation into Johannine Gnosticism* (Leuven: Peeters, 1998), esp. 32–5; Schäferdiek, "The Acts of John," 212–214.

[136] See esp. Lalleman, *Acts of John*, 32–5; cf. also Czachesz, *Commission Narratives*, 120–2.

[137] Schäferdiek, "Acts of John," 212.

[138] Taylor, *Christians and the Holy Places*, 149.

[139] Cf. Marvin W. Meyer, Introduction to "The Letter of Peter to Philip," in *The Nag Hammadi Library in English*, 3rd ed., ed. James M. Robinson (San Francisco: HarperCollins, 1990), 431–33 (433).

[140] Trans. from Frederik Wisse, trans., "The Letter of Perter to Philip," in *The Nag Hammadi Library in English*, 3rd ed., ed. James M. Robinson (San Francisco: HarperCollins, 1990), 434–437. All subsequent translations of this text are drawn from this source unless otherwise indicated.

[141] The issues surrounding the definitions of "Gnosticism," "Gnostics," and "gnosis" are complex. For a brief overview of "gnosis" in early Christianity, see Christoph Markschies, *Gnosis: An Introduction*, trans. John Bowden (London and New York: T&T Clark, [2001] 2003), 13–27. Although these categories are not without problems, these issues are beyond the purview of the present project. It is sufficient to observe that the traditions discussed here, typically identified with "gnosis" or "Gnosticism," are heterodox, or at least quite different from the Nicene Christianity that emerges as a politically dominant force within early Christianity in the fourth century CE. Whether or not there was a dominant stream of Christianity that could be considered "orthodox" in the second or third centuries is also an issue that is beyond the urview of this project. For our purposes, it is

A somewhat similar scenario involving the risen Jesus teaching on the Mount of Olives is presented in *The Sophia of Jesus Christ*, in which the risen Jesus and a group of disciples including the Twelve along with seven women are taught by Jesus on "the mountain called 'Of Olives' in Galilee" (91.20).[142] This curious Galilean location of the Mount of Olives, which is in actuality located just outside Jerusalem, may be the result of a conflation of the Galilean mountain where the resurrected Jesus meets his disciples in Matt 28:16 and the Mount of Olives, where the resurrected Jesus goes with his disciples prior to his ascension in Luke 24:40 (cf. Acts 1:12).

The Mount of Olives was thus remembered in early Christianity as a place connected to Jesus' teaching, and especially esoteric teaching rather than exoteric or public teaching. This was already the case in the synoptic tradition, as in Mark 13:3, the audience for Jesus' eschatological teaching consists only of a select group from among the Twelve, Peter, James, John, and Andrew. The role played by the Mount of Olives as a site for Jesus' esoteric teaching in "heterodox" Christian texts contributes to that mnemonic matrix, and should be seen in *commemorative* continuum between the synoptic tradition in the first century C.E. and the construction of the Eleona under Helena and Constantine in the fourth century C.E., even if it is not necessarily in *theological* continuity with the synoptic tradition nor with the Nicene church. As Walker observes, the authors of these texts "will most probably have referred to this mount, not because they had personally visited it, but because it was the biblical mountain *par excellence*, associated canonically with revelation both of the future and of the heavenly realm; it could therefore be used by absentee writers as a natural authenticating touch for extra-canonical material."[143]

As it stands, the only direct reference to a cave associated with Jesus' teaching prior to Eusebius comes from the passage from the *Acts of John* discussed above. Some scholars (e.g., Walker and Bagatti) have posited an actual cave that was known to the author of the *Acts of John* that was already associated with Jesus' teaching,[144] though it has also been suggested that the detail of the cave was contributed by the *Acts of John* to the tradition and that an actual cave should not be presumed.[145] The appearance of a cave in the tradition's memory of Jesus' teaching on the Mount of Olives is a natural development, since it serves to localize the tradition and anchor it to a particular spot where it supposedly "happened." That said, it is nevertheless true that the references to the Mount of Olives in early Christian apocryphal literature would naturally have contributed to and impacted the memory of Jesus connected to the site, regardless of whether the authors of those texts had any topographical knowledge or firsthand

---

enough to acknowledge that the streams of Christian thought represented by the texts in question would have stood at some distance from the Nicene Christianity of the Constantinian era.

[142] Trans. from Douglas M. Parrot, trans., "Eugnostos the Blessed and The Sophia of Jesus Christ," in in *The Nag Hammadi Library in English*, 3rd ed., ed. James M. Robinson (San Francisco: HarperCollins, 1990), 222–43.

[143] Walker, *Holy City*, 207.

[144] Ibid.; John Wilkinson, "Christian Pilgrims in Jerusalem during the Byzantine Period," *PEQ* 108, no. 2 (1976): 74–101 (84); cf. Bagatti, *Church from the Gentiles*, 61–3.

[145] Taylor, *Christians and the Holy Places*, 146–7.

experience of the place.[146] It is in this way that they were a part of the developing mnemonic matrix of the site.

The core of the tradition being remembered is, nevertheless, Jesus' esoteric teaching on the Mount of Olives. Thus, the Jesus-memory that attached itself to the place was that of Jesus *as a teacher*. This memory was developed in new directions by the apocryphal writings in the second and third centuries. Since it is localized only generally on the Mount of Olives in the canonical gospels, this memory of Jesus teaching was likely to receive a more specific localization, and it is difficult to know whether the detail of the cave originated from the *Acts of John*, whether it predates that text, or if the agreement in detail between Eusebius (along with the eventual location of the Eleona) and the *Acts of John* is mere coincidence. What matters for our purposes is simply the fact that it was localized at all and, moreover, that the Mount of Olives became a place in early Christian memory, which was tied to the memory of Jesus as a teacher.

The Mount of Olives in *Demonstratio Evangelica*

In his *Demonstratio Evangelica*, which was written prior to the construction of the Constantinian commemorative structures on the mountain, Eusebius discusses the Mount of Olives and the significance of its place within the Jesus tradition and in early Christianity. In interpreting the passage from Zech 14:4 discussed above, he writes, "And the words, 'And his feet shall stand in that day on the Mount of Olives, which is before Jerusalem to the eastward,' what else can they mean than that the Lord God, that is to say the Word of God Himself, will stand, and stand firm, upon His Church, which is here metaphorically called the Mount of Olives?" (*Dem. Evang.* 6.18.28).

Here, Eusebius metaphorically interprets the Mount of Olives as the Church. This plays into his "New Jerusalem" theology, as the Mount of Olives, and thus the Church, is symbolically pitted against Jerusalem. Eusebius goes on to write that

> this Mount of Olives is said to be over against Jerusalem, because it was established by God after the fall of Jerusalem, instead of the old earthly Jerusalem and its worship. For as Scripture said above with reference to Jerusalem: "The city shall be taken, and the nations that are her enemies and foes shall be gathered together against her, and her spoils shall be divided," it could not say that the feet of the Lord should stand upon Jerusalem. How could that be, once it were destroyed? But it says that they will stand with them that depart from it to the mount opposite the city called the Mount of Olives. And this, too, the prophet Ezekiel anticipates by the Holy Spirit and foretells. (*Dem. Evang.* 6.18.29)[147]

This is followed with a citation of Ezek 11:22–23 (discussed above) as Eusebius' evidence for his claim. The ideology represented in this passage is reminiscent of Eusebius'

---

[146] Cf. Walker, *Holy City*, 208.
[147] Translation from Ferrar, *Proof of the Gospel*, 29.

presentation of the Church of the Holy Sepulchre in opposition to the Jewish Temple, which we have discussed previously in Chapters 3 and 4. In his understanding, the Mount of Olives, which he symbolically understands to be the Church, was established as the place where the presence of God, represented by "the feet of the Lord" in Zech 14:4 and the Holy Spirit in Ezek 11:23, would stand. The Church, presented here as the Mount of Olives, is explicitly "over against Jerusalem" and is established in opposition to "old earthly Jerusalem and its worship." Here, we see a site strongly connected with the memory of Jesus, which would soon receive an imperial commemorative church complex, being presented as a successor to the "old" Jerusalem, by which he means Jewish Jerusalem, and standing in opposition to it. Thus, the Mount of Olives, along with the Holy Sepulchre complex, played an ideological role in the discourse of interreligious competition in fourth-century Palestine.

According to Eusebius, the Mount of Olives had become a place of Christian gathering and worship:

> believers in Christ all congregate from all parts of the world, not as of old time because of the glory of Jerusalem, nor that they may worship in the ancient Temple at Jerusalem, but they rest there that they may learn both about the city being taken and devastated as the prophets foretold, and that they may worship at the Mount of Olives opposite to the city, whither the glory of the Lord migrated when it left the former city. (*Dem. Evang.* 6.18.29)

This statement is particularly interesting, since it strongly implies that Christians were already visiting the Mount of Olives as a place of worship and as a place where the destruction of Jerusalem was remembered before the construction of an imperial commemorative monument on the site.[148]

The mention here of learning about the destruction of Jerusalem indicates that there was some sort of oral tradition being passed on at the place, which Eusebius identifies with the foretelling of the prophets. However, this was almost certainly done in concert with and reinforcement of the Jesus tradition, since the Mount of Olives is the place where Jesus' prophecies about the destruction of Jerusalem were localized, both in the Olivet discourse (Mark 13; Matt 24:1–44) as well as in the Lukan narrative of Jesus weeping over Jerusalem (Luke 19:37, 41–44) as he came down from the Mount of Olives to Jerusalem. The fact that Christian commemorative activity was already occurring on the Mount of Olives before the construction of the Constantinian edifices on the site shows that the construction of the Eleona and the Imbomon were a part of an already ongoing process of the crystallization of memory of Jesus at the Mount of Olives. However, this does not warrant any conclusions about the antiquity of the use of the place as a site of Christian worship and teaching before Eusebius' time, nor does it speak in any clear way to the authenticity of the tradition site as a place where Jesus taught.[149]

---

[148] Cf. ibid., 202–3.
[149] For a similar cautionary statement, see Taylor, *Christians and the Holy Places*, 152–3.

Eusebius goes on to connect the site specifically with the Jesus tradition:

> There stood in truth according to the common and received account the feet of our Lord and Savior, Himself the Word of God, through that tabernacle of humanity He had borne up the Mount of Olives to the cave that is shewn there; there He prayed and delivered to His disciples on the summit of the Mount of Olives the mysteries of His end, and thence He made His Ascension into heaven, as Luke tells us in the Acts of the Apostles. (*Dem. Evang.* 6.18.29–30)

There are several traditional elements that demand our attention. Eusebius mentions a cave where Jesus prayed. Along with this he mentions teachings delivered to the disciples concerning "the mysteries of his end," which is set on the summit of the Mount of Olives, and finally, Jesus' ascension.

Apart from the ascension, which Eusebius cites in the form in which it appears in Acts 1:9–11, it is difficult to determine precisely which Jesus traditions or narratives Eusebius is referring to here. None of the narratives mention Jesus praying in a cave prior to the ascension, but Luke 22:39–40 might be taken to imply that Jesus habitually went to the Mount of Olives to pray.[150] The eschatological teaching discourse most clearly situated on the Mount of Olives is the Olivet discourse (Mark 13; Matt 24:1–44), but as Taylor rightly observes, these "mysteries" are passed on earlier in the Synoptic narratives, not immediately prior to the ascension.[151] As some scholars have noted, Eusebius elsewhere locates the saying about the destruction of the Temple in Matt 24:2 ("not one stone will be left here upon another") in the Temple complex rather than on the Mount of Olives,[152] which may indicate that Eusebius did not think that the eschatological discourse about the destruction of the Temple took place on the Mount of Olives at all. This, however, could simply be because Luke situates this saying in the Temple precincts (21:6). There are, thus, two locations in the tradition associated with this prediction. This may be the reason underlying Eusebius' confusion or reluctance surrounding the precise identification of the teaching that took place on the Mount of Olives.

It is possible that Eusebius has conflated the apocryphal tradition in the *Acts of John* discussed above, which is set in a cave on the Mount of Olives, with the ascension narrative in Luke-Acts.[153] However, this solution does not have as much explanatory power as we might like, as what Eusebius describes does not match the *Acts of John* narrative almost at all save for the setting of the cave and the very general theme of teaching mysteries. Another possibility is that Eusebius might be referring to the answer to the question about the restoration of the kingdom that Jesus gives right before the ascension in Acts (1:6–8). This is a strong candidate, since it involves eschatological mysteries, and since Eusebius cites the verses depicting the ascension that directly follow this saying. We must, however, admit that no cave is mentioned in this narrative and that the ascension *literally* follows this saying, as he was taken from them "when he had said this" (Acts 1:9; Greek ταῦτα εἰπὼν βλεπόντων).

---

[150] Cf. Walker, *Holy City*, 209.
[151] Taylor, *Christians and the Holy Places*, 148.
[152] *Theoph.* 4.35. See Walker, *Holy City*, 204; Cameron and Hall, *Life of Constantine*, 294.
[153] Cf. Taylor, *Christians and the Holy Places*, 148.

There is ultimately no certainty to be had about the referent of Eusebius' description here. However, in my opinion, though it is somewhat speculative, it is likely that he has the teaching of Acts 1:7–8 in mind, though he has relocated the tradition within a particular cave that in Eusebius' time was used to locate the memory of Jesus' eschatological teaching, specifically Mark 13 and Matt 24:1–44, on the Mount of Olives. The idea that Jesus taught in a cave on the Mount of Olives may have been a detail that first appeared in text in the *Acts of John*. In this way, it may have contributed to the development of the memory of Jesus' teaching on the mountain. However, that does not necessitate a conclusion that the cave that Eusebius referred to, which is presumably the one which would eventually be enshrined in the Eleona Church, was associated with the discourse from the *Acts of John* in the fourth century. It is much more likely that it was associated with the Olivet discourse. This is strongly implied by Eusebius' discussion of the Mount of Olives, which depicts it as a place where the destruction of Jerusalem was remembered.

Eusebius clearly mentions two places on the Mount of Olives: the cave and the summit. The cave is where the memory of the prayer and teaching was apparently localized, while the summit is where the ascension was localized.[154] This is particularly significant, given that monumental commemorative architecture would soon crown and preserve both sites.

Eusebius' use of Old Testament passages in his interpretation of the memory of Jesus attached to the Mount of Olives deserves some attention here. He understood the ascension as a fulfilment of Zech 14:4 ("his feet shall stand on the Mount of Olives").[155] Given the eschatological context of this passage in Zechariah, particularly its reference to the fall of Jerusalem (Zech 14:2), and that the discussion of Jesus' activity on the Mount of Olives as fulfilment of Zech 14:4 immediately follows Eusebius' unfortunate supersessionist interpretation of Ezek 11:22–23, the implications of the connection that is drawn between Zech 14:4 and the ascension for Eusebius' supersessionist ideology are clear.

We should recall that the act of remembering is *interpretive*, and the past is remembered in light of the present. In Eusebius' discussion of the Mount of Olives, we see how the early Christian memory of Jesus' actions at that place were interpreted in light of the present reality of religious competition in the fourth century CE. The hope that Jerusalem would be restored to the Jewish people, a hope that would come to a head with Julian the Apostate's failed project to rebuild the Temple, apparently remained alive in the minds of Jews in the East in the fourth century CE.[156] John Chrysostom, for example, writes that the Jews in Syrian Antioch were bragging that they would "get their city back again" (*Adv. Jud.* 7.1.4). The ruination of Jerusalem and the presence of Christian worship on the Mount of Olives represented, in Eusebius' mind, proof of the victory of Christianity and of the truth of the gospel.[157]

---

[154] Cf. Walker, *Holy City*, 209.
[155] See also ibid.
[156] On this, see for example Robert L. Wilkin, *John Chrysostom and the Jews: Rhetoric and Reality in the Late Fourth Century* (Eugene: Wipf and Stock, [1983] 2004), 146.
[157] Cf. similar comments on the Holy Sepulchre, in Finkelstein, *Specter of the Jews*, 112.

The Bordeaux Pilgrim's Experience of the Mount of Olives

By the time of the Bordeaux Pilgrim's journey in 333 CE, less than ten years after Eusebius had written the *Demonstratio Evangelica*, the Constantinian construction project on the Mount of Olives was already underway. Several minor topographical features had also begun to function as *lieux de mémoire*. Although no commemorative architecture marked these spots at the time of Constantine, the Bordeaux Pilgrim mentions several markers that were connected to several of the events that took place on the Mount of Olives, including "a rock where Judas Iscariot betrayed Christ" (*Itin. Burd.* 594), "the palm-tree from which children took branches and strewed them in Christ's path" (595), and "the vault in which was laid Lazarus, whom the Lord raised" (596). This demonstrates the manner in which memory could attach itself to any recognizable feature as a way to mark the past in the present.

The Pilgrim of Bordeaux recounts their experience of the commemorative sites on the Mount of Olives in the following manner:

> On the Mount of Olives, where the Lord taught before his passion, a basilica has been built by command of Constantine. And not far off is the Hillock ("Imbomon")[158] where the Lord went up to pray, and where there appeared Moses and Elijah, when he took Peter and John apart with him. (*Itin. Burd.* 595–6)[159]

According to the Bordeaux Pilgrim, the Constantinian basilica on the Mount of Olives commemorates the place where Jesus taught "before his passion." This basilica must be the Eleona, the only Constantinian basilica that would have existed on the Mount of Olives at this time,[160] the same basilica that Eusebius describes (*Life of Constantine*, 3.43.3).

The Bordeaux Pilgrim writes that the site commemorated by the Eleona is the place where Jesus taught "before his passion." It is most likely that they have the Olivet discourse in mind. This chronological placement of the teaching event commemorated by the cave where the Eleona would be built differs from Eusebius' description of the teaching as taking place before the ascension. The Bordeaux Pilgrim's witness appears to represent the common tradition that visitors to the site would have attached to the Eleona, and it should probably be given priority over that of Eusebius in this case. This is all the more reasonable when we consider the fact that the Bordeaux Pilgrim's description of the teaching commemorated at the Eleona has a clear traditional referent, while the same cannot be said for Eusebius' presentation of the same. It is most likely that the Mount of Olives cave was identified, at least in the mainstream, as the place where the Olivet discourse was remembered.

---

[158] See Wilkinson, *Egeria's Travels*, 14–15.
[159] Translation from ibid., 32.
[160] As Wilkinson notes, the basilica would not yet have been dedicated when the pilgrim visited it (*Egeria's Travels*, 32 n. 2), though construction would have been underway, and had apparently progressed far enough that it was recognizable as a basilica.

Adomnan, writing as late as the seventh century, provides some agreement with the Pilgrim's witness, as he specifically identifies the Olivet discourse as the teaching commemorated by the Eleona.[161] In discussing the teaching commemorated by the Eleona, Adomnan writes that "we must take care to ask what address this was, when it took place, and to which particular disciples the Lord was speaking" (*de loc. sanct.* 1.25.2–3). This implies that, even as late as the seventh century, some confusion persisted about the memory associated with the site.[162] At the same time, it also indicates that the mainstream identification, which is probably the tradition that the Constantinian monument was intended to remember, had continued to persist in its connection to the place through the centuries.[163]

The Pilgrim identifies the Imbomon on the summit of the Mount of Olives as the site of the Transfiguration (Mark 9:2–8; Matt 17:1–8; Luke 9:28–36; 2 Pet 1:17–18). However, this identification is problematic; since none of the evangelists locate the Transfiguration on the Mount of Olives, nor anywhere near the Jerusalem area. Although it has been suggested that the Transfiguration may have been commemorated at the Mount of Olives in the fourth century,[164] this is unlikely, as Cyril identifies Mount Tabor as the location of the Transfiguration (*Cat.* 12.16).[165] Moreover, given that the Mount of Olives is identified as the site of the ascension in Acts 1:12 (cf. Luke 24:50) and that the Imbomon is clearly connected to the ascension in the Jerusalem liturgy as witnessed by Egeria (*Itin. Eger.* 39.3–4; 43.5–6), the best explanation is that the Bordeaux Pilgrim is mistaken in this identification.

The very fact that there is such a high level of confusion about the events that were commemorated by the primary Christian sites on the Mount of Olives in the fourth century demonstrates the fluid nature of memory, even when it is anchored to place. Memory can be slippery: identifications can be altered,[166] added to,[167] or forgotten altogether.[168] In this case, the core tradition being remembered is that of Jesus' role as a teacher, and his act of teaching on the Mount of Olives, though the content of the teaching is obscure. The confusion surrounding the memory of the site continues to his day. The partially rebuilt church that exists presently on the site, which incorporates the architectural footprint and elements of the Eleona, is called the "Pater Noster Church"[169] and now commemorates the Lord's Prayer.

---

[161] Adomnan, *de loc. sanct.* 1.25.1–6.
[162] Cf. Taylor, *Christians and the Holy Places*, 150.
[163] This is all the more remarkable given the destruction of the Eleona by the Persians in 614 CE.
[164] Clemens Kopp, *The Holy Places of the Gospels*, trans. Ronald Wells (New York: Herder and Herder, 1963), 411–13.
[165] Cf. Walker, *Holy City*, 214.
[166] As seen with the Mount of Olive traditions.
[167] As with the Adamic traditions remembered at Golgotha discussed in an earlier chapter.
[168] Consider, for example, the peculiar case of the "Anchor Church" on Mount Berenice near Tiberias. It was likely a Byzantine commemorative church, but the object of its commemoration has been lost over time and is now obscure. See Yizhar Hirschfeld, "Imperial Building Activity during the Reign of Justinian and Pilgrimage to the Holy Land in Light of the Excavations on Mt. Berenice, Tiberias," *Revue Biblique* 106, no. 2 (1999): 236–49; cf. Yizhar Hirschfeld, "The Anchor Church at the Summit of Mt. Berenice, Tiberias," *Biblical Archaeologist* 57, no. 3 (1994): 122–33.
[169] See Vincent and Abel, *Jérusalem Nouvelle*, 338–9.

The earliest connection of the site to the Lord's Prayer dates to the Crusader period[170] and should be understood as a commemoration of the teaching of the Prayer, but not an identification of where the teaching took place, since neither Matthew nor Luke place it near Jerusalem.[171] This shows the potential fluidity of place-based memory over time and that the processes of interpretation in remembrance are ongoing through history so long as there is something being remembered. The Christian memory of Jesus at the Mount of Olives has not been static over the centuries. Rather, it has shifted to such a degree that, at the present-day site, the commemoration of the Lord's Prayer has completely overshadowed and obscured the memory of the Olivet discourse, despite the fact that the canonical gospels situate the Olivet discourse on the Mount of Olives and the Lord's Prayer in Galilee. It seems that Christian memory can disagree with both historical tradition and with canonical Scripture, and it can be persistent in that disagreement over a long period of time.

The Eleona and the Imbomon

Christian commemoration on the Mount of Olives was bifocal, with memory coalescing around the cave where Jesus taught and the summit from which he ascended.[172] Fittingly, in the fourth century, two commemorative structures were built at the top of the Mount of Olives: the Eleona and the Imbomon. These two structures were located less than a hundred meters away from one another,[173] and one would most likely have been clearly visible from the other.

We have already discussed Eusebius' narration of the construction of the Constantinian commemorative complex on the Mount of Olives (in *Life of Constantine*, 3.43.3).

Eusebius bears witness to the bifocal nature of Christian memory of Jesus at the Mount of Olives. He references two different places on the Mount of Olives and two events in the remembered life of Jesus. The first event is the ascension ("the journey into heaven of the Savior"), and the second is the initiation of Jesus' followers "in ineffable mysteries." The two locations are "the ridges at the peak" of the Mount of Olives, where

---

[170] For an overview of this and other rebuilding projects and transformations of Jerusalem holy sites in this period, see Bernard Hamilton, "Rebuilding Zion: The Holy Places of Jerusalem in the Twelfth Century," *Studies in Church History* 14 (1977): 105–16.

[171] Matthew situates the teaching of the Lord's Prayer, which is found in the Sermon on the Mount, on a mountain in Galilee (Matt 4:23–5:1, 6:9–13). The Sermon on the Mount was traditionally located near Tabgha in antiquity, and was marked by a commemorative chapel as early as the fourth century. Luke places it within the travel narrative (Luke 11:1–4), well before Jesus arrives at the Mount of Olives (which is not until 19:29). On the Chapel of the Beatitudes, marking the traditional site of the Sermon on the Mount, see Bellarmino Bagatti, *Ancient Christian Villages of Galilee* (Jerusalem: Franciscan Printing Press, 2001), 72–4; Bellarmino Bagatti, "La cappella sul monte delle Beatitudini," *Revista d'Archeologia Cristiana* 14 (1937): 43–91; cf. Wilkinson, *Egeria's Travels*, 41–3.

[172] Cf. Walker, *Holy City*, 213.

[173] I am basing this on a calculation of the distance between the remains of the Eleona, which are located at the modern-day Pater Noster church, and the remains of the Imbomon at the modern-day Chapel of the Ascension.

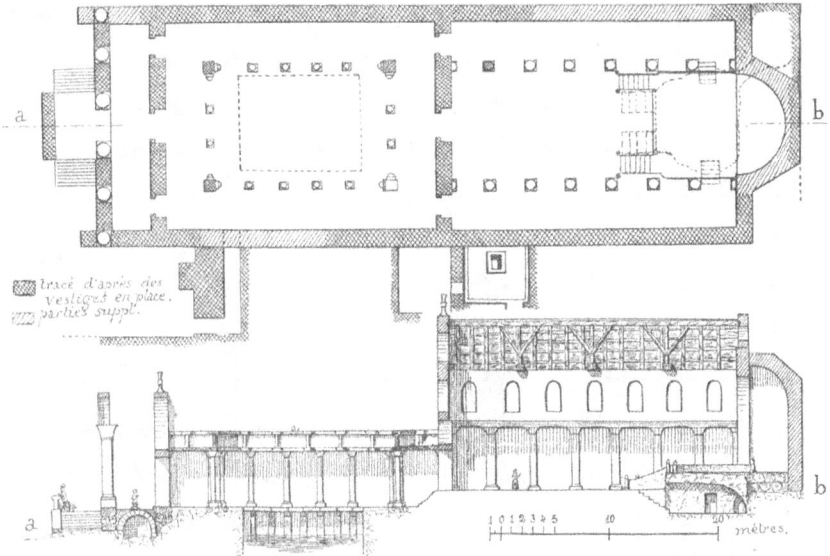

Figure 3 Floor plan of the Eleona.

Source: Louis-Hugues Vicent, "L'Église de L'Éléona," *Revue Biblique* 8 (1910): 219–65 (259).

Helena "raised the sacred house of the church," and the "shrine for prayer," which is located "just there" (Greek κἀνταῦθα). I take this to indicate that there were two commemorative sites located in roughly the same area on the Mount of Olives,[174] each remembering a different event.

It is worth observing that Eusebius specifically uses the language of commemorative architecture for the structure that Helena built in memory of Jesus' ascension, calling it a *mnēmē*, literally meaning a "memory" or "remembrance." This term is translated here by Cameron and Hall as "monument,"[175] which has the appropriate valence of an architectural structure built for the purposes of remembering. The use of this particular term to describe the structure indicates that Eusebius himself thought of the building as preserving a memory of Jesus' ascension in architectural form.

The Eleona commemorated Jesus' teaching on the Mount of Olives, while the Imbomon commemorated the ascension. There is some question as to the date of the Imbomon, as some have proposed that it is not Constantinian but was constructed later in the fourth century, and thus separately from the Eleona.[176] The primary impetus for this late dating of the Imbomon comes from the early sixth-century *Life of Peter the Iberian*,[177] which depicts the building of the Church of the Ascension by

---

[174] In general agreement with Shalev-Hurvitz, *Holy Sites Encircled*, 92.
[175] Cameron and Hall, *Life of Constantine*, 137.
[176] E.g., Vincent and Abel, *Jérusalem Nouvelle*, 378; Virgilio C. Corbo, *Richerche archeologiche al Monte degli Ulivi*, Publications of the Studium Biblicum Franciscanum 16 (Jerusalem: Franciscan Printing Press, 1965), 135; Bagatti, *Church from the Gentiles*, 219; Walker, *Holy City*, 214–15.
[177] On the date, see Wilkinson, *Jerusalem Pilgrims*, 8.

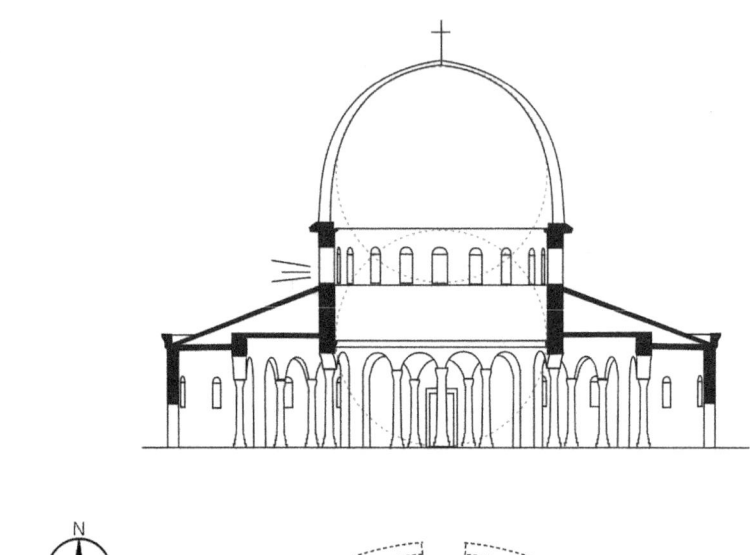

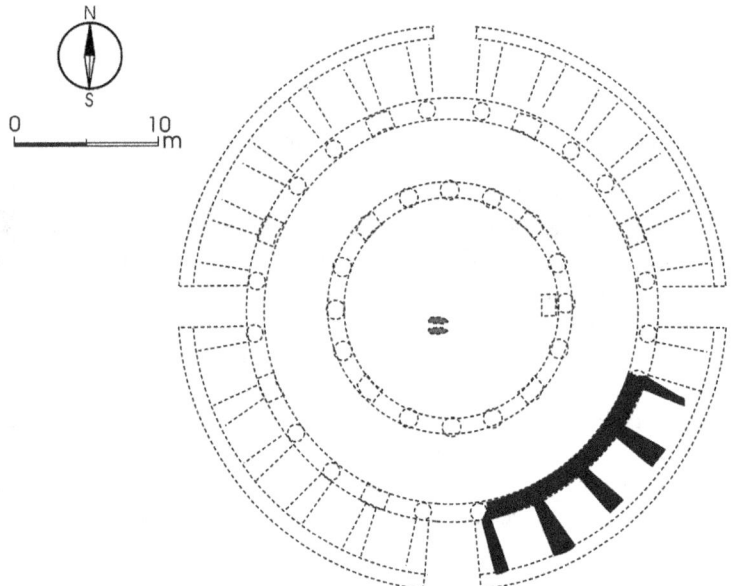

Figure 4 Floor plan and reconstruction of the Church of the Ascension.

Source: Courtesy of Vered Shalev-Hurvitz and Oxford University Press. From Vered Shalev-Hurvitz, *Holy Sites Encircled: The Early Byzantine Concentric Church of Jerusalem*, Oxford Studies in Byzantium (Oxford: Oxford University Press, 2015), fig. 7.

a woman by the name of Poemenia in the late fourth century.[178] However, Shalev-Hurvitz has convincingly argued, in agreement with an earlier position advanced by

---

[178] John Rufus, *The Lives of Peter the Iberian, Theodosius of Jerusalem, and the Monk Romanus* (Atlanta: Society of Biblical Literature, 2008), 43. On the date of Poemenia's activity, see Shalev-Hurvitz, *Holy Sites Encircled*, 99–101.

André Grabar,[179] that the construction of the Church of the Acension (the Imbomon) should be attributed to Helena and Constantine, since earlier evidence attributed the church to one or both of them.[180]

As we have already seen above, Eusebius appears to indicate two monumental structures built by Helena or Constantine on the Mount of Olives. Furthermore, Paulinus of Nola and Sulpicius Severus both attributed the building of the Church of the Ascension to Helena, not Poemenia.[181] Given the close physical location of the two sites, the fact that Eusebius seems to envision two closely connected and located sites, and that Egeria (as we will see below) depicts the two sites as closely connected in the liturgy of Jerusalem, the suggestion proposed by Grabar and followed by Shalev-Hurvitz that the Eleona and the Imbomon are two churches within a single complex that dates to the time of Constantine and Helena is both reasonable and likely.[182]

The form of the Eleona can be reconstructed to some degree on the basis of the archaeological evidence.[183] We will focus on the broad contours of the architectural form rather than the details, which are difficult to determine.[184] The ancient building, located less than one hundred meters away from the summit of the Mount of Olives,[185] is dated by the excavators to the Constantinian era and identified with some confidence as the Eleona.[186]

The Eleona was basilical in form.[187] Its entrance was located on the western side of the building, featuring a staircase leading to a portico. From the portico, a visitor would have encountered a monumental triple entrance into a large atrium. Through another set of triple doors, one would have entered from the atrium into the basilical sanctuary. The Eleona basilica featured a nave and two aisles, demarcated by two

---

[179] Grabar, *Martyrium*, 282–91.
[180] Shalev-Hurvitz, *Holy Sites Encircled*, 90–1, 102–6.
[181] Paulinus of Nola, *Epist.* 31.4, English translation in P. G. Walsh (trans.), *Letters of St. Paulinus of Nola*, 2 vols., Ancient Christian Writers (New York: Newman Press, 1967) 2: 130; Sulpicius Severus, *Chronica* 2.33.5 (NPNF II. 11:274). Cf. Shalev-Hurvitz, *Holy Sites Encircled*, 103.
[182] Shalev-Hurvitz, *Holy Sites Encircled*, 101–2, 105; Grabar, *Martyrium*, 282–91. See also the discussion in Hanswulf Bloedhorn, "Die Eleona und das Imbomon in Jerusalem: eine Doppelkirchenanlage auf dem Ölberg?" in *Akten des XII internationalen Kongresses für christliche Archäologie*, ed. Ernst Dassmann and Josef Engemann (Vatican City: Pontificio Istituto di Archeologia Cristiana, 1995), 568–71.
[183] See esp. Louis-Hugues Vincent, "L'Église de L'Éléona," *Revue Biblique* 7 (1910): 573–74; Vincent, "L'Église de L'Éléona," *Revue Biblique* 8 (1911): 219–65; Félix-Marie Abel, "Mont des Oliviers: ruine de la grotte de L'Éléona," *Revue Biblique* 27 (1914): 55–8; Vincent and Abel, *Jérusalem Nouvelle*, 337–74; Louis-Hugues Vincent, "L'Éléona: Sanctuaire Primitif de L'Ascension," *Revue Biblique* 64, no. 1 (1957): 48–71; Bagatti, *Church from the Gentiles*, 184–90.
[184] On this, see Bagatti, *Church from the Gentiles*, 184–6. The trench method used in the excavation complicates the reconstruction.
[185] Today, the summit is marked by the Chapel (or Mosque) of the Ascension.
[186] Cf. Vincent, "L'Éléona: Sanctuaire Primitif de L'Ascension," 49.
[187] See the reconstructions in Vincent and Abel, *Jérusalem Nouvelle*, 349–60; cf. Bagatti, *Church from the Gentiles*, 184–90. These reconstructions are the primary basis for the discussion to follow, which will assume that, even if some specific details might be debatable or difficult to reconstruct, these reconstructions are essentially accurate depictions of the form of the Eleona. Although this is not to place to discuss this matter, it is important to acknowledge the problems involved in the reconstruction of this building, stemming in some measure from the excavation method used to uncover it, as discussed by Bagatti, *Church from the Gentiles*, 184–6.

rows of columns. Remains of the apse were discovered within a grotto located at the eastern end of the church. The grotto is presumably the cave mentioned in the sources discussed above that was remembered as the site of Jesus' teaching. The use of the apse to mark the primary commemorative space, the "very place" where Jesus taught, is notable. The Martyrium did not use its apse to mark commemorative space but rather to orient the congregation toward the Anastasis. The use of the apse in the Eleona as a marker of the venerated spot is much more similar to the function of the polygonal structure in the Church of the Nativity, which also marked a grotto.

Egeria describes the Eleona as a "very beautiful church" (*Itin. Eger.* 25.11), and we should imagine that it was elegantly decorated much like its siblings, the Church of the Holy Sepulchre and the Church of the Nativity. Some elements of the decoration of the Eleona have been preserved, including a basket column capital and remnants of mosaic pavement.[188] Although little of the décor has survived, these minor elements nevertheless give us some sense of the imperial grandeur of the edifice as it would have existed in the fourth century.

The excavations carried out by Virgilio Corbo revealed that the fourth-century Church of the Ascension (or "Imbomon") consisted of a round complex featuring a circular domed structure.[189] Shalev-Hurvitz has recently proposed that the dome would have spanned 14.80 m and stood at a height of 10.46 m,[190] and that it was surrounded by two colonnaded ambulatories, one interior and exterior.[191] This reconstruction has the advantage of matching the plan of the Church of the Ascension as described by Arculf.[192] It would thus, as Shalev-Hurvitz notes, have boasted the first double-tier ambulatory in Palestine,[193] as well as an impressive dome, which would have been particularly visible in Jerusalem and the surrounding region given its elevation on the Mount of Olives. Jerome mentions a cross on top of the Mount of Olives,[194] which he describes as "sparkling."[195] It is likely that this refers to a decorative metal cross that surmounted the Church of the Ascension or was somewhere on its premises.

The central plan of the Imbomon allowed it to mark a particular spot at the very center of the structure. This was, according to the sources, the place where tradition placed the ascension of Jesus.[196] Paulinus of Nola writes of the purported imprint of "the divine feet" contained within the Church of the Ascension, describing a spot in the church "retaining its natural green appearance of turf."[197] According to Paulinus, this

---

[188] Cf. Bagatti, *Church from the Gentiles*, 185–6.
[189] Published in Corbo, *Richerche archeologiche al Monte degli Ulivi*. See esp. the plan on p. 149, fig. 107. See also Bagatti, *Church from the Gentiles*, 219–23.
[190] Shalev-Hurvitz, *Holy Sites Encircled*, 114.
[191] Ibid., 113–14.
[192] See Adomnan, *De Locis Sanctis*, 1.23.
[193] Shalev-Hurvitz, *Holy Sites Encircled*, 114.
[194] On this cross, see Galit Noga-Banai, "Das Kreuz Auf Dem Ölberg: Mögliche Frühe Bildbezeugungens," *Römische Quartalschrift Für Christliche Altertumskunde Und Kirchengeschichte* 102, nos. 1–2 (2007): 141–54.
[195] Jerome, *Ep.* 108, 12.1.
[196] See, e.g., *Itin. Eger.* 31.1.
[197] Paulinus of Nola, *Ep.* 31.4. Translation from Walsh, *Letters of St. Paulinus of Nola*, 2: 130. Subsequent citations are also from this translation unless otherwise stated. This letter was written to Sulpicius Severus. See also Sulpicius Severus' comments on this tradition, in *Chronica* 2.33.6–8.

was because that spot miraculously rejects any pavement, leaving the footprints "both visible and accessible to worshippers ... so that one can truly say: 'We have adored in the place where His feet stood'" (*Ep.* 31.4).[198] Although this feature is curiously omitted from the descriptions of our usual sources for Palestine in the fourth century (Eusebius, Cyril, Egeria, Jerome, and the Bordeaux Pilgrim), it is reasonable to think that it describes an actual venerated spot that existed in the Church of the Ascension.[199] His discussion of the spot's miraculous rejection of pavement is best understood as a supernatural etiological explanation of the oddity of the venerated place being unpaved. In reality, it is quite possible that the spot was intentionally left unpaved in order to preserve "the very spot" where tradition held that Jesus ascended from the summit of the Mount of Olives.

If the hypothesis originally proposed by Grabar and recently revitalized by Shalev-Hurvitz is correct, and I am persuaded that it is, the Imbomon and the Eleona were two focal points of a large church complex spanning around 100 m (give or take) on the top of the Mount of Olives.[200] Two sites were commemorated here through architecture, the first being a place where tradition held that Jesus taught, and the other being the place remembered as the site of Jesus' ascension. Each was marked by a topographical feature that was incorporated into the architecture. The Eleona incorporated a cave that had come to mark the place where Jesus taught his disciples, while something resembling footprints marked the place of the ascension. Here, we see topographical features attracting memory and serving to locate events narrated in the gospels in real space, thus anchoring the memory to the spaces that they occupied. Paulinus' use of Ps 131:7 LXX here is telling, since it expresses a desire to worship at the very places where gospel stories had taken place.

The iconography of the architecture of the Mount of Olives commemorative complex including both the Eleona and the Imbomon draws a natural and inevitable comparison with the Church of the Holy Sepulchre. Like the Church of the Holy Sepulchre, the Mount of Olives complex was bifocal, commemorating two traditional sites of Jesus-memory. Moreover, like the Church of the Holy Sepulchre, the Mount of Olives complex included both a basilica and a domed structure with a central plan. It would also seem as though both included a noteworthy decorative cross, at least by the end of the fourth century.

The iconographic connections between the Mount of Olives complex and the Church of the Holy Sepulchre communicated that these two constructions were two of a kind, that both fulfilled a similar function. That function was, as the sources pertaining to both structures show, to commemorate key events of the life of Jesus as they were remembered by the church and to locate them within the actual space of fourth-century Jerusalem.

We have already highlighted the architectural iconography of the rotunda and the basilica in our discussion of the Church of the Holy Sepulchre. Suffice it to

---

[198] Adapting Ps 131:7 LXX.
[199] It is worth noting that visitors to the Chapel (or Mosque) of the Ascension today can still view purported imprints of Jesus' footprints in a stone slab.
[200] Cf. Taylor, "Christian Archaeology in Palestine," 376.

say that much of the same could be said of the use of these forms in the Mount of Olives complex as for the Church of the Holy Sepulchre, and there is no need to cover the same ground again here. However, it is worth reminding ourselves of the Roman symbolism of domed rotundas, which represented the cosmos, with the dome symbolizing heaven.[201] The symbolism of the dome as heaven is particularly fitting for the Imbomon, as the place where Jesus was supposed to have ascended to heaven. The story was thus representationally told through the iconography of the building, through the presence of the footprints marking the place where Jesus stood, and the dome symbolizing the place to which he ascended from that very spot. The footprints also served as a visible reminder to visitors of the incarnation and the purportedly historical nature of the events that pilgrims came to Jerusalem to remember. As Sulpicius Severus wrote, the footprints marked soil that had been trodden by God.[202] There, visitors could literally worship, as his friend Paulinus put it, "where His feet stood" (*Ep*. 31.4).

Egeria's Experience of the Space of the Eleona and Imbomon

Egeria provides a window into the role that the Eleona and the Imbomon played in the liturgical life of the Jerusalem church. She recounts several instances of communal worship that took place at the Mount of Olives,[203] which help us to imagine how the space was used in the commemoration of Jesus through liturgy and worship. Egeria frequently describes services beginning at the Eleona and then moving from there to the Imbomon, or vice versa.[204] This regular movement back and forth from the two sites further solidifies the connection between the two places in the liturgical life of the church, despite the events that they commemorate having no direct connection to one another save for the fact that both are set on the Mount of Olives. This movement from one to the other is best understood as processions that took place within the confines of a single ecclesiastical complex.

Egeria recalls a gathering at the Eleona that took place on the first day of the paschal week (or "Great Week"), which corresponds to Palm Sunday (*Itin. Eger*. 30.3–31.1). She identifies the Eleona as the place "where there is the cave in which the Lord taught" (30.3). According to Egeria, hymns and antiphons "appropriate to that day and place" were recited (31.1) along with readings. This service took place from the seventh to ninth hours, when the congregation would then relocate to the Imbomon, where further hymns, antiphons, readings, and prayers that are again "appropriate to the place and day" were performed (31.1). Unfortunately, Egeria does not specify the readings that took place at the Eleona nor the Imbomon. We should note that the transition from the Eleona to the Imbomon would have made particularly good sense if the two were part of one large complex on the Mount of Olives.

---

[201] Cf. Johnson, *Imperial Mausoleum*, 182–3.
[202] *Chronica* 2.33.
[203] *Itin. Eger*. 25.11, 30.3–31.1, 33.1, 35.1–4, 39.1–3, 40.1, 43.3–6.
[204] Ibid., 31.1, 35.1–4, 40.1, 43.5–6.

Although the Armenian Lectionary (AL) preserves this service as well, it too does not list the readings.[205] As McGowan and Bradshaw rightly observe, "it is difficult to imagine what readings 'appropriate' to the Imbomon on this day might have been."[206] However, the AL does list Matt 20:29–21:17 as the gospel reading for the service that preceded the gathering at the Mount of Olives, which took place at the Martyrium (cf. *Itin. Eger.* 30.1–3). This reading, which describes Jesus' travels as he neared and entered Jerusalem, is appropriate for the occasion and also mentions that Jesus came to Mount of Olives, from which he descended to enter the city (Matt 21:1). This would have set the stage for the Jerusalem congregation's own journey to the Mount of Olives for the celebration at the Eleona.

Following the service at the Imbomon, Egeria writes that

> when the eleventh hour begins, there is read that passage from the gospel were children with branches and palms meet the Lord, saying, "Blessed in the One who comes in the name of the Lord." And immediately the bishop rises and all the people go forward from there entirely on foot from the summit of the Mount of Olives. For all the people [go] before him with hymns and antiphons, continually responding, "Blessed is the One who comes in the name of the Lord." And there are very many children in these places … all carrying branches, some of palm, others of olive; and so the bishop is led in the same way as the Lord was led then. (*Itin. Eger.* 31.2)

This describes a reenactment of the events of Jesus' "triumphal" entry into the city (Matt 21:1–10 and parallels), with the bishop playing the role of Jesus. Egeria specifies that the bishop "is led in the same way as the Lord," which indicates that it was a *conscious* reenactment of the triumphal entry. The Mount of Olives is the setting for several events in the life of Jesus according to the canonical evangelists, and as such, it was itself a *lieu de mémoire*, around which multiple Christian traditions coalesced. This is true even now, as the Mount of Olives today is dotted with Christian pilgrimage sites. Even though the Eleona and the Imbomon, as monuments, remember events that are not directly connected to the triumphal entry, their location on the Mount of Olives meant that they could function in commemorative rituals connected to that place in general. A commemorative church could be used to remember more than one event.

Egeria mentions that this procession began with a gospel reading narrating the triumphal entry. Although she does not identify which evangelist's version was used, a clue might be found in the mention of the children here. None of the canonical accounts of the triumphal entry specifically mention children carrying branches.[207] However, McGowan and Bradshaw note that Matt 21:15 depicts children crying "Hosanna to the Son of David" in the Temple precincts.[208] Moreover, as mentioned

---

[205] Refer to Wilkinson, *Egeria's Travels*, 184; cf. the comments of McGowan and Bradshaw, *Pilgrimage of Egeria*, 168.
[206] McGowan and Bradshaw, *Pilgrimage of Egeria*, 168.
[207] Cf. Wilkinson, *Egeria's Travels*, 152 n. 1; McGowan and Bradshaw, *Pilgrimage of Egeria*, 168.
[208] McGowan and Bradshaw, *Pilgrimage of Egeria*, 168.

above, the AL indicates that the reading from that day included Matt 20:29–21:17, which makes it all the more likely that Matthew's version was utilized.

The procession went from the summit of the Mount of Olives (the Imbomon) and terminated at the Anastasis, where *Lucernare* is held including a prayer service at the Cross before the people are finally dismissed (*Itin. Eger.* 31.4). It is surely significant that the terminal point of the reenactment is the Anastasis, given that Jesus' triumphal entry ended at the Temple (Matt 21:12). Given that the AL indicates that the gospel reading for that day ended at 21:17, it would have included the narrative of the (so-called) "cleansing" of the Temple (21:12–17). This would have set up both a parallel and contrast between the Temple and the Church of the Holy Sepulchre, Eusebius' "New Jerusalem," in the minds of the Jerusalemite congregants. The Anastasis, as the place where Jesus offered his once-for-all sacrifice, stood in for the Temple as the destination of the procession. However, it also provided a contrast with the Temple, as the original Temple was criticized in the gospel reading for that day as a "den of robbers" (Matt 21:13) and was a place where Jesus met opposition from the priests of his day (21:15). Thus, we should imagine that this procession from the Mount of Olives leveraged the memory of Jesus in service of the supersessionist ideology of the Jerusalem church through the subtle substitution of the Anastasis for the Temple.

Reenactments are a type of commemorative event, with "strong meanings relating to society and identity," meanings that could be contested by different stakeholder groups.[209] The reenactment of the triumphal entry described by Egeria was staged by the ecclesiastical authorities, with the bishop of Jerusalem playing the role of Jesus, and made use of imperial ecclesiastical space. It was, then, a ritual with institutional and official support that served the formation of the identity of the Christian community of Jerusalem through the memory of Jesus' fateful entry into their city three centuries prior.

According to Egeria, on the third day of Holy Week, a late night service took place at the Eleona after the daily service at the Church of the Holy Sepulchre (*Itin. Eger.* 33.1–2). During this service, "the bishop enters into the cave in which the Lord was accustomed to teach the disciples, and he takes the gospel book, and, standing, the bishop himself reads the words of the Lord that are written in the Gospel according to Matthew, that is, where he says, 'See, let no one lead you astray.'" The reading was followed with prayer and blessings prior to the dismissal of the people.

The discourse referred to here is Matt 24:4–26:2.[210] As discussed previously, this is the passage that is most likely commemorated by construction of the Eleona. The fact that this particular passage was read in the cave at the Eleona is particularly strong evidence that it is the tradition most associated with that cave. This reading ritual is performed within the cave itself and clearly associates the place with the scriptural narrative. It is important to recognize that this particular passage, as discussed above,

---

[209] Warwick Frost and Jenny Laing, *Commemorative Events: Memory, Identities, Conflicts* (London: Routledge, 2013), 86.

[210] Indeed, the AL lists the reading as 24:1–26:2 (Wilkinson, *Egeria's Travels*, 184), cf. McGowan and Bradshaw, *Pilgrimage of Egeria*, 170. It is possible that the reading would have included the introductory verses (24:1–3) in the fourth century as well.

deals with the destruction of the "old" Jerusalem, particularly the Temple. Given the role that commemorative rituals play in identity formation, along with the "New Jerusalem" ideology associated with Constantine's Jerusalemite building projects, it is crucial to consider this reading, performed in the very place where the teaching event that it describes was understood to have taken place, as an instantiation of identity formation through commemoration that would have contributed to the matrix of religious competition in fourth-century Palestine. This comes into even sharper focus when we recall Eusebius' deployment of the Mount of Olives as a symbol representing the triumph of Christianity over Judaism within his anti-Jewish exegesis.

The public reading of Matt 24:4–26:2 within the space of the cave would also have served to solidify the association of the cave with that particular tradition. As we have discussed above, there were other apocryphal traditions depicting Jesus teaching on the Mount of Olives, and there was some confusion about what teaching was commemorated at the cave. The act of reading the Matthean Olivet discourse at the cave served to fix the identification of the teaching that took place at the cave. This too is a sort of identity formation, insofar as it would have excluded the sort of heterodox teachings set on the Mount of Olives as seen in the apocryphal material discussed above.

A commemorative service remembering the ascension took place on the Sunday fifty days after Pascha, during the celebration of Pentecost.[211] This service follows a celebration of the descent of the Holy Spirit on Pentecost (Acts 2:1–21), which took place on Sion.[212] That evening, the people gathered at the Imbomon, and according to Egeria, "that passage from the gospel is also read where it speaks of the Lord's ascension; then there is a reading from the Acts of the Apostles where it speaks of the Lord's ascension into heaven after the resurrection" (*Itin. Eger.* 43.5). The readings that she refers to are Luke 24:50–53 and Acts 1:6–11. What Egeria describes here is a commemorative ritual,[213] a "rite fixed and performed" meant not only to remind the participants of the past but also to re-present it, giving the past event that it commemorated a "ceremonially embodied form."[214] It is a "narrative made flesh,"[215] rehearsed in the place where it was traditionally believed that the original event had taken place. Locating the scriptural event of Jesus' ascension within the real world of fourth-century Jerusalem and celebrating it in tandem with a festival remembering the birth of the Jerusalem church would have greatly contributed to the formation of the identity of the fourth-century Jerusalem church. Jesus' words at the ascension in Acts 1:7–8 place Jerusalem

---

[211] *Itin. Eger.* 42.1, 43.5. The ascension is commonly associated with the fortieth day after Pascha, not the fiftieth, in keeping with Acts 1:3. However, McGowan and Bradshaw observe that the AL lists the New Testament readings for this particular service as Acts 2:1–21 and John 16:5b–15, which are unrelated to the ascension. Moreover, Egeria clearly identifies the ascension narrative as a reading for that day (Luke 24:50–53; Acts 1:6–11). Thus, McGowan and Bradshaw suggest that the readings were changed between Egeria's time and the time of the AL as the celebration of the ascension moved to the fortieth day from the fiftieth (*Pilgrimage of Egeria*, 185), probably in order to reflect Acts 1:3.

[212] *Itin. Eger.* 43.3.

[213] See Connerton, *How Societies Remember*, 41–71.

[214] Borrowing the language of ibid., 43.

[215] Again, to borrow the language of ibid., 47.

at the center of the church's mission, which would have undoubtedly strengthened the social cohesion of the Jerusalemite Christian community, as they were read at the very place where they were supposed to have been delivered.

Conclusion

Our examination of the role of Bethlehem and the Mount of Olives in the early Christian memory of Jesus has demonstrated how traditions can develop when they are attached to place. Place functions symbolically to denote meaning within the tradition. Thus, Bethlehem has significance and meaning beyond just being the place of Jesus' birth, and the Mount of Olives has significance beyond its identification as the site of Jesus' ascension and teaching. Moreover, the development of the cave tradition at Bethlehem shows how canonical narratives can attract and lead to the normalization of apocryphal elements through the need to specifically situate a past event within real space. Thus, topographical features such as caves could be vested with memory and so take on meaning. As we saw with Justin's interpretation of the cave tradition, these topographical elements, though unmentioned in the canonical narratives, could contribute to the theological or ideological understanding of the commemorated event. Thus, the topography could be vested not only with memory but also with Christological significance.

All of the sites that we have discussed thus far commemorate events that are depicted in the canonical gospels. They all correspond to some canonical event. However, the details of the narratives told by or associated with those sites can incorporate or attract noncanonical elements. For example, the event remembered by the Church of the Nativity is the birth of Jesus, which is canonical. However, the detail that the birth took place is a cave is not canonical. Similarly, the event of the crucifixion at Golgotha is canonical, while the burial of Adam at the same place is not. Thus, at the earliest commemorative sites, while the core of the remembered tradition had some canonical basis, extracanonical tradition could accrue around them. This phenomenon can be explained through recourse to the nature of remembering. Because remembering is by nature an interpretive process, the canonical event being remembered could be further interpreted by the memory of the community, resulting in the incorporation of details and traditions that are extrinsic to, though not excluded by, the canonical event.

While the prominence of sources with some connection to Palestine in the development of the traditions that we have discussed thus far is not surprising, the fact that Palestinian sources are so prominent alerts us to the role of Palestinian Christians in the development of the memory of place. Previous scholarship has tended to focus on the role played by Jewish Christians in the development of commemorative sites connected to the life of Jesus prior to the fourth century. However, our discussion of this period has been continually driven by Gentile Christian sources. This highlights the importance of early Gentile Christians in pre-Constantinian Palestine, such as Justin and Origen, in the development of local traditions.

The construction of the church complexes at Bethlehem and on the Mount of Olives carried the commemoration of Jesus in new directions. The addition of these sites to the Church of the Holy Sepulchre fundamentally altered how the Holy Sepulchre functioned within the Jerusalem church's collective remembering of Jesus. Egeria depicts the Jerusalemite gatherings moving back and forth from the Holy Sepulchre complex, especially to the sites at Bethlehem and to the Mount of Olives. The Church of the Holy Sepulchre itself commemorated the death and resurrection of Jesus. With the addition of these two new sites, the combined commemorative force of the three of them bore witness to the life of Jesus through pilgrimage and the liturgical activity of the church.

6

Galilee: "There They Will See Me"

The memory of Jesus presented in the canonical gospels is concentrated primarily around two regions: Jerusalem and Galilee. It is thus no surprise that Galilee was and is host to its own collection of *lieux de mémoire*, places where Jesus-memory have coalesced and taken root. Not long after the construction of commemorative churches in the Jerusalem area, efforts began throughout Galilee to give shape to that Jesus-memory in architectural form. By the end of the fourth century, Galilee positively abounded with commemorative sites related to the life of Jesus. Although our primary discussion has focused on the memories that were eventually crystalized in the triad of Constantinian commemorative churches located in the region in and around Jerusalem, it is worthwhile to consider, however briefly, the memories of Jesus that were likewise captured in stone in the fourth century.

The addition of Galilean places to the Jerusalem-area commemorative churches transformed the narrative told through the experience of the "holy sites" through pilgrimage. If the trio of the Holy Sepulchre, Church of the Nativity, and Church of the Ascension formed an architectural instantiation of the Nicene Creed, what happened when the Galilean sites were added to that core? When all of the commemorative churches of fourth-century Palestine are considered together, we are presented with a telling of the life of Jesus. This could be understood as a kind of experiential gospel, the story of Jesus not penned in ink upon papyrus, but in stone upon the Land itself. The Galilean churches complete the narrative of the life of Jesus by telling the story of his ministry. This was a gospel that was experienced through travel and reenactment rather than through reading. In the words of Walker, "Those who emphasize the humanity of Jesus find in [Galilee] the ordinariness and the earthy reality of that human life … Jerusalem may speak of the Resurrection of the Redemption; but Galilee can speak of Christ's humanity and of the Incarnation."[1]

According to Michael Kammen, "societies in fact reconstruct their pasts rather than faithfully record them."[2] The selection and presentation of sites on which to build commemorative churches is itself a kind of history writing, the reconstruction of the

---

[1] Walker, *Holy City*, 135.
[2] Michael Kammen, *Mystic Chords of Memory: The Transformation of Tradition in American Culture* (New York: Vintage, 1993), 3.

life of Jesus through the erection of monuments, a history that could be consumed by locals and by pilgrims such as Egeria. This was, to be sure, a selection process, by which places and stories to be commemorated were curated by the ecclesiastical funding of church building on those sites. That selection process can be understood as an instantiation of official memory constructed by imperial, local, or ecclesiastical authorities as a means of asserting its influence on public memory. However, as we will see, vernacular memory was nevertheless at work here in Galilee alongside official memory in the formation of that public memory. Furthermore, the construction of churches at specific geographical or topographical locations allowed for the evangelical narrative to be both explicated and controlled by the authorities responsible for the construction of those churches. The new Galilean commemorative churches developed the pilgrims' "map" of Galilee, providing landmarks of interest to them where before there was little to hold their interest.[3]

It is necessary to limit the scope of our investigation at this point. We are, in this project, concerned primarily with sites of Jesus-memory that received commemorative churches in the age of Constantine, roughly three centuries after the life of Jesus, giving or taking a decade or so. While this chronological scope is somewhat artificial, it does allow for limits to be set on the data, making it manageable. The Constantinian age provides a convenient bookend, as it was in those years that memory began to take tangible form in stone. There are a great number of Galilean commemorative sites, and not all of them fall within the chronological limits of our study, which means that we will have to be selective. Moreover, time and length constraints dictate that this chapter will need to be broad rather than deep. Nevertheless, a study of the memory of Jesus in place cannot be complete without giving at least some consideration to the emergence of Galilean *lieux de mémoire*, places that remember the events of the life of Jesus. In this chapter, we will conduct a very brief survey of some of the earliest commemorative churches in Galilee in order to examine how they contributed to the memory and interpretation of the events of the life of Jesus. The sites examined will include Tabgha, Nazareth, and the Mount of Beatitudes.

Constantinian Church Building in Galilee?

Epiphanius recounts a narrative about a Jew from Tiberias who had been "converted to Christ" (*Pan.* 30.3.8) and during the reign of Constantine was "awarded the rank of count by the Emperor [Constantine] himself, and was authorized to build a church for Christ in Tiberias itself, and in Diocaesarea [Sepphoris], Capernaum and the other towns" (*Pan.* 30.4.1).[4] According to Epiphanius, while at Constantine's court, Joseph

---

[3] Leyerle notes that the Bordeaux Pilgrim shows little interest in Galilee, since it was still "undeveloped" for Christian pilgrimage, resulting in a notable silence in the Bordeaux Pilgrim's account so far as Galilee is concerned: "On this map, Galilee is quite blank." See Leyerle, "Early Christian Perceptions," 345–57 (348).

[4] Translation from Frank Williams (trans.), *The Panarion of Epiphanius of Salamis: Book I (Sects 1–46)* (Leiden: Brill, 1987), 122. Subsequent translations of Epiphanius' *Panarion* in this chapter are drawn from the same source unless otherwise stated.

requested "permission by imperial rescript to build Christ's churches in the Jewish towns and villages where no one had ever been able to found churches, since there were no Greeks, Samaritans or Christians among the population. This <rule> of having no gentiles among them is observed especially at Tiberias, Diocaesarea, Sepphoris, Nazareth and Capernaum" (*Pan.* 30.11.9–10). Constantine apparently granted this request, since Epiphanius informs us that Joseph received an imperial letter and authorization along with his title before returning to Galilee (*Pan.* 30.12.1).

There is no clear indication in what Epiphanius writes that all or any of the churches that Joseph built were *commemorative* churches. He calls them "churches of Christ" (*Pan.* 30.11.9; Greek Χριστοῦ ἐκκλησίας), but this could simply be a way of referring to Christian assembly places rather than churches specifically dedicated to specific memories of the events of Jesus' life. Of the four places mentioned, both Nazareth and Capernaum are closely tied to the life of Jesus in the gospel narratives. The other two, Sepphoris and Tiberias, were urban centers in Galilee, so Joseph's designs to build churches in those places might have had more to do with their status as influential Galilean population centers rather than with their connections to the events of the life of Jesus. Sepphoris is not mentioned in the gospels at all, while Tiberias is only mentioned in passing (John 6:1, 23, 21:1) and is never the setting for any events in the canonical gospels.[5] However, in a section of Peter the Deacon's *Liber de locis sanctis* that makes use of the otherwise lost Galilean segment of Egeria's *Itinerarium*,[6] mention is made of a church in Tiberias "where once stood the house of the apostles James and John" (*de loc. sanct.* V2). If this reference is drawn from Egeria and not some later source, then it is possible that the "small church" that Joseph built on the former site of the unfinished Hadrianeum was or would be associated with the memory of James and John, as also suggested by Joan Taylor.[7] It is perhaps even possible, though this is no more than mere speculation, that Joseph's Tiberian church was also where the story of the call of James and John (Mark 1:18–20; Matt 4:21–22; cf. Luke 5:10) on the lake nearby would have been remembered.

To summarize the data presented by Epiphanius, this narrative presents a scenario in which an imperial official holding the rank of *comēs* (*Pan.* 30.5.6), a Galilean Jew who had become a Christ-believer, was given authorization by Constantine himself to construct churches in Jewish locales in Galilee.[8] Epiphanius initially names

---

[5] Of these three references, two are to the "Sea of Tiberias" (6:1, 21:1). Only John 6:23 refers to the city itself, as it describes "some boats from Tiberias." On this, see Jordan J. Ryan, "Tiberias," in *The Lexham Bible Dictionary*, ed. John D. Barry, David Bomar, Derek R. Brown, Rachel Klippenstein, Douglas Mangum, Carrie Sinclair Wolcott, Lazarus Wentz, Elliot Ritzema, and Wendy Widder (Bellingham, WA: Lexham Press, 2016), n.p.

[6] See Wilkinson, *Egeria's Travels*, 86; cf. McGowan and Bradshaw, *Pilgrimage of Egeria*, 16–17. Note, however, McGowan and Bradshaw's cautionary statement about this material, since it is difficult to know what comes from Egeria's work and what comes from elsewhere.

[7] Cf. Taylor, *Christians and the Holy Places*, 289. As Taylor rightly points out, the location of the "small church" in what would have been a corner of the old Hadrianeum would not necessarily rule out the possibility that the church was built on a site associated with James and John, since "the presence of a pagan temple did nothing to dissuade Christians from believing a Christian site lay buried beneath it, and, after the examples of Mamre, Bethlehem, and Golgotha, may even have encouraged the belief" (289).

[8] For an in-depth study of this episode and its relevance to the study of Jewish-Christian relations, particularly in Galilee, see Stephen Craft Goranson, "The Joseph of Tiberias Episode in

Tiberias, Diocaesarea (Sepphoris), and Capernaum as well as "the other towns" as places where Joseph was authorized to build churches in *Pan.* 30.4.1, but later also mentions Nazareth among the places where Joseph aspired to construct churches in *Pan.* 30.11.10. Of these places, Epiphanius only specifically relates the story of the construction of a church at Tiberias (*Pan.* 30.12.2-9), though he implies that Joseph built others in calling this his "first foundation" (*Pan.* 30.12.2). If we infer the basic scenario summarized above as a historical core from Epiphanius' account,[9] we must nevertheless acknowledge that Epiphanius does not tell us that Joseph was successful in constructing churches at all four of these places. However, as we will see, there is at least some archaeological evidence for the existence of churches in the regions of Capernaum and Nazareth.

Capernaum

The region of Capernaum was host to a number of Christian buildings in the fourth century. No mention is made of Capernaum in the writings of the Bordeaux Pilgrim (*c.*333 CE).[10] In the entry for Capernaum in his *Onomasticon*, Eusebius describes the location of Capernaum but mentions no churches or Christian presence there. However, the segment of Peter the Deacon's *de locis sanctis* describing Galilean sites, which likely relies on the missing Galilean section of Egeria's *Itinerarium*, describes at least two, and perhaps as many as three or four, commemorative churches in the region of Capernaum.[11]

The well-known building in Capernaum that was commemorated as the house of Peter is certainly mentioned: "in Capernaum the house of the prince of the apostles has been made into a church, with its original walls still standing. It is where the Lord healed the paralytic" (*de loc. sanct.* V2). Similarly, the Church of the Multiplication at the Heptapegon (Tabgha) is mentioned with some degree of certainty. After mentioning a field by the sea near Capernaum with seven springs, the author writes, "this is the field where the Lord fed the people with the five loaves and the two fishes. In face the stone on which the Lord places the bread has now been made into an altar" (*de loc. sanct.* V3). That a church building is envisioned here is indicated by the mention of the altar.[12] Beyond these two fairly certain references, the author refers to "some

---

Epiphanius: Studies in Jewish and Christian Relations" (PhD diss., Duke University, Durham, 2010); cf. also Stephen Goranson, "Joseph of Tiberias Revisited: Orthodoxies and Heresies in Fourth-Century Galilee," in *Galilee Through the Centuries: Confluence of Cultures*, ed. Eric M. Meyers, Duke Judaic Studies Series 1 (Winona Lake: Eisenbrauns, 1999), 335-43.

[9] An examination of the historical plausibility and accuracy of Epiphanius' account of Joseph's building activities is beyond the scope of this study. However, this question has been explored in detail by Goranson, "Joseph of Tiberias Episode," 73-125. While we must acknowledge that there are legendary aspects of Epiphanius' Joseph of Tiberias narrative, the basic scenario of Joseph's construction activities is plausible and generally credible (cf. Goranson, "Joseph of Tiberias Revisited," 339).

[10] Cf. Leyerle, "Early Christian Perceptions," 347-8.

[11] On this cluster of churches, see the helpful summaries in Stanislao Loffreda, *The Sanctuaries of Tabgha* (Jerusalem: Franciscan Printing Press, 1975); cf. also Wilkinson, *Egeria's Travels*, 38-41, figs. 18-20.

[12] See ibid., 24-5.

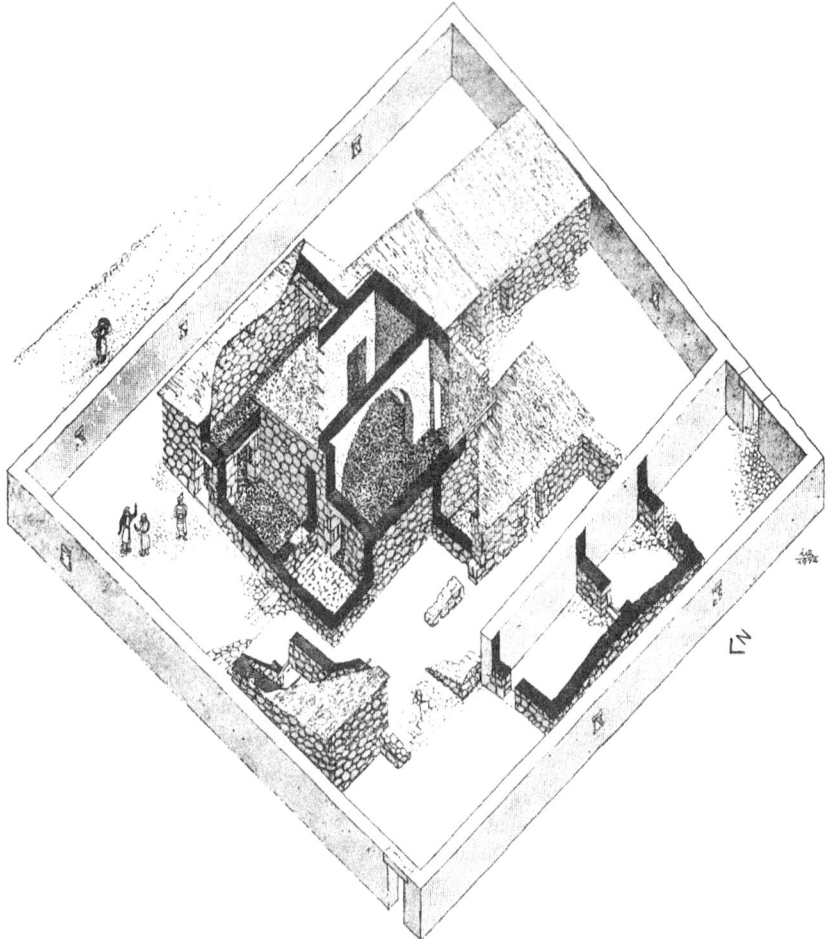

Figure 5 Reconstruction of the fourth-century Church of the House of Peter by Virgilio Corbo.

Source: Courtesy of Franciscan Printing Press.

stone steps where the Lord stood," (V2), which are likely those at the Sanctuary of the Primacy, which is also at the Heptapegon, and to place nearby where there is "a cave to which the Savior climbed and spoke the Beatitudes," (V3), which fairly certainly refers to the spot where the Beatitudes were commemorated in antiquity. This spot is only about a hundred meters from the Church of the Multiplication and features a cave. The Chapel of the Beatitudes was built there sometime in the fourth century,[13] though there is no mention of a building at this site in *de locis sanctis*.[14]

---

[13] See, e.g., Bellarmino Bagatti, *Ancient Christian Villages of Galilee* (Jerusalem: Franciscan Printing Press, 2001), 72–4; cf. Bagatti, *Church from the Gentiles*, 216–217.

[14] Cf. Wilkinson, *Egeria's Travels*, 41.

There is some discussion in scholarship about the use of Peter the Deacon's text as a witness to Egeria's travels in Galilee,[15] since it is difficult to know what exactly comes from Peter himself, or from his other sources, which include Bede's *de locis sanctis*, as well as an unknown guidebook dating to the period of the Latin Kingdom of Jerusalem.[16] However, we may be fairly confident that this segment (V2–V3) has an Egerian core. First, this segment appears in a greater section whose order, as Wilkinson notes, is determined by Egeria's travels rather than on the order of Bede as per Peter's usual practice.[17] Second, while early pilgrims to Capernaum report seeing the house of Peter,[18] references in pilgrim writings after the Arab conquest make mention of the house of "John the Evangelist" rather than that of Peter.[19] We should, then, consider why Peter the Deacon, writing in the twelfth century, would associate it with "the prince of the Apostles" (Peter) and not with John the Evangelist. Third, and most importantly, Peter the Deacon's text mentions that the original walls of the house of Peter ("the prince of the Apostles") are still standing (V2).

The archaeological record shows that, in the fourth century, the building in question was essentially a kind of *domus ecclesia*,[20] which is to say, an insula that had been converted for semi-public gatherings, and which had been separated from the rest of the surrounding village by an enclosure wall.[21] The insula itself dated back beyond the first century CE, as far as the Late Hellenistic period, and so, regardless of whether the insula ever contained the dwelling of Peter the Apostle, the notion that its walls were original could easily be claimed in the fourth century. However, in the second half of the fifth century, the *domus ecclesia* was destroyed, and an octagonal, central-planned commemorative church was built where the insula had previously stood.[22] Thus, the description of a house at Capernaum associated with Peter that had been turned into a church and whose original walls were still standing fits with what we know from the archaeological record of this site during the fourth century, when Egeria would have

---

[15] See, e.g., McGowan and Bradshaw, *Pilgrimage of Egeria*, 16–17.
[16] Wilkinson, *Egeria's Travels*, 86.
[17] Cf. ibid.
[18] See *Itin. Piac.* 7.
[19] Epiphanius the Monk, *Hag.*, 10.1 (circa ninth century C.E.); Hygeburg, *Vita S. Will.*, 14 (circa eighth century CE). See also Wilkinson, *Jerusalem Pilgrims*, 292.
[20] We should note, however, that Taylor is correct in saying that the term "house-church" may be misleading, since it was not an owner-occupied home used for Christian assembly but, rather, a Christian gathering place that had been formed out of the component parts of houses belonging to the same insula (*Christians and the Holy Places*, 274).
[21] See the summaries in Stanislao Loffreda, *Recovering Capharnaum*, 2nd ed. (Jerusalem: Franciscan Printing Press, 1993), 50–66; Anders Runesson, "Architecture, Conflict, and Identity Formation: Jews and Christians in Capernaum from the First to the Sixth Century," in *Religion, Ethnicity, and Identity in Ancient Galilee: A Region in Transition*, ed. Jürgen Zangenberg, Harold W. Attridge, and Dale Martin, WUNT 210 (Tübingen: Mohr Siebeck, 2007), 231–57 (240–3). See also Taylor, 269–84; cf. Joan E. Taylor, "Capernaum and its 'Jewish Christians': A Re-Examination of the Franciscan Excavations," *Bulletin of the Anglo-Israel Archaeological Society* 9 (1989–90): 7–28; and Bagatti, *Church from the Circumcision*, 128–32. For fuller reports, see Virgilio C. Corbo, *The House of St. Peter at Capernaum*, trans. S. Saller, LA 18 (1969): 5–54; Virgilio C. Corbo, *Cafarnao I: Gli edifice della città* (Jerusalem: Franciscan Printing Press, 1975). My summary below follows the sources listed here.
[22] Discussion of this intriguing later edifice is beyond the scope of our project. See, however, the recent work of Shalev-Hurvitz, *Holy Sites Encircled*, 267–73.

visited Galilee, but not at the time of Peter the Deacon or his other, later sources. As a result, this section describing Capernaum and its environs almost certainly contains an Egerian core dating back to the fourth century, though we must also admit that we cannot know what has been changed by Peter the Deacon, nor what he may have added from his other sources. For our purposes, we will regard it as Egerian, but with the caveat that there may be things changed or added to it that we cannot detect.

Although the fourth-century Church of the House of Peter did not have the typical form of Christian commemorative architecture of its period, there were nevertheless commemorative elements communicated through the architecture. The structure was focused on one particular assembly area, deemed room 1 by the excavators. This room, measuring 5.8 m × 6.4 m,[23] was located in an insula, insula 1 (also called the *insula sacra* by the excavators), which was originally constructed in the Late Hellenistic period. During the latter half of the first century CE, the floor of room 1 was plastered with six successive layers of beaten lime.[24] This was the only lime floor in this part of Capernaum dated to this time, which led the excavators to conclude that room 1 had a special function, particularly that of a gathering place.[25]

Sometime in the fourth century, insula 1 was made into a compound, separated from the surrounding dwellings by the construction of an enclosure wall.[26] Room 1 was located roughly at the center of the compound. As such, it was the focal point of the new complex. The room was extensively modified at this time, with the addition of polychrome pavement[27] and a plastered arch dividing the room into two segments. The walls were also plastered and painted at this time. The paint was primarily red, dark orange, and white with green, sky blue, ocher, and black accents.[28] Decorative motifs included fruits (such as pomegranates) and cruciform flowers.[29] This vibrant decoration alone would have marked it off from the other domestic space in the immediate area.[30] Graffiti, primarily in Greek, but also some Syriac and possibly Latin,[31] indicate the presence of Christian pilgrims who had come from elsewhere to visit this place. The inscribing of pilgrimage graffiti is itself a commemorative activity.[32] At the very least,

---

[23] Measurements are drawn in this case from the summary by Taylor, *Christians and the Holy Places*, 273.
[24] Corbo, *Gli edifici*, 97–8; Loffreda, *Capharnaum*, 57. See, however, Taylor, *Christians and the Holy Places*, 281–4, who challenges the excavators' dating.
[25] Corbo, *Gli edifici*, 97–8; Loffreda, *Capharnaum*, 57.
[26] See Virgilio Corbo, *The House of Saint Peter at Capharnaum*, trans. Sylvester Saller (Jerusalem: Franciscan Printing Press, 1972), 61–74.
[27] On this pavement and its stratigraphical relationship to earlier floors, see Corbo, *Gli edifici*, 79–98.
[28] Corbo, *House of Saint Peter*, 67–9.
[29] Ibid., 69.
[30] While this sort of fresco painting, particularly with these colors, is hardly unknown or uncommon during the Roman and early Byzantine periods, the decoration of this particular room was unique in this particular context.
[31] See Emmanuel Testa, *Cafarno IV: I Graffiti della Casa di S. Pietro* (Jerusalem: Franciscan Printing Press, 1972). Testa identified some possible Aramaic graffiti (93–104, nos. 95–104), though these identifications have been convincingly challenged by Taylor, *Christians and the Holy Places*, 285–8.
[32] On the function of pilgrimage graffiti, see Eva-Maria Butz and Alfons Zettler, "Pilgrim's Devotion?: Christian Graffiti from Antiquity to the Middle Ages," in *Travel, Pilgrimage and Social Interaction from Antiquity to the Middle Ages*, ed. Jenni Kuuliala and Jussi Rantala (New York: Routledge, 2020), 141–64. See also Ann Marie Yasin, "Prayers on Site: the Materiality

the presence of the graffiti marks room 1 as a pilgrimage destination, a place where commemorative activity took place.

Could this *domus ecclesia*, the Church of the House of Peter, be the church built by Joseph of Tiberias in Capernaum, as some scholars have suggested?[33] Taylor observes that the date of the building fits with Joseph's building activity (*c.*330–337 CE) and that the use of lime matches a curious detail mentioned in Epiphanius' account of Joseph, which involved Joseph constructing seven lime kilns in Tiberias for his building project in that city.[34] However, beyond the fourth century date and the use of lime for the floors, we must admit there is no clear evidence that would lead us to definitively connect this church with Joseph's imperial-authorized building program. Furthermore, we would need to be able to securely date the structure to the period of Joseph's activity in the fourth century. Corbo dates the transformation of the structure around the middle of the fourth century.[35] However, Loffreda states elsewhere that the transformation took place in the late fourth century.[36] Naturally, if it was constructed in the late fourth century, it would postdate Joseph's activity. We also need to be able to address the matter of whether there is any continuity of the fourth-century *domus ecclesia* with the previous usage of the space. In the late first century, and up to its transformation in the fourth century, room 1 was paved, and no household vessels associated with daily life that one would expect in a dwelling space were discovered in that space during that period.[37] The conversion but preservation of the space in the fourth century seems to indicate a desire for continuity, which is confirmed by Egeria's statement to the effect that the structure had its original walls.

The Church of the House of Peter was a commemorative church, despite the fact that its fourth-century iteration lacked the monumental grandeur of the Church of the Nativity or the Church of the Holy Sepulchre. Although the structure was associated with the dwelling place of Peter, there is evidence that the site commemorated Jesus' miracles in Capernaum. Jerome writes that Paula, on her pilgrimage, went through "Cana and Capernaum, which witnessed his miracles" (*Ep.* 108.13.5).[38] The miracle in Cana that Jerome references here is undoubtedly the turning of water into wine (John 2:1–11), since this is the only dominical miracle specifically associated with Cana in the tradition. However, a number of different miracles took place at Capernaum: the exorcism of a man with an unclean spirit in the synagogue (Mark 1:21–27; Luke 4:31–37), the healing of Peter's mother-in-law along with many others at the house of Simon (Peter) and Andrew (Mark 1:29–34; Matt 8:14–17; Luke 4:38–41), the healing of a paralytic (Mark 2:1–12; Matt 9:2–8; Luke 5:17–26), and the healing of a man with a

---

of Devotional Graffiti and the Production of Early Christian Sacred Space," in *Viewing Inscriptions in the Late Antique and Medieval World*, ed. Antony Eastmond (Cambridge: Cambridge University Press, 2015), 36–60.

[33] Most notably Corbo, *Gli edifici*, 71–2; Taylor, *Christians and the Holy Places*, 288–90.
[34] Taylor, *Christians and the Holy Places*, 288.
[35] Corbo, *Gli edifici*, 73.
[36] Loffreda, *Capharnaum*, 58.
[37] Ibid., 57; cf. Runesson, "Architecture," 240.
[38] Translation from Wilkinson, *Jerusalem Pilgrims*, 89.

withered hand in the synagogue (Mark 3:1–6; Matt 12:9–14; Luke 6:6–11).[39] It could very well be that all of these miracles were remembered at Capernaum in antiquity.[40] However, while the events of Mark 1:21–27 and 3:1–6 are set in the synagogue, the healing of Peter's mother-in-law (and the other subsequent healings in that narrative) is set specifically in the house of Simon (that is, Peter) and Andrew (Mark 1:29). The healing of the paralytic is set in a house where Jesus was staying in Capernaum.[41] Although this is not clearly identified as Peter's house in the biblical narrative, the Church of the House of Peter is apparently where the event was commemorated in the fourth century, as Egeria informs us that this is "where the Lord healed the paralytic" (*de loc. sanct.* V3). We may conclude from this that the Church of the House of Peter had a *dominical* commemorative function and that gospel events connected with the life of Jesus (and not Peter only) were remembered there, particularly the healing of the paralytic (Mark 2:1–12), and almost certainly also the healing of Peter's mother-in-law and the others that followed (Mark 1:29–34).

Peter's house is significant within the synoptic narrative precisely because *it was the site where Jesus performed a miracle*. That significance, it seems, was not lost on the pilgrims who traveled to the site in the fourth century. In fact, the evidence drawn from Jerome's account of Paula's pilgrimage and from Egeria's travels suggests that Capernaum was a place where Jesus' miracles were generally remembered and that the Church of the House of Peter is the specific site where Christians remembered them.

The iconography of the architecture of the fourth-century Church of the House of Peter is somewhat unique among the known commemorative churches in Palestine of this period. Rather than being a new construction enshrining, incorporating, or marking the venerated first-century remains, the primary assembly space of the Church of the House of Peter actually *was* room 1, the first-century dwelling space. Granted, it had been renovated, and the surrounding insula had been altered such that the compound was now focused on room 1, but it was nevertheless the same space. It commemorated the site of Peter's house and the miracle that Jesus performed there by presenting itself *as the very same building*. Congregants and pilgrims could thus see themselves in direct continuity with a space that had once welcomed Jesus and his disciples, including James and John (Mark 1:29). Moreover, it was the house of Simon (i.e., Peter) and Andrew. By retaining the essential form of that space, the Church of the House of Peter communicated the message that "where once they dwelled, we now dwell." This would have had an impact on identity formation and would have helped to emphasize the continuity of the faith of pilgrims and congregants with the faith of

---

[39] Mark 3:1 reads "Again he entered the synagogue." The scenes of Mark 2 are set in the region of Capernaum (Mark 2:1), and the last (and only specific) synagogue that Jesus had entered at that point in the Markan narrative was the synagogue in Capernaum (Mark 1:21). On the location of this miracle within the synagogue at Capernaum, see Ryan, *Role of the Synagogue*, 232–3.

[40] Indeed, the modern church that has been built over the ancient (House) Church of St. Peter at Capernaum contains artwork commemorating the various scenes set in Capernaum in the canonical gospels.

[41] There is some ambiguity in translation as to whether this was Jesus' home or a place where he was staying. Note also the variants in the Greek, as some manuscripts read ἠκούσθη ὅτι ἐν οἴκῳ ἐστίν, while others read εἰς οἰκον rather than ἐν οἴκῳ.

the apostles who once dwelt in this house, and moreover, with the life and works of Jesus himself.

Egeria's description of this building as "the house of the prince of the apostles … with its original walls still standing" (*de loc. sanct.* V2) is telling. Visitors recognized it as preserving the original walls of the first-century dwelling. Moreover, Egeria's subsequent identification of the place as the site "where the Lord healed the paralytic" further solidifies its function as a site of dominical memory, where Jesus' Capernaum-based miracles were remembered. It was not merely a new building on the spot where Peter dwelled, where Jesus healed his mother-in-law, and where he healed the paralytic. It was, at least to pilgrims such as Egeria, the actual building where these things took place. The result is that, regardless of the "authenticity" of the house, the space represented a direct connection between the Christian community of the fourth century and the life of Jesus and his earliest followers of the first century. It was a place where memory became present, where biblical narrative became reality. No other commemorative church in Palestine had quite this level of direct spatial connection to the first-century world of Jesus. The traditional tomb of Jesus, for example, had been thoroughly altered and enshrined in an imperial rotunda. The fact that Egeria notes the persistence of the original walls of the Church of the House of Peter shows that the direct connection to the past presented in the architecture of the place was a significant element of the experience of this place.

To put this in terms related to the theory of commemoration, the Church of the House of Peter creates a narrative that speaks to the collective identity of early Christians through creating a direct link between the fourth-century pilgrims and worshippers who visited or used the site and the founding figures of the tradition, particularly Jesus and Peter, who were understood to have used that very same space.[42] It seeks to address the "who we are" question of Christian identity by pointing to the origins of the movement in this very village, in this very space, and, moreover, *within these very walls*. "Who we are" is thus bound up with "where we come from,"[43] which the Church of the House of Peter locates within its very space, space once occupied by Peter and visited by Jesus himself.

The identification of the Church of the House of Peter as the site where Jesus healed the paralytic man (Egeria, in Peter the Deacon, *de loc. sanct.* V2; Mark 2:1–12), despite the fact that none of the canonical evangelists locate this narrative in Peter's house, is a datum worth considering. It certainly represents a development in the tradition. In the earliest account, in Mark 2:1–12, we are simply told that Jesus was "at home" (NRSV) or "in a house" (Greek ἐν οἴκῳ). We are not informed as to the identity of the owner of the dwelling. The other synoptic evangelists are no more precise. Matthew simply locates this event in Jesus' "own town" (9:1; Greek τὴν ἰδίαν πόλιν), which is understood to be Capernaum (cf. Matt 4:13). No mention is made of the house setting. In fact, the Matthean version of the story does not specifically require an indoor setting at all, since the roof incident is omitted.[44] Luke does not specifically locate the story in

---

[42] On this, see Foote and Azaryahu, "Geography of Memory," 127.
[43] Cf. ibid.
[44] On the significance of this omission, see (e.g.) Ulrich Luz, *Matthew: A Commentary*, 3 vols., Hermeneia (Minneapolis: Fortress, 2001), 2:27; Craig A. Evans, *Matthew*, NCBC (Cambridge: Cambridge University Press, 2012), 199–200.

Capernaum, though he does include the element of the paralyzed man being lowered through the roof (Luke 5:17–26). Suffice it to say that there is no canonical evidence that this narrative took place in Peter's house.

What, then, is the significance of the identification of Peter's house as the setting of this narrative? As mentioned above, Capernaum was the site of a number of miracle stories in the canonical Jesus tradition. The fact that this miracle was commemorated in the space of the Church of the House of Peter indicates that it had become a place for the commemoration of these miracles. Moreover, Peter the Deacon's text goes on to mention that (in Capernaum) "there also is the synagogue where the Lord cured a man possessed by the devil (Mark 1:23). The way in is up many stairs, and it is made of dressed stone" (*de loc. sanct.* V2). The monumental limestone synagogue that currently stands in ancient Capernaum is probably best dated to the fifth or sixth century CE.[45] Thus, it was not yet constructed when Egeria visited Galilee in the fourth century. We are thus presented with two possibilities: i) the reference to the Capernaum synagogue in Peter the Deacon's text is not Egerian and comes from some later source, or ii) it is Egerian, but does not refer to the limestone synagogue. I am inclined to regard the passage as Egerian. It seems to be consistent with and follow from what is said just previous about the Church of the House of Peter, which is necessarily dated prior to the construction of the octagonal commemorative church in the fifth century. More importantly, the description of the way in being "up many steps" does not match the archaeological record of the limestone synagogue, whose entrance is certainly not up many steps.[46] Thus, this testimony likely describes a synagogue building that existed prior to the limestone synagogue.

The existence of a black basalt pavement, measuring approximately 20 m × 8 m,[47] discovered underneath the limestone synagogue suggests that there was a large public building on the same location prior to the construction of the limestone synagogue.[48] The initial construction of the pavement is best dated to the first century CE, as it lies on top of an even earlier stratum in which coins and pottery from the Hellenistic period were found.[49] The excavators have suggested that this pavement belonged to an earlier

---

[45] See Stanislao Loffreda, "Potsherds from a Sealed Level of the Synagogue at Capharnaum," *Liber Annuus* 29 (1979): 215–20; Loffreda, "The Late Chronology of the Synagogue of Capernaum," in *Ancient Synagogues Revealed*, ed. Lee I. Levine (Jerusalem: Israel Exploration Society, 1981), 52–6; Loffreda, *Capharnaum*, 32–49. The date of this structure has been a matter of some debate. There is no need to delve into this matter here. For a review of the relevant issues, see Runesson, "Architecture," 235–7. However, it should be acknowledged that the ceramic and numismatic evidence, coming from a sealed stratum, should be given priority in dating, which leads us toward a date in the fifth century, as perhaps even the sixth century, as argued by Jodi Magness, "The Question of the Synagogue: The Problem of Typology," in *Judaism in Antiquity*, part 3: *Where We Stand: Issues and Debates in Ancient Judaism*, vol. 4: *The Special Problem of the Ancient Synagogue*, HdO 55, ed. Alan J. Avery-Peck and Jacob Neusner (Leiden: Brill, 2001), 1–48 (22–3). Magness's argument that the latest coins discovered beneath the synagogue's courtyard, dated to the second reign of Zeno (476–491), pointing toward *terminus post quem* of 491 is particularly significant. At the very least, the evidence seems to point to the late fifth century, and perhaps even the sixth.

[46] Cf. Wilkinson, *Egeria's Travels*, 97 n. 8.

[47] Stefano De Luca, "Capernaum," in *The Oxford Encyclopedia of the Bible and Archaeology* (ed. Daniel M. Master; New York: Oxford University Press, 2013), 1: 168–78 (174).

[48] For summaries of this complex issue, see Loffreda, *Capaharnaum*, esp. 93.

[49] Ibid., 45.

synagogue building, and others have subsequently followed this identification.[50] It is most likely that this earlier building is what Egeria describes. Even if the identification of the basalt platform as a synagogue is incorrect, it is nevertheless possible that the synagogue that she refers to here has not yet been discovered[51] and lies somewhere else in the village.

A number of canonical narratives involve the synagogue in Capernaum,[52] including several healing miracles (Mark 1:21-28, 3:1-6; Luke 4:31-37, 7:5-9). That Egeria specifically connects the synagogue to the curing of "a man possessed by the devil" is significant, precisely because it further solidifies Capernaum as a *lieu de mémoire* where Jesus' healing ministry was commemorated. The twin sites of the Church of the House of Peter and the synagogue thus served to tether and locate the memory of Jesus' identity as a miracle-working healer, which is a significant dimension of his portrayal in the canonical tradition. Notably, this key aspect of Jesus' remembered life is missing from the Nicene Creed of 325 and from the commemorative narrative told by the Jerusalem-area triad of the Church of the Holy Sepulchre, the Church of the Nativity, and the Eleona-Ascension complex.

This facet of Jesus' remembered life and identity was added to the commemorative narrative expressed through place and pilgrimage *without* the construction of new imperial monuments. Instead, it was attached to a previously existing structure that had been renovated and altered for Christian assembly purposes and to a previously existing *Jewish* structure. Both could, in the fourth century, be plausibly identified as the actual buildings where the remembered events attached to the place of Capernaum occurred. In the case of the synagogue, we must note the lack of mention of the Jewish character or use of the building in Egeria's time.[53] This fits into the overarching ideology of supersession that we have seen present elsewhere in the activity of early Christian commemoration-in-situ in Palestine.[54] The presence of Jews is constructed only in the

---

[50] Corbo, "Resti della sinagoga," 3: 313-57; Loffreda, *Capharnaum*, 43-9; James F. Strange and Hershel Shanks, "Synagogue Where Jesus Preached Found at Capernaum," *BAR* 9, no. 6 (1983): 24-31; Donald D. Binder, *Into the Temple Courts* (Atlanta: SBL Press, 1998), 186-93 (esp. 189-90); Michael Avi-Yonah, "Editor's Note," *IEJ* 23 (1973): 43-5 (cf. Avi-Yonah, "Some Comments," 60-2); Runesson, "Architecture," 231-57; Stephen K. Catto, *Reconstructing the First-Century Synagogue: A Critical Analysis of Current Research*, LNTS 363 (London: T&T Clark, 2007), 99-102; De Luca, "Capernaum," 174; Lee I. Levine, "The Synagogues of Galilee," in *Galilee in the Late Second Temple and Mishnaic Periods: Life, Culture, and Society*, vol. 1 of *Galilee in the Late Second Temple and Mishnaic Periods*, ed. David A. Fiensy and James Riley Strange; Fortress Press, 2014), 129-50 (144-5). Although this is not the place to discuss the matter, the identification of the basalt pavement as an earlier synagogue has been challenged, most notably by Magness, "The Question," 18-26. For the present purposes of this study, we will follow the excavators in the identification of the basalt platform as an earlier synagogue. Good support for this position is also to be found in Runesson, "Architecture," 237-9.

[51] It is worth noting the multiple direct references to a synagogue at Capernaum in the first century, including a clear reference in Luke 7:5 to this synagogue as a building (see also Mark 1:21-28; John 6:59).

[52] Mark 1:21-29, 3:1-6; Luke 4:31-37, 7:5-9; John 6:25-59.

[53] See also Andrew S. Jacobs, "Visible Ghosts and Invisible Demons: The Place of Jews in Early Christian *Terra Sancta*," in *Galilee through the Centuries: Confluence of Cultures*, ed. Eric M. Meyers (Winona Lake: Eisenbrauns, 1999), 359-75.

[54] On this, see (e.g.) Leyerle, "Early Christian Perceptions of the Galilee," 351-2. According to Leyerly, "Egeria's blindness to contemporary Jewish life is thus doubly endorsed by her perception of the testimony of the land as well as that of apocryphal scripture."

mention of the synagogue, which is itself only of interest to Egeria because of its place within the gospel narratives. The Jews of Capernaum themselves remain invisible in Egeria's account of the place.[55]

The Heptapegon

Several other commemorative churches whose foundations have been dated to the fourth century were also located on the outskirts of Capernaum, at a place called the Heptapegon, named for its seven springs. Three dominical events were commemorated here: the miracle of the multiplication of the fish and loaves (Mark 6:30–44; Matt 14:13–21; Luke 9:10–17; John 6:1–14), the resurrection appearance of Jesus to his disciples on the shores of the Sea of Galilee (John 21:4), and the delivery of the Beatitudes (Matt 5:1–12; cf. Luke 6:20–26).[56] All three appear in Peter the Deacon's account, in the section usually ascribed to Egeria:

> Not far away from there (Capernaum) are some stone steps where the Lord stood. And in the same place by the sea is a grassy field with plenty of hay and many palm trees. By them are seven springs, each flowing strongly. And this is the field where the Lord fed the people with the five loaves and the two fishes. In fact the stone on which the Lord placed the bread has now been made into an altar. People who go there take away small pieces of the stone to bring them prosperity, and they are very effective … Near there on a mountain is the cave to which the Savior climbed and spoke the Beatitudes."[57]

The location of this site is in the vicinity of Capernaum, a fact that would continue to be noted by other witnesses in antiquity and through the medieval periods.[58] The three sites mentioned above are all included. The reference to the Lord standing on some steps probably refers to John 21:4, in which Jesus is depicted standing on the beach. We should note that the author, probably Egeria, mentions a stone on which Jesus was said to have placed the bread during the Feeding of the Five Thousand, a physical feature of the site that had become a marker, attracting memory and commemorative activity.

The ancient Church of the Multiplication at Tabgha has been discovered and excavated. It is indeed located in the vicinity of Capernaum, about 1.8 miles (3 km) away from Capernaum, just southwest or counterclockwise down the shore of the lake. This location is curious, particularly when compared to the accounts of the Feeding

---

[55] Jacobs, "Visible Ghosts," 369.
[56] See esp. Stanislao Loffreda, *Scavi di-et Tabgha*, Collectio Minor 7 (Jerusalem: Franciscan Printing Press, 1970); Schneider, *Church of the Multiplying*; Pixner, *Paths of the Messiah*, 77–114.
[57] Peter the Deacon, *de loc. sanct.* V2–V3, probably following Egeria. As per usual, translation from Wilkinson, *Egeria's Travels*, 97–9.
[58] See the catalog and discussion of these sources in E. W. G. Masterman, "The Site of Capernaum," *PEQ* 39:3 (1907): 220–9 (225–7). The earliest of these sources discussed by Masterman is Theodosius, *Topography of the Holy Land*, 2, which mentions the distance between Capernaum and the Heptapegon ("Seven Springs") as just two miles.

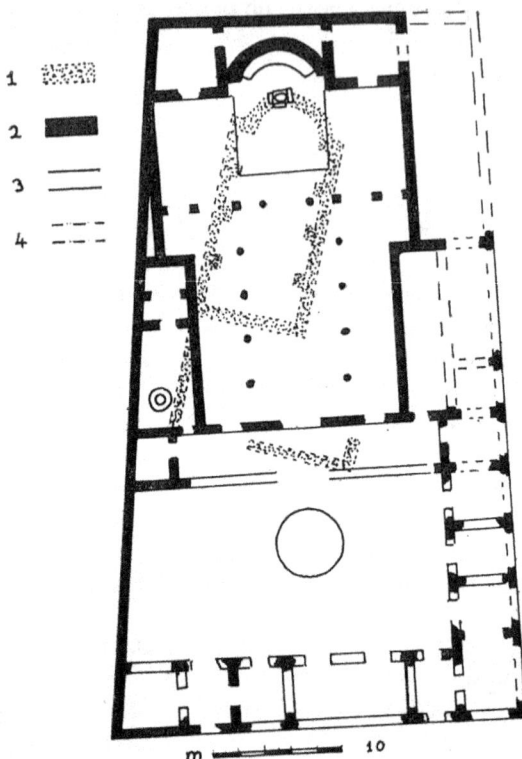

Figure 6 The fourth-century Church of the Multiplication superimposed on the fifth-century structure.

Source: Stanislao Loffreda, *The Sanctuaries of Tabgha* (Jerusalem: Franciscan Printing Press, 1975), fig. 6. Courtesy of Franciscan Printing Press.

of the Five Thousand in the canonical gospels.[59] The synoptic evangelists describe the site as a "deserted place" (Mark 6:31–32 and parallels; Greek *erēmos*). This much might suit the location of the Church of the Multiplication, as Tabgha is located *outside* Capernaum, in an area that was not apparently settled in the first century CE. Luke situates the Feeding of the Five Thousand at a deserted place in the region of Bethsaida (9:10, 12). John locates the event near a mountain (6:3, 15). Initially, John depicts Jesus and his disciples as sitting down "up the mountain" (6:3), but when the crowds arrive, they are shown sitting down at a place with a great deal of grass (v. 10), which may indicate a change in location,[60] since v. 15 says that Jesus "withdrew again to the

---

[59] See also Gordon Franz, "The Feedings of the Multitudes: When, Where, and Why?" in *Lexham Geographic Commentary on the Gospels*, ed. Barry J. Beitzel (Bellingham: Lexham, [2016] 2017), 239–43.

[60] Though, naturally, there could be grass on top of the mountain, as is the case in that region.

mountain by himself" when he realized that the people planned to make him king by force. Most importantly, in vv. 16–17, that evening, "his disciples went down to the sea, got into a boat, and started *across the sea to Capernaum*" (emphasis my own). This implies that the Feeding of the Five Thousand took place not in the vicinity of Capernaum but across the lake from Capernaum. This is not the place to combine or reconcile the details provided by the evangelists.[61] Suffice it to say, there is presently some disagreement as to the location of early Roman Bethsaida, with some locating it at et-Tell and others at el-Araj,[62] which may also impact how we interpret the data.

Tabgha, and the Church of the Multiplication, is not at Bethsaida,[63] and certainly not across the lake from Capernaum. Leaving questions about authenticity aside, this is a curious case in which the location of the site where the event was commemorated disagrees with the canonical accounts. We cannot know why this is the case with any certainty, but the fact that the location of the traditional site disagrees with the canonical location is a relevant datum in and of itself. This indicates that the traditional site of the Feeding of the Five Thousand at Tabgha is probably best understood as symbolic and representational. It represents the memory of Jesus' public ministry in the lake region of Galilee. It is quite likely that the feature of the boulder in the grassy field attracted strands of memory, which congealed around it and eventually crystallized in the form of the commemorative churches built around it. The fact that the Heptapegon cannot be the location of the Feeding of the Five Thousand as envisioned in the canonical narratives does not, however, necessitate that the site was selected to commemorate or represent this tradition only in the fourth century. We cannot know how or when the tradition came to be located here, save that it can have been no later than the fourth century.

Two successive churches were built on the site in antiquity.[64] The second, which featured the stunning mosaics that have been incorporated into and can be seen in the modern Church of the Multiplication, was initially constructed in the fifth century.[65] The earlier church is dated by the excavator, A. M. Schneider,[66] to the middle of the fourth

---

[61] Instead, see Franz, "Feedings of the Multitudes," 239–43.
[62] See, e.g., R. Steven Notley, "Et-Tell Is *Not* Bethsaida," *Near Eastern Archaeology* 70, no. 4 (2007): 220–30; Rami Arav, "Bethsaida – A Response to Steven Notley," *Near Easter Archaeology* 72, no. 2 (2011): 92–100. Ongoing excavations at el-Araj will likely speak more to this matter as discoveries are made and published.
[63] Nor is it part of the region controlled by Bethsaida, cf. Franz, "Feedings of the Multitudes," 241–2.
[64] See Schneider, *Church of the Multiplying*, 20–3; Asher Ovadiah, *Corpus of Byzantine Churches in the Holy Land* (Bonn: Hanstein, 1970), 56–9 (nos. 46a and 46b).
[65] See the discussion and finds throughout Schneider, *Church of the Multiplying*, esp. the summary on p. 80; cf. Loffreda, *Scavi di et-Tabgha*; cf. also the summary in Loffreda, *Sanctuaries of Tabgha*, esp. 36. Schneider dates the second church at Tabgha (the "basilica") to "the closing years of the fourth century," but a date in the fifth century seems more likely, cf. Ovadiah, *Byzantine Churches*, 58–9. In association with the date of the earlier church, the excavators mention finds dated to the fourth century including coins, though Schneider writes that the coins "were not generally found in the Chapel itself," (*Church of the Multiplying*, 23), which is somewhat cryptic. One of the most significant diagnostic finds mentioned by the excavators is an oil lamp dated to "the first half of the fourth century" (23).
[66] As Steven Fine notes in a forthcoming piece, Schneider copublished *Die Stadtmauer on Iznik (Nicaea)* with Walter Karnapp under the "Archäologisches Institut des Deutschen Reiches" imprint, which featured a swastika on the title page. Fine also notes that Schneider served as a military interpreter

century CE.⁶⁷ Schneider specifically dates it "most probably to the period of the *comes* Joseph."⁶⁸ Following Schneider, Bargil Pixner has suggested that this, not the Church of the House of Peter, is where Joseph's plan of building a church at Capernaum was realized.⁶⁹ However, in 1970, Loffreda conducted a reexamination of the foundations of the first church,⁷⁰ during which he discovered a coin dated to the reign of Honorius (*c*.395–404 CE) among the cracks of the foundations.⁷¹ According to Loffreda, it was found in a context that excluded the possibility of it being an intrusion.⁷² Admittedly, it is problematic to date a structure based on a single find, especially when we consider earthquakes and other such disturbances. However, this discovery does point toward a *terminus post quem* in the very last years of the fourth century (395 CE),⁷³ which complicates the hypothesis that the original Church of the Multiplication at Tabgha was built by Joseph of Tiberias. Indeed, as Goranson observes, Joseph was already elderly in 355-360 when he met Epiphanius,⁷⁴ so to connect him with a building constructed in the last decade of the fourth century would be a stretch.

The first Church of the Multiplication was a chapel,⁷⁵ meaning a small edifice constructed for Christian assembly whose interior space consists of a nave with no aisles.⁷⁶ It measures 15.5 m in length and 9.5 m in width. The chapel features a single apse, with a depth of 2.6 m. In the area of the choir,⁷⁷ the excavators discovered a large piece of limestone lying on the bare ground. It was located in the center of the area right in front of the apse, making this stone the focal point of the church. Because it was found lying on the ground the excavators believed that it was brought there from somewhere else. Thus, it is possible that the stone came from some other place entirely, or, more likely, it was simply dug out of the ground from nearby and placed

---

in Romania and Greece during the Second World War. See Steven Fine, "'For the Glory of the Holy House': The Sardis Synagogue and the History of Judaism in Roman Antiquity," in *The Synagogue at Sardis, Sardis Report* 9, ed. Andrew Seager, Marcus L. Rautman, and Vanessa Rousseau (Cambridge, MA: Harvard University Press, 2021). Schneider's work as a military interpreter during the Second World War is confirmed in his biographical commemorative obituary, written by Franz Babinger, "Alfons Maria Schneider (1896-1952)," *Zeitschrift der Deutschen Morgenländischen Gesellschaft* 103 (1953): 1–8 (5). Babinger's account indicates that Schneider was not happy about doing this work in an occupied nation ("aber die Tätigkeit im besetzten Gebiet eines Landes, dem seine Neigungen galten, widerstrebten seinem innersten Wesen"). We should nevertheless note that he did this work. Babinger also states that the "Hitler years" were the worst of Schneider's life (4). I am in no position to evaluate how Schneider felt about his work as a military interpreter in an occupied nation during the Second World War in his (to use Babinger's term) "inner being." However, since we will be discussing his work pertaining to Judaism, Christianity, and Jewish Christianity, it is a matter of scholarly and ethical responsibility to acknowledge Schneider's connections to the Nazi regime.

67 Schneider, *Church of the Multiplying*, 20–3, 80; Ovadiah, *Byzantine Churches*, 56.
68 Schneider, *Church of the Multiplying*, 80.
69 Pixner, *Paths of the Messiah*, 103.
70 Stanislao Loffreda, "Sondaggio nella Chiesa della Moltiplicatione di Pani a Tabgha," *Liber Annuus* 20 (1970): 370–80.
71 Ibid., 378; Loffreda, *Sanctuaries of Tabgha*, 24–5.
72 Loffreda, "Sondaggio," 378.
73 Ibid., 379. Loffreda generally still holds to a date in the fourth century (*Sanctuaries of Tabgha*, 24).
74 Goranson, "Joseph of Tiberias Episode," 138–9.
75 The description here is based on that given by the excavators, in Schneider, *Church of the Multiplying*, 20–3.
76 Cf. the basic definition used by Bagatti, *Church from the Gentiles*, 191.
77 "Choir" here follows Schneider's language. To be a little bit more precise, he means the area between the nave and the apse, about where the altar was likely located.

at the focal point of the chapel. A piece of this same stone was discovered under the altar of the fifth-century basilica. It was probably the focus of commemorative activity for both churches. This stone is almost certainly "the stone on which the Lord placed the bread" mentioned by Egeria.[78] The fact that it was *placed* in the spot in which it was featured in the fourth century and then a piece of it was moved again and placed under the altar of the fifth century church shows that the activity of commemorative was not so much about the "actual spot" where Jesus performed the miracle so much as it was about representing and commemorating the miracle. The Tabgha chapel, with its "holy stone,"[79] provided a discernable focal point for the memory and affect that was generated by the commemoration of the Feeding of the Five Thousand.

The Tabgha chapel was, thus, a reproduction and representation of a significant miraculous event in the remembered life of Jesus. Combined with the commemorative life-of-Jesus churches in the Jerusalem area, it and the other Galilean commemorative churches added additional facets and narratives to the representation of Jesus' life and ministry expressed through the commemorative churches of Palestine. Like the other commemorative churches, it functioned as a "witness" in the minds those who visited it, a witness to the authenticity and to the reality of Jesus' Galilean miracle-working ministry.[80] It did so through the presentation of the site, the building's architecture, and, most importantly, the presence of the "holy stone." It is difficult to know much about what sort of commemorative took place at Tabgha. Unlike the Sepulchre, Nativity, and Ascension churches, we have no record of the liturgy that took place there in the fourth century. Egeria does mention, however, that people who go to Tabgha "take away small pieces of the stone to bring them prosperity, and they are very effective."[81] This speaks to the commemorative function of the stone. Its purported magical properties and usage are derivative of its connection to Jesus and to the miraculous multiplication of the loaves and fishes. In the mind of the ancient pilgrims, the stone was effective in bringing people prosperity precisely because it was the authentic stone upon which Jesus multiplied bread and fish, enough to feed five thousand people. Through this practice of taking away small pieces of the stone, its effectiveness was multiplied, and thus its witness to the miraculous ministry of Jesus, much like the two fish and five loaves of the tradition that it commemorated.

Was the Chapel of the Multiplication at Tabgha Built by Joseph of Tiberias?

The churches built by Joseph were built by an imperial official with the express authorization of the emperor himself.[82] If the Chapel of the Multiplication at Tabgha was the church built at Capernaum by Joseph of Tiberias,[83] then it would qualify as an imperial monument, its small size notwithstanding.

---

[78] Peter the Deacon, *de loc. sanct.*, V3; cf. Wilkinson, *Egeria's Travels*, 98 n. 2.
[79] This is the term used by Schneider to refer to this stone (*Church of the Multiplying*, 21, illustration 2b).
[80] On this aspect of the geography of memory, see Foote and Azaryahu, "Geography of Memory," 128.
[81] In Peter the Deacon, *de loc. sanct.*, V3.
[82] This assumes, of course, that Joseph actually did build churches, and that some level of historical reality is attested by Epiphanius' narrative.
[83] As argued by Pixner, *Paths of the Messiah*, 102–3; suggested also by Schneider, *Church of the Multiplying*, 77–8, 80; cf. also Mordechai Aviam and Jacob Ashkenazi, "Late Antique Pilgrim Monasteries in Galilean *Loca Sancta*," *Liber Annuus* 64 (2014): 559–73 (565).

As Schneider acknowledges, it is difficult to know if the chapel can be confidently dated to the time of Joseph, [84] and by extension, prior to the writing of Epiphanius' *Panarion*. The paucity of archaeological finds from the excavation of the fourth-century chapel published by the original excavators is unfortunate. However, he nevertheless suggests that the chapel probably dates to Joseph's time.[85] Presumably, Joseph's building projects took place prior to his move to Scythopolis, where he hosted Eusebius of Vercelli during his banishment by order of Constantius (Epiphanius, *Pan.* 30.5), c.355–6.[86] If we are confident in assigning the testimony of the "holy stone" being used as an altar preserved by Peter the Deacon to Egeria, then the chapel must have certainly existed prior to her travels in Palestine (c.381–4).[87] While it is not impossible that the stone was simply at the site of the Heptapegon in the open air, Egeria's statement that it had been "made into an altar" (*de loc. sanct.* V3) suggests that it had been incorporated into a church building. Moreover, the fact that the stone was *brought* to the site where it was incorporated into the chapel also suggests that it came from elsewhere and may not have even been at the Heptapegon until the chapel was constructed.

Pixner points to a Greek funerary inscription for someone by the name of Joseph (Greek *Iōsēpos*) discovered during the excavation of the chapel as evidence that Joseph of Tiberias constructed the building and was later buried there.[88] This is significant potential evidence to be sure. However, it is far from decisive. Pixner interprets the find as belonging to the first church (fourth century CE) on the site.[89] However, the excavator describes the inscription as being on "a basalt block, 1.18 m. long, 0.40 m. wide and 0.47 m. thick, among the flags of the pavement of the western entrance of the atrium."[90] This seems to describe the stone as being part of the pavement used in the atrium entrance. This would mean that it belonged to the fifth century, since the fifth-century church had an atrium,[91] while the excavator says nothing about an atrium for the fourth-century chapel.[92] Of course, the fact that the block bearing the inscription was used in the pavement belonging to the fifth-century church does not rule out the possibility that it came originally from the fourth-century chapel and was reused in the rebuilt basilica.[93] Moreover, it is possible that, if the Joseph referred to in the inscription was indeed Joseph of Tiberias, he could have been reburied under the later church when the first chapel was dismantled. All we can say for the time being is that this inscription may but does not conclusively refer to Joseph of Tiberias. Dating issues aside, we cannot know for certain whether the Joseph of the Tabgha funerary inscription is Joseph of Tiberias.

---

[84] A date "as early as 352," in Schneider, *Church of the Multiplying*, 78. See also B. Gauer, "Ein neuer Fund in der Brotvermehrungskirche zu Tabgha," *Das Heilige Land* 80 (1936): 60.
[85] Schneider, *Church of the Multiplying*, 80.
[86] Ibid., 123.
[87] On the date of Egeria's travels, see Devos, "Le date," 165–84; Wilkinson, *Egeria's Travels*, 169–71; McGowan and Bradshaw, *Pilgrimage of Egeria*, 22–7.
[88] Pixner, *Paths of the Messiah*, 103. The find is published in Schneider, *Church of the Multiplying*, 33 (no. 24).
[89] Pixner, *Paths of the Messiah*, 103.
[90] Schneider, *Church of the Multiplying*, 33.
[91] Ibid., 11.
[92] Compare ibid. with 20–3, cf. also Plan II, which does not clearly depict an atrium.
[93] Cf. Goranson, "Joseph of Tiberias Episode," 137.

Further difficulties exist with Pixner's identification of Joseph buried at Tabgha with Joseph of Tiberias. As Goranson has noted, the title *komēs* is missing from the inscription, which would be a curious omission for a memorial of someone of that rank.[94] Also missing is any mention of church-building activity.[95]

The Chapel of the Multiplication does seem to be the sort of structure that one might imagine being funded by a wealthy patron, especially since the Chapel of the Multiplication was not located in a major settlement. The Church of the House of Peter presumably had some local community that might have contributed to its renovations, though this could also have been undertaken or aided by a patron. The form of the chapel itself, with its nave and apse, is a sort of basilica in miniature. If someone such as Joseph of Tiberias wanted to build a church commemorating an event in the life of Jesus, it is natural that he would have looked to the commemorative churches built by Constantine himself for architectural patterns and inspiration. The apsed form of the Martyrion and the Eleona may have provided just that. Despite its small size, the Chapel of the Multiplication may have been intended to invoke the form of the imperial commemorative monuments, which it did in miniature. However, it is also similar, as Schneider notes, to chapels in nearby Hauran.[96]

Ultimately, there is no evidence at either the Church of the House of Peter nor the Chapel of the Multiplication that conclusively shows that either of them is the church that was built at Capernaum by Joseph of Tiberias. More importantly, both would need to be shown to date to the time of Joseph of Tiberias in the mid-fourth century in order to be viable candidates. This is an open question for both sites at present. For the Chapel of the Multiplication, the discovery of the coin from the reign of Honorius calls the viability of a mid-fourth-century date into question. Furthermore, we cannot know for certain that a man named Joseph even built a church at Capernaum at all. While it is not impossible for one or both of these structures to have been built by Joseph, the evidence is not clear enough to draw a conclusion with any confidence.

Remembering the Miracle of the Multiplication of Fish and Loaves

The miracle of the multiplication of fish and loaves was already remembered in light of the Exodus miracle of the manna from heaven (Exod 16:1–36; Num 11:1–19) within the Fourth Gospel (John 6:25–34). This tradition of interpreting the miracle in connection with Moses and the Exodus narrative carried over to early Patristic exegesis in the Eastern Mediterranean world. Cyril of Alexandria notes the "harmony" between miracle of the manna and the feeding of the multitudes:

> The feeding of the multitudes in the desert by Christ is worthy of all admiration. But it is also profitable in another way. We can plainly see that these new miracles are in harmony with those of ancient times. They are the acts of one and the same

---

[94] Ibid., 136.
[95] Ibid., 136–7.
[96] Schneider, *Church of the Multiplying*, 23.

power. He rained manna in the desert upon the Israelites. He gave them bread from heaven. "Man did eat angels' food," according to the words of praise in the Psalms. But look! He has again abundantly supplied food to those who needed food in the desert. He brought it down, as it were, from heaven. Multiplying that small amount of food many times and feeding so large a multitude, so to speak, with nothing, is like that first miracle.[97]

Origen makes a connection to the Exodus narrative in a different manner. Mark 6:40 describes the crowd being seated in groups of hundreds and of fifties. Origen interprets the groups of fifty in light of the Jubilee, which took place every fifty years, and of the feast of Pentecost, that is, Shavuot (*Comm. Matt.* 11.3).

The connections to Moses drawn in the interpretation of the miracle of the multiplication of the fish and the loaves are particularly interesting given the localization of the Sermon on the Mount in the foothills near Tabgha. The parallel between Jesus' Sermon and the Mosaic Sinai event was not lost on the ancient church. Chromatius draws attention to "both laws" (the Sinaitic law and the Sermon on the Mount) as being given on mountains, noting however that at Sinai the people were forbidden from drawing close, while at the unnamed mountain of 5:1, "all are invited that they might hear."[98] The topographical connection between the commemorative sites associated with the Sermon on the Mount and the Feeding of the Five Thousand may have served to solidify the parallel between Jesus and Moses drawn in the canonical narrative of Jesus' ministry.

Egeria makes mention of "a cave to which the Savior climbed and spoke the Beatitudes," located on a mountain near the seven springs of Tabgha.[99] In 1935, Bellarmino Bagatti excavated a small church with a single nave dated to the early Byzantine period, built over a cave, which has been reasonably identified as the place where the Beatitudes (and thus the Sermons) were localized and commemorated by at least the fourth century.[100] Its location is noteworthy, as it is situated on the slope of the foothill of a mountain near et Tabgha,[101] a very short way up the hill, overlooking the flatter area below the mountain where Tabgha is located. Just above the cave is a level stretch, just beyond which the mountain rises steeply.[102]

The Sermon on the Mount's closest narrative parallel in the canonical tradition, Luke's so-called Sermon on the Plain takes place not on a mountain but on a "level

---

[97] *Commentary on Luke*, Homily 48. Translation from Cyril of Alexandria, *Commentary on the Gospel of St. Luke*, trans. R. Payne Smith (Long Island: Studion, 1983), 215.
[98] Chromatius, *Tractate on Matthew*, 17.1.3-4. Translation from Manlio Simonetti, ed., *Matthew 1–13*, Ancient Christian Commentary on Scripture, New Testament 1a (Downers Grove: InterVarsity, 2001), 77.
[99] Peter the Deacon, *de loc. sanct.*, V3.
[100] Bagatti, *Ancient Christian Villages of Galilee*, 72–4; Bagatti, "La cappella sul monte," 43–91; cf. Wilkinson, *Egeria's Travels*, 41–3. Note that it is dated as late as the sixth century by Ovadiah (*Byzantine Churches*, 59–60).
[101] As Bagatti says, it is "on the farthest slopes of the mountain called Mount of Beatitudes" (*Ancient Christian Villages*, 72).
[102] See also Augustine Wand, "Along the North Shore of the Sea of Galilee: A Topographical and Archaeological Study," *CBQ* 5, no. 4 (1943): 430–44 (435–6).

place" (Luke 6:17; Greek τόπου πεδινοῦ).[103] Interestingly, the apparent problem posed by this difference in the description of the locations of the Lukan and Matthean Sermons is through the location of an early commemorative site. The situation of the localization of the Sermon event in early Christian commemoration is a resourceful harmonization of the Lukan and Matthean Sermons, making use of the topography to provide a solution to the problem caused by the difference in setting.[104] However, the harmonization, though ingenious, is not entirely successful. The topography matches the description in Luke 6:17 of a "level place" but imperfectly fits the description in Matt 5:1 of Jesus "going up" (ἀνέβη) the mountain, as it is only a short way up the slope of the mountain's foot. This curious attempt at harmonization in early Christian commemorative topography demonstrates the connection between gospel texts and the experience of the real world of Galilee in the minds of fourth-century Christians. Moreover, it shows us the potential function of the geography of memory in exegesis and the creation of historical narrative.

Nazareth

By the fourth century, Nazareth had become a site of Christian commemorative activity. However, the evidence, both literary and material, pertaining to the commemoration of Jesus at Nazareth from the first to the fourth centuries CE is complex and difficult to interpret. As mentioned above, according to Epiphanius, Joseph of Tiberias received permission to build a church at Nazareth (*Pan.* 30.11.9–10, 30.12.1). There is fairly clear evidence that Nazareth had become a part of the typical itinerary of pilgrims in Galilee in the latter decades of the fourth century. Jerome tells us that Paula "went quickly on through Nazareth, the nurse of the Lord" prior to visiting Cana and Capernaum (*Ep.* 108.13.5).[105] The Galilean section of Peter the Deacon's *de locis sanctis*, which is typically regarded as derived from Egeria,[106] mentions several events and sites:

> There is a big and very splendid cave in which she [that is, Holy Mary] lived. An altar has been placed there, *and there, within the* actual cave, is the place from which she drew water. Inside the city the synagogue, where the Lord read the book of Isaiah, is now a church, but the spring from which Holy Mary used to take water is outside the village.[107]

---

[103] There is, however, a mountain setting in Mark 3:13, which also functions as a symbolic place of gathering.
[104] Pace Wand, "Along the North Shore," 442. Wand sees this topography as providing "the key for the solution" to the problem of the difference in setting of Matt 5:1 and Luke 6:17. However, it is better understood as an ingenious attempt at harmonization rather than as a solution to the problem altogether.
[105] Translation from Wilkinson, *Jerusalem Pilgrims*, 89.
[106] On the likelihood of Egerian testimony underlying the Nazareth portion of *de loc. sanct.* (T), see Wilkinson, *Egeria's Travels*, 96 n. 5, n. 7.
[107] *de loc. sanct.*, T. Translation from Wilkinson, *Egeria's Travels*, 96. Emphasis original to Wilkinson's translation.

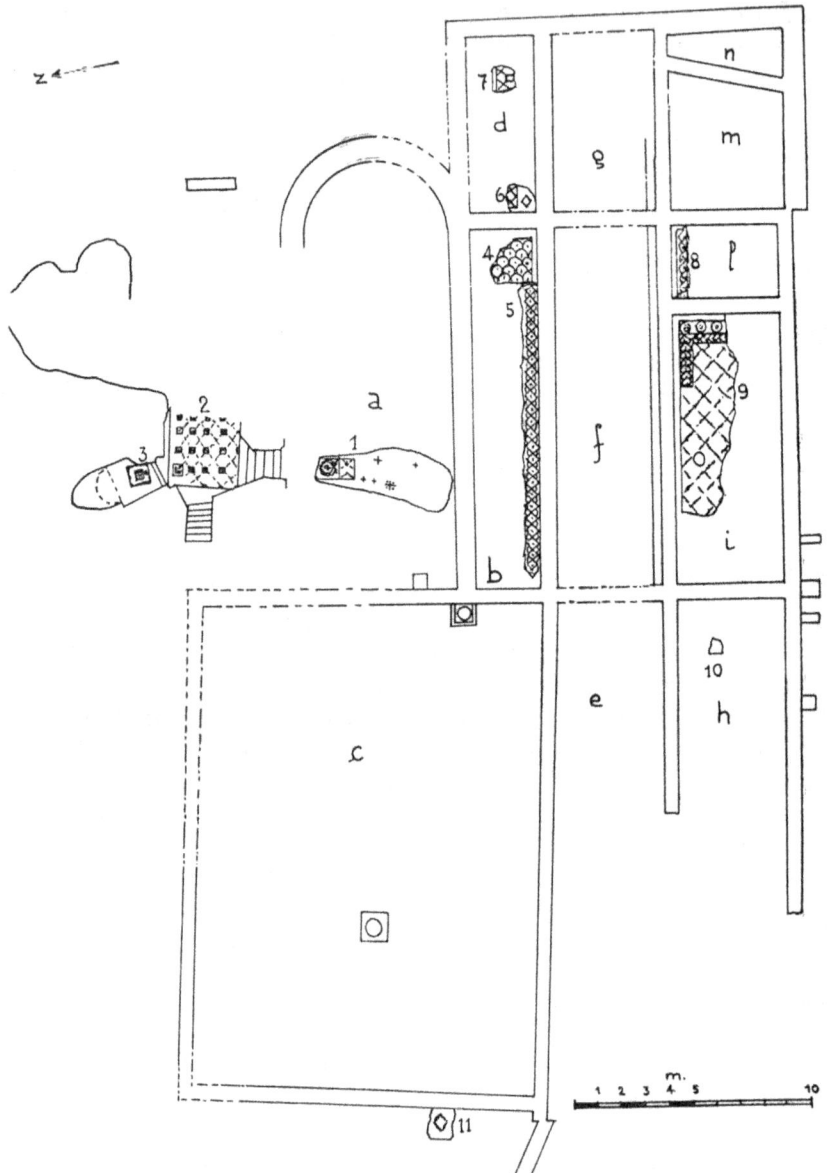

Figure 7 Floor plan of the excavations at the Church of the Annunciation at Nazareth.

Source: From Bellarmino Bagatti, *Excavations in Nazareth*, 2 vols. (Jerusalem: Franciscan Printing Press), fig. 49. Courtesy of Franciscan Printing Press.

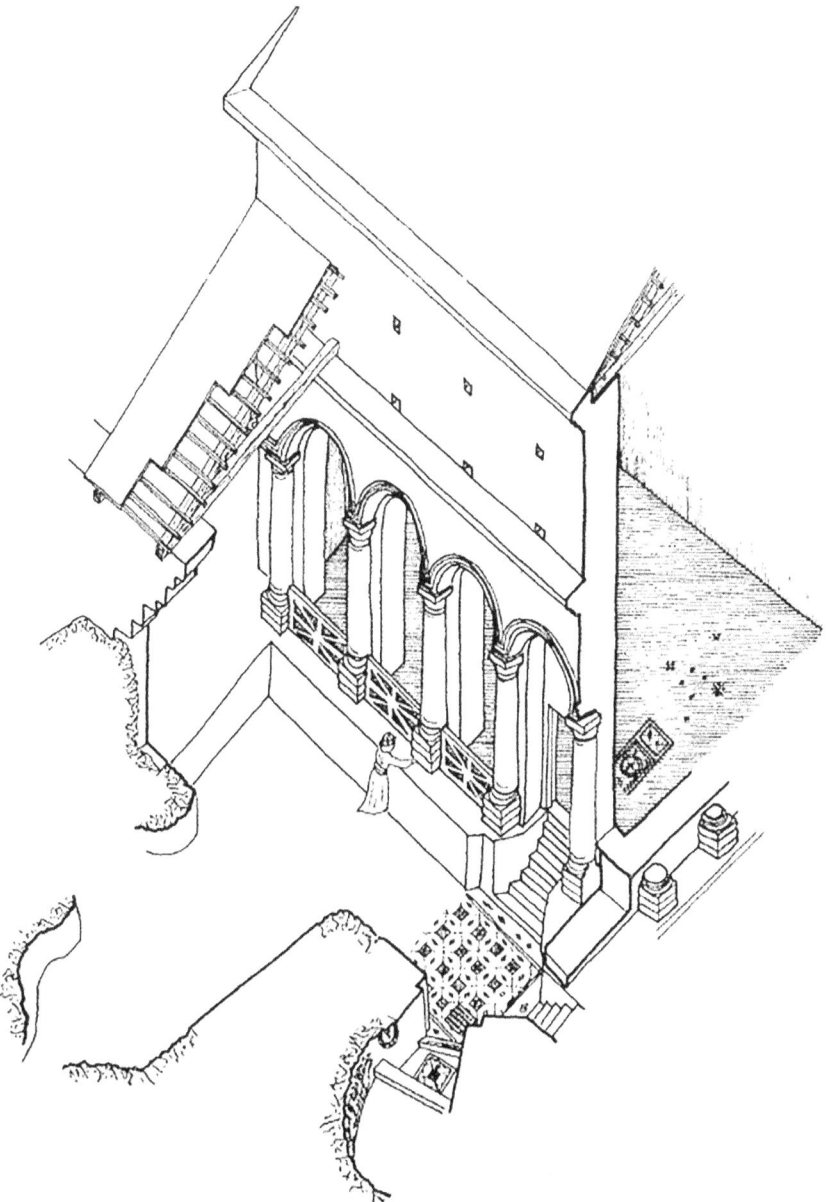

Figure 8 Reconstruction of the early Church of the Annunciation.

Source: Illustration by Eugenio Alliata. From Virgilio Corbo, "La chiesa-sinagoga dell'annonziata a Nazaret," *Liber Annuus* 37 (1987): 335–348 (fig. 2).

Based on the evidence at hand, it is reasonable to infer that *someone* had undertaken Christian commemorative construction projects at Nazareth prior to the journeys of Egeria and Paula. Even if we did not have the evidence from *de locis sanctis*, Paula's visit to Nazareth indicates that Christian commemoration of Jesus took place there in some form before the end of the century.

Both Egeria and Jerome provide us with some hints as to what was specifically commemorated at Nazareth. As we will see, Nazareth was most strongly remembered in early Christianity as the place where Jesus came of age, where the annunciation to Mary took place, and as the hometown of his parents and other family members. Egeria mentions at least two sites: the home of Mary with a place from which she (Mary) drew water, and the synagogue where Jesus read from the book of Isaiah. She also mentions a spring from which Mary used to take water, but it is unclear as to whether or not this is the same as the place as the cave identified as Mary's home, since the memory of Mary drawing water was also located there. The canonical event remembered by the "synagogue" that had become a church is undoubtedly Luke 4:16–30. The home of Mary could be broadly understood as an instantiation of the memory of Mary in general, and it is quite likely that it served this function. We should recognize a canonical connection here insofar as Luke sets the annunciation of Jesus' coming birth to Mary in Nazareth (1:26–27). However, the mention of Mary drawing water has no clear canonical referent.

The Protevangelium of James includes a version of the annunciation to Mary (Prot. Jas. 11), which depicts Mary filling a pitcher with water as she is addressed by a celestial voice, which says, "Greetings, favored one! The Lord is with you. You are blessed among women" (11:1). This greeting contains echoes of canonical greetings of Mary in the Lukan nativity narrative, particularly Gabriel's greeting in Luke 1:28 and Elizabeth's greeting in Luke 1:42. In the Protevangelium's version of the nativity, after hearing the greeting, Mary returns to her home where an angel appears to her and foretells the birth of Jesus in language that echoes both the Lukan annunciation to Mary (Luke 1:26–38) and the Matthean annunciation to Joseph (Matt 1:20–21).

The Protevangelium's annunciation narrative is a reception and expansion of the canonical annunciation narratives. Its relationship to the fourth-century commemorative site of Mary's home in Nazareth is certainly noteworthy. The site of Mary's home at Nazareth very clearly commemorated the annunciation to Mary. This commemorative tradition continues to this day in the form of the modern Basilica of the Annunciation at Nazareth. However, while the narrative of the annunciation to Mary is itself canonical, the commemoration at the site of Mary's home also incorporated traditional elements from beyond the canonical narrative. As we have already seen at both Golgotha and at Bethlehem, commemorative sites facilitated the transmission of apocryphal traditions. Typically, the core tradition being commemorated has a canonical referent, but apocryphal elements may be included in the presentation of the site (as with the cave at Bethlehem) or be otherwise attached through oral or literary discussion of the sites of commemoration (as with the burial place of Adam at Golgotha). In the case of the home of Mary at Nazareth, the detail mentioned in Prot. Jas. 11 of Mary drawing water in connection with the memory of the annunciation was represented at the site itself through the presentation of the place from which she drew the water.

Jerome mentions that Nazareth was "the nurse of the Lord." This represents the fact that Nazareth was remembered as Jesus' home prior to beginning his ministry, a detail mentioned in several places in the canonical gospels.[108] This fact is frequently discussed and mentioned in early Christian writings.[109] Moreover, Nazareth is often featured in early Christian apocrypha as a setting for narratives about Jesus' childhood or about his parents.[110] Nazareth was naturally also connected to Jesus' other family members in general in early Christian literature.[111]

The Early Commemorative Church at Nazareth

Excavations undertaken in the mid-twentieth century in preparation for the construction of the modern Basilica of the Annunciation uncovered the remains of a Byzantine commemorative church that was decorated richly with mosaic floors.[112] This ancient church was built in connection with a grotto that was remembered as the site of the annunciation of Jesus' birth to Mary, and thus as the house of Mary.[113] Although the canonical narrative of the annunciation as told in Luke 1:26–38 is not explicitly set in Mary's house, the Protevangelium of James specifically depicts Mary in her house when the angel appears to her (11:1–2). The fact that both Egeria and the Piacenza Pilgrim mention that the grotto was understood to be Mary's dwelling place further indicates the influence of the Protevangelium on early Christian commemorative sites, as well as the role of commemorative churches in the preservation and dissemination of extra-canonical traditions.

The Byzantine church, whose remains can now be visited in the lower church of the modern Basilica of the Annunciation, was constructed no earlier than the fifth century CE.[114] However, remains of an earlier church were discovered beneath the fifth-century edifice.[115] Bagatti dates its construction to the middle of the third century,[116] but a date

---

[108] Mark 1:9; Matt 2:23, 21:11; Luke 2:39, 51, 4:16; John 1:45–46.
[109] See, e.g., Epiphanius, *Panarion*, 29.5.6.
[110] E.g., Nazareth is the assumed setting of the Infancy Gospel of Thomas, and is specifically identified as the setting in some manuscripts of the text.
[111] E.g., Eusebius, *Hist. Eccl.* 1.7.14.
[112] Bellarmino Bagatti, *Excavations in Nazareth*, 2 vols., trans. Eugenio Hoade, Publications of the Studium Biblicum Franciscanum 17 (Jerusalem: Franciscan Printing Press, 1969), 2: 77–114.
[113] Cf. Egeria, in Peter the Deacon, *de loc. sanct.*, T; *Itin. Piac.* 5.
[114] Excavations beneath the floor revealed finds dating up to but not later than the fifth century CE, according to Bagatti, *Excavations in Nazareth*, 136.
[115] Bagatti, *Excavations in Nazareth*, 114–73. See also Bagatti, *Church from the Circumcision*, 125–8; Bagatti, *Ancient Christian Villages of Galilee*, 24; Virgilio Corbo and Eugenio Alliata, "La chiesa-sinagoga dell'annonziata a Nazaret," *Liber Annuus* 37 (1987): 335–48; Ken Dark, *Roman-Period and Byzantine Nazareth and Its Hinterland* (Abingdon: Routledge, 2020), 125–7; James F. Strange, "Nazareth," in *The Archaeological Record From Cities, Towns, and Villages*, vol. 2 of *Galilee in the Late Second Temple and Mishnaic Periods*, ed. David A. Fiensy and James Riley Strange (Minneapolis: Fortress, 2015), 167–80 (175–7); and Taylor, *Christians and the Holy Places*, 253–7.
[116] Bagatti, *Excavations in Nazareth*, 173. The rationale for the third-century date is based on the style of the mouldings of the architectural elements of the earlier church as well as on a questionable analysis of the graffiti, neither of which would hold up in light of modern scholarly advances. As the study of Galilean synagogues has shown, architectural style is not always a reliable index for dating buildings. This is particularly true now that so many synagogue buildings originally dated to earlier

in the fourth century is more likely.[117] This earlier church, which we will refer to here as the "earlier church at Nazareth" for lack of a better name, will be the focus of the brief discussion to follow.

The remains of the earlier church at Nazareth were discovered in a poor state of preservation, likely due in no small measure to the construction of the new church at the same site in the fifth century. A brief catalogue of the elements of the earlier church will help us to imagine it as best as we can.

1. Remains of some walls that predate the fifth-century Byzantine church were discovered.[118] However, it is difficult to discern the form or shape of the building from the walls that remain. One significant section of a wall belonging to the earlier church was reused as a stylobate in the fifth-century church, in which it was conspicuously higher than the mosaic pavements.[119] Other drafted stones likely belonging to the earlier church were discovered out of context, reused in the fifth-century church.[120] Many of these stones were plastered with white plaster.[121] The primary material used was *nari* stone with white lime plaster.[122]
2. Fragments of painted plaster belonging to the earlier church were found in fill within a basin located under the mosaic floor of the central nave of the fifth-century church.[123] The plaster was colored primarily with red and green with some

centuries are now dated considerably later. For a summary of some of these issues, see Magness, "Question of the Synagogue," 1–48.

[117] Cf. Corbo, "Chiesa-sinagoga," 340–3; Taylor, *Christians and the Holy Places*, 265; Dark, *Nazareth and Its Hinterland*, 125–6. In general, I am convinced by the dating of the earlier church to the mid-fourth century (note that both Corbo and Taylor place its construction in the first half of the fourth century). There are few good contexts from which datable, diagnostic material could have been excavated from the remains of the earlier church. A coin was found in layer c of the plaster in one of the grottoes (the one somewhat tendentiously identified as a "martyrium" by the excavators), which Bagatti identified as belonging to Constans (*Excavations in Nazareth*, 210), though Taylor has suggested that it is probably Constantius II (since he ruled in the East from 337 to 361). Meyers and Strange have suggested that the coin dates to the reign of Constantine, which would be even earlier, in Eric M. Meyers and James F. Strange, *Archaeology, the Rabbis and Early Christianity* (London: SCM, 1981), 133–4. This leaves the possibility open that the lower layers of plaster could predate the Constantinian age. However, as Taylor observes, the coin provides a *terminus ante quem* for that layer of the plaster but does not exclude the possibility that the coin might predate the plaster by a significant amount of time. A large number of architectural elements of the earlier church were discovered in a basin (although identified by Bagatti as a baptismal basin [*Excavations in Nazareth*, 120–3], it is in fact clearly a winepress, cf. Taylor, *Christians and the Holy Places*, 244–51). The earliest literary mentions of architectural space for specifically Christian gathering in Nazareth date to mid- or late fourth century (Epiphanius, *Panarion*, 30.11.10, discussing events that took place c.340 CE; Egeria, in Peter the Deacon, *de loc. sanct.*, T), while no mention is made of Christian architecture in Nazareth by the Bordeaux Pilgrim nor by Eusebius. As we shall see below, Egeria's description of an altar in the cave where Mary lived matches the archaeological remains of the earlier church at Nazareth. See also Taylor, *Christians and the Holy Places*, 226–8. All of this, combined with the stratigraphic evidence, points toward a Christian building constructed in the mid-fourth century that was eventually destroyed to make way for a larger church sometime in the fifth century.
[118] Bagatti, *Excavations in Nazareth*, 115–19.
[119] Ibid., 115.
[120] Ibid., 118.
[121] Ibid.
[122] Based on inferences from ibid., 119, 141.
[123] Ibid., 120, 123–31.

white stripes,[124] exhibiting some floral motifs, while some pieces also exhibit some grey, orange, and violet.[125] Graffiti, mostly in Greek, were incised on the plaster. As Bagatti has noted, the painted plaster discovered at Nazareth is similar to that found at the Church of the House of Peter in Capernaum.[126]

3. A significant number of major architectural fragments belonging to the earlier church were excavated beneath the convent of the Byzantine (fifth century) church. Bagatti writes that "some seventy big architectonic pieces that once belonged to an older building" were found beneath the convent.[127] These architectural fragments, as depicted in the drawings and photographs published by Bagatti, are clearly derived from a monumental, public structure.[128] Included among the fragments are (1) capitals, (2) column shafts, (3) column bases, (4) arch imposts, (5) cornices, (6) thresholds, and (7) jambs belonging to either windows or doors.

4. Fragments of white marble were also discovered underneath the Byzantine convent. According to Bagatti, the excavation collected "many fragments of white marble, cut in slabs of 1 cm. thickness or more, according to the case, and smoothed on both sides. Some fragments have a round corner and sometimes lime attached, showing that they adorned the walls or were part of the pavement or some furniture."[129] The marble was found in the same context as the architectural fragments mentioned above, along with an assemblage of datable diagnostic material that Bagatti dated "prior to the Byzantine period,"[130] which could further support a fourth-century date. The presence of a significant amount of marble differentiates this edifice at Nazareth from those at Tabgha and Capernaum that we have discussed above. In addition to these marble fragments, the base of a marble post from an altar and fragments of a small marble column, including part of a capital ornamented with concentric circles were also discovered.[131] Furthermore, Bagatti suggests that two marble Corinthian capitals discovered out of context in "relatively modern masonry" might hypothetically also belong to the earlier church.[132] However, Taylor has questioned their inclusion with the materials of the earlier church, "since the early Christian structure was not built with any marble."[133] As we have seen, there was some marble in the structure, but nothing monumental that we might connect these capitals to. Suffice it to say, it is not clear that the marble capitals date to the time of the earlier church.

---

[124] Ibid., pl. 2 (cf. 120).
[125] Ibid., 120 (cf. pl. 3).
[126] Ibid., 130–1.
[127] Ibid., 140. According to Strange, there were only about two dozen pieces ("Nazareth," 176), but this number is probably based only on the fragments published by Bagatti.
[128] Bagatti, *Excavations in Nazareth*, figs. 84–96.
[129] Ibid., 139.
[130] Ibid.
[131] Ibid., 145 (figs. 95–6).
[132] Ibid., 169.
[133] Taylor, *Christians and the Holy Places*, 257.

5. The earlier church included the Grotto of the Annunciation (numbered 31 in the report), the place regarded as the house of Mary in which the event of annunciation to Mary was commemorated.[134] There was an east-facing apse carved out of the rock of this grotto.[135] It is quite likely that this is the place where the altar mentioned by Egeria was placed in the earlier church.[136]
6. A second grotto (no. 29), referred to as the Grotto of Conon (though a good case has been made by Alliata that it should instead be called the "Grotto of Valeria") after a mosaic naming the deacon Conon,[137] which was likely added at a slightly later time.[138] This grotto was plastered, and features a fresco of a garden and a painted inscription.[139] The inscription is of a clearly Christian character, including the phrase "Lord Christ, save your servant Valeria [Greek Οὐλεριαν]."[140] This grotto featured a plastered bench, which concealed a small trough 3.5 feet in height with a stone slab next to it, understood to be a stepping stone to the trough, with a small round hole next to the slab.[141] Ken Dark has recently suggested that this might be "an altar built above a reliquary, overlaying a venerated grave … The 'small round hold' would then be used to either take or drain away liquid, whether functionally or liturgically."[142] This is a strong suggestion and fits squarely with the archaeological evidence of the early Christian martyr cult as elaborated and studied by Ramsay MacMullen.[143] MacMullen's work has drawn attention to holes used in martyr shrines for the pouring of libations. Perhaps this hole in the Grotto of Valeria had a liturgical function, though that need not necessarily be the case, particularly since it would seem that the hole was not located on the reliquary itself.
7. Some mosaic floors may be associated with the earlier church.[144]
8. Graffiti were incised into the architectural elements of the earlier church. An extended discussion of the graffiti is neither possible nor necessary here. The most noteworthy of the graffiti found on the architectural elements was a Greek inscription scratched into one of the column bases. This particular inscription reads "X̅E̅ MAPIA," best understood as "Hail Mary" (Greek XAIPE MAPIA).[145] Meyers and Strange, however, have suggested that "Christ, Mary" might be a preferable reading.[146] Whichever reading is correct, the name "Mary" (Greek MAPIA) is certain. The graffito is potential evidence of the Marian connection at the site, as witnessed already in the fourth century by Egeria (as seen above).

---

[134] Cf. Egeria, in Peter the Deacon, *de loc. sanct.*, T.
[135] Bagatti, *Excavations in Nazareth*, 176–7. See also the helpful summary in Taylor, *Christians and the Holy Places*, 254–5, and the reconstruction by Corbo and Alliata, "Chiesa-sinagoga," 334, 338.
[136] Egeria, in Peter the Deacon, *de loc. sanct.*, T; cf. Taylor, *Christians and the Holy Places*, 254–5.
[137] Bagatti, *Excavations in Nazareth*, 100–3.
[138] On the date of the mosaic, see Taylor, *Christians and the Holy Places*, 242–3.
[139] Bagatti, *Excavations in Nazareth*, 192–9 (fig. 151, pls. 9.2, 10).
[140] See transcription in ibid., 197.
[141] Ibid., 186.
[142] Dark, *Nazareth and Its Hinterland*, 126.
[143] MacMullen, *Second Church*, 104–11 (e.g.).
[144] Corbo, "Chiesa-sinagoga," 337.
[145] Bagatti, *Excavations at Nazareth*, 155–6.
[146] Meyers and Strange, *Archaeology, the Rabbis and Early Christianity*, 133–4.

In my opinion, Bagatti's reading of "Hail Mary" is likely correct. It is a short citation from the wording of Luke 1:28 and serves to further connect the site to the event that was commemorated there. Another graffito incised on in the plaster of one of the columns includes the phrase "under the holy place [of] M..." (Greek ΥΠΟ ΑΓΙΩ ΤΟΠΟ Μ...).[147] Unfortunately, the rest of the final word is missing. Bagatti supplies "Mary" (Greek ΜΑΡΙΑΣ) for the final word, resulting in a reading of "under the holy place of Mary." Given the literary evidence concerning the site's connection to Mary, and the "Hail Mary" graffito, this is a reasonable suggestion.

What may we conclude about the form of the structure? Corbo has reconstructed the structure based on the extant evidence, and his reconstruction makes very good sense of the evidence.[148] Based on the fact that the column bases featured significant amounts of graffiti, Corbo ingeniously suggested that they were located roughly at eye level for the people who incised the graffiti into them. Corbo envisioned the cave being cut away from the rock and walls being to extend the area. The Grotto of the Annunciation was the focus of the building, with the Grotto of Valeria accessible just to the west of it as well. The columns rested on a low wall to the south of the Grotto of the Annunciation that ran east-west, supporting a series of archways and forming a sort of elevated transenna before the area of the grottos. This supported the roof, which rested over the cave complex. To the south of the transenna was an open hall, separated from the grottoes by the transenna. The grottos were accessed from the hall by a staircase. Corbo suggests that the building was entered from the west side. The whole structure would have measured 16 m × 20 m.[149]

Analysis of the Early Church of the Annunciation

The early Church of the Annunciation is the most unique of the early commemorative churches in Palestine in terms of form and design. There are a few notable features to comment on. The architectural elements and scale reflect a public building.[150] The entire structure is focused upon the Grotto of the Annunciation, the site remembered as the place where the events narrated in Luke 1:28–38 and *Prot. Jas.* 11 took place. The structure was mostly oriented north-south, with the hall and the "forecourt" formed by the walled area between the Grotto of the Annunciations and the transenna constituting gathering space facing the Grotto, which formed a long orienting space similar to an apse. However, the Grotto of the Annunciation featured an apse carved into its *east* wall, despite the grotto being longer on its north-south axis than its east-west axis. Moreover, the building was likely entered from the west. We might say that the architecture was oriented north-south but that foot traffic was probably oriented

---

[147] Bagatti, *Excavations in Nazareth*, 151.
[148] Corbo, "Chiesa-sinagoga," 336–40. See also the summary in Taylor, *Christians and the Holy Places*, 252–7, which largely follows and supports Corbo's reconstruction.
[149] Cf. Taylor, *Christians and the Holy Places*, 256.
[150] Cf. Dark, *Nazareth and Its Hinterland*, 125.

west-east. That having been said, however we understand the orientation of the building, the focal point was clearly the Grotto of the Annunciation, where the apse and the altar were located. The Grotto of Valeria (or Conon) provided a secondary *lieu de mémoire*, much like martyr chapels located in apsed basilicas of the Byzantine period.

One of the noteworthy features of this particular edifice is that it designates the commemorative space of the Grotto of the Annunciation without using a typical basilical form, nor a rotunda or other central plan structure. Like the Church of the Nativity and the Eleona, the commemorated space is a natural cave. However, the early Church of the Annunciation used a different architectural strategy entirely in order to create and present the sacred space of the Grotto within its structure. It is entirely unconventional and without parallel in architectural form.[151] Because of this, it is extremely difficult to say much about the iconography of its architecture. Perhaps the closest *conceptual* parallel to the early Church of the Annunciation is the fourth-century Church of the House of Peter at Capernaum, insofar as both are attempts to commemorate a place remembered as the home of an important New Testament figure closely connected to Jesus. Although the evidence is far from clear that the Grotto of the Annunciation was used as a home in the first century, let alone Mary's home, it was regarded by those who visited it in the fourth century as the place where she lived. As with the Church of the House of Peter, the fourth-century structure was designed to mark off the commemorative "living space" from the surrounding area. The parallel is thus more conceptual than it is strictly architectural.

The decoration and quality of the construction is noteworthy. While the early Church of the Annunciation certainly lacks the imperial grandeur of the Church of the Holy Sepulchre or the Church of the Nativity, the use of marble and mosaics, along with frescos and well-cut ashlars would have required funding. This is all the more so given that it was located in a rural area.[152] Thus, I would agree with Dark's recent statement that "the most likely origin for an architecturally elaborate Christian building in a fourth-century rural context is that it was constructed on the orders of a wealthy Christian patron."[153] If this is the case, it is possible that the early Church of the Annunciation was actually constructed by Joseph of Tiberias, as suggested by several scholars.[154] While certainty is far from possible, it does fit the profile in terms of date and construction of a structure built by a wealthy Christian patron with a minor imperial title such as Joseph.

---

[151] Cf. ibid., 126.
[152] Ibid., 126. Taylor questions whether there was a significant Jewish Christian or Gentile Christian population in Nazareth at all prior to the age of Constantine (*Christians and the Holy Places*, 221–30). If there was no significant local Christian community, outside funding would be all the more necessary. Goranson, however, is more willing to accept some Christian presence prior to the fourth century ("Joseph of Tiberias Episode," 105–12, esp. 110).
[153] Dark, *Nazareth and Its Hinterland*, 126.
[154] E.g., Corbo, "Chiesa-sinagoga," 340–3; Taylor, *Christians and the Holy Places*, 267, cf. Joan E. Taylor, "A Graffito Depicting John the Baptist in Nazareth," *PEQ* 119 (1987): 142–8; Dark, *Nazareth and Its Hinterland*, 126. Goranson, however, is more skeptical ("Joseph of Tiberias Episode," 112).

The unconventional architecture of the site further problematizes the identification of the building as a "synagogue-church" used by Jewish Christians.[155] This identification has already rightly been challenged by Taylor,[156] and there is no need to repeat her arguments again here. However, I might add that typical synagogue architecture of the first four centuries CE in Israel-Palestine differs greatly from what we see at the early Church of the Annunciation.[157] Typical synagogue architecture from this time consisted of a primary assembly hall with benches located along three or four of the walls with columns located in the central area supporting a clerestory ceiling. Synagogues were designed for discussion, and so the focus was typically at the center of the room. Synagogues after the Second Temple period could also feature Torah niches or arks and *bamot*. None of these features matches what we see in the early Church of the Annunciation. In fact, Bagatti's initial suggestion that the building was a synagogue-church was based on architectural similarities that he saw in the architectural fragments to synagogues. However, since further architectural analysis demonstrates the differences between the building in question and early synagogues, the identification should be seriously called into question.

Like other commemorative churches, the Church of the Annunciation served to locate the narrative of the annunciation to Mary within actual space. It also asserted and reminded visitors and locals of the origins of Jesus at Nazareth. Moreover, it was likely the first commemorative structure with a direct Marian connection, such that we should understand it as being a site remembering Mary while simultaneously rooting Jesus within his *patris*. That it was understood to be built on the site of Mary's home is significant, since this raises some of the same issues that we addressed with the Church of the House of Peter earlier in this chapter. The cave, remembered as Mary's house, was fully incorporated into the commemorative structure, which was built around it.

As the site of the annunciation, there is a sense in which this "house" could be understood as the place where the Christian faith began, the place where the news of the coming of Jesus was first proclaimed. It would have been closely tied to the origins of Christianity in the eyes of its beholders. Visitors would thus be able to draw a direct connection between themselves and the origins of the Christian faith, thereby contributing to the formation of their identity as Christians by being in the very place (in their understanding) where the mother of Jesus lived, and where she first received news about the child that she would bear. This would again serve to define "who we are" as "where we come from."[158] As Halbwachs writes, the function of religious memory is not the preservation of the past so much as to "reconstruct it with the aid of material

---

[155] See Bagatti, *Excavations in Nazareth*, 172, 173; Corbo, "Chiesa-sinagoga" (see the title of the article itself).
[156] Taylor, *Christians the Holy Places*, 256–7.
[157] See, for an overview, e.g., Anders Runesson, Donald Binder, and Birger Olsson, *The Ancient Synagogue from Its Origins to 200 C.E.: A Source Book* (Leiden: Brill, 2008); Rachel Hachlili, *Ancient Synagogues – Archaeology and Art: New Discoveries and Current Research*, HdO 105 (Leiden: Brill, 2013); Lee I. Levine, *The Ancient Synagogue: The First Thousand Years*, 2nd ed. (New Haven: Yale University Press, 2005). The present author has written on early synagogue architecture elsewhere, in Ryan, *Role of the Synagogue*, 61–78.
[158] Cf. Foote and Azaryahu, "Geography of Memory," 127.

traces, rites, texts, and traditions left behind by that past, and with the aid moreover of recent psychological and social data, that is to say, the present."[159]

While we know little about the rituals that took place at the early Church of the Annunciation, there are a few things that we might be able to infer. The material evidence of the altar post and Egeria's witness to the presence of an altar at the site is an indication of liturgical activity at the site. Moreover, the "Hail Mary" graffito strongly points toward the use of the Lukan annunciation narrative in the space of the building. We can envision a scenario similar to that at the Church of the Holy Sepulchre, wherein the foundational scriptural texts for the site were read regularly, probably weekly, at the "very place" where the narrative of the text was believed to have occurred. Text likely guided and formed the interpretation and understanding of the place here as at the Holy Sepulchre. Hence, the two examples of graffiti mentioning Mary, combined with Egeria's testimony that the place was understood as Mary's house, indicate that the commemorative activity at the site was guided by a sacred narrative. While the use of Luke 1:26-38 is to be expected, it is important to recognize the role played by *Prot. Jas.* 11 as well. Egeria's discussion of the site clearly indicates a level of familiarity with traditions found in the Protevangelium. There is no way to know precisely how these traditions were used or circulated in connection with the site. We cannot know, for example, whether it was ever read in a liturgical capacity at the site. However, it is clear that the annunciation traditions contained in *Prot. Jas.* 11 colored the experience of the place. These traditions may have spread orally or through homilies (as with the homily that Jerome heard that included the tradition of the burial of Adam at Golgotha, in *Comm. Eph.* 5:14), even if they were not incorporated into liturgical readings.

The place of the early Church of the Annunciation within Jewish-Christian relations is complex. The material culture of Nazareth is primarily Jewish in character, at least prior to the construction of the earlier church.[160] This is further supported by the scant literary evidence, which suggests a primarily Jewish population. Epiphanius claims that Joseph requested to build a church at Nazareth because it was a thoroughly Jewish town with no Gentiles among them (*Pan.* 30.11.9-10). We must grant that this may be overstated, but it does nevertheless fit the evidence. A few centuries later, the Piacenza Pilgrim also writes about Nazareth as though Jews still made up the majority of its population (*Itin. Piac.* 5).[161]

By virtue of being built in a Jewish village, the early Church of the Annunciation acknowledged the Jewish origins of the Christian tradition, while simultaneously laying claim to those origins in supersessionist fashion by staking out a Gentile Christian space within Jewish territory through the presence of its monumental architecture. Its location in a Jewish village was a means of encoding Palestinian Jews into the sacred geography of the Christian "the Holy Land."[162] There is certainly room for overlap between Jewish and Christian identity, which we might imagine as a sliding

---

[159] Halbwachs, *On Collective Memory*, 119. See also Leyerle, "Landscape as Cartography," 119-43.
[160] See Dark, *Nazareth and its Hinterland*, 94-115. This is made even clearer by Strange's summary of the data, as he notes the presence of typical elements of Galilean Jewish material culture, including Herodian oil lamps, chalkstone vessels, and limestone ossuaries (Strange, "Nazareth," 175-6).
[161] Cf. Jacobs, "Visible Ghosts," 373-4.
[162] Cf, the language used by Jacobs, "Visible Ghosts," 359-75 (367).

scale. While it is important not to draw hard lines between the categories of "Jewish" and "Christian," the Gentile languages used for the inscriptions at the site, and the non-Jewish identity of the pilgrims that we can place at the site (Egeria and Paula) prior to the construction of the larger basilical church, indicate that the early Church of the Annunciation was a foothold for Gentile Christianity within a Jewish locale. That is to say, the identity and culture of the site itself was much closer to "Gentile Christian" than "Jewish" on the sliding scale of identity. Granted, this does not in itself exclude or ignore the presence of Jewish Christians at the site.

Epiphanius indicates that the rationale for building a Christian church at Nazareth came out of a desire to found a church in a place where there were (ostensibly) no Greeks, Samaritans, or Christians, where the supposed "rule" of having no Gentiles among the population was particularly observed (*Pan.* 30.11.9–10). Goranson is astute in his observation that this does not exclude the presence of "Jewish Christians," which we might understand as people whose Christian and Jewish identities overlapped, since Epiphanius did not consider such groups to be Christian.[163] If there is only a kernel of historical reality behind Epiphanius' Joseph of Tiberias narrative, the notion that a church was built in Nazareth by a wealthy patron in order to establish an "orthodox" Christian presence in a Jewish locale may be it, since it does seem to reflect the evidence presented above. As Goranson has pointed out, if there were Jewish Christians at Nazareth, it is quite possible that the construction of the early church at Nazareth would not have been welcomed by them nor by the local Jewish population.[164] The evidence that Epiphanius provides furthers the image that is already emerging from the data concerning Jewish-Christian relations.

The construction of the early Church of the Annunciation leveraged the scriptural and Jewish past of the Christian tradition in order to gain a foothold in the Jewish locale of Nazareth, thus contributing to the supersessionist Gentile-Christianization of the "Holy Land," a project that we have already seen set in motion by the Constantinian construction of the "New Jerusalem" earlier in the fourth century. This continued well into the sixth century, in which the Piacenza Pilgrim's visit to Nazareth (*Itin. Piac.* 5) treats the local Jewish population and synagogue as set pieces for Christian imagination and piety. According to the Piacenza Pilgrim, the Jewish synagogue at Nazareth held the book in which Jesus "wrote his ABC," as well as the bench on which he sat. This bench could only be lifted and moved by "Christians" while "Jews are completely unable to move it." This indicates that Christians were present in Jewish communal space for the purposes of tourism and pilgrimage. The performative inability of Jews to lift the bench in the synagogue (whether physically acted out or orally transmitted) is symbolic of "orthodox" Christian triumphalism over its Jewish heritage. The pilgrim's reference to the Jewish women of Nazareth being the most beautiful in the land as a result of their kinship to Mary exemplifies the manner in which the Jews of Nazareth in his present day were understood and beheld through

---

[163] Goranson, "Joseph of Tiberias Episode," 73.
[164] Ibid., 112.

the lens of the Christian scriptural past. They were, as Jacobs incisively puts it, "part of the 'exhibit' itself."[165]

Conclusions: The Galilean Life-of-Jesus Churches

The fourth century saw a boom in the construction of life-of-Jesus churches in Galilee following on the heels of the advent of the Jerusalem-area commemorative churches. No commemorative churches in Galilee can be confidently dated prior to the construction of the Church of the Holy Sepulchre.[166] However, by the end of the fourth century, churches were erected in Galilee commemorating such events as the feeding of the five thousand, the delivery of the Sermon on the Mount, and the annunciation. Whether it was originally built as a *commemorative* church or not, the Church of the House of Peter certainly had a commemorative function and was closely tied to memories of Jesus' miracle-working ministry in Capernaum.

If the initial Constantinian trio of the Holy Sepulchre, Church of the Nativity, and Church of the Ascension formed an architectural instantiation of the Nicene Creed, what happened when the Galilean sites were added to that core? When all of the life-of-Jesus churches of fourth-century Palestine are considered together, we are presented with a mnemonic narrative, a sort of experiential gospel not penned in ink upon papyrus but in stone upon the Land itself. This represents an attempt by the imperial, orthodox Christianity of the fourth century to reconstruct its past in order to construct its present identity.[167] The selection and presentation of sites on which to build commemorative churches is itself a kind of history writing, the reconstruction of the life of Jesus through the erection of monuments, a history that could be consumed by locals and by pilgrims such as Egeria. This was. That selection process, with its apparent preference in the fourth century for sites with canonical basis, can be understood as official memory constructed by imperial, local, or ecclesiastical authorities as a means of asserting its influence on public memory. Nevertheless, we see vernacular memory at work alongside that official memory in the formation of public memory.

Some of the traditions attached to places that Egeria recounts in her travels in Galilee have no canonical or certain textual counterpart: she mentions a field where Jesus ate with his disciples and rested his arm upon a rock (*de loc. sanct.* P3), a mountain spring with healing properties that Jesus blessed (*de loc. sanct.* P3), and a story about a synagogue that Jesus cursed (*de loc. sanct.* V4). It is worth observing that, in these cases, the tradition is attached to a topographical marker or, in the case of the cursed synagogue, ruins that have become a part of the local landscape. However, no church instantiating official memory was constructed at any of these sites. It goes almost without saying that history writing through commemorative church building

---

[165] On this, see also Jacobs, "Visible Ghosts," 374.
[166] Although there is good reason to think that the Christian building at Capernaum that existed in the fourth century was in continuity with an earlier Christian gathering place that had existed on that site for centuries prior, it is not quite appropriate to call such a structure a commemorative church.
[167] On how societies reconstruct the past, see Kammen, *Mystic Chords of Memory*, 3.

is a selective process. Commemorative churches require funding, and authorities, whether local, episcopal, or imperial, select sites on which to construct them. Nevertheless, sites commemorating, preserving, inspiring, or facilitating traditions like these existed and were visited by pilgrims such as Egeria. This demonstrates that pilgrimage was one manner in which apocryphal traditions could be encountered and disseminated.

In general, traditions that can be traced to canonical sources lie at the core of the Galilean traditional sites that we have examined: the miracles in Capernaum, the multiplication of the bread and the loaves, and the annunciation to Mary. However, as we have seen with other sites, such as the Church of the Nativity, extracanonical traditions could also be represented and preserved or disseminated at sites with commemorative churches. This is exemplified by the extracanonical elements of the annunciation tradition that were represented within the space of the Church of the Annunciation.

The role of the Galilean life-of-Jesus commemorative sites within Jewish-Christian relations is complex[168] and is an area that could continue to benefit from further research. The presence of "Christian" sites commemorating the life-of-Jesus within locales with populations that were primarily Jewish, such as Capernaum and Nazareth, is a tacit acknowledgement of the Jewish roots of the Christian tradition and of its founder, Jesus of Nazareth. However, we have also seen some indications that the construction of a church such as the one at Nazareth may have been tied to attempts to stake a claim to the Jewish heritage of the Christian faith, and perhaps also to Jewish territory.

The situations at Capernaum and Nazareth are further complicated by questions about the dates of the sites and the religio-ethnic composition of the people who regularly used them. For Capernaum in particular, the fourth-century renovation of the "insula sacra" can be interpreted as renovations undertaken by a local community, who could have identified as both Jews and as Christ-followers that inhabited and used the site prior to the renovations.[169] Epiphanius' idea that there was no "church" at Capernaum before the mid-fourth century could be taken to mean that there was no *orthodox* church there, as understood by Epiphanius. The multilingual graffiti at the site could be evidence of outside visitors to the site (pilgrims) rather than as the work of the people who regularly and traditionally gathered there. A group of local Jewish Christ-followers would have related to the Jewish community of Capernaum in a very different way than a group of Gentile Christian pilgrims who had come from far-off regions might have. Local Jewish Christ-followers may have been perceived as a subset but part of the local Jewish community, whereas Gentile pilgrims from elsewhere would clearly be outsiders.

---

[168] See, e.g., Goranson, "Joseph of Tiberias Episode," Leyerle, "Landscape as Cartography," Jacobs, "Visible Ghosts," Runesson, "Architecture." More recently, see also Eyal Ben-Eliyahu, *Identity and Territory: Jewish Perceptions of Space in Antiquity* (Oakland: University of California Press, 2019), 110–54 (esp. 142–54). A promising project dealing with Jewish-Christian relations in Capernaum is also currently being undertaken by Wally V. Cirafesi.

[169] As convincingly argued by Runesson, "Architecture," 245–7.

The Galilean life-of-Jesus churches present us with more pieces of the puzzle that is the landscape of Jesus-memory and tradition in Eretz Israel-Palestine from the first to the fourth centuries. Their addition to the triad of the Sepulchre, Nativity, and Eleona-Ascension in the south and their inclusion on pilgrimage itineraries would have served to further round out the mnemonic, narrative role played by the pilgrims' encounter with sites connected to the story of Jesus' life.

7

Conclusion

Our study of the reception, memory, and commemoration of key places connected to the life of Jesus has revealed much about each individual site of memory. It has also revealed some broader trends and patterns that contribute intriguing new elements to our understanding of the reception of Jesus traditions in Palestine over the first few centuries of the Common Era. By tracking the reception histories of life-of-Jesus sites of memory from the time of the New Testament to the Constantinian age, we have seen that places connected to major events in the Jesus tradition took on theological, exegetical, and Christological significance. Place functions symbolically to denote meaning within the tradition. Often, places associated with key events in the life of Jesus took on significance beyond the events that they were primarily connected with. Golgotha became a representation of the Pauline Adam-Christ typology and a symbol of the redemptive power of Jesus' death for humanity. The tomb of Jesus was understood as the new Holy of Holies, which is reminiscent of the Christological imagery of Hebrews 9. The nativity cave at Bethlehem was the "high cave of the strong rock" of the messianic prophecy of LXX Isa 33:16. Jesus' ascension from the Mount of Olives was unfortunately leveraged for supersessionist ideology by Eusebius, who connected the site to the fall of Jerusalem in Zech 14:2–4, through the mention of the Mount of Olives in v. 4. These are just a few of the examples that we have seen, all of which point toward the theological, exegetical, and Christological meaning ascribed to and symbolized by these places in early Christian memory.

The places themselves were also widely understood to bear witness to the events that they commemorated. This is a natural function of commemorative sites. Visitors understood themselves to be able to stand where the feet of Jesus himself had stood, an idea further supported aided by the citation of LXX Ps 131:7 in connection with pilgrimage activities.[1] They were, to those who visited or frequented them, the very places where the foundational narrative of their faith happened. This contributed to identity formation, allowing pilgrims and the Christians of Palestine to define who they were in light of the narrative of the life of Jesus,[2] the foundational narrative of the Christian tradition. That foundational narrative was mediated and retold through the

---

[1] Eusebius, *Life of Constantine*, 3.42.2; Paulinus of Nola, *Ep.* 31.4.
[2] Foote and Azaryahu, "Geography of Memory," 127.

iconography, symbolism, liturgy, accreted traditions, and representation of the biblical narrative of the commemorative churches.

Our study has highlighted the ways in which places associated with important events in the life of Jesus could function as "sites of memory" (*lieux de mémoire*) well before official commemorative structures were built at them. Topographical features, such as caves, rocks,[3] and springs could attract commemorative activity without architecture. More importantly, places can attract memory without needing to be experienced in actual space and time. Sites like Golgotha and the Mount of Olives have a conceptual and literary existence as sites of memory beyond their physical, geographical presence. Places do not have to be physically experienced in order to be receptacles and vehicles for memory. The very idea of a place such as Golgotha can attract interpretation and create meaning.

Places connected to the life of Jesus in Christian memory often functioned as vehicles and receptacles for the preservation of traditions, both canonical and apocryphal. Golgotha was widely remembered as the place where Adam was buried as well as the site of Jesus' crucifixion; Jesus' birthplace was associated with a cave as per the infancy narrative of the *Protevangelium of James*; and details of the Church of the Annunciation at Nazareth similarly drew on traditional elements found in the *Protevangelium of James* but not in the canonical narratives. In the cases of the tradition of Adam's burial at Golgotha and the nativity cave at Bethlehem, these traditional elements were associated with these places prior to the construction of the Constantinian commemorative churches. Other minor extracanonical traditions that we have observed include such things as the imprint of Jesus' feet being stamped into the rock of the Mount of Olives as he ascended from there, and the notion that Jesus performed the multiplication of the fish and the loaves on a stone table. The minor sites in Galilee mentioned by Egeria that were marked only by a topographical feature, including the field in which Jesus ate with his disciples and rested his arm on a rock (*de loc. sanct.* P3), the mountain stream that Jesus blessed (*de loc. sanct.* P3), and the ruined synagogue that Jesus cursed (*de loc. sanct.* V4) are all further examples of apocryphal traditions attached to places that were encountered and disseminated through the commemorative activity of pilgrimage. It does seem as though, in the fourth century at least, identified places connected to traditions whose core stemmed from the canonical narrative were preferred as sites for commemorative church building. This is perhaps the result of official memory, constructed by ecclesiastical and imperial authority, asserting itself in the formation of public memory. However, this did not stop monuments from including elements drawn from extracanonical traditions. Nor did it prevent extracanonical traditions from attaching themselves to places, even

---

[3] As at Tabgha. Moreover, although we have not discussed it at length in this work, the commemorative "hanging chapel" at Kursi, which is traditionally associated with the exorcism of the "Gerasene" demoniac and the subsequent miracle of the swine (Mark 5:1–20; cf. Matt 8:28–34 and Luke 8:26–39), appeared to include a large rock, which was the focus of commemorative activity. See Vassilios Tzaferis, *The Excavations of Kursi-Gergesa* (Jerusalem: Israel Exploration Society, 1983), esp. 49–51; Tzaferis, "The Early Christian Monastery at Kursi," 77–9 (79); Pixner, *Paths of the Messiah*, 152–5. That the rock was the focus of commemorative activity even before the chapel was built is suggested by Origen, *Commentary on John*, 6.24 (on John 1:28).

when such traditions were not explicitly reflected in the architecture. We are reminded especially here of the popularity of the tradition of Adam's burial at Golgotha, despite no architecture or space being dedicated to Adam in the Church of the Holy Sepulchre until the time of Modestus. Contemporary readers who have visited Israel-Palestine in our own times are likely well aware that life-of-Jesus sites still have a tendency to attract and accrete satellite traditions, most of which are extracanonical. Indeed, some traditions that are passed on to pilgrims today are the same very that were passed on to their spiritual forebears in antiquity.

Furthermore, the precise geographical location of a site identified as the setting of an event in the life of Jesus could be considered extracanonical. This is particularly true of sites such as the traditional site of the delivery of the beatitudes, or the site of the miracle of the multiplication of the fish and loaves at Tabgha. In these cases, the traditional site actually appears to disagree with the canonical accounts. The location of the multiplication of the fish and loaves at Tabgha is a complicated matter and is difficult to comprehend. However, the location of the Chapel of the Beatitudes is likely meant to be an ingenious attempt at harmonizing the Matthean Sermon on the Mount and the Lukan Sermon on the Plain. In both cases, the location of the traditional site provides additional information about the site not clearly indicated by the canonical narratives, and in the case of the Chapel of the Beatitudes, the traditional site attempts to clarify an interpretive difficulty.

The architecture of commemorative churches built at sites connected to events in the life of Jesus communicates meaning and requires interpretation as much as the literary evidence does. By considering the iconography of the architecture of a commemorative church, and approaching it as a monument intended to convey meaning that can be grasped and interpreted, we have seen how architecture contributes to the reception of Jesus. Architecture can contribute theological, historical, and political claims about Jesus. This is especially acute in the Church of the Holy Sepulchre, which enshrined and remembered the places of Jesus' crucifixion and burial using imperial forms mixed with inspiration drawn from biblical architecture. The use of public scripture reading, teaching, and liturgy within the space of the earliest commemorative churches would have provided guidance to help visitors and congregants to interpret the place. Guides and guidebooks (such as the *Breviarius*) may have also facilitated interpretation.

The monuments dedicated to events in the life of Jesus were not politically neutral. The interpretation of Jesus presented especially by the Constantinian commemorative churches was bound up with imperial ideology. As we have seen, the Church of the Holy Sepulchre, the monument to the resurrection of Jesus, commemorated not only the victory of Jesus over death but also the victory of Constantine over his political opponents. The joint celebration of the dedication of this central shrine and Constantine's tricenalia is surely significant and demonstrates the degree to which the Constantinian monuments commemorated their imperial builder alongside Jesus of Nazareth. Memory of Jesus could be co-opted for the purposes of political propaganda.

Our study has also highlighted the complex interface between the memory of Jesus through place and Jewish-Christian relations. Commemorative activity helped the Christian communities of Palestine as well as pilgrims from abroad to define and form their identity in light of the movement's origins in the "Holy Land" and in relationship to the life of the movement's founder, Jesus of Nazareth. In the context of Jerusalem, the construction of the commemorative churches fed into the supersessionist "New Jerusalem" ideology of the triumph of Christianity over Judaism. This was reflected in the very architecture of the Church of the Holy Sepulchre, which presented itself as a new Jerusalem Temple, its splendor intentionally contrasted with the barrenness of Mount Moriah. The combination of the Church of the Nativity with the Davidic tomb at Bethlehem on pilgrim itineraries presented a tacit claim to the Christian inheritance of David's legacy. At Nazareth, the construction of the small but nevertheless monumental Church of the Annunciation in a small Jewish village may have functioned in part as an acknowledgment of Jesus' Jewish roots, but it was also as a claim upon Jewish territory.

This study has been selective. The data pool is both deep and rich. Due to the constraints of time and space, there are a number of places that could have been explored but were not. For example, the Cenacle and the memory of the Upper Room,[4] Kursi and the memory of the miracle of the swine, and the Tomb of Lazarus come to mind as examples of places that might have more to contribute to our knowledge and understanding of the memory of Jesus in place, pilgrimage, and early holy sites. Although we have examined a broad swathe of evidence in this study, we have only just scratched the surface of what the data has to offer. Further research might also examine the sum total of traditions and life-of-Jesus commemorative sites mentioned in pilgrim itineraries to try to discern what sort of narrative and memory of Jesus' life emerges from them.

What can we reiterate about the Jesus constructed and remembered by the *lieux de mémoire* that we have examined in this study? Much has been covered up to this point, but we may mention just a few things here. The Jesus remembered by the *lieux de mémoire* is the incarnate Son of God, the Messiah of Israel and heir to David's legacy. He was the new Adam, and his emotionally impactful death was understood as a sacrifice offered by himself, and his blood washed away the sin of humanity, represented by Adam. The Jesus remembered by the *lieux de mémoire* is the risen Jesus, who triumphed over death. This Jesus ascended from the Mount of Olives, which was understood by Eusebius as a sign of the judgment of the "old" Jewish Jerusalem of Jesus' day (*Dem. Evang.* 6.18.29, combining Zech 14:1–4 and Ezek 11:22–23). This same Jesus also taught his followers on the same mountain about the coming fall of Jerusalem. He was a miracle worker who hailed from Nazareth Galilee, who healed the sick and fed the hungry by the Sea of Galilee. These memories are expressed by our *lieux de mémoire* through a combination of architecture, liturgy, pilgrimage, patristic exegesis, and other similar modes of communication.

As previous scholarship has already determined, the Jesus of the Constantinian triad of the Church of the Holy Sepulchre, the Church of the Nativity, and the Church of the Ascension is the "Lord Jesus Christ" of the Nicene Creed. The core events commemorated by those three monuments are the very same biographical details found in the Nicene Creed of 325. They include the incarnation ("[he] came down and was incarnate and was made man"), the passion ("he suffered"), the resurrection ("he

---

[4] Our understanding of this site has lately been advanced by a recent study, David Christian Clausen, *The Upper Room and the Tomb of David* (Jefferson: McFarland, 2016).

Figure 9 The modern Church of the Holy Sepulchre.
Source: Photo courtesy of Anders Runesson.

rose again"), and the ascension ("[he] ascended into heaven"). However, by the close of the fourth century, other monuments commemorating more events in the life of Jesus were added to these three. As a result, the narrative experienced by the pilgrims who visited the life-of-Jesus churches of Palestine was much expanded beyond the biographical details of the Creed, all of which were situated in the Jerusalem area. The addition in particular of the Galilean commemorative churches presented a fuller narrative of Jesus' life and ministry, including his Galilean miracle-working ministry. Egeria also indicates that Jesus' synagogue ministry was remembered in some form in fourth-century Capernaum (*de loc. sanct.* V3). The inclusion of these traditions resulted in a narrative told by the sum of commemorative churches that approximated a specific retelling of the life of Jesus, a novel sort of "gospel," one that was written in stone upon the land rather than in ink upon the page, telling a narrative that could be experienced through the senses by those who visited them.

Gallery of Additional Photos

Figure 10 Façade of the Church of the Holy Sepulchre.
Source: Photo courtesy of the author.

Figure 11 The Anastasis and Aedicule in the modern Church of the Holy Sepulchre.
Source: Photo courtesy of the author.

Figure 12 The Chapel of Adam.
Source: Photo courtesy of the author.

Figure 13 Heavily reconstructed stairway from the monumental entrance to the Constantinian Church of the Holy Sepulchre in the Russian Hospice in Jerusalem.

Source: Photo courtesy of the author.

Figure 14 The modern Church of the Nativity.
Source: Photo courtesy of Anders Runesson.

Figure 15 Interior of the Church of the Nativity.
Source: Photo courtesy of Anders Runesson.

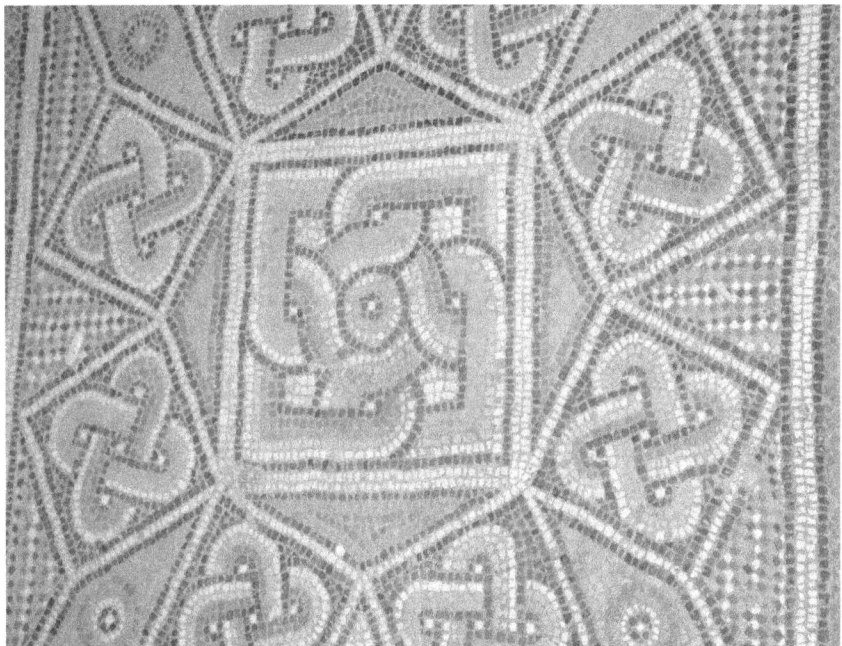

Figure 16 Mosaic floor beneath the current floor of the Church of the Nativity.
Source: Photo courtesy of the author.

Figure 17 Reconstructed façade of the Eleona.
Source: Photo courtesy of the author.

Figure 18 Reconstructed interior of the Eleona (now the Pater Noster Church).
Source: Photo courtesy of the author.

Figure 19 Reconstructed Apse of the Eleona.
Source: Photo courtesy of the author.

Gallery of Additional Photos 231

Figure 20 Grotto of the Eleona.
Source: Photo courtesy of the author.

Figure 21 The Chapel of the Ascension.
Source: Photo courtesy of the author.

Figure 22 Remains of the Byzantine Church of the Ascension (Imbomon).
Source: Photo courtesy of the author.

Figure 23 Jesus' footprint in the Chapel of the Ascension.
Source: Photo courtesy of the author.

Figure 24 Modern Church of the Multiplication interior, Tabgha (based on the plan of the fifth-century Church of the Multiplication).

Source: Photo courtesy of the author.

Figure 25 The altar and "holy rock" at the Church of the Multiplication, Tabgha.

Source: Photo courtesy of the author.

Figure 26 Archaeological remains of the ancient Church of the Annunciation in the modern-day Basilica of the Annunciation.

Source: Photo courtesy of the author.

Bibliography

Abel, Félix-Marie. "Mont des Oliviers: ruine de la grotte de L'Éléona." *Revue Biblique* 27 (1914): 55–8.
Adelman, Rachel. *The Return of the Repressed: Pirqe De-Rabbi Elizer and the Pseudepigrapha*. JSJSupp 140. Leiden: Brill, 2009.
Africanus, Julius. *Chronographiae*. Edited by Martin Wallraff. Die Griechischen Christlichen Schriftsteller der ersten Jahrhunderte Neue Folge 15. Berlin: Walter de Gruyter, 2007.
Ahmed, Sara. *The Cultural Politics of Emotion*. Edinburgh: Edinburgh University Press, 2004.
Alexander, Philip S. "Jerusalem as the *Omphalos* of the World: On the History of a Geographical Concept." *Judaism* 46, no. 2 (1997): 147–58.
Alexander, Loveday. "Memory and Tradition in the Hellenistic Schools." Pages 113–54 in *Jesus and Memory*. Edited by Werner H. Kelber and Samuel Byrskog. Waco: Baylor, 2009.
Allert, Craig D. *Revelation, Truth, Canon and Interpretation: Studies in Justin Martyr's Dialogue with Trypho*. Supplements to Vigilae Christianae 64. Leiden: Brill, 2002.
Amar, Joseph. P., trans. *A Metrical Homily on Holy Mar Ephrem by Mar Jacob of Serugh*. Turnhout: Brepols, 1995.
Anderson, F. I. "2 (Slavonic Apocalypse of) Enoch." Pages 1: 91–221 in *The Old Testament Pseudepigrapha*. 2 vols. Edited by James J. Charlesworth. Peabody: Hendrickson, 1983.
Angeloni, Alessandra. "The Interpretation of Wall Stratigraphy of the North Transept of the Holy Sepulchre in Jerusalem." Pages 47–67 in *Jerusalem – The Holy Sepulchre: Research and Investigations (2007–2011)*. Edited by Grazia Tucci. Florence: Altralinea Edizioni, 2019.
Angeloni, Alessandra, and Carmelo Pappalardo. "The Archaeological and Historical Context of the Basilica of the Holy Sepulchre in Jerusalem." Pages 25–45 in *Jerusalem – The Holy Sepulchre: Research and Investigations (2007–2011)*. Edited by Grazia Tucci. Florence: Altralinea Edizioni, 2019.
Apostolopoulou, M., E. T. Delegou, Emm. Alexakis, M. Kalofonou, K. C. Lampropoulos, E. Aggelakopoulou, A. Bakolas, and A. Moropoulou. "Study of the Historical Mortars of the Holy Aedicule as a Basis for the Design, Application and Assessment of Repair Mortars: A Multispectral Approach Applied on the Holy Aedicule." *Construction & Building Materials* 181 (2018): 618–37.
Apowitzer, Victor. "Les Elements Juifs dans la legend du Golgotha." *REJ* (1924): 145–62.
Arav, Rami. "Bethsaida – A Response to Steven Notley." *Near Eastern Archaeology* 72, no. 2 (2011): 92–100.
Armstrong, Gregory T. "Constantine's Churches: Symbol and Structure." *Journal of the Society of Architectural Historians* 33, no. 1 (1974): 5–16.
Armstrong, Jonathan J., trans. "Translator's Introduction." Pages xxvii–xxix in *Eusebius of Caesarea: Commentary on Isaiah*. Edited by Joel C. Elowsky. Ancient Christian Texts. Downers Grove: IVP Academic, 2013.

Attridge, Harold W. "Melchizedek in Some Early Christian Texts and 2 Enoch." Pages 387–410 in *New Perspectives on 2 Enoch: No Longer Slavonic Only*. Edited by Andrei A. Orlov and Gabriele Boccaccini. Associate Editor Jason Zurawski. Studia Judaeoslavica 4. Leiden: Brill, 2012.

Avi-Yonah, Michael. "Editor's Note." *Israel Exploration Journal* 23 (1973): 43–5.

Aviam, Mordechai, and Jacob Ashkenazi. "Late Antique Pilgrim Monasteries in Galilean *Loca Sancta*." *Liber Annuus* 64 (2014): 559–73.

Avigad, Nahman. *Discovering Jerusalem*. Nashville: Nelson, 1983.

Babinger, Franz. "Alfons Maria Schneider (1896-1952)." *Zeitschrift der Deutschen Morgenländischen Gesellschaft* 103 (1953): 1–8.

Bacci, Michele. *The Mystic Cave: A History of the Nativity Church in Bethlehem*. Conviva 1. Viella: Masaryk University, 2017.

Bacci, Michele, Giovanna Bianchi, Stefano Campana, and Giuseppe Fichera. "Historical and Archaeological Analysis of the Church of the Nativity." *Journal of Cultural Heritage* 13 (2012): 5–26.

Bagatti, Bellarmino. "La cappella sul monte delle Beatitudini." *Revista d'Archeologia Cristiana* 14 (1937): 43–91.

Bagatti, Bellarmino. *Gli antichi edifice sacri di Betlemme in seguito agli scavi e restauri practicati dalla Custodia di Terra Santa (1948-1951)*. Jerusalem: Franciscan Printing Press, 1952.

Bagatti, Bellarmino. "Recenti Scavi a Betlemme." *Liber Annuus* 18 (1968): 181–237.

Bagatti, Bellarmino. *Excavations in Nazareth*. 2 vols. Translated by Eugenio Hoade. Publications of the Studium Biblicum Franciscanum 17. Jerusalem: Franciscan Printing Press, 1969.

Bagatti, Bellarmino. "Note sull'iconografia di Adamo sotto il Calvario." *Liber Annuus* 27 (1977): 5–32.

Bagatti, Bellarmino. *The Church from the Gentiles in Palestine: History and Archaeology*. Repr. ed. Translated by Eugene Hoade. SBF Collectio Minor 4. Jerusalem: Franciscan Printing Press, [1970] 1984.

Bagatti, Bellarmino. *Ancient Christian Villages of Galilee*. Jerusalem: Franciscan Printing Press, 2001.

Bagatti, Bellarmino. *The Church from the Circumcision: History and Archaeology of the Judaeo-Christians*. Repr. ed. Translated by Eugene Hoade. Jerusalem: Franciscan Printing Press, [1971] 2004.

Bagatti, Bellarmino, and Emmanuel Testa. *Il Golgota e la Croce: ricerche storico-archeologiche*. Collectio Minor 21. Jerusalem: Franciscan Printing Press, 1978.

Bain, Andrew M. *Passion and Resurrection Narratives: Post-Nicene Latin Interpretations*. Eugene: Wipf and Stock, 2018.

Baker, Margaret. "Jerusalem the Golden: Vision and Memory of the Church." *Journal for the Study of the Christian Church* 5, no. 1 (2005): 1–10.

Barkley, Gary Wayne, trans. *Origen: Homilies on Leviticus*, The Fathers of the Church. Washington, DC: Catholic University of America Press, 1990.

Barnes, T. D. "The Composition of Eusebius' *Onomasticon*." *JTS* 26, no. 2 (1975): 412–15.

Barrett, C. K. *The Gospel According to St. John*. 2nd ed. Philadelphia: Westminster, 1978.

Barton, John. *Holy Writings, Sacred Text: The Canon in Early Christianity*. Louisville: Westminster John Knox, 1997.

Barzun, Jacques, and Henry F. Graff. "A Medley of Mysteries: A Number of Dogs That Didn't Bark." Pages 213–31 in *The Historian as Detective: Essays on Evidence*. Edited by Robin W. Winks. New York: Harper Torchbooks, 1970.

Ben-Eliyahu, Eyal. *Identity and Territory: Jewish Perceptions of Space in Antiquity.* Oakland: University of California Press, 2019.

Bernabei, Mauro, and Jarno Bontadi. "Dendochronological Analysis of the Timber Structure of the Church of the Nativity in Bethlehem." *Journal of Cultural Heritage* 13 (2012): 54–60.

Betz, Hans Dieter. "Hero Worship and Christian Beliefs: Observations from the History of Religion on Philostratus's Heroikos." Pages 25–47 in *Philostratus's Heroikos: Religion and Cultural Identity in the Third Century C.E.* Edited by Ellen Bradshaw Aitken and Jennifer K. Berenson MacLean. Society of Biblical Literature Writings from the Greco-Roman World 6. Leiden: Brill, 2004.

Biddle, Martin. *The Tomb of Christ.* Stroud: Sutton, 2000.

Bildstein, Moshe B. "Polemics against Death Defilement in Third-Century Christian Sources." Pages 373–84 in *Studia Patristica Vol. LXIII.* Edited by Markus Vinzent. Leuven: Peeters, 2013.

Bildstein, Moshe B. *Purity, Community, and Ritual in Early Christianity. Oxford Studies in the Abrahamic Religions.* Oxford: Oxford University Press, 2017.

Binder, Donald D. *Into the Temple Courts.* Atlanta: SBL Press, 1998.

Bloch, Marc. *The Historian's Craft.* Translated by Peter Putnam. New York: Alfred A. Knopf, 1953.

Bloedhorn, Hanswulf. "Die Eleona und das Imbomon in Jerusalem: eine Doppelkirchenanlage auf dem Ölberg?" Pages 568–71 in *Akten des XII internationalen Kongresses für christliche Archäologie.* Edited by Ernst Dassmann and Josef Engemann. Vatican City: Pontificio Istituto di Archeologia Cristiana, 1995.

Bock, Darrell L. *Luke.* 2 vols. BECNT. Grand Rapids: Baker, 1994.

Bodnar, John. *Remaking America: Public Memory, Commemoration, and Patriotism in the Twentieth Century.* Princeton: Princeton University Press, 1992.

Boomer, Megan, and Robert G. Ousterhout. "The Church of the Holy Sepulchre." Pages 169–84 in *Routledge Handbook on Jerusalem.* Edited by Suleiman A. Mourad, Naomi Koltun-Fromm, and Bedross Der Matossian. New York: Routledge, 2018.

Böttrich, Christfried. *Weltweisheit, Menschheitsethik, Urkult: Studien zum slavischen Henochbuch.* WUNT R.2, 50. Tübingen: Mohr Siebeck, 1992.

Böttrich, Christfried. "The 'Book of the Secrets of Enoch' (2 En): Between Jewish Origin and Christian Transmission." Pages 37–67 in *New Perspectives on 2 Enoch: No Longer Slavonic Only.* Edited by Andrei A. Orlov and Gabriele Boccaccini. Associate Editor Jason Zurawski. Studia Judaeoslavica 4. Leiden: Brill, 2012.

Bovon, François. "The Suspension of Time in Chapter 18 of the Protevangelium of Jacobi." Pages 393–405 in *The Future of Early Christianity: Essays in Honour of Helmut Koester.* Edited by Birger A. Pearson. Minneapolis: Fortress, 1991.

Bradshaw, Paul F. *Daily Prayer in the Early Church: A Study of the Origin and Early Development of the Divine Office.* Repr. ed. Eugene: Wipf and Stock, 1981.

Broadhurst, Laurence. "Melito of Sardis, the Second Sophistic, and 'Israel.'" Pages 49–74 in *Rhetoric and Reality in Early Christianities.* Edited by Willi Braun. Waterloo: Wilfred Laurier University Press, 2005.

Brock, Sebastian P. "The Transmission of Ephrem's *madrashe* in the Syriac Liturgical Tradition." Pages 490–505 in *Studia Patristica* 33. Edited by E. A. Livingstone. Leuven: Peeters, 1997.

Broshi, Magen, and Gabriel Barkay. "Excavations in the Chapel of St. Vartan in the Church of the Holy Sepulchre." *IEJ* 35, no. 2 (1985): 108–28.

Brown, Raymond E. *The Birth of the Messiah: A Commentary on the Infancy Narratives in Matthew and Luke*. Garden City: Image, 1979.
Brown, Raymond E. "The Burial of Jesus (Mark 15:42–47)." *CBQ* 50, no. 2 (1988): 238–45.
Brown, Raymond E. *The Death of the Messiah*. 2 vols. ABRL. New York: Doubleday, 1994.
Bruner, Frederick Dale. *The Gospel of John: A Commentary*. Grand Rapids: Eerdmans, 2012.
Butz, Eva-Maria, and Alfons Zettler. "Pilgrim's Devotion?: Christian Graffiti from Antiquity to the Middle Ages." Pages 141–64 in *Travel, Pilgrimage and Social Interaction from Antiquity to the Middle Ages*. Edited by Jenni Kuuliala and Jussi Rantala. New York: Routledge, 2020.
Cain, Andrew. *Jerome's Epitaph on Paula: A Commentary on the Epitaphum Sanctae Paulae*. Oxford Early Christian Texts. Oxford: Oxford University Press, 2013.
Cameron, Averil, and Stuart G. Hall. *Life of Constantine*. Clarendon Ancient History Series. Oxford: Clarendon Press, 1999.
Carroll, John T. *Luke: A Commentary*. NTL. Louisville: Westminster John Knox, 2012.
Carson, D. A. *The Gospel According to John*. PNTC. Grand Rapids: Eerdmans, 1991.
Cary, Earnest, trans. *Dio Cassius: Roman History*. 9 vols. Loeb Classical Library. New York: Macmillan, 1914–27.
Catto, Stephen K. *Reconstructing the First-Century Synagogue: A Critical Analysis of Current Research*. LNTS 363. London: T&T Clark, 2007.
Chadwick, Henry, trans. *Origen: Contra Celsum*. Cambridge: Cambridge University Press, 1953.
Clausen, David Christian. *The Upper Room and the Tomb of David*. Jefferson: McFarland, 2016.
Cohick, Lynn H. "Melito of Sardis's *PERI PASCHA* and Its 'Israel'." *Harvard Theological Review* 91, no. 4 (1998): 351–72.
Cohick, Lynn H. *The Peri Pascha Attributed to Melito of Sardis: Setting, Purpose, and Sources*. Brown Judaic Studies 327. Providence: Brown Judaic Studies, 2000.
Collingwood, R. G. *The Idea of History*. Rev. and enl. ed. Edited by Jan van der Dussen. Oxford: Clarendon Press, [1946] 1993.
Connerton, Paul. *How Societies Remember*. Cambridge: Cambridge University Press, 1989.
Corbo, Virgilio. "Gli edifici della Santa Anastasi a Gerusalemme." *Liber Annuus* 12 (1962): 221–316.
Corbo, Virgilio C. *Richerche archeologiche al Monte degli Ulivi*. Publications of the Studium Biblicum Franciscanum 16. Jerusalem: Franciscan Printing Press, 1965.
Corbo, Virgilio. *The House of Saint Peter at Capharnaum*. Translated by Sylvester Saller. Jerusalem: Franciscan Printing Press, 1972.
Corbo, Virgilio C. *Cafarnao I: Gli edifice della città*. Jerusalem: Franciscan Printing Press, 1975.
Corbo, Virgilio C. *Il Santo sepolcro di Gerusalemme*. 3 vols. Jerusalem: Franciscan Printing Press, 1981–2.
Corbo, Virgilio. "A proposito di presunti scavi stratigrafici al S. Sepolcro." *Liber Annuus* 34 (1984): 409–16.
Corbo, Virgilio, and Eugenio Alliata. "La chiesa-sinagoga dell'annonziata a Nazaret." *Liber Annuus* 37 (1987): 335–48.
Corke-Webster, James. *Eusebius and Empire: Constructing Church and Rome in the Ecclesiastical History*. Cambridge: Cambridge University Press, 2019.
Coüasnon, Charles. *The Church of the Holy Sepulchre in Jerusalem*. Translated by John-Paul Beverley and Claude Ross. New York: Oxford University Press, 1974.

Curtis, John Briggs. "An Investigation of the Mount of Olives in the Judaeo-Christian Tradition." *Hebrew Union College Annual* 28 (1957): 137–80.
Czachesz, István. *Commission Narratives: A Comparative Study of the Canonical and Apocryphal Acts*. Studies on Early Christian Apocrypha 8. Leuven: Peeters, 2007.
Cyril of Alexandria. *Commentary on the Gospel of St. Luke*. Translated by R. Payne Smith. Long Island: Studion, 1983.
Dalman, Gustaf. *Arbeit und Sitte in Palästina*. Band VI. Zeltleben, Vieh- und Milchwirtshaft, *Jagd, Fischfang*. Hildeshiem: Olms, [1939] 1987.
Dark, Ken. *Roman-Period and Byzantine Nazareth and Its Hinterland*. Abingdon: Routledge, 2020.
Davidson Kelly, John Norman. *Jerome: His Life, Writings, and Controversies*. New York: Duckworth, 1975.
Davies, Penelope J. E. *Death and the Emperor: Roman Imperial Funerary Monuments from Augustus to Marcus Aurelius*. Austin: University of Texas Press, 2004.
de Blaauw, Sible. "The Church Atrium as a Ritual Space: The Cathedral of Tyre and St Peter's in Rome." Pages 30–43 in *Ritual and Space in the Middle Ages*. Edited by Frances Andrews, Harlaxton Medieval Studies 21. Lincolnshire: Paul Watkins, 2011.
de Jonge, Marinus. "The Literary Development of the *Life of Adam and Eve*." Pages 239–49 in *Literature on Adam & Eve: Collected Essays*. Edited by Gary Anderson, Michael Stone, and Johannes Tromp. Leiden: Brill, 2000.
de Jonge, Marinus. *Pseudepigrapha of the Old Testament as Part of Christian Literature: The Case of the* Testaments of the Twelve Patriarchs *and the* Greek Life of Adam and Eve. Leiden: Brill, 2003.
de Jonge, Marinus, and Johannes Tromp. *The Life of Adam and Eve and Related Literature*. Guides to Apocrypha and Pseudepigrapha. Sheffield: Sheffield Academic, 1997.
De Luca, Stefano. "Capernaum." Pages 1: 168–78 in *The Oxford Encyclopedia of the Bible and Archaeology*. Edited by Daniel M. Master. New York: Oxford University Press, 2013.
del Álamo, Elizabeth Valdez. "The Iconography of Architecture." Pages 377–89 in *The Routledge Companion to Medieval Iconography*. Edited by Colum Hourihane. London: Routledge, 2016.
de Strycker, Émile. *La forme la plus ancienne du Protévangile de Jacques*. Subsidia Hagiographica 33. Bruxelles: Société des Bollandists, 1961.
Devos, Paul. "Le date due voyage d'Égérie." *Analecta Bollandiana* 85 (1967): 165–94.
Dochhorn, Jan. *Die Apokalypse des Mose*. Tübingen: Mohr Siebeck, 2005.
Dodd, C. H. *Historical Tradition in the Fourth Gospel*. Cambridge: Cambridge University Press, 1963.
Donner, Herbert. *The Mosaic Map of Madaba: An Introductory Guide*. Palaestina Antiqua 7. Kampen: Pharos, 1992.
Donohoe, Janet. *Remembering Places: A Phenomenological Study of the Relationship between Memory and Place*. Lanham: Lexington, 2014.
Douglass, Laurie. "A New Look at the *Itinerarium Burdigalense*." *JECS* 4 (1996): 313–33.
Doval, Alexis James. *Cyril of Jerusalem, Mystagogue: The Authorship of the Mystagogic Catecheses*. Patristic Monograph Series 17. Washington, DC: Catholic University of America Press, 2001.
Dow, Lois Katherine. "Eternal Jerusalem: Jerusalem/Zion in Biblical Theology with Special Attention to 'New Jerusalem' as the Name for the Final State in Revelation 21–22." PhD diss., McMaster Divinity College, 2008.

Drake, H. A. "When Was the 'De Laudibus Constantini' Delivered?" *Historia* 24, no. 2 (1975): 345–56.
Drake, H. A. *In Praise of Constantine: A Historical Study and New Translation of Eusebius' Tricennial Orations*. Classical Studies 15. Berkeley: University of California Publications, 1976.
Drijvers, Jan Willem. *Cyril of Jerusalem: Bishop and City*. Supplements to Vigiliae Christianae. Leiden: Brill, 2004.
Drobner, Hubertus R. "Eine pseudo-athanasianische Osterpredigt (CPG II. 2247) über die Wahrheit Gottes und ihre Erfüllung." Pages 43–51 in *Christian Faith and Greek Philosophy in Late Antiquity*. Edited by Lionel R. Wickham, Caroline P. Ammel, assisted by Erica C.D. Hunter. Leiden: Brill, 1993.
Dunn, James D. G. *Jesus Remembered*. Christianity in the Making 1. Grand Rapids: Eerdmans, 2003.
Eastman, David L. "Martyria." Pages 89–104 in *The Oxford Handbook of Early Christian Archaeology*. Edited by David K. Pettigrew, William R. Caraher, and Thomas W. Davis. Oxford: Oxford University Press, 2019.
Edwards, James R. *The Gospel According to Luke*. PNTC. Grand Rapids: Eerdmans, 2015.
Elowsky, Joel C., ed. *John 11–21*. Ancient Christian Commentary on Scripture 4b. Downers Grove: InterVarsity Press, 2007.
Esche, Sigrid. *Adam und Eva: Sündenfall und Erlösung*. Düsseldorf: L. Schwann, 1957.
Etheridge, John Wesley. *The Targums of Onkelos and Jonathan ben Uzziel on the Pentateuch: With the Fragments of the Jerusalem Targum from the Chaldee*. London: Longman, Green, Longman, and Roberts, 1862.
Evans, Craig A. *Matthew*. NCBC. Cambridge: Cambridge University Press, 2012.
Falls, Thomas B., trans. *Saint Justin Martyr: The First Apology, The Second Apology, Dialogue With Trypho, Exhortation to the Greeks, Discourse to the Greeks, The Monarchy or the Rule of God*. The Fathers of the Church 6. Repr. ed. Washington, DC: Catholic University of America Press, [1948] 2008.
Ferrar, W. J., trans. *The Proof of the Gospel*. 2 vols. Eugene: Wipf and Stock, [1920] 2001.
Fiensy, David A. "The Galilean House in the Late Second Temple and Mishnaic Periods." Pages 216–41 in *Galilee in the Late Second Temple and Mishnaic Periods*. Vol. 1. *Life, Culture, and Society*. Edited by David A. Fiensy and James Riley Strange. Minneapolis: Fortress, 2014.
Fine, Steven. "'For the Glory of the Holy House': The Sardis Synagogue and the History of Judaism in Roman Antiquity." In *The Synagogue at Sardis, Sardis Report* 9. Edited by Andrew Seager, Marcus L. Rautman, and Vanessa Rousseau. Cambridge, MA: Harvard University Press, 2021.
Finkelstein, Ari. *The Specter of the Jews: Emperor Julian and the Rhetoric of Ethnicity in Syrian Antioch*. Oakland: University of California Press, 2018.
Fitzmyer, Joseph A. *The Gospel According to Luke*. 3 vols. AYB 28. New York: Doubleday, 1981.
Fokkelman, Jan. *Reading Biblical Narrative: A Practical Guide*. Leiden: Deo, 1999.
Foote, Kenneth E., and Maoz Azaryahu. "Toward a Geography of Memory: Geographical Dimensions of Public Memory and Commemoration." *Journal of Political and Military Sociology* 35, no. 1 (2007): 125–44.
Foreman, Benjamin A. "Luke's Birth Narrative: Reconstructing the Real Story." Pages 10–18 in *Lexham Geographic Commentary on the Gospels*. Edited by Barry J. Beitzel. Bellingham: Lexham Press, [2016] 2017.

Foreman, Benjamin A. "Matthew's Birth Narrative." Pages 19–29 in *Lexham Geographic Commentary on the Gospels*. Edited by Barry J. Beitzel. Bellingham: Lexham Press, [2016] 2017.

Foster, Paul, trans. *The Gospel of Peter: Introduction, Critical Edition and Commentary*. TENT 4. Leiden: Brill, 2010.

France, R. T. *The Gospel of Mark: A Commentary on the Greek Text*. NIGTC. Grand Rapids: Eerdmans, 2002.

Franz, Gordon. "The Feedings of the Multitudes: When, Where, and Why?" N.p. in *Lexham Geographic Commentary on the Gospels*. Edited by Barry J. Beitzel and Kristopher A. Lyle. Bellingham: Lexham, [2016] 2017.

Freeman-Grenville, G. S. P., Rupert L. Chapman III, and Joan E. Taylor, eds. *The Onomasticon by Eusebius of Caesarea*. Jerusalem: Carta, 2003.

Fremantle, W. H. *St. Jerome: Letters and Select Works*. NPNF 2.6. New York: Christian Literature, 1892.

Frost, Warwick, and Jenny Laing. *Commemorative Events: Memory, Identities, Conflicts*. London: Routledge, 2013.

Gafni, Isaiah. *Jews and Judaism in the Rabbinic Era: Image and Reality – History and Historiography*. TSAJ 173. Tübingen: Mohr Siebeck, 2019.

Garbarino, Osvaldo. "Il Santo Sepolcro di Gerusalemme. Appunti di ricercar storico-architettonica." *Liber Annuus* 55 (2005): 239–314.

Gauer, B. "Ein neuer Fund in der Brotvermehrungskirche zu Tabgha." *Das Heilige Land* 80 (1936): 60.

Georgopoulos, A., E. Lambrou, G. Pantazis, P. Agrafiotis, A. Papadaki, L. Kotoula, K. Lampropoulos, E. Delegou, M. Apostolopoulou, M. Alexakis, and A. Moropoulou. "Merging Geometric Documentation with Materials Characterization and Analysis of the History of the Holy Aedicule in the Church of the Holy Sepulchre in Jerusalem." *The International Archives of the Photogrammetry, Remote Sensing and Spatial Information Sciences* 42, no. 5 (2017): 487–94.

Gerding, Henrik. "The Tomb of Caecilia Metella: Tumulus, Tropaeum and Thymele." PhD diss., Lund University, Lund, 2010.

Gervers, Michael. "The Iconography of the Cave in Christian and Mithraic Tradition." Pages 579–99 in *Mysteria Mithrae*. Edited by Ugo Bianchi. Études préliminaires aux religions orientales dans l'Empire romain 80. Leiden: Brill, 1979.

Giblin, Charles Homer. "Reflections on the Sign of the Manger." *CBQ* 29 (1967): 87–101.

Gibson, Jennifer L., and Rabun M. Taylor. "Atrium." Pages 1: 142–3 in *Eerdmans Encyclopedia of Early Christian Art*. 3 vols. Edited by Paul Corby Finney. Grand Rapids: Eerdmans, 2016.

Gibson, Shimon, and Joan E. Taylor. *Beneath the Church of the Holy Sepulchre, Jerusalem: The Archaeology and Early History of Traditional Golgotha*. London: Palestine Exploration Fund, 1994.

Gifford, Edwin Hamilton, trans. "The Catechetical Lectures of S. Cyril, Archbishop of Jerusalem." Pages 1–298 in *Cyril of Jerusalem, Gregory Nazianzen*. Edited by Philip Schaff. NPNF 2.7. New York: Christian Literature, 1893.

Ginzberg, Louis. *The Legends of the Jews*. 2 vols. Reissue ed. Translated by Henrietta Szold and Paul Radin. Philadelphia: Jewish Publication Society of America, 2003.

Gleschen, Charles A. "Enoch and Melchizedek: The Concern for Supra-Human Priestly Mediators in 2 Enoch." Pages 369–85 in *New Perspectives on 2 Enoch: No Longer Slavonic Only*. Edited by Andrei A. Orlov and Gabriele Boccaccini. Associate Editor Jason Zurawski. Studia Judaeoslavica 4. Leiden: Brill, 2012.

Goranson, Stephen Craft. "Joseph of Tiberias Revisited: Orthodoxies and Heresies in Fourth-Century Galilee." Pages 335–43 in *Galilee through the Centuries: Confluence of Cultures*. Edited by Eric M. Meyers. Duke Judaic Studies Series 1. Winona Lake: Eisenbrauns, 1999.

Goranson, Stephen Craft. "The Joseph of Tiberias Episode in Epiphanius: Studies in Jewish and Christian Relations." PhD diss., Duke University, Durham, 2010.

Grabar, André. *Martyrium: Recherches sur le culte des reliques et l'art chrétien antique*. 2 vols. Paris: Collège de France, 1943–6.

Grabar, André. "La Fresque des saintes femmes au tombeau à Doura." *Cahiers Archéologiques* 8 (1956): 9–26.

Grafton, Anthony, and Megan Williams. *Christianity and the Transformation of the Book: Origen, Eusebius and the Library of Caesarea*. Cambridge, MA: Harvard University Press, 2008.

Grappe, Christian. "Les deux anges de Jean 20:12: Signes de la presence mystérieuse du Logos (à la lumière du targum d'Ex 25:22)?" *Revue d'Histoire et de Philosophies Religieuses* 89 (2009): 169–77.

Green, Joel B. *The Gospel of Luke*. NICNT. Grand Rapids: Eerdmans, 1997.

Grundmann, Walter. *Das Evangelium nach Markus*. THKNT 3. Berlin: Evangelische Verlagsanstalt, 1977.

Grypeou, Emmanouela, and Helen Spurling. *The Book of Genesis in Late Antiquity: Encounters between Jewish and Christian Exegesis*. Jewish and Christian Perspectives 24. Leiden: Brill, 2013.

Hachlili, Rachel. *Jewish Funerary Customs, Practices and Rites in the Second Temple Period*. JSJSupp 94. Leiden: Brill, 2005.

Hachlili, Rachel. *Ancient Synagogues – Archaeology and Art: New Discoveries and Current Research*. HdO 105. Leiden: Brill, 2013.

Halbwachs, Maurice. *La Topographie Légendaire des Évangiles en Terre Sainte: Étude de Mémoire Collective*. Paris: Presses Universitaires de France, 1941.

Halbwachs, Maurice. *On Collective Memory*. Translated by Lewis A. Coser. Chicago: University of Chicago Press, 1992.

Hamilton, Bernard. "Rebuilding Zion: The Holy Places of Jerusalem in the Twelfth Century." *Studies in Church History* 14 (1977): 105–16.

Hamilton, R. W. "Excavations in the Atrium of the Church of the Nativity." *Quarterly of the Department of Antiquities in Palestine* 3 (1934): 1–8.

Hamilton, R. W. *The Church of the Nativity, Bethlehem: A Guide*. Jerusalem: Government of Palestine Department of Antiquities, 1947.

Hammel, C. P. "Adam in Origen." Pages 62–93 in *The Making of Orthodoxy: Essays in Honour of Henry Chadwick*. Edited by Rowan Williams. New York: Cambridge University Press, 1989.

Hanhart, Karel. *The Open Tomb: A New Approach, Mark's Passover Haggadah*. Collegeville: Liturgical Press, 1995.

Hanson, R. P. C. *Origen's Doctrine of Tradition*. Repr. Eugene: Wipf and Stock, [1954] 2004.

Harvey, A. E. "Melito and Jerusalem." *JTS* 17, no. 2 (1966): 401–4.

Harvey, Susan A. "Revisiting the Daughters of the Covenant: Women's Choirs and Sacred Song in Ancient Syriac Christianity." *Hugoye* 8, no. 2 (2005): n.p.

Harvey, William. *Structural Survey of the Church of the Nativity, Bethlehem*. Oxford: Oxford University Press, 1935.

Harvey, William. "The Early Basilica at Bethlehem." *PEQ* 68, no. 1 (1936): 28–33.

Haskins, Ekaterina. "Between Archive and Participation: Public Memory in a Digital Age." *Rhetoric Society Quarterly* 37, no. 4 (2007): 401–22.

Hayward, C. T. R. *Jerome's Hebrew Questions on Genesis: Translated with an Introduction and Commentary*. Oxford Early Christian Studies. Oxford: Clarendon Press, 1995.

Heine, Ronald E. *The Commentaries of Origen and Jerome on St. Paul's Epistle to the Ephesians*. Oxford: Oxford University Press, 2003.

Heine, Ronald E. *The Commentary of Origen on the Gospel of St. Matthew: Translated with Introduction and Brief Annotations by Ronald E. Heine*. Oxford Early Christian Texts. Oxford: Oxford University Press, 2018.

Hess, Aaron. "In Digital Remembrance: Vernacular Memory and the Rhetorical Construction of Web Memorials." *Media, Culture & Society* 29, no. 5 (2007): 812–30.

Hirschfeld, Yizhar. "The Anchor Church at the Summit of Mt. Berenice, Tiberias." *Biblical Archaeologist* 57, no. 3 (1994): 122–33.

Hirschfeld, Yizhar. "Imperial Building Activity during the Reign of Justinian and Pilgrimage to the Holy Land in Light of the Excavations on Mt. Berenice, Tiberias." *Revue Biblique* 106, no. 2 (1999): 236–49.

Hock, Ronald F. *The Infancy Gospels of James and Thomas*. The Scholar's Bible 2. Santa Rosa: Polebridge, 1995.

Hoelscher, Stephen, and Derek H. Alderman. "Memory and Place: Geographies of a Critical Relationship." *Social and Cultural Geography* 5, no. 3 (2004): 347–55.

Hollerich, M. J. *Eusebius of Caesarea's Commentary on Isaiah*. Oxford Early Christian Studies. Oxford: Clarendon Press, 1999.

Hugger, V. "Mai's Lukaskommentar und der Traktat De passione athanasianisches Gut?" *Zeitschrift für katholische Theologie* 43 (1919): 732–41.

Hunt, E. D. "Constantine and Jerusalem." *Journal of Ecclesiastical History* 48, no. 3 (1997): 405–24.

Hunt, E. D. *Holy Land Pilgrimage in the Later Roman Empire AD 312–460*. Oxford: Clarendon Press, 2002.

Irshai, Oded. "The Christian Appropriation of Jerusalem in the Fourth Century: The Case of the Bordeaux Pilgrim." *JQR* 99, no. 4 (2009): 465–86.

Irwin-Zarecka, Iwona. *Frames of Remembrance: The Dynamics of Collective Memory*. New Brunswick: Transaction, 1994.

Isenberg, Wesley W. *The Nag Hammadi Library in English*. Rev. ed. Edited by James M. Robinson. Leiden: Brill, 1990.

Jacobs, Andrew S. "Visible Ghosts and Invisible Demons: The Place of Jews in Early Christian *Terra Sancta*." Pages 359–75 in *Galilee through the Centuries: Confluence of Cultures*. Edited by Eric M. Meyers. Winona Lake: Eisenbrauns, 1999.

Jacobs, Andrew S. "'The Most Beautiful Jewesses in the Land': Imperial Travel in the Early Christian Holy Land." *Religion* 32 (2002): 205–25.

Jacobs, Andrew S. *The Remains of the Jews: The Holy Land and Christian Empire*. Stanford: Stanford University Press, 2004.

Jacobs, Andrew S. *Epiphanius of Cyprus: A Cultural Biography of Late Antiquity*. Oakland: University of California Press, 2016.

Jeremias, Joachim. *Golgotha*. ΑΓΓΕΛΟΣ 1. Leipzig: E. Pfeiffer, 1926.

Jeremias, Joachim. "Golgotha und der heilige Felsen." *ΑΓΓΕΛΟΣ* 2 (1926): 78.

Johnson, M. D. "Life of Adam and Eve: A New Translation and Introduction." Pages 249–95 in *The Old Testament Pseudepigrapha*. 2 vols. Edited by James J. Charlesworth. Vol. 2. Peabody: Hendrickson, 1983.

Johnson, Mark J. *The Imperial Mausoleum in Late Antiquity*. Cambridge: Cambridge University Press, 2014.

Kadari, Adiel. "Interreligious Aspects in the Burial of Adam in *Pirkei de-Rabbi Eliezer*." Pages 82–103 in *Religious Stories in Transformation: Conflict, Revision and Reception*. Edited by Alberdina Houtman, Tamar Kadari, Marcel Poorthuis, Vered Tohar. Jewish and Christian Perspectives 31. Leiden: Brill, 2016.

Kammen, Michael. *Mystic Chords of Memory: The Transformation of Tradition in American Culture*. New York: Vintage, 1993.

Kateusz, Ally. *Mary and Early Christian Women: Hidden Leadership*. Cham: Palgrave Macmillan, 2019.

Keener, Craig S. "The Nativity Cave and Gentile Myths." *Journal of Greco-Roman Christianity and Judaism* 7 (2010): 59–67.

Keightley, Georgia Masters. "Christian Collective Memory and Paul's Knowledge of Jesus." Pages 129–50 in *Memory, Tradition, and Text: Uses of the Past in Early Christianity*. Edited by Alan Kirk and Tom Thatcher. Semeia 52. Atlanta: Society of Biblical Literature, 2005.

Keith, Chris, and Anthony Le Donne, eds. *Jesus, Criteria, and the Demise of Authenticity*. London: T&T Clark International, 2012.

Keith, Chris. *The Pericope Adulterae, the Gospel of John, and the Literacy of Jesus*. Leiden: Brill, 2009.

Keith, Chris. *Jesus' Literacy: Scribal Culture and the Teacher from Galilee*. LNTS 413. London: T&T Clark, 2011.

Keith, Chris. *Jesus against the Scribal Elite*. Grand Rapids: Baker, 2014.

Kelhoffer, James A. *Miracle and Mission. The Authentication of Missionaries and Their Message in the Longer Ending of Mark*. WUNT 2/112. Tübingen: Mohr Siebeck, 2000.

Kelley, Justin L. *The Church of the Holy Sepulchre in Text and Archaeology: A Survey and Analysis of Past Excavations with a Collection of Principal Historical Sources*. Oxford: Archaeopress, 2019.

Kenyon, Kathleen. *Digging Up Jerusalem*. New York: Praeger, 1974.

Kirk, Alan. "The Johannine Jesus in the Gospel of Peter." Pages 313–22 in *Jesus in Johannine Tradition*. Edited by Robert Tomson Fortna and Tom Thatcher. Louisville: Westminster John Knox, 2001.

Kirk, Alan. "Cognition, Commemoration, and Tradition: Memory and the Historiography of Jesus Research." *Early Christianity* 6 (2015): 285–310.

Kirk, Alan. *Memory and the Jesus Tradition*. Reception of Jesus in the First Three Centuries 2. London: T&T Clark, 2018.

Klaver, Sanne. "The Brides of Christ: 'The Women in Procession' in the Baptistery of Dura-Europos." *Eastern Christian Art* 9 (2012–2013): 63–78.

Klink, Edward W. III. *John*. Zondervan Exegetical Commentary on the New Testament. Grand Rapids: Zondervan, 2016.

Kloner, Amos, and Sherry Whetstone. "A Burial Complex of the Second Temple Period on Mount Scopus, Jerusalem." Pages 193–270 in *Viewing Ancient Jewish Art and Archaeology: Vehinnei Rachel, Essays in Honor of Rachel Hachlili*. Edited by Ann E. Killebrew and Gabriele Faßbeck. JSJSupp 172. Leiden: Brill, 2016.

Kloner, Amos, and Boaz Zissu. *The Necropolis of Jerusalem in the Second Temple Period*. Leuven: Peeters, 2007.

Koester, Helmut. "On Heroes, Tombs, and Early Christianity: An Epilogue." Pages 259–64 in *Flavius Philostratus: Heroikos*. Translated by Ellen Bradshaw Aitken and Jennifer K. Berenson MacLean. Society of Biblical Literature Writings from the Greco-Roman World 1. Leiden: Brill, 2004.

Kopp, Clemens. *The Holy Places of the Gospels*. Translated by Ronald Wells. New York: Herder and Herder, 1963.

Köstenberger, Andreas J. *John*. BECNT. Grand Rapids: Baker, 2004.

Kraabel, A. Thomas. "Melito the Bishop and the Synagogue at Sardis Text and Context." Pages 77–85 in *Studies Presented to George M. A Hanfmann*. Edited by David G Mitten, John G Pedley, and Jane A. Scott. Cambridge: Harvard University Press, 1971.

Kraeling, Carl H., with C. Bradford Welles. *The Excavations at Dura-Europos. Final Report VIII, Part II: The Christian Building*. New Haven: Dura Europos Publications, 1967.

Krautheimer, Richard. "Introduction to an 'Iconography of Mediaeval Architecture.'" *Journal of the Wartburg and Courtald Institutes* 5 (1942): 1–33.

Krautheimer, Richard. "The Carolingian Revival of Early Christian Architecture." *The Art Bulletin* 24, no. 1 (1942): 1–38.

Krautheimer, Richard. *Early Christian and Byzantine Architecture*. New Haven: Yale University Press, 1992.

Kretschmar, Georg. "Festkalender und Memorialstatten Jerusalems in altkirchlicher Zeit." Pages 39–111 in *Jerusalemer Heiligtumstraditionen in altkirchlicher und fruhislamischer Zeit*. Edited by Heribert Busse and Gerog Kretschmar, Abhandlungen des Deutschen Palastinavereins 8. Wiesbaden: Otto Harrassowitz, 1987.

Kretschmar, Georg. "Kreuz und Auferstehung Jesu Christi. Das Zeugnis der Heiligen Stätten." *Erbe und Auftrag* 54 (1978): 423–31; 55 (1979): 12–26.

Krewson, William L. *Jerome and the Jews: Innovative Supersessionism*. Eugene: Wipf and Stock, 2017.

Laato, Anni Maria. "What Makes the Holy Land Holy? A Debate between Paula, Eustochium, and Marcella (Jerome, Ep. 46)." Pages 169–99 in *Holy Places and Cult*. Edited by Erkki Koskenniemi and J. Cornelis de Vos. Studies in the Reception History of the Bible 5. Winona Lake: Eisenbrauns, 2014.

Lake, Kirsopp, and J. E. L. Oulton. *The Ecclesiastical History*. 2 vols. The Loeb Classical Library. London; New York; Cambridge, MA: William Heinemann; G. P. Putnam's Sons; Harvard University Press, 1926-32.

Lalleman, Pieter J. *The Acts of John: A Two-Stage Initiation into Johannine Gnosticism*. Leuven: Peeters, 1998.

Lampropoulos, Kyriakos C., Antonia Moropoulou, and Manolis Korres. "Ground Penetrating Radar Prospection of the Construction Phases of the Holy Aedicula of the Holy Sepulchre in Correlation with Architectural Analysis." *Construction and Building Materials* 155 (2017): 307–22.

Le Donne, Anthony. "Theological Memory Distortion in the Jesus Tradition: A Study in Social Memory Theory." Pages 163–77 in *Memory in the Bible and Antiquity*. Edited by Loren T. Stuckenbruck, Stephen C. Barton, and Benjamin G. Wold. WUNT 212. Tübingen: Mohr Siebeck, 2007.

Le Donne, Anthony. *The Historiographical Jesus: Memory, Typology, and the Son of David*. Waco: Baylor, 2009.

Le Donne, Anthony. *Historical Jesus: What Can We Know and How Can We Know It?* Grand Rapids: Eerdmans, 2011.

Le Donne, Anthony. "The Problem of Selectivity in Memory Research: A Response to Zeba Crook." *Journal for the Study of the Historical Jesus* 11, no. 1 (2013): 77–97.

Lee, Samuel. *Eusebius on the Theophaneia*. Cambridge: Cambridge University Press, 1843.

Leonhard, Clemens. "Observations on the Date of the Syriac Cave of Treasures." Pages 3: 255–88 in *The World of the Aramaeans: Studies in Honour of Paul-Eugène Dion*.

3 vols. Edited by P. M. Michèle Daviau, John W. Wevers, and Michael Weigl. JSOT 326. Sheffield: Sheffield Academic, 2001.

Leonhard, Clemens. *The Jewish Pesach and the Origins of the Christian Easter: Open Questions in Current Research*. Berlin: De Gruyter, 2006.

Levine, Amy-Jill, and Ben Witherington III. *The Gospel of Luke*. NCBC. Cambridge: Cambridge University Press, 2018.

Levine, Lee I. *The Ancient Synagogue: The First Thousand Years*. 2nd ed. New Haven: Yale University Press, 2005.

Levine, Lee I. "The Synagogues of Galilee." Pages 129–50 in *Galilee in the Late Second Temple* and *Mishnaic Periods: Life, Culture, and Society*. Vol. 1 of Galilee in the Late Second Temple and Mishnaic Periods. Edited by David A. Fiensy and James Riley Strange. Fortress Press, 2014.

Levinson, Sanford. *Written in Stone: Public Monuments in Changing Societies*. 2nd ed. Durham: Duke University Press, 2018.

Leyerle, Blake. "Landscape as Cartography in Early Christian Pilgrimage Narratives." *JAAR* 64, no. 1 (1996): 119–43.

Leyerle, Blake. "Pilgrims to the Land: Early Christian Perceptions of Galilee." Pages 345–57 in *Galilee through the Centuries: Confluence of Cultures*. Edited by Eric M. Meyers. Winona Lake: Eisenbrauns, 1999.

Lieu, Judith M. *Image and Reality: The Jews in the World of Christians in the Second Century*. Edinburgh: T&T Clark, 1996.

Limor, Ora. "Reading Sacred Space: Egeria, Paula,and the Christian Holy Land." Pages 1–15 in *De Sion exibit lex et verbum domini de Hierusalem: Essays on Medieval Law, Liturgy, and Literature in Honour of Amnon Linde*. Edited by Yitzhak Hen. Cultural Encounters in Late Antiquity and the Middle Ages 1. Turnhout: Brepols, 2001.

Lipatov, Nikolai A. "The Problem of the Authorship of the Commentary on the prophet Isaiah Attributed to St. Basil the Great." Pages 42–8 in *Studia Patristica*. Vol. XXVII: Cappadocian Fathers, Greek Authors After Nicaea, Augustine, Donatism, and Pelagianism. Edited by Elizabeth A. Livingstone. Leuven: Peeters, 1993.

Lipatov, Nikolai A., trans. *St. Basil the Great: Commentary on the Prophet Isaiah*. Texts and Studies in the History of Theology 7. Mandelbachtal: Edition Cicero, 2001.

Lipatov-Chicherin, Nikolai. "Early Christian Tradition about Adam's Burial on Golgotha and Origen." Pages 151–78 in *Origeniana Duodecima: Origen's Legacy in the Holy Land - A Tale of Three Cities: Jerusalem, Caesarea and Bethlehem*. Proceedings of the 12th International Origen Congress, Jerusalem, June 25–29, 2017. Edited by Brouria Bitton-Ashkelony, Oded Irshai, Aryeh Kofsky, H. Newman, and Lorenzo Perrone. Leuven: Peeters, 2019.

Loffreda, Stanislao. *Scavi di et-Tabgha*. Collectio Minor 7. Jerusalem: Franciscan Printing Press, 1970.

Loffreda, Stanislao. *The Sanctuaries of Tabgha*. Jerusalem: Franciscan Printing Press, 1975.

Loffreda, Stanislao. "Potsherds from a Sealed Level of the Synagogue at Capharnaum." *Liber Annuus* 29 (1979): 215–20.

Loffreda, Stanislao. "The Late Chronology of the Synagogue of Capernaum." Pages 52–6 in *Ancient Synagogues Revealed*. Edited by Lee I. Levine; Jerusalem: Israel Exploration Society, 1981.

Loffreda, Stanislao. "Sondaggio nella Chiesa della Moltiplicatione di Pani a Tabgha." *Liber Annuus* 20 (1970): 370–80.

Loffreda, Stanislao. *Recovering Capharnaum*. 2nd ed. Jerusalem: Franciscan Printing Press, 1993.

Lunn, Nicholas P. "Jesus, the Ark, and the Day of Atonement: Intertextual Echoes in John 19:38-20:18." *JETS* 52 (2009): 731–46.
Luz, Ulrich. *Matthew: A Commentary*. 3 vols. Hermeneia. Minneapolis: Fortress, 2001.
Macaskill, Grant. "2 Enoch: Manuscripts, Recensions, and Original Language." Pages 83–101 in *New Perspectives on 2 Enoch: No Longer Slavonic Only*. Edited by Andrei A. Orlov and Gabriele Boccaccini. Associate Editor Jason Zurawski. Studia Judaeoslavica 4. Leiden: Brill, 2012.
MacMullen, Ramsay. *The Second Church: Popular Christianity A.D. 200–400*. Writings from the Greco-Roman World Supplement Series 1. Atlanta: Society of Biblical Literature, 2009.
Magliano-Tromp, Johannes. "Adamic Traditions in 2 Enoch and in the Books of Adam and Eve." Pages 283–304 in *New Perspectives on 2 Enoch: No Longer Slavonic Only*. Edited by Andrei A. Orlov and Gabriele Boccaccini. Associate Editor Jason Zurawski. Studia Judaeoslavica 4. Leiden: Brill, 2012.
Magness, Jodi. "The Question of the Synagogue: The Problem of Typology." Pages 1–48 in *Judaism in Antiquity*. Part 3: Where We Stand: Issues and Debates in Ancient Judaism. Vol. 4: The Special Problem of the Ancient Synagogue. HdO 55. Edited by Alan J. Avery-Peck and Jacob Neusner. Leiden: Brill, 2001.
Magness, Jodi. "Sweet Memory: Archaeological Evidence of Jesus in Jerusalem." Pages 324–43 in *Memory in Ancient Rome and Early Christianity*. Edited by Karl Galinsky. Oxford: Oxford University Press, 2016.
Mancini, Ignazio. "Adamo sotto il Calvario." *Terra Santa* 41 (1965): 277–82.
Mancini, Ignazio. *Archeological Discoveries Relative to the Judeo-Christians*. Jerusalem: Franciscan Printing Press, 1984.
Markschies, Christoph. *Gnosis: An Introduction*. Translated by John Bowden. London: T&T Clark, [2003] 2003.
Markus, R. A. "How on Earth Could Places Become Holy?: Origins of the Christian Idea of Holy Places." *Journal of Early Christian Studies* 2, no. 3 (1994): 257–71.
Mason, Steve. "O Little Town of… Nazareth?" *Bible Review* 16, no. 1 (2000): 32–9, 51–3.
Masterman, E. W. G. "The Site of Capernaum." *PEQ* 39, no. 3 (1907): 220–29.
Mateos, Juan. "La vigile cathédrale chez Egérie." *OCP* 27 (1961): 281–312.
McCane, Byron R. *Roll Back the Stone: Death and Burial in the World of Jesus*. Harrisburg: Trinity Press International, 2003.
McCurrach, Catherine Carver. "'Renovatio' Reconsidered: Richard Krautheimer and the Iconography of Architecture." *Gesta* 50, no. 1 (2011): 41–69.
McGowan, Anne, and Paul F. Bradshaw. *The Pilgrimage of Egeria: A New Translation of the Itinerarium Egeriae with Introduction and Commentary*. Alcuin Club Collections 93. Collegeville: Liturgical Press Academic, 2018.
McGrath, James F. *The Burial of Jesus: History and Faith*. Englewood: Patheos Press, 2012.
McGuckin, John Anthony, ed. *The Westminster Handbook to Origen*. Westminster Handbooks to Christian Theology. Louisville: John Knox, 2004.
McIntyre, Gwynaeth. *Imperial Cult*. Leiden: Brill, 2019.
McKinion, Steven A., ed. *Isaiah 1–39*. Ancient Christian Commentary on Scripture: Old Testament 10. Downers Grove: InterVarsity, 2004.
McVey, Kathleen E., trans. *Ephrem the Syrian: Hymns*. Classics of Western Spirituality. New York: Paulist Press, 1989.
Menk, Otto, and Merin Meiser. *Das Leben Adams und Evas*. Jüdische Schriften aus hellenistisch-römischer Zeit 2,5. Gütersloh: Gütersloher Verlagshaus, 1998.
Meyer, Ben F. *Critical Realism and the New Testament*. Allison Park: Pickwick, 1989.

Meyer, Marvin W. "The Letter of Peter to Philip." Pages 431–33 in *The Nag Hammadi Library in English*. 3rd ed. Edited by James M. Robinson. San Francisco: HarperCollins, 1990.

Meyers, Eric M., and James F. Strange. *Archaeology, the Rabbis and Early Christianity*. London: SCM, 1981.

Minov, Sergey. "Date and Provenance of the Syriac Cave of Treasures: A Reappraisal." *Hugoye* 20, no. 1 (2017): 129–229.

Montero, Roberto López. "La antropología teológica del *Carmen Adversus Marcionem* del Pseudo-Tertuliano." *Salmanticensis* 60 (2013): 257–303.

Morehouse, Nathaniel J. *Death's Dominion: Power, Identity, and Memory at the Fourth-Century Martyr Shrine*. Studies in Ancient Religion and Culture. Sheffield: Equinox, 2016.

Moropoulou, Antonia, Calliope Maria Farmakidi, Kyriakos Lampropoulos, and Maria Apostolopoulou. "Interdisciplinary Planning and Scientific Support to Rehabilitate and Preserve the Values of the Holy Aedicule of the Holy Sepulchre in Interrelation with Social Accessibility." *Sociology and Anthropology* 6, no. 6 (2018): 534–46.

Moropoulou, A., N. Zacharias, E. T. Delegou, M. Apostolopoulou, E. Palamara, and A. Kolaiti. "OSL Mortar Dating to Elucidate the Construction History of the Tomb Chamber of the Holy Aedicule of the Holy Sepulchre in Jerusalem." *Journal of Archaeological Science: Reports* 19 (2018): 80–91.

Moropoulou, Antonia, Ekaterini T. Delegou, Maria Apostolopoulou, Aikaterini Kolaiti, Christos Papatrechas, George Economou, and Constantinos Mavrogonatos. "The White Marbles of the Tomb of Christ in Jerusalem: Characterization and Provenance." *Sustainability* 11 (2019): 1–32.

Murphy O'Connor, Jerome. "Argument for the Holy Sepulchre." *Revue Biblique* 117, no. 1 (2010): 74.

Murphy O'Connor, Jerome. "Bethlehem… Of Course." *Bible Review* 16, no. 1 (2000): 40–5.

Murphy O'Connor, Jerome. *Keys to Jerusalem: Collected Essays*. Oxford: Oxford University Press, 2012.

Nautin, Pierre. *Origène: sa vie et son œuvre*. Paris: Beauchesne, 1977.

Nautin, Pierre. "La Date des commentaires de Jérôme sur les épîtres pauliniennes." *Revue d'Histoire Ecclésiastique de Louvain* 74, no. 1 (1979): 5–12.

Nir, Rivka. "The Aromatic Fragrances of Paradise in the *Greek Life of Adam and Eve* and the Christian Origin of the Composition." *Novum Testamentum* 46, no. 1 (2004): 20–45.

Noga-Banai, Galit. "Das Kreuz Auf Dem Ölberg: Mögliche Frühe Bildbezeugungens." *Römische Quartalschrift Für Christliche Altertumskunde Und Kirchengeschichte* 102, nos. 1–2 (2007): 141–54.

Nora, Pierre. "Between Memory and History: Les Lieux De Mémoire." *Representations* 26 (1989): 7–24.

Nora, Pierre. *Realms of Memory: The Construction of the French Past*. Translated by Arthur Goldhammer. New York: Columbia University Press, 1996.

Notley, R. Steven. "Et-Tell Is *Not* Bethsaida." *Near Eastern Archaeology* 70, no. 4 (2007): 220–30.

Oakeshott, Michael. *Experience and Its Modes*. Repr. ed. Cambridge: Cambridge University Press, [1933] 1994.

Olley, John W. *'Righteousness' in the Septuagint of Isaiah: A Contextual Study*. Ann Arbor: Society of Biblical Literature, 1979.

Orlov, Andrei A. "The Sacerdotal Traditions of 2 Enoch and the Date of the Text." Pages 103–16 in *New Perspectives on 2 Enoch: No Longer Slavonic Only*. Edited by Andrei A. Orlov and Gabriele Boccacini. Associate Editor Jason Zurawski. Studia Judaeoslavica 4. Leiden: Brill, 2012.

Ousterhout, Robert. "New Temples and New Solomons: The Rhetoric of Byzantine Architecture." Pages 223–53 in *The Old Testament in Byzantium*. Edited by Paul Magdalino and Robert Nelson. Dumbarton Oaks Byzantine Symposia and Colloquia. Washington, DC: Dumbarton Oaks, 2010.

Ovadiah, Asher. *Corpus of the Byzantine Churches in the Holy Land*. Bonn: Hanstein, 1970.

Parrot, Douglas M., trans. "Eugnostos the Blessed and The Sophia of Jesus Christ." Pages 222–43 in *The Nag Hammadi Library in English*. 3rd ed. Edited by James M. Robinson. San Francisco: HarperCollins (1990): 222–243.

Patrich, Joseph. "An Overview of the Archaeological Work in the Church of the Holy Sepulchre." Pages 138–61 in *The Archaeology and History of the Church of the Redeemer and the Muristan in Jerusalem*. Edited by Dieter Vieweger and Shimon Gibson. Oxford: Archaeopress, 2016.

Patrich, Joseph. "The Early Church of the Holy Sepulchre in the Light of Excavations and Restoration." Pages 101–17 in *Ancient Churches Revealed*. Edited by Yoram Tsafrir. Jerusalem: Israel Exploration Society, 1993.

Pelak, Cynthia Fabrizio. "Institutionalizing Counter-Memories of the U.S. Civil Rights Movement: The National Civil Rights Museum and an Application of the Interest-Convergence Principle." *Sociological Forum* 30, no. 2 (2015): 305–27.

Peppard, Michael. *The World's Oldest Church: Bible, Art, and Ritual at Dura-Europos, Syria, Synkrisis*. New Haven: Yale University Press, 2016.

Perkins, Pheme. "Apocryphal Gospels and the Historical Jesus." Pages 663–90 in *Jesus Research: New Methodologies and Perceptions – The Second Princeton-Prague Symposium on Jesus Research*. Edited by James H. Charlesworth with Brian Rhea and Petr Pokorný. Grand Rapids: Eerdmans, 2014.

Perkins, Ann. *The Art of Dura-Europos*. Oxford: Clarendon Press, 1973.

Peterson, William L. "Tatian the Assyrian." Pages 125–58 in *A Companion to Second-Century Christian 'Heretics'*. Edited by Antti Marjanen and Petri Luomanen. Leiden: Brill, 2008.

Pickett, Jordan, and Oliver Nicholson. "Octagonal Buildings." Page 1095 in *The Oxford Dictionary of Late Antiquity*. Edited by Oliver Nicholson. Oxford: Oxford University Press, 2018.

Pixner, Bargil. *Paths of the Messiah and Sites of the Early Church from Galilee to Jerusalem: Jesus and Jewish Christianity in Light of Archaeological Discoveries*. Edited by Rainer Riesner. Translated by Keith Myrick, Sam Randall, and Miriam Randall. San Francisco: Ignatius Press, [1991] 2010.

Pollman, Karla. *Das Carmen adversus Marcionitas. Einleitung, Text, Übersetzung und Kommentar*. Göttingen: Vandenhoeck & Ruprecht, 1991.

Pryor, John W. "John 4:44 and the *Patris* of Jesus." *CBQ* 49, no. 2 (1987): 254–63.

Quasten, Johannes. *Patrology*. Vol. 3. Allen: Christian Classics, 1983.

Ramelli, Ilaria L. E. "Basil and Apokatastasis: New Findings." *Journal of Early Christian History* 4, no. 2 (2014): 116–36.

Ramsay, William Mitchell. *Was Christ Born at Bethlehem: A Study on the Credibility of St. Luke*. New York: Putnam, 1898.

Reuling, Hanneke. "The Christian and the Rabbinic Adam: Genesis Rabbah and Patristic Exegesis of Gen 3:17–19." Pages 63–74 in *The Exegetical Encounter Between Jews and*

Christians in Late Antiquity. Edited by Emmanouela Grypeou and Helen Spurling. Leiden: Brill, 2009.

Richardson, Ernest Cushing, trans. *Eusebius: Church History, Life of Constantine the Great, and Oration in Praise of Constantine*. Edited by Schaff, Philip and Henry Wace. Vol. 1. A Select Library of the Nicene and Post-Nicene Fathers of the Christian Church, Second Series. New York: Christian Literature Company, 1890.

Richmond, Ernest T. "Basilica of the Nativity, Discovery of the Remains of an Earlier Church." *Quarterly of the Department of Antiquities in Palestine* 5 (1936): 75–81; 6 (1937): 63–72.

Riesner, Rainer. "Archaeology and Geography." Pages 45–59 in *Dictionary of Jesus and the Gospels*. 2nd ed. Edited by Joel B. Green, Jeannine K. Brown, and Nicholas Perrin. Downers Grove: IVP Academic 2013.

Riesner, Rainer. "Golgota und die Archäologie." *Bible und Kirche* 40 (1985): 21–6.

Rosenthal, Renate, and Malka Hershkovitz. "Tabgha." *IEJ* 30 (1980): 207.

Rubin, Ze'ev. "The Church of the Holy Sepulchre and the Conflict between the Sees of Caesarea and Jerusalem." Pages 79–105 in *The Jerusalem Cathedra*. Edited by Lee Levine. Jerusalem: Yad Izhak Ben-Zvi, 1982.

Rufus, John. *The Lives of Peter the Iberian, Theodosius of Jerusalem, and the Monk Romanus*. Atlanta: Society of Biblical Literature, 2008.

Runesson, Anders. "Architecture, Conflict, and Identity Formation: Jews and Christians in Capernaum from the First to the Sixth Century." Pages 231–57 in *Religion, Ethnicity, and Identity in Ancient Galilee: A Region in Transition*. Edited by Jürgen Zangenberg, Harold W. Attridge, and Dale Martin. WUNT 210. Tübingen: Mohr Siebeck, 2007.

Runesson, Anders, Donald Binder, and Birger Olsson. *The Ancient Synagogue from Its Origins to 200 C.E.: A Source Book*. Leiden: Brill, 2008.

Ryan, Jordan. "Golgotha and the Burial of Adam between Jewish and Christian Tradition." *Scandinavian Jewish Studies* 32, no. 1 (2021): 3–29.

Ryan, Jordan J. "Jesus at the Crossroads of Inference and Imagination: The Relevance of R.G. Collingwood's Philosophy of History for Current Methodological Discussions in Historical Jesus Research." *Journal for the Study of the Historical Jesus* 13 (2015): 66–89.

Ryan, Jordan J. "Tiberias." N.p. in *The Lexham Bible Dictionary*. Edited by John D. Barry, David Bomar, Derek R. Brown, Rachel Klippenstein, Douglas Mangum, Carrie Sinclair Wolcott, Lazarus Wentz, Elliot Ritzema, and Wendy Widder. Bellingham, WA: Lexham Press, 2016.

Ryan, Jordan J. *The Role of the Synagogue in the Aims of Jesus*. Minneapolis: Fortress, 2017.

Sakamoto, Rumi. "Mobilizing Affect for Collective War Memory." *Cultural Studies* 29, no. 2 (2015): 158–84.

Schäferdiek, Knut. "The Acts of John." Pages 2: 188–215 in *New Testament Apocrypha*. 2 vols. Edited by Wilhelm Schneemelcher. Translated by Robert McLachlan Wilson. Philadelphia: Westminster, 1964.

Schaper, Joachim. "The Messiah in the Garden: John 19.38–41, (Royal) Gardens, and Messianic Concepts." Pages 17–27 in *Paradise in Antiquity*. Edited by Markus Bockmuehl and Guy G. Strousma. Cambridge: Cambridge University Press, 2010.

Schenk, Thomas O. *St. Jerome: Commentary on Matthew*. The Fathers of the Church 117. Washington, DC: Catholic University of America Press, 2008.

Schick, Conrad. "Notes from Jerusalem." *PEFQS* 19, no. 3 (1887): 156–70.

Schlatter, Adolf. *Der Evangelist Matthäus*. Stuttgart: Calwer Verlag, 1948.

Schneemelcher, Wilhelm, trans. *New Testament Apocrypha*.

Schneider, Alfons M. *The Church of the Multiplying of the Loaves and Fishes at Tabgha on the Lake of Gennesaret and Its Mosaics*. Edited by Archibald Alexander Gordon. London: Ouseley, 1937.

Schrenk, Thomas P., trans. *Origen: Commentary on the Epistle to the Romans, Books 1–5.* FC 103. Washington DC: Catholic University of America Press, 2001.

Schwartz, Barry. *Abraham Lincoln and the Forge of National Memory.* Chicago: University of Chicago Press, 2000.

Schwartz, Barry. "Christian Origins: Historical Truth and Social Memory." Pages 43–56 in *Memory, Tradition, and Text: Uses of the Past in Early Christianity.* Edited by Alan Kirk and Tom Thatcher. Semeia. Atlanta: Society of Biblical Literature, 2005.

Schwartz, Seth. *Imperialism and Jewish Society, 200 B.C.E. to 640 C.E.* (*Jews, Christians, and Muslims from the Ancient to the Modern World*). Princeton: Princeton University Press, 2001.

Schwartz, Barry. "The Social Context of Commemoration: A Study in Collective Memory." *Social Forces* 61, no. 2 (1982): 374–402.

Serr, Marcel, and Dieter Vieweger. "Is the Holy Sepulchre Church Authentic?" *Biblical Archaeology Review* 42, no. 3 (2016): 28–30, 66.

Seston, William. "L'Église et le baptistère de Doura-Europos." *Annales de l'École des Hautes Études de Gand* 1 (1937): 161–77.

Shalev-Hurvitz, Vered. *Holy Sites Encircled: The Early Byzantine Concentric Church of Jerusalem.* Oxford Studies in Byzantium. Oxford: Oxford University Press, 2015.

Simonetti, Manlio, ed. *Matthew 1–13.* Ancient Christian Commentary on Scripture, New Testament 1a. Downers Grove: InterVarsity, 2001.

Sivan, Higath. "Who Was Egeria? Piety and Pilgrimage in the Age of Gratian." *Harvard Theological Review* 81 (1988): 59–72.

Skarsaune, Oskar. *In the Shadow of the Temple: Jewish Influences on Early Christianity.* Downers Grove: IVP Academic, 2002.

Sloane, David Charles. "Roadside Shrines and Granite Sketches: Diversifying the Vernacular Landscape of Memory." *Perspectives in Vernacular Architecture* 12 (2005): 64–81.

Smid, Harm R. *Protevangelium Jacobi: A Commentary.* Translated by G. E. Van Baaren-Pape. Apocrypha Novi Testamenti 1. Assen: Van Gorcum, 1965.

Smith, Daniel A. "'Look, the Place Where They Put Him' (Mk 16:6): The Space of Jesus' Tomb in Early Christian Memory." *HTS* 70, no. 1 (2014): 1–8.

Smith, Daniel A. *Revisiting the Empty Tomb: The Early History of Easter.* Minneapolis: Fortress Press, 2010.

Smith, H. D., ed. *Ante-Nicene Exegesis of the Gospels.* 6 vols. London: SPCK, 1925–9.

Smith, Jonathan Z. *To Take Place: Toward Theory in Ritual.* Chicago: University of Chicago Press, 1987.

Smit, Peter-Ben. "Incense Revisited: Reviewing the Evidence For Incense as a Clue to the Christian Provenance of the *Greek Life of Adam and Eve*." *Novum Testamentum* 46, no. 4 (2004): 369–75.

Sosa Siliezar, Carlos Raúl. *Creation Imagery in the Gospel of John.* LNTS 546. London: T&T Clark, 2015.

Spieser, Jean-Michel. "En Suivant Eusèbe Au Saint-Sépulcre." *Antiquité Tardive* 22 (2014): 95–103.

Stewart, Charles Anthony. "Churches." Pages 127–46 in *The Oxford Handbook of Early Christian Archaeology.* Edited by David K. Pettigrew, William R. Caraher, and Thomas W. Davis. Oxford: Oxford University Press, 2019.

Stewart-Sykes, Alistair. *On Pascha: With the Fragments of Melito and Other Material Related to the Quartodecimans.* Crestwood: St. Vladimir's Seminary Press, 2001.

Strack, Hermann Leberecht, and Günter Stemberger. *Introduction to the Talmud and Midrash*. 2nd ed. Translated by Markus Bockmuehl. Minneapolis: Fortress, [1982] 1996.

Strange, James F. "Nazareth." Pages 167–80 in *The Archaeological Record From Cities, Towns, and Villages*. Vol. 2 of *Galilee in the Late Second Temple and Mishnaic Periods*. Edited by David A. Fiensy and James Riley Strange. Minneapolis: Fortress, 2015.

Strange, James F., and Hershel Shanks. "Synagogue Where Jesus Preached Found at Capernaum." *Biblical Archaeology Review* 9, no. 6 (1983): 24–31.

Sweet, Anne Marie. "A Religio-Historical Study of the Greek Life of Adam and Eve." PhD diss., University of Notre Dame, 1992.

Taylor, Miriam S. *Anti-Judaism & Early Christian Identity: A Critique of the Scholarly Consensus*. Leiden: Brill, 1995.

Taylor, Joan E. "A Graffito Depicting John the Baptist in Nazareth." *PEQ* 119 (1987): 142–8.

Taylor, Joan E. "Capernaum and its 'Jewish Christians': A Re-Examination of the Franciscan Excavations." *Bulletin of the Anglo-Israel Archaeological Society* 9 (1989–90): 7–28.

Taylor, Joan E. *Christians and the Holy Places*. Oxford: Clarendon Press, 1993.

Taylor, Joan E. "Golgotha: A Reconsideration of the Evidence for the Sites of Jesus' Crucifixion and Burial." *NTS* 44, no. 2 (1998): 180–203.

Taylor, Joan E. "Introduction." Pages 1–8 in *The Onomasticon by Eusebius of Caesarea*. Edited by G. S. P. Freeman-Grenville, Rupert L. Chapman III, and Joan E. Taylor. Jerusalem: Carta, 2003.

Taylor, Joan E. "Christian Archaeology in Palestine." Pages 369–89 in *The Oxford Handbook of Early Christian Archaeology*. Edited by David K. Pettegrew, William R. Caraher, and Thomas W. Davis. Oxford: Oxford University Press, 2019.

Testa, Emmanuel. *Cafarno IV: I Graffiti della Casa di S. Pietro*. Jerusalem: Franciscan Printing Press, 1972.

Toepel, Alexander. "Adamic Traditions in Early Christianity and Rabbinic Literature." Pages 302–24 in *New Perspectives on 2 Enoch: No Longer Slavonic Only*. Edited by Andrei A. Orlov and Gabriele Boccaccini. Leiden: Brill, 2012.

Thilo, Georgius, and Hermannus Hagen, eds. *In Vergilii carmina comentarii. Servii Grammatici qui feruntur in Vergilii carmina commentarii*. Leipzig: B. G. Teubner, 1881.

Trigg, Joseph W. *Origen*. The Early Church Fathers. New York: Routledge, 1998.

Tromp, Johannes. *The Life of Adam and Eve in Greek: A Critical Edition*. Pseudepigrapha Veteris Testamenti Graece. Leiden: Brill, 2005.

Tromp, Johannes. "The Textual History of the *Life of Adam and Eve* in the Light of a Newly Discovered Latin Text-Form." *Journal for the Study of Judaism* 33, no. 1 (2002): 28–41.

Troxel, Ronald L. *LXX-Isaiah as Translation and Interpretation: The Strategies of the Translator of the Septuagint of Isaiah*. JSJSupp 124. Leiden: Brill, 2008.

Truc, Gérôme. "Memory of Places and Places of Memory: For a Halbwachsian Socio-Ethnography of Collective Memory." *International Social Science Journal* 62, nos. 203–4 (2011): 147–59.

Tsafrir, Yoram. "The Development of Ecclesiastical Architecture in Palestine." Pages 5–6 in *Ancient Churches Revealed*. Edited by Yoram Tsafrir. Jerusalem: Israel Exploration Society, 1993.

Tucci, Grazia, ed. *Jerusalem – The Holy Sepulchre: Research and Investigations (2007–2011)*. Florence: Altralinea Edizioni, 2019.

Tzaferis, Vassilios. "The Archaeological Excavation at Shepherds' Field." *Liber Annuus* 25 (1975): 5–52.
Tzaferis, Vassilios. *The Excavations of Kursi-Gergesa*. Jerusalem: Israel Exploration Society, 1983.
Tzaferis, Vassilios. "The Early Christian Monastery at Kursi." Pages 77–9 in *Ancient Churches Revealed*. Edited by Yoram Tsafrir. Jerusalem: Israel Exploration Society, 1993.
Tzaferis, Vassilios. "The Early Christian Holy Site at Shepherds' Field." Pages 204–6 in *Ancient Churches Revealed*. Edited by Yoram Tsafrir. Jerusalem: Israel Exploration Society, 1993.
Vanden Eykel, Eric M. *"But Their Faces Were All Looking Up": Author and Reader in the Protevangelium of James*. The Reception of Jesus in the First Three Centuries 1. London: T&T Clark, 2015.
VanMaaren, John. "The Adam-Christ Typology in Paul and Its Development in the Early Church Fathers." *Tyndale Bulletin* 64, no. 2 (2013): 275–97.
Vieweger, Dieter, and Gabriele Förder-Hoff. *The Archaeological Park under the Church of the Redeemer in Jerusalem*. Jerusalem: German Protestant Institute of Archaeology, 2013.
Vieweger, Dieter. "Archaeological Park & Museum: Durch die Zeiten." *Bible and Interpretation* (2013): n.p.
Vincent, Louis-Hugues. "L'Église de L'Éléona." *Revue Biblique* 7 (1910): 573–74.
Vincent, Louis-Hugues. "L'Église de L'Éléona." *Revue Biblique* 8 (1911): 219–65.
Vincent, Louis-Hugues. "Le sanctuaire de la Nativité d'après les fouilles récentes." *Revue Biblique* 45 (1936–7): 544–74; 46 (1936–7): 93–121.
Vincent, Louis-Hugues. "L'Éléona: Sanctuaire Primitif de L'Ascension." *Revue Biblique* 64, no. 1 (1957): 48–71.
Vincent, Hugues, and Félix-Marie Abel. *Bethléem, le sanctuaire de la nativité*. Paris: Gabalda, 1914.
Vincent, Louis-Hugues, and Félix-Marie Abel. *Jérusalem Nouvelle*, Book II. Jérusalem: Recherches de topographie, d'aechéologie et d'histoire. Paris: Gabalda, 1922.
von Wahlde, Urban C. "The References to the Time and Place of the Crucifixion in the *Peri Pascha* of Melito of Sardis." *JTS* 60 (2009): 556–69.
von Wahlde, Urban C. *The Gospel and Letters of John*. 3 vols. Eerdmans Critical Commentary. Grand Rapids: Eerdmans, 2010.
von Wahlde, Urban C. "The Gospel of John and Archaeology." Pages 101–20 in *The Oxford Handbook of Johannine Studies*. Oxford: Oxford University Press, 2018.
Vriezen, Karel. *Die Ausgrabungen unter der Erlöserkirche im Muristan, Jerusalem (1970–1974)*. Abhandlungen des Deutschen Palästina-Vereins 19. Wiesbaden: Harrassowitz, 1994.
Vuong, Lily C. *Gender and Purity in the Protevangelium of James*. WUNT 2. Reihe 358. Tübingen: Mohr Siebeck, 2013.
Vuong, Lily C. *The Protevangelium of James*. Early Christian Apocrypha 7. Eugene: Cascade, 2019.
Waitz, Hans. *Das Pseudotertullianische Gedicht Adversus Marcionem: ein Beitrag zur Geschichte der alchristlichen Litteratur sowie zur Quellenkritik des Marcionitisus*. Darmstadt: Johannes Waitz, 1901.
Walker, P. W. L. *Holy City, Holy Places?: Christian Attitudes to Jerusalem and the Holy Land in the Fourth Century*. Oxford Early Christian Studies. Oxford: Clarendon Press, 1990.

Walsh, P. G., trans. *Letters of St. Paulinus of Nola.* 2 vols. Ancient Christian Writers. New York: Newman Press 1967.

Wand, Augustine. "Along the North Shore of the Sea of Galilee: A Topographical and Archaeological Study." *CBQ* 5, no. 4 (1943): 430–44.

Weingarten, Susan. "Was the Pilgrim from Bordeaux a Woman? A Reply to Laurie Douglass." *Journal of Early Christian Studies* 7, no. 2 (1999): 291–7.

Weyermann, Maja. "The Typologies of Adam-Christ and Eve-Mary and Their Relationship to One Another." *Anglican Theological Review* 84, no. 3 (2002): 609–26.

White, Hayden. *Metahistory: The Historical Imagination in Nineteenth-Century Europe.* 4th ed. Maryland: Johns Hopkins University Press, [1973] 2014.

Wieviorka, Annette. *The Era of the Witness.* Translated by Jared Stark. Ithaca: Cornell University Press, 2006.

Wilken, Robert L. *The Land Called Holy: Palestine in Christian History and Thought.* New Haven: Yale University Press, 1992.

Wilken, Robert L. "Eusebius and the Christian Holy Land." Pages 736–55 in *Eusebius, Christianity, and Judaism.* Edited by Harold W. Attridge and Gohei Hata. Detroit: Wayne State University Press, 1992.

Wilken, Robert L. *John Chrysostom and the Jews: Rhetoric and Reality in the Late Fourth Century.* Eugene: Wipf and Stock, [1983] 2004.

Wilkinson, John. "Christian Pilgrims in Jerusalem during the Byzantine Period." *PEQ* 108, no. 2 (1976): 74–101.

Wilkinson, John. "Review of Joan E. Taylor, *Christians and the Holy Places.*" *JTS* 45, no. 1 (1994): 304.

Wilkinson, John. "L'Apport de Saint Jérome a la Topographie." *Revue Biblique* 81, no. 2 (1974): 245–57.

Wilkinson, John. "Constantinian Churches in Palestine." Pages 23–7 in *Ancient Churches Revealed.* Edited by Yoram Tsafrir. Jerusalem: Israel Exploration, 1993.

Wilkinson, John. *Egeria's Travels.* 3rd ed. Warminster: Aris & Philipps, 2002.

Wilkinson, John. *Jerusalem Pilgrims before the Crusades.* Warminster: Aris & Philipps, 2002.

Williams, Frank, trans. *The* Panarion *of Epiphanius of Salamis: Book I (Sects 1–46).* Leiden: Brill, 1987.

Williams, Frank, trans. *The* Panarion *of Epiphanius of Salamis.* 2nd ed. Leiden: Brill, 2009.

Williams, George Huntston. "Christology and Church-State Relations in the Fourth Century." *Church History* 20, no. 3 (1951): 3–33.

Wilson, C. W. *Golgotha and the Holy Sepulchre.* London: Palestine Exploration Fund, 1906.

Wilson, Stephen G. "Passover, Easter, and Anti-Judaism." Pages 337–55 in *To See Ourselves as Others See Us.* Edited by Jacob Neusner and Ernest S. Frerichs. Atlanta: Scholars Press, 1985.

Winfeld-Hansen, Hemming. "Centrally Planned Structures." Pages 289–93 in *The Eerdmans Encyclopedia of Early Christian Art and Archaeology.* Edited by Paul Corbey Finney. Grand Rapids: Eerdmans, 2017.

Winks, Robin W. *The Historian as Detective: Essays on Evidence.* New York: Harper Torchbooks, 1970.

Wisse, Frederik, trans. "The Letter of Perter to Philip " Pages 434–7 in *The Nag Hammadi Library in English.* 3rd ed. Edited by James M. Robinson. San Francisco: HarperCollins, 1990.

Wright, Paul H. "The Birthplace of Jesus and the Journeys of His First Visitors." Pages 1–9 in *Lexham Geographic Commentary on the Gospels*. Edited by Barry J. Beitzel. Bellingham: Lexham Press, 2016, 2017.

Wyatt, Nicolas. "'Supposing Him to Be the Gardener' (John 20,15) A Study of the Paradise Motif in John." *Zeitschrift für die Neutestamentliche Wissenschaft* 81 (1990): 21–38.

Yarnold, Edward. "Who Planned the Churches at the Christian Holy Places in the Holy Land?" Pages 105–9 in *Studia Patristica* 18.1. Edited by E. A. Livingstone. Leuven: Peeters, 1989.

Yarnold, Edward. *Cyril of Jerusalem*. London: Routledge, 2000.

Yasin, Ann Marie. "Prayers on Site: the Materiality of Devotional Graffiti and the Production of Early Christian Sacred Space." Pages 36–60 in *Viewing Inscriptions in the Late Antique and Medieval World*. Edited by Antony Eastmond. Cambridge: Cambridge University Press, 2015.

Zelizer, Barbie. "Reading the Past against the Grain: The Shape of Memory Studies." *Critical Studies in Mass Media* 12 (1995): 214–39.

Zemler-Cizewski, Wanda. "The Apocryphal Life of Adam and Eve: Recent Scholarly Work." *ATR* 86, no. 4 (2004): 671–7.

Zervos, George Themelis. "Dating the Protevangelium of James: The Justin Martyr Connection." Pages 415–34 in *Society of Biblical Literature 1994 Seminar Papers*. Edited by E. Lovering. Atlanta: Scholars Press, 1994.

Zervos, George Themelis. *The Protevangelium of James*. 2 vols. London: T&T Clark, 2019.

Index of Authors

Abel, F. 104, 106–08, 114, 140–41, 146, 154, 169, 171, 173
Adelman, R. 31
Africanus, J. 28–29
Aggelakopoulou, E. 111
Agrafiotis, P. 104–06
Ahmed, S. 62
Alderman, D. 99
Alexakis, M. 104–06, 111
Alexander, P. 36, 56, 87
Alexander, L. 6
Allert, C. 140
Alliata, E. 205, 207, 210
Anderson, F. 35–36
Angeloni, A. 111, 116, 118
Apostolopoulou, M. 104–06, 111, 115, 118
Apowitzer, V. 35
Arav, R. 197
Armstrong, G. 126
Armstrong J. 85, 90
Ashkenazi, J. 199
Attridge, H. 36, 87, 188, 197
Avi-Yonah, M. 194
Aviam, M. 199
Avigad, N. 72, 103
Azaryahu, M. 13–14, 129–30, 192, 199, 213, 219

Babinger, F. 198
Bacci, M. 115, 140, 149–50, 152–56
Bagatti, B. 29–30, 37–38, 43, 74, 111, 114–15, 117, 119, 148–50, 154–55, 159, 163, 170–71, 173–74, 187–88, 198, 202, 204, 207–11, 213
Bain, A. 43
Baker, M. 89–90
Bakolas, A. 111
Barkay, G. 111
Barkley, G. 77
Barnes, T. 51

Barrett, C. 68–69
Barton, J. 143
Barzun, J. 7
Ben-Eliyahu, E. 217
Bernabei, M. 153
Betz, H. 66
Bianchi, G. 141, 154
Biddle, M. 23–24, 86, 88, 104–09, 119
Bildstein, M. 77–78
Binder, D. 194, 213
Bloch, M. 7
Bloedhorn, H. 173
Bock, D. 5
Bodnar, J. 5, 13–14, 61, 96
Bontadi, J. 153
Boomer, M. 114–15
Böttrich, C. 36
Bovon, F. 145
Bradshaw, P. 60, 92–94, 177–79, 185, 188, 200
Broadhurst, L. 26
Brock, S. 46
Broshi, M. 111
Brown, R. 20–21, 66, 68–69, 71–72, 75, 110, 135–39
Bruner, F. 68
Butz, E. 189

Cain, A. 92
Cameron, A. 80–81, 84–85, 88, 90, 114, 131, 153, 161, 166, 171
Campana, S. 154
Carroll, J. 139
Carson, D. 68
Cary, E. 124
Catto, S. 194
Chadwick, H. 77–78, 148
Chapman III, R. 51
Clausen, D. 222
Cohick, L. 23, 26

Collingwood, R. 6–7, 15
Connerton, P. 13, 95–96, 179
Corbo, V. 103–04, 108, 111, 113, 116–17, 171, 174, 187–90, 194, 205, 207–08, 210–13
Corke-Webster, J. 80, 91
Coüasnon, C. 84, 110–14, 116–20
Curtis, J. 160
Czachesz, I. 161–62

Dalman, G. 140
Dark, K. 207–08, 210–12, 214
Davidson Kelly, J. 42
Davies, P. 124–26
de Blaauw, S. 112
de Jonge, M. 32–34, 75–76
De Luca, S. 193–94
del Álamo, E. 16, 101
Delegou, E. 104–06, 111, 115
de Strycker, É. 144
Devos, P. 60, 200
Dochhorn, J. 33–34
Dodd, C. 67
Donner, H. 111
Donohoe, J. 101–02, 121, 129–30
Douglass, L. 58
Doval, A. 54
Dow, L. 32–33
Drake, H. 74, 80–81
Drijvers, J. 54–57
Drobner, H. 45
Dunn, J. 7

Eastman, D. 113
Economou, G. 115
Edwards, J. 5, 137–38
Elowsky, J. 78
Esche, S. 43
Etheridge, J. 33
Evans, C. 192

Falls, T. 140
Farmakidi, C. 105
Förder-Hoff, G. 103
Ferrar, W. 150, 164
Fichera, G. 154
Fiensy, D. 138, 194, 207
Fine, S. 197–98
Finkelstein, A. 127, 167

Fitzmyer, J. 5, 137–39
Fokkelman, J. 69
Foote, K. 13–14, 129–30, 192, 199, 213, 219
Foreman, B. 137–38
Foster, P. 71, 75
France, R. 21
Franz, G. 196–98
Freeman-Grenville, G. 51
Fremantle, W. 41
Frost, W. 178

Gafni, I. 35–36
Garbarino, O. 111
Gauer, B. 200
Georgopoulos, A. 104–06
Gerding, H. 123
Gervers, M. 141
Giblin, C. 138–39
Gibson, J. 112
Gibson, S. 55, 58, 84–85, 97, 103–04, 108–09, 111–14, 116–119
Gifford, E. 73
Ginzberg, L. 35–36
Gleschen, C. 36
Goranson, S. 185–86, 198, 200–01, 212, 215, 217
Grabar, A. 79, 117, 173, 175
Graff, H. 7
Grafton, A. 52
Grappe, C. 76
Green, J. 139
Grundmann, W. 22
Grypeou, E. 27–28, 31–32, 40, 42–45

Hachlili, R. 105, 107, 108, 213
Hagen, H. 124
Halbwachs, M. 9–12, 213–14
Hall, S. 80–81, 84–85, 88, 90, 114, 131, 153, 161, 166, 171
Hamilton, B. 170
Hamilton, R. 154–55
Hammel, C. 27
Hanhart, K. 22
Hanson, R. 34
Harvey, A. 23–25
Harvey, S. 46
Harvey, W. 115, 153–55
Haskins, E. 13
Hayward, C. 42

Heine, R. 26–27, 37, 41–42, 77
Hershkovitz, M. 143
Hess, A. 13
Hirschfeld, Y. 169
Hock, R. 145–47
Hoelscher, S. 99
Hollerich, M. 90–91
Hugger, V. 45
Hunt, E. 89–90, 117–18

Irshai, O. 87
Irwin-Zarecka, I. 95
Isenberg, W. 72

Jacobs, A. 40, 87, 194–95, 214, 216–17
Jeremias, J. 26, 43, 48
Johnson, M. D. 32–33, 35
Johnson, M. J. 123–24, 156–57, 176

Kadari, A. 35
Kalofonou, M. 111
Kammen, M. 183, 216
Kateusz, A. 93
Keener, C. 142
Keightley, G. 95
Keith, C. 6, 8–10, 159
Kelhoffer, J. 160
Kelley, J. 104–06, 109, 111, 117
Kenyon, K. 103
Kirk, A. 8, 61, 71
Klaver, S. 79
Klink, E. 21–22, 68
Kloner, A. 104–05, 107
Koester, H. 66
Kolaiti, A. 105, 115
Kopp, C. 169
Korres, M. 104, 111
Köstenberger, A. 68
Kotoula, L. 104–06
Kraabel, A. 26
Kraeling, C. 79
Krautheimer, R. 15–16, 101, 112–13, 118, 121–23
Kretschmar, G. 29
Krewson, W. 30, 42, 45

Laato, A. 45
Laing, J. 178
Lake, K. 23

Lalleman, P. 162
Lambrou, E. 104–06
Lampropoulos, K. 104–07, 111
Le Donne, A. 6, 9–10, 142
Lee, S. 81
Leonhard, C. 30, 93
Levine, A. 139
Levine, L. 86, 194, 213
Levinson, S. 101
Leyerle, C. 5, 58, 184, 186, 194, 214, 217
Lieu, J. 26
Limor, O. 87
Lipatov, N. 47
Lipatov-Chicherin, N. 28–29, 42, 45, 48
Loffreda, S. 143, 186, 188–90, 193–98
Lunn, N. 67
Luz, U. 192

Macaskill, G. 35
MacMullen, R. 77, 114, 210
Magliano-Tromp, J. 36
Magness, J. 68, 193–94, 208
Mancini, I. 29–30, 38
Markschies, C. 162
Markus, R. 4
Mason, S. 135
Masterman, E. 195
Mateos, J. 93
Mavrogonatos, C. 115
McCane, B. 66, 75
McCurrach, C. 15–16
McGowan, A. 60, 92–94, 177–79, 185, 188, 200
McGrath, J. 66
McGuckin, J. 27
McIntyre, G. 125
McKinion, S. 47
McVey, K. 46
Meiser, M. 33
Menk, O. 33
Meyer, B. 15
Meyer, M. 162
Meyers, E. 208, 210
Minov, S. 30
Montero, R. 47
Morehouse, N. 83
Moropoulou, A. 104–06, 111, 115
Murphy-O'Connor, J. 23, 51–52, 72, 84, 86, 103, 105, 107, 109, 119, 135, 159

Nautin, P. 37, 42
Nicholson, O. 123
Nir, R. 33, 34
Noga-Banai, G. 174
Nora, P. 9
Notley, R. 197

Oakeshott, M. 7
Olley, J. 141
Olsson, B. 213
Orlov, A. 36
Oulton, J. 23
Ousterhout, R. 114–115, 128
Ovadiah, A. 197–98, 202

Palamara, E. 105
Pantazis, G. 104–06
Papadaki, A. 104–06
Papatrechas, C. 115
Pappalardo, C. 111
Parrot, D. 163
Patrich, J. 111–12, 114, 116
Pelak, C. 13–14, 61
Peppard, M. 79–80
Perkins, A. 79
Perkins, P. 71
Peterson, W. 38
Pickett, J. 123
Pixner, B. 143, 195, 198–200, 220
Pollman, K. 47
Pryor, J. 136

Quasten, J. 81

Ramelli, I. 47
Ramsay, W. 77, 135, 210
Reuling, H. 72
Richardson, E. 53–54, 81–83
Richmond, E. 136, 154
Riesner, R. 86, 138
Rosenthal, R. 143
Rubin, Z. 86, 113
Rufus, J. 172
Runesson, A. 188, 190, 193–94, 213, 217, 223, 228
Ryan, J. 6, 8, 185, 191, 213

Sakamoto, R. 62–63
Schäferdiek, K. 161–62

Schaper, J. 69
Schenk, T. 43
Schick, C. 104
Schlatter, A. 22
Schneemelcher, W. 161
Schneider, A. 143, 195, 197–201
Schrenk, T. 28
Schwartz, B. 9–10, 12–13
Serr, M. 72, 103
Seston, W. 79
Shalev-Hurvitz, V. 8, 59, 82, 84, 87, 89, 91, 100, 113–14, 117–19, 123–24, 132, 155–57, 171–75, 188
Simonetti, M. 202
Sivan, H. 92
Skarsaune, O. 29
Sloane, D. 13
Smid, H. 145–46
Smith, D. 65–67, 75, 96
Smith, H. 78
Smith, J. 62–63
Smit, P. 34
Sosa Siliezar, C. 68, 70, 73
Spieser, J. 53
Spurling, H. 27–28, 31–32, 40, 42–45
Stemberger, G. 31
Stewart, C. 113, 121–22
Stewart-Sykes, A. 23–24
Strack, H. 31
Strange, J. F. 194, 208, 209, 210, 214
Sweet, A. 33, 75

Taylor, J. 21, 24–25, 27, 30, 31, 44, 49, 51, 55, 58, 72, 74, 86, 97, 103, 110, 123, 125, 142, 149, 151, 159, 162–63, 165–66, 169, 175, 185, 188–190, 207–213
Taylor, M. 26
Taylor, R. 55, 58, 84–85, 97, 103–04, 108–09, 111–14, 116–119
Testa, E. 29, 30, 74, 189
Toepel, A. 31
Thilo, G. 124
Trigg, J. 37
Tromp, J. 32–34, 36, 75–76
Troxel, R. 141
Truc, G. 3
Tsafrir, Y. 113
Tucci, G. 111
Tzaferis, V. 114, 136, 220

Vanden Eykel, E. 144, 146–48
VanMaaren, J. 27
Vieweger, D. 72, 103, 111
Vincent, L. 104, 106–08, 114, 140–41, 146, 154, 169, 171, 173
von Wahlde, U. 25, 69
Vriezen, K. 103
Vuong, L. 144–47

Waitz, H. 47
Walker, P. 39, 53, 55, 57, 59, 81–82, 86, 108, 110, 113, 116, 118, 161, 163–164, 166–67, 169–71, 183
Walsh, P. 173–74
Wand, A. 202–03
Weingarten, S. 58
Welles, C. 79
Weyermann, M. 28
Whetstone, S. 107
White, H. 69
Wieviorka, A. 102
Wilken, R. 85, 87, 167
Wilkinson, J. 52, 55, 57–60, 90, 92, 94, 111–12, 114, 119, 127–29, 131, 149, 157, 159, 163, 168, 170–71, 177–78, 185–88, 190, 193, 195, 199–200, 202–03
Williams, F. 39–40, 184
Williams, G. 53–54
Williams, M. 52
Wilson, C. 46
Wilson, S. 26
Winfeld-Hansen, H. 156–57
Winks, R. 7
Wisse, F. 162
Witherington III, B. 139
Wright, P. 137–39
Wyatt, N. 68–69

Yarnold, E. 37, 54–57, 73, 116
Yasin, A. 189

Zacharias, N. 105
Zelizer, B. 10
Zemler-Cizewski, W. 33
Zervos, G. 143–44
Zettler, A. 189
Zissu, B. 104–05, 107

Index of References

Old Testament

Genesis
2–3	68, 74
2:9	69
3:19	32
35:19	138, 152
35:19–20 LXX	142

Exodus
1:15 LXX	145
1:15–21	145
1:15–22	145
2:7–10	145
3:5	67
13:21–22	147
14	116
14:19	147
14:24	147
14:26	116
14:27–29	116
14:27–31	116
16:1–36	201
16:10	147
19:16 LXX	147
25:18	67
25:18–22	67
25:20	67
33:9–10	147

Numbers
11:1–19	201
16:42	147
19:11–20	77
24:17	147

Leviticus
16	129

Joshua
14:15	43, 44 (Vulg.), 45

1 Samuel
4:4	67
16:11	137
17:14–15	137
17:20	137
17:28	137
17:34	137

2 Samuel
5:2	137, 147, 148, 150
6:20	70
15:30	160

1 Kings
2:10	71
6–7	89
6:21	128
8	127
8:1–2	127
11:7	160
11:43	158

2 Kings
5:26 LXX	68
23:13–14	160

Nehemiah
3:16	70, 71

Psalms
2:1–2	61
16:8–11	61
50	158
73–83	158
73:12 LXX	56
80:1	67
118:22	73
131 LXX	151, 153
131:5	151, 153
131:6	151, 152

131:7 LXX	153, 175, 219

Ecclesiastes
2:5 LXX	68

Isaiah
1:3 LXX	138
8:14	73
28:16	73
33 LXX	141
33:13–19 LXX	141
33:16 LXX	140, 141, 142, 145, 219
51:1 LXX	73
53:7–8	61

Jeremiah
14:8	139
31:15	138, 142, 144

Lamentations
3:53 LXX	73

Ezekiel
11:22–23	164, 167, 222
11:23	160, 165
40	90
40–42	127
43:1–2	160
43:1–5	127

Daniel
2:34	141
7:13–14	161
12:4	75

Amos
9:14 LXX	68

Micah
5:2	137, 142, 147, 148, 150, 151, 152

Zechariah
14:1–5	160
14:1–4	222
14:2	167
14:2–4	219
14:4	164, 165, 167

LXX

4 Kingdoms
21:18	70
21:26	70

Canticles
2:10	108
2:14	108

Old Testament Apocrypha

2 Esdras
13:16 LXX	70

Old Testament Pseudepigrapha

2 Enoch
64:2	36
68:5	36
70:17	36
71:35	35
71:34	36
71:34–37	36
71:35–36	35, 36

Greek Life of Adam and Eve
5:3	32, 34
28–29	34
29:6	34
33	34
33:4	32, 34
38:4	32, 59
38:3–4	34
40	34
40:3–4	32, 59
40:6	32, 35, 49
42:1	75

Latin Life of Adam and Eve
30:2	32
45:2	32, 34

Jubilees
4:29	29, 49

Dead Sea Scrolls

4Q554 Frag. 3 Col. 2.15	128

Index of References

New Testament

Matthew
1:1	139
1:1–17	136
1:6	139
1:20	139
1:20–21	206
1:23	156
2:1	142
2:1–6	135
2:1–8	147
2:2	125
2:3–6	147
2:5–6	135, 137, 142, 148
2:6	141, 147, 150
2:16	138, 145
2:18	138, 141, 144
2:23	207
4:12	20
4:13	20, 192
4:16	147
4:21–22	185
4:23–5:1	170
5:1	202, 203
5:1–12	195
6:9–13	170
8:14–17	190
8:28–34	220
9:1	192
9:2–8	190
12:9–14	191
12:23	139
13:54	136
14:13	5, 143
14:13–21	16, 195
16:13	3
17:1–8	169
20:29–21:17	177, 178
21:1	159, 177
21:1–10	177
21:6	166
21:9	139
21:11	207
21:12	178
21:12–17	178
21:13	178
21:15	139, 177, 178
21:42	73
24:1–2	127
24:1–44	165, 166, 167
24:2	166
24:3–25:36	160, 161
24:4–26:2	178, 179
26:36	20, 22, 160
27:20–23	127
27:25	127
27:32	68
27:33	21, 32, 51
27:59–60	77
27:60	72, 78, 107
27:62–66	66
27:66	75
28:2–7	88
28:6	83
28:9–10	67
28:16	163
28:22	66

Mark
1:9	207
1:18–20	185
1:21	20, 191
1:21–27	190, 191
1:21–28	194
1:21–29	194
1:23	193
1:29	191
1:29–34	190, 191
1:31–32	5
2	191
2:1	191
2:1–12	190, 191, 192
3:1	191
3:1–6	191, 194
3:13	203
4:13	192
5:1–20	220
6:1	135
6:4	135
6:30–44	16, 195
6:31–32	196
6:32–35	143
6:40	202
8:27	3
9:1	192
9:2–8	169
10:33	22

10:47–48	139	2:39	207
11:1	159	2:51	207
12:10	73	3:23–38	136
13	165, 166, 167	3:31	139
13:1–2	127	4:16	136, 207
13:2	22	4:16–30	139, 206
13:3	163	4:31–37	190, 194
13:3–36	160, 161	4:38–41	190
14:3–7	160	5:10	185
14:26–31	159	5:17–26	190, 193
14:32	20, 22, 159, 160	6:6–11	191
14:58	23	6:17	203
15:2	125	6:20–26	195
15:9–15	127	7:5	194
15:20	24, 68	7:5–9	194
15:22	21, 22, 51	8:26–39	220
15:29	23	9:10	143, 196
15:32	125	9:10–11	5
15:42–16:8	94	9:10–17	16, 143, 195
15:45–46	107	9:12	196
16:1	93, 94, 107	9:28–36	169
16:1–8	66, 94	10:34–35	99
16:4	66	10:38–42	160
16:5	107	11:1–4	170
16:5–7	88	13:21	127
16:6	22, 66	19:29	159, 170
16:7	66	19:37	159, 165
16:8	66	19:41–44	165
16:14	160	20:17	73
16:19	160	21:5–6	127
		21:6	166
Luke		21:7–36	160
1:26–27	206	21:37	159
1:26–38	206, 207	22:39	20, 159, 160
1:28	206, 211	22:39–40	166
1:28–38	211, 214	23:33	20, 21
1:32	139	23:53	73, 107
1:42	206	23:56	93, 94
1:79	147	24:1	93, 94
2:1	144, 145	24:1–12	94
2:1–7	135	24:4	67
2:4	135, 136, 137, 138, 145	24:4–7	88
		24:12	66
2:7	138, 139	24:40	163
2:11	136, 137	24:50	160, 169
2:15	137	24:50–53	179
2:15–16	135		
2:16	138	John	
2:32	147	1:1–5	146

1:1-9	147	19:41	49, 50, 68, 69, 70, 72, 74, 78, 103, 107
1:5	146		
1:14	156	19:41-42	67, 76
1:28	220	20:2-4	66
1:45-46	207	20:5-7	66
1:49	70	20:6	66
2:1-11	190	20:12	67
3:19	146	20:12-13	88
5:2	3	20:14-18	67
6:1	185	20:19	127
6:1-14	195	21:1	185
6:1-15	16	21:4	195
6:3	196		
6:10	196	Acts	
6:15	196	1:3	179
6:16-17	197	1:6-8	166
6:23	185	1:6-11	179
6:25-34	201	1:7-8	167, 179
6:25-59	194	1:8b	121
6:59	3, 194	1:9	160, 166
7:53-8:11	159	1:9-11	166
8:1	159	1:12	160, 163, 169
8:12	146, 147	2:1-21	179
9:5	147	2:25-28	61
11:1-44	160	2:29	70
11:9	147	2:29-36	121
12:13	70	4:25-26	61
12:28-36	147	8:32-33	61
12:35	146	9:37	75
12:46	146, 147	13:29	20
15:1	74		
16:5b-15	179	Romans	
18:1	68, 69, 70	5:12-21	49, 62
18:26	68, 69, 70	6:4	78, 79
18:33	70, 125	8:11	88
18:39	70, 125		
19:2	125	1 Corinthians	
19:3	70	1:23	20, 73
19:12	125	11:3	27, 56
19:14	125	15:4	20
19:14-15	70	15:12-23	88
19:17	21, 52, 68	15:12-27	88
19:19	70, 125	15:21-22	49, 62
19:20	67, 68	15:22	27, 49
19:21	125	15:45-49	49, 62
19:30	61	15:54-57	88
19:34	40		
19:39-40	107	Galatians	
		2:9	121

Index of References

Ephesians	
1:22	27
5:14	40, 41, 42, 49, 50, 62

Colossians	
1:15	56
1:18	27, 56, 78, 88
2:10	56, 57

1 Thessalonians	
2:14–15	127
4:14	88

Hebrews	
9	219
9–10	128
9:1–10:18	90
9:7	129
9:11–12	128
9:12	128
9:24	90
12:22	90
13:11	68
13:12	68, 72

1 Peter	
2:6	73
2:7–8	73
2:8	73

2 Peter	
1:17–18	168

1 John	
5:6	40

Revelation	
1:5	126
5:5	75
5–8	75
17:14	126
19:16	126
21–22	133
21:2	127
21:10–14	121
21:14	121
21:19	128
21:21	121
22:2	69

New Testament Apocrypha

Acts of John	
94–102	162
97	161
97–102	161, 162
98	162
99	162
101	162

Cave of Treasures	
23:15–18	37
23:19–23	37

Gospel of Peter	
6.23	75
6.24	71, 75
8.33	75
9.37	75
9.39	76
12.50–54	75

Protoevangelium of James	
11	206, 211, 214
11:1	206
11:1–2	207
15–16	145
15:2	145
16:3	145
17	145
17:1	144, 145
17:1–11	144
17:6	145
17:6–18:1	143
17:10	145
18:2	145
18:3–11	145
18:10	145
18:11	146
19:1–12	146
19:12–15	145
19:13	147
19:13–15	145
19:13–16a	146
19:15	146
19:15–16	147
19:16	145, 146

19:18–20:12	146
21:2–9	147
21:4–8	147
21:10	147
22:1–2	144
22:2	145

Rabbinic Texts

Genesis Rabbah
14:2	59
14:8	35
58:4	32, 44
58:9	32, 44

Midrash on Psalms
92:6	32

Pesiqta Rabbati
43:2	32

Pirqe Rabbi Eliezer
23	32
31	32

Mishnah and Talmudic Texts

b. Erub
53a	32, 44

m. Sabbat
23:5	75

y. Nazir
7.56b	35, 59

Targumic Texts

Targum Pseudo-Jonathan
3	33

Nag Hammadi Codices

Gospel of Philip
73:9–15	71

Letter of Peter to Philip
133.14–17	162
134.10–18	162
135.5–138.3	162

The Sophia of Jesus Christ
91.20	163

Classical and Ancient Christian Writings

Adomnan
De Locis Sanctis
1.23	174
1.25.1–6	169
1.25.2–3	169
3–4	92
4.4	158

Ambrose
De Obitus Theodosii
43–8	76

Expositio Evangelii secundum Lucam
10.114	46

Basil of Caesarea
Commentary on Isaiah
5.141	29, 47, 48

Bede
On the Holy Places
2.1	92, 131

Bernard the Monk
A Journey to the Holy Places and Babylon
11	131
314	92

Breviarius
1	112
1–2	130
2	59, 116, 117

Cassius Deo
Roman History
53.27.2–4	124

Chromatius
Tractate on Matthew
17.1.3–4	202

Cicero
De finibus
5.1.2   126

Cyril of Alexandria
Commentary on Luke
Homily 48   202

Cyril of Jerusalem
Catechetical Lectures
1.1   54
4.10   54, 55, 57
5.10   54
10.19   54, 55
12.16   169
13   55
13.1   57
13.4   54, 55
13.8   73
13.9   57
13.13   55
13.19   73
13.20   57
13.22   54, 55, 57
13.23   54, 56
13.26   54
13.28   37, 54, 56
13.35   73, 74
13.37   57
13.38   57
13.38–39   56
13.39   54, 55
14   125
14.5   72, 103
14.6   54, 113
14.9   108
14.11   74
14.14   118
14.22   66, 118
15.22   57
16.4   54

Mystagogic Catecheses
1.2   116
1.3   116

Itinerarium Egeriae
16.5–6   158

24.1–12   92
24.3   129
24.7   116
24.9   129
24.10   92, 94
25.1   60, 91
25.6   60, 91
25.8   60, 89, 116, 128
25.8–9   128
25.9   89, 91, 115
25.10   60
25.11   60, 174, 176
27.2   116
27.3   60
30.1   60, 113
30.1–3   177
30.3   176
30.3–31.1   176
31.1   174, 176
31.2   177
31.4   178
33.1   176
33.1–2   178
34   94
35.1–4   176
36.3   94
37.1   60
37.2   60
37.4   117
37.4–5   116, 117
37.4–7   86, 117
37.5   60, 62
37.6   61
37.6–7   61
37.7   94
39.1–3   176
39.3–4   169
40.1   176
42.1   179
43.3   179
43.3–6   176
43.5   179
43.5–6   169, 176
48.1–2   118

Ephrem
Hymn on Virginity
16   46

Epiphanius
Diatessaron
51.25	39

Panarion
29.5.6	207
30.3.8	184
30.4.1	184, 186
30.5	200
30.5.6	185
30.11.9	185
30.11.9–10	185, 203, 214, 215
30.11.10	186, 208
30.12.1	185, 203
30.12.2	186
30.12.2–9	186
46	38
46.5.1	39
46.5.1–9	39
46.5.7	40
46.5.8	40
46.5.9	40

Epiphanius the Monk
Hag.
10.1	188

Eucherius
Letter to Faustus
5–6	112, 113, 131

Eusebius
Commentary in Psalms
54.7–12	53

De Laudibus Constantini
9.16	82
11–18	81
11.2	82
18.1	82

Demonstratio Evangelica
1.1.4	150
3.2.97	150
6.13.275	150
6.18.28	164
6.18.29	164, 165, 222
6.28.29–30	166
7.2.341	150, 151
7.2.341–4	151
7.2.346–9	151
7.2.347	151, 152
7.2.348	152

Historia ecclesiastica
1.7.14	207
6.2–3	52
6.8	52
6.16	52
6.19	52
6.23–26	52
6.24–25	52
6.32	52
6.36	52
10.4	112, 121

Life of Constantine
3.25	53, 84
3.25–40	53
3.26	109
3.26.1–2	110
3.26.1–3	110
3.26.2	85
3.26.2–3	109
3.26.3	85
3.27	85
3.28	85, 87
3.30–2	86, 102
3.30.1	86
3.31–32	115
3.31.1–2	89
3.33	54, 127
3.33–34	119
3.33.1	91
3.33.2	91
3.33.3	88
3.34	118
3.34–40	128
3.35	116
3.36	89, 115, 128
3.36–38	113
3.37	114
3.38	114, 121
3.39	112
3.40	128
3.41	152
3.41–43	135, 152
3.41.1	152

3.42	152	*Commentary on Matthew*	
3.42.1	152	27:53	39
3.42.2	219		
3.42.2–43.2	153	*Epistle 46*	
3.43.1	153	3	41, 50
3.43.3	168, 170		
4.33	80	*Epistle 58*	
4.40.1	83	3	109, 110, 149, 156
4.41–42	81		
4.43	81, 152	*Epistle 108*	
4.43–5	81	1	92
4.45	81	9.2	116
4.45.1	80	11	32, 44
4.47	118	12.1	174
30.1	131	13.5	190, 203
31.1	122		
41.1	148	*Liber Locorum*	
43.3	161	75.23	44

Onomasticon *Quaestionum hebraicarum liber in Genesim*
74	86	23.2	44
74.19–21	28, 51		

Theophania Josephus
Antiquities
3.61	81	7.392	159
4.35	166	16.179–83	70

Gregory of Nyssa *Jewish War*
On the Nativity of Christ
1141.43	148	5.146	72
		5.4.2	103

Hyeburg Justin Martyr
Vita S. Will. *Dialogue with Trypho*
14	188	70.2	140, 141
		78.1	142
Jachintus the Presbyter		78.5	142
Pilgrimage		78.5–6	140, 145
10	131	78.6	141
		78.8	142

John Chrysostom
Adversus Judaeas Melito of Sardis
7.1.4	167	*Peri Pascha*	
		72	24
Homiliae in Joannem		93	24
85	46	94	24, 25

Jerome Origen
Commentary on Ephesians *Commentary on John*
5:14	41, 50, 214	6.24	220

Commentary on Matthew
11.3	202
126	27, 49
143	77, 78

Commentary on Romans
5.1.7	28

Contra Celsum
1.51	148, 149, 150
5.61, 65	37
II, 69	77

Homiliae in Jeremiam
20.2	37

Paulus
Opinions
1.21	77

Paulinus of Nola
Epistles
31.4	173, 174, 175, 176, 219

Peter the Deacon
de locis sanctis (Egerian fragments)
P3	216, 220
T	203, 207, 208, 210
V2	185, 186, 187, 188, 192, 193
V2–V3	195
V3	186, 187, 191, 199, 200, 202, 223
V4	216, 220

Piacenza Pigrim
Itinerarium Piacenza
5	207, 214
7	188
29	158

Travels
19	131

Pilgrim of Bordeaux
Itinerarium Burdigalense
571	57
594	58, 112, 115, 168
595	168
595–6	168
596	168
598	138, 152, 158

Ps.-Athanasius
De passione et cruce Domini 45

Ps.-Tertullian
Carmen adversus Marcionem
2.4	46

Rufinus
Historia ecclesiastica
9.6	109
10.7–8	76

Socrates Scholasticus
Historia ecclesiastica
1	76
1.17	109, 110
17	76

Sozomen
Historia ecclesiastica
2.1	76, 109
4.25.2	56

Sulpicius Severus
Chronica
2.33.6–8	174

Theodoret
Historia ecclesiastica
2.22	56

www.ingramcontent.com/pod-product-compliance
Lightning Source LLC
Chambersburg PA
CBHW072127290426
44111CB00012B/1807